LATINAS AND AFRICAN AMERICAN WOMEN AT WORK

LATINAS AND AFRICAN AMERICAN WOMEN AT WORK

Race, Gender, and Economic Inequality

WITHDRAW

Irene Browne
Editor

Russell Sage Foundation / New York

The Russell Sage Foundation

The Russell Sage Foundation, one of the oldest of America's general purpose foundations, was established in 1907 by Mrs. Margaret Olivia Sage for "the improvement of social and living conditions in the United States." The Foundation seeks to fulfill this mandate by fostering the development and dissemination of knowledge about the country's political, social, and economic problems. While the Foundation endeavors to assure the accuracy and objectivity of each book it publishes, the conclusions and interpretations in Russell Sage Foundation publications are those of the authors and not of the Foundation, its Trustees, or its staff. Publication by Russell Sage, therefore, does not imply Foundation endorsement.

Library of Congress Cataloging-in-Publication Data

Latinas and African American women at work: race, gender, and economic
  inequality / Irene Browne, editor
    p. cm.
  Includes bibliographical references and index.
  ISBN 0–87154–147–5
    1. Afro-American women—Employment. 2. Hispanic American women—
  Employment. I. Browne, Irene.
  HD6057.5.U5A37 1999   98-19536
  331.4'089'96073—dc21   CIP

RUSSELL SAGE FOUNDATION
112 East 64th Street, New York, New York 10021
10 9 8 7 6 5 4 3 2 1

To the memory of my mother, Mary Ann Browne

Contents

Contributors

IRENE BROWNE is associate professor of sociology and women's studies at Emory University.

DELORES P. ALDRIDGE is Grace Towns Hamilton Professor of Sociology and African American Studies at Emory University. She is also associate director of the Program in Women's Health Service Research at the Center for Evaluation Sciences, Emory University.

JOHN BOUND is professor of economics at the University of Michigan. He is also research affiliate of the Population Studies Center at the University of Michigan and the National Bureau of Economic Reseach, Cambridge, Massachusetts.

CAMILLE Z. CHARLES is assistant professor of sociology at the University of Pennsylvania.

KAREN CHRISTOPHER is doctoral candidate in sociology at the University of Arizona, Tucson.

AIXA N. CINTRÓN-VÉLEZ is assistant professor in the Department of Urban Studies and Planning at the Massachusetts Institute of Technology. She is also affiliated with the Women's Studies Program at the Massachusetts Institute of Technology.

MARY CORCORAN is professor of public policy, political science, social work, and women's studies at the University of Michigan.

LAURA DRESSER is research director at the Center on Wisconsin Strategy at the University of Wisconsin-Madison.

KATHRYN EDIN is assistant professor of sociology at the University of Pennsylvania.

PAULA ENGLAND is professor of sociology at the University of Arizona, Tucson.

SUSAN GONZÁLEZ BAKER is assistant professor in the Department of Sociology, University of Texas at Austin. She is also faculty affiliate at the University of Texas Population Research Center and at the University of Texas Center for Mexican-American Studies.

COLLEEN M. HEFLIN is doctoral candidate in the Sociology Department at the University of Michigan.

ELIZABETH HIGGINBOTHAM is professor in the Department of Sociology and Criminal Justice at the University of Delaware.

IVY KENNELLY is doctoral candidate in sociology at the University of Georgia.

JOYA MISRA is assistant professor in the Department of Sociology at the University of Georgia.

KATHLEEN MULLAN HARRIS is associate chair and associate professor in the Sociology Department at the University of North Carolina at Chapel Hill. She is also a faculty fellow at the Carolina Population Center at the University of North Carolina.

LORI L. REID is post-doctoral fellow at the Institute for Social Research at the University of Michigan, Ann Arbor.

BARBARA F. RESKIN is professor of sociology at Harvard University.

BELINDA L. REYES is policy analyst at the Public Policy Institute of California.

LYNN WEBER is director of the Women's Studies Program and professor of sociology at the University of South Carolina.

Introduction

Latinas and African American Women in the U.S. Labor Market

Irene Browne

More than thirty years after the passage of the landmark Civil Rights Act of 1964, economic inequality in the United States continues to be inextricably linked to both race and gender. The groups facing the greatest risk of poverty and lowest wages are Latinas and African American women.[1] And their plight appears to be getting worse. Women of color are increasingly responsible for supporting their families at a time when all individuals at the bottom of the income distribution are slipping further behind those at the top (Danziger and Gottschalk 1993; Levy and Murnane 1992). The economic prospects for Latinas and African American women who have few marketable skills are especially bleak, as shifts in the industrial mix of the economy and the rising demand for highly educated workers are pulling wages and employment rates downward for the unskilled (Holzer and Vroman 1992).

Despite their acute economic vulnerability, very little is known about the underlying conditions shaping labor market disadvantage among Latinas and African American women. The majority of studies investigating the relationship between race and industrial restructuring focus on men, with particular emphases on the problems of joblessness and falling wages among black men (Holzer 1991). Economic hardship among Latinas and African American women is often framed as a welfare issue or as a problem of the lack of a male wage earner rather than a question of female labor market dynamics (Mead 1992; Wilson 1987). Studies of racial inequality in the labor market that do consider women tend to use theories developed from male employment patterns, which leads to conflicting and inconclusive results (Bluestone, Stevenson, and Tilly 1992; Ihlanfeldt and Sjoquist 1989).

It is not surprising that Latinas and African American women are relatively scarce in studies of race and rising inequality in the labor market. In the late 1970s and early 1980s, black and white employment and wage inequality in the labor market was a problem confronting primarily men—

particularly young men (Bound and Freeman 1992). While black male joblessness was growing and the wage gap between blacks and whites was widening among men, the position of women was actually improving. By 1979, earnings for African American women were approaching white women's earnings, and the two groups had similar rates of employment (England 1992). Labor force participation among Latinas was also increasing, and the earnings gap between white women and Latinas was closing (Bean and Tienda 1987). Although the race- and ethnicity-based gap in wages among women narrowed throughout the 1970s, all groups of women continued to earn less than men did (England and Browne 1992). Among the employed, for instance, black men outearned white women. Thus it was gender inequality, rather than racial or ethnic inequality, that distinguished the overall labor market patterns of Latinas and African American women during the late 1970s.

As the 1980s approached, the labor market future of women of color therefore appeared to be much brighter than that of their male counterparts. By the end of the 1980s, however, indications were that something quite different had transpired, and a few researchers began to uncover a dismaying trend. There were reports that the advancements in the labor market status of African American women had stalled or reversed direction in the 1980s, creating especially harsh consequences for the most economically vulnerable—the young, the unskilled, and single parents (Corcoran and Parrott 1992). Although Latinas continued to show economic mobility, some groups were suffering the effects of industrial restructuring within large cities and were facing rising unemployment and poverty (Moore and Pinderhughes 1993; Ortíz 1996).

Because the slowdown in economic progress among some Latinas and the growing disadvantage for African American women have been recent, and because economic theories on race and labor market inequality tend to be based on male experiences, little is known about the dynamics underlying the employment prospects of Latinas and African American women. Any explanation of patterns of female labor market activity must consider two fundamental differences between women's and men's lives. First, jobs continue to be segregated by sex, with women concentrated in service occupations and industries (Reskin 1993). Second, women are primarily responsible for raising children and increasingly are the sole family heads. Yet the racial stratification in U.S. society, which includes residential segregation and discrimination, suggests that job segregation and family structure should play out differently for women depending on their race or ethnicity (Glenn 1985). Unfortunately, we lack both the empirical studies and the appropriate theoretical models to explain adequately how race and gender *combine* to create labor market inequality for Latinas and African American women.

A literature on race, gender, and economic inequality exists within the interdisciplinary fields of African American studies, Chicano or Latino studies, and women's studies, but these contributions have not been systematically incorporated into policy debates or writings on the impact of industrial restructuring on labor markets. Feminist scholars in particular have been attempting to develop new theoretical insights in the study of women of color, offering trenchant critiques of the biases in economic and sociological traditions that assume male experiences as normative and render female experiences marginal or invisible (Beasley 1994; England and Kilbourne 1990). For instance, theories of racial inequality in labor markets often presuppose a "typical male worker," who continuously works for pay throughout his lifetime in a full-time job and can find employment across a wide range of occupations and industries. Blue-collar jobs have historically been his mainstay, and his family life interferes little with his "work" life.

The "typical female worker" does not fit this model, partly because women's employment histories vary so much. A woman often moves in and out of the labor force or engages in part-time employment as she cares for her children. She is most likely to be employed in a clerical job or to find herself in one of the "female-dominated" occupations. Not only is she concentrated with other women in sectors where men are absent, but the experiences and opportunities she encounters on the job are qualitatively distinct from those of her male counterpart (Hochschild 1983; Williams 1992). And her family situation is intimately tied to her attachment to the labor force.

Although debates on the relationship between race and gender are at the heart of current feminist theorizing in the United States, feminist scholarship has not been integrated into the labor market literature (some post-Marxist work is an exception to this; see, for instance, Beasley 1994). In addition, there is a methodological divide between the labor market literature and feminist scholarship, as the feminist claims are most often supported by ethnographic, case study, or descriptive research. Thus quantitative approaches to the intersection of gender, race, and class are rare (but see Kilbourne, England, and Beron 1994 and Tomaskovic-Devey 1993).

The studies of Latinas and African American women that emerge from the different corners of the social sciences thus tend to appear as rich ethnographic studies (Hondagneu-Sotelo 1994; Romero 1992; Rollins 1985; Zavella 1987), investigations within particular locales (Tomaskovic-Devey 1993; Zsembik and Peek 1994), or single chapters in volumes on the labor market and women (Stromberg and Harkess 1988); African Americans (Jennings 1992); or Latinos (Bean and Tienda 1987; Knouse, Rosenfeld, and Culbertson 1992). Few comprehensive investigations provide a comparative perspective on Latinas and African American women and speak to the current debates on the labor market problems that industrial restructuring has generated for these women.[2]

The question remains: Is the story of the labor market fortunes of Latinas and African American women over the past quarter century one of expansion and progress or of stagnation and decline? The literature suggests an answer that is not "either/or" but rather "both/and" (Hondagneu-Sotelo 1997; King 1988). Changing populations and opportunities have been accompanied by growing diversity among groups of women, producing important contingencies in the ways that race or ethnicity combines with gender to ameliorate or intensify labor market disadvantage. Thus far, knowledge of these contingencies remains incomplete. To understand where Latinas and African American women stand in relation to the eroding labor market position of men of color, scholars must construct analyses for women that parallel existing analyses for men and train their sights on aggregate trends. Also necessary is attention to the diversity among women, with consideration of particular groups whose severe deprivation may be hidden within the broader patterns (Hondagneu-Sotelo 1997).

The chapters in this book contribute to the accomplishment of both these tasks. The authors build upon and often challenge the prominent frameworks currently used to explain the position of Latinas and African American women in the U.S. labor market. Below I review these frameworks. I first set the stage by describing patterns in female employment and wages, the increasing racial or ethnic diversity within the U.S. population, and the changing structure of the U.S. economy. I then turn to the theoretical debates about how race or ethnicity and gender affect women's experiences in the labor market. Finally, I highlight the contributions of this volume to these debates.

EMPLOYMENT AND WAGE PROFILES OF LATINAS AND AFRICAN AMERICAN WOMEN

The overall picture of wages and employment creates an impression of progress for Latinas, African American women, and white women. Real wages among all groups of Latinas rose steadily between 1969 and 1996 (table I.1). The wages earned by African American women increased sharply in the 1970s compared with the much more modest increases for white women. Thus, scholars in the early 1980s had reason to be optimistic about the labor market prospects for African American women in relation to white women and to expect the imminent elimination of racial inequality in women's wages.

Many trace the improvements in earnings among Latinas and African American women during the 1970s to increases in their years of education and experience and to their entry into better-paying clerical jobs as they departed domestic service and agricultural work (King 1993; Bean and Tienda 1987; O'Neill 1985). Barriers to employment mobility also lifted

Table I.1 / Median Annual Earnings Among Individuals Employed Full-Time, Full-Year, by Gender and Race or Ethnicity, 1969 to 1996

Gender and Race or Ethnicity[a]	1969	1979	1989	1996
Women				
African American	17,101	21,190	21,890	21,000
Mexican-origin	9,619	11,638	18,980	17,000
Puerto Rican	14,322	14,713	22,776	22,000
Cuban	10,643	14,058	22,738	22,000
Central and South American	11,319	12,978	18,154	18,720
Other Latina	10,305	10,256	22,775	18,300
White[a]	21,376	21,622	24,041	25,000
Men				
African American	25,651	25,945	26,572	26,000
Mexican-origin	21,590	20,780	22,776	19,900
Puerto Rican	21,590	20,903	27,609	25,000
Cuban	23,727	24,659	30,368	28,000
Central and South American	25,865	21,622	23,408	20,000
Other Latino	25,865	24,140	29,102	26,000
White[a]	36,767	38,912	37,456	35,000

Sources: Bean and Tienda (1987, table 10.8); U.S. Department of Commerce (1992, 1998).
[a]Earnings in real (1996) dollars.
[b]White, non-Hispanic.

during the 1970s with the passage of the Civil Rights Act of 1964 and the enforcement of equal opportunity legislation (Leonard 1994; Wilson 1996, 193). Wages were expected to rise with the retirement of older cohorts of Latinos and African Americans whose labor market position was forged during times of extreme racial discrimination (Smith 1984).

During the 1980s and through the 1990s, the progress for African American women appears to have stalled, however, as their wages barely trickled upward. In contrast, Latinas and white women experienced much steeper increases in their wages between 1979 and 1989.[3] While Latinas' wages fell slightly in the 1990s, earnings for white women continued to rise. Men's earnings showed distinctly different patterns from those of women, dropping or rising only slightly in the 1970s among all groups, improving between 1979 and 1989 and then falling in the 1990s.[4] In every decade, wages remained higher for men than for coethnic women (women from the same race or ethnic group).

Wage inequality among women appears as a variegated landscape, with the shape and extent of the wage gap differing over time and across race and ethnic groups (table I.2). In 1979, for instance, African American women earned nearly as much (98 percent) as white women did, while African American women earned only 82 percent of the wages earned by

Table I.2 / Earnings Gap, by Gender and Race or Ethnicity, 1969 to 1996

| | Earnings as a Ratio of the Earnings of | | | | | | | |
| | White Women | | | | Coethnic Men[a] | | | |
Women[b]	1969	1979	1989	1996	1969	1979	1989	1996
African American	.80	.98	.91	.85	.67	.82	.83	.81
Mexican-origin	.45	.54	.79	.68	.45	.54	.83	.85
Puerto Rican	.67	.68	.95	.88	.66	.70	.75	.88
Cuban	.63	.65	.95	.88	.57	.57	.75	.79
Central and South American	.67	.60	.76	.75	.55	.60	.62	.94
Other Latina	.61	.60	.95	.73	.50	.54	.78	.70
White[c]	—	—	—	—	.58	.56	.64	.71

Source: Ratios computed from median earnings estimates reported in table I.1.
[a]Men of the same race or ethnicity as the women in each group. For instance, the African American men are coethnic with respect to African American women; Mexican-origin men are coethnic with respect to Mexican-origin women.
[b]Aged sixteen to sixty-four.
[c]Non-Hispanic.

their male counterparts. By the end of the next decade, however, the gender gap had closed while the race-based gap had widened. In contrast, all groups of Latinas saw a reduction in wage inequality as the gap between their earnings and those of white women and coethnic men narrowed.

Employment and unemployment rates also tell a mixed story of expanding employment opportunities alongside continued disadvantages for Latinas and African American women. Among all groups of women, employment increased between 1979 and 1996; among men, it decreased (table I.3). Although a growing number of women were working during that period, some found it more difficult to obtain a job in the 1990s. Unemployment rates fell among all groups of women between 1979 and 1989 but then rose among Latinas and remained constant among white women. Thus, while Latinas achieved wage gains in the 1980s, their advances were tempered by a rising unemployment rate. African American women, in contrast, were slightly more able to find employment in 1996 than in 1989. For most women, the gender gap in unemployment favored men, so that male unemployment rates were lower than female rates (Mexican-origin and Cuban individuals were the exception to this pattern). The wage and unemployment figures in table I.3 also reveal an enduring advantage of white women vis-à-vis Latinas and African American women in the labor market. In every year, white women not only earned the highest wages among women but were also much more likely to find a job when they were searching for paid work. Unemployment rates for white women in 1996 were less than half the rate for Latinas and African American women.

Table I.3 / Employment and Unemployment Rates by Gender and Race or Ethnicity, 1979 to 1996 (Percent)

Gender and Race or Ethnicity[a]	Employed			Unemployed		
	1979	1989	1996	1979	1989	1996
Women						
African American	49.3	54.6	57.1	10.8	9.8	8.7
Latina	43.6	54.9	50.2	8.9	8.0	9.2
Mexican	43.5	50.8	49.3	9.9	8.8	9.7
Puerto Rican	31.9	40.2	45.3	9.3	8.5	10.0
Cuban	50.9	48.0	50.0	7.9	5.9	8.3
White	47.4	54.9	57.0	5.0	4.0	4.3
Men						
African American	69.0	67.0	65.5	9.1	10.0	9.4
Latino	80.4	79.4	77.3	5.7	6.6	6.9
Mexican	83.3	80.4	78.7	5.4	8.8	7.0
Puerto Rican	71.9	72.8	68.5	9.9	8.5	7.0
Cuban	79.1	75.3	70.9	4.9	5.3	6.3
White	77.3	75.4	74.2	3.6	3.9	4.1

Sources: U.S. Department of Labor (1980, tables 44, 45; 1990, tables 39, 40; 1996, tables 5, 6).
[a]In 1979, individuals aged sixteen to nineteen were not included in the reports. Therefore, the table includes only women and men aged twenty to sixty-four to allow comparability across years. Note that employment rates are higher for every group when individuals aged sixteen to nineteen are included. For instance, the unemployment rate in 1995 was 10.2 percent among African American women aged sixteen to sixty-four.

The unemployment figures suggest that Latinas and African American women may still be facing barriers in the labor market that belie the rosy image portrayed in the general wage trends. The broad earnings profiles may actually mask disadvantage within races or ethnic groups of women, and substantial pockets of growing wage inequality between women may be hidden in the composite numbers. Feminist scholars would look to social class as a third dimension of inequality and argue that disadvantage by gender and by race or ethnicity may vary along class lines (King 1988). In particular, poor and working-class women of color are vulnerable to "multiple jeopardy" stemming from their gender, race or ethnicity, and class combined (King 1988).

Economists interpret "education" as an indicator of "skill" rather than as the more complex sociological concept of "social class." From either theoretical orientation, the data reveal that education represents a salient axis of inequality—one that appears to have grown in importance for women during the 1970s and the 1980s. The data in table I.4 provide a simple indication of how women at the lowest end of the educational distribution have fared in relation to coethnic women at the highest end. With one exception (the "other Latina" group), the education-related discrepancy in wages

Table I.4 / **Earnings Gap between Women at Lowest and Highest Education Levels, by Race and Ethnicity, 1969 to 1996**

Group[a]	Median Earnings of Women with Less Than Twelve Years of Education as a Ratio of Median Earnings of Women with at Least Sixteen Years of Education			
	1969	1979	1989	1996
African American	.42	.60	.48	.50
Mexican-origin	.30	.46	.47	.36
Puerto Rican	.60	.57	.50	.44
Cuban	.63	.56	.44	.43
Central and South American	.68	.65	.47	.40
Other Latina	.41	.41	.47	.47
White	.51	.63	.49	.44

Sources: Bean and Tienda (1997, table 10.8); U.S. Department of Commerce (1992, 1998).
[a]Includes only women employed full-time, full-year.

widened between 1979 and 1996 among Latinas, African American, and white women.

Thus, consistent with trends occurring within the labor market as a whole in the 1980s, wage inequality between women with the least education and women with the most education grew, with the gap especially pronounced for young workers (Blau and Beller 1992; Karoly 1993). More comprehensive studies of the growing disparity in wages show that the underlying patterns of increasing wage inequality between "low-skilled" and "high-skilled" workers have differed by gender *and* by race or ethnicity (Karoly 1993; Morris, Bernhardt, and Handcock 1994). Among the least educated, for instance, men's wages eroded more rapidly than women's did (Blau and Beller 1992). In addition, black and white women experienced earnings declines at the bottom of the distribution and earnings gains at the top (Blau and Beller 1992). Latinas achieved increases at both ends, but the rise was faster among those at the top (Karoly 1993). The evidence therefore suggests that Latinas and African American women may be under the sway of distinctive forces that are creating inequality within their ranks and fueling their declining labor market status in relation to white women (Karoly 1993; Morris, Bernhardt, and Handcock 1994). Because of the complexity of these trends, the determinants of these contrasting pathways are not fully known.

WHY DOES RACIAL AND ETHNIC INEQUALITY PERSIST IN THE LABOR MARKET?

Latina, black, and white women are located in different sectors of local labor markets, bring differing sets of skills into their jobs, and potentially encounter different types of reception by employers, coworkers, and customers. Scholars are just beginning to appreciate the diversity among black women and Latinas in terms of their personal and family characteristics—skill and education levels, age, status as head of the family, social resources—their class background, and their exposure to local labor market opportunities. The patterns of inequality among Latinas and black women thus vary within these groups and appear to be linked to the substantial changes altering the landscape of the social and economic institutions within the United States. Debates over the causes of the continued advantage that non-Hispanic whites enjoy in the labor market center on several key processes: population changes, industrial restructuring, disarticulation, and discrimination.

The Increasing Diversity of the U.S. Population

The labor market fortunes of Latinas and African American women occur within a backdrop of a society marked by racial inequality. In 1944, Myrdal derided the "treatment" of African Americans as "America's greatest failure" (2021) that was engendering a fundamental social struggle. Fifty years later, this struggle continues; African Americans are segregated into predominantly black neighborhoods (Massey and Denton 1993); their children often attend schools that provide woeful preparation (Farkas and Vicknair 1996; Orfield 1992); and over one-third of African American families live in poverty (U.S. Department of Commerce 1997).

Although many of Myrdal's insights about the disjuncture between the ethos of equality and social conditions for African Americans are relevant today (Clayton 1996), the simple black-white distinction of "race" is now inadequate to characterize the U.S. population and the dynamics of social inequality. First, many African Americans have entered the middle class, so that there are wide economic disparities within the African American community (Wilson 1978). Second, gender is recognized as an important axis of inequality that intersects with race (Collins 1990; King 1988; Baca Zinn and Dill 1996). For instance, African American men and women hold jobs in quite different occupations and industries. African American women are employed within the female-dominated service sectors of urban areas, with clerical work representing the largest single occupational category that they fill (Reskin and Padavic 1993).

Third, conceptualizations of "race/ethnicity" are supplanting older notions of "race" to capture the "multiethnic" diversity within the United States (Bobo and Suh 1996; Nelson and Tienda 1985). Latinos and Latinas represent one of the most rapidly growing "ethnic" groups in the United States. Between 1990 and 1994 alone, the Latino and Latina population increased by approximately 28 percent, reaching over 10 percent of the U.S. population (Day 1996). Social scientists estimate that if current immigration and fertility trends continue, by 2010 Latinos and Latinas will surpass African Americans to become the second largest race or ethnic group living in the United States (Day 1996). Approximately one-third of Latinos and Latinas in the United States are immigrants, and Latinas sustain the highest fertility rates of any major race or ethnic group in the United States (U.S. Department of Commerce 1997).

While "Latino" or "Hispanic" is considered a single ethnic category for political purposes and bureaucratic record-keeping, many question the utility of a single analytic construct, arguing that race or ethnicity is not just a demographic descriptor but a theoretical construct that is forged through political, social, and cultural contestations (Nelson and Tienda 1985). That is, "ethnicity" is a socially produced category, changing with social conditions.[5] The groups that fall under the cognomen "Latino" vary widely in their experiences, identities, characteristics, histories, cultural heritage, and place in local economies (Bean and Tienda 1987). Consequently, the labor market profiles of Latinas vary by their national origin and nativity (Bean and Tienda 1987).

Men and women of Mexican origin constitute the largest group of Latinos and Latinas. According to Nelson and Tienda (1985), a main force drawing Mexicans into the United States has been the need for cheap labor. Concentrated in the Southwest, the Mexican-origin population is rapidly increasing as a result of the recent influx of immigrants. The new arrivals tend to have low levels of education and are hired to fill the worst jobs within the fields and factories of California, Arizona, New Mexico, and Texas. Those who were born in the United States or who arrived there as children occupy a different niche in the economies of the Southwest (Ortíz 1996). Although they have made some inroads into professional and managerial positions, Mexican Americans whose families have been in the United States for several generations are still concentrated in relatively low-status occupations (Knouse, Rosenfeld, and Culbertson 1992; Ortíz 1996; Scott 1996). Overall, Mexican-origin women are overrepresented in agricultural and manufacturing employment.

In contrast to individuals of Mexican origin, Puerto Ricans reside primarily in the large cities of the Northeast and Midwest and share a distinctive set of historical circumstances (Bean and Tienda 1987). The commonwealth status of Puerto Rico allows unrestricted migration between the island and the U.S. mainland. Puerto Ricans have sought employment on the mainland as economic opportunities on the island have evaporated with rapid industrialization and have become the second largest group of Latinos in the United States They have flowed into the economies of cities such as New York and Chicago as low-wage workers (Bean and Tienda 1987; Nelson and Tienda 1997).

The circumstances bringing Mexicans and Puerto Ricans to the mainland United States are grounded in economic hardship and economic necessity. These groups have encountered barriers to advancement in the labor market from several directions, including the low levels of human capital they possess, the types of jobs that are available to them, their limited political clout, and the degree of prejudice they endure from their neighbors, employers, and fellow workers (Bean and Tienda 1987; Dovidio et al. 1992).

Cubans, the third largest group of Latinos, are distinguished by their relative economic success and by the welcome that they received from the U.S. government following the Cuban revolution in 1959. Middle- and upper-class Cubans fled the Castro regime in the 1960s. They settled in Miami, Chicago, and New York with the assistance of government programs that developed as part of the U.S. anti-Communist policy agenda. In Miami especially, Cubans created an enclave economy that generated capital for Cuban entrepreneurs and provided jobs to newly arrived Cuban workers (Portes and Bach 1985). The relatively salubrious employment opportunities for Cubans are reflected in the small wage gaps between Cubans and non-Hispanic whites of the same gender (table I.1).

Many Latinos and Latinas from Central America entered the United States as political refugees in the 1980s, fleeing war, violence, and political repression (Moore and Pinderhughes 1993). However, their status has been much more tenuous than that of Cubans. These groups have lacked economic and political resources and have often found employment in the lowest-paying sectors of local economies. Latinos and Latinas from Central and South America and the Caribbean represent 12 percent of the U.S. Latino and Latina population (U.S. Department of Commerce 1998a, b).

The geographic concentration of African Americans and groups of Latinos and Latinas in particular urban centers and regions implies that their labor market fates will be shaped by labor market conditions within distinct local areas. Changes in the structure of opportunities within those areas should thus affect their labor market profiles relatively strongly.

Changes in the Economy

Current studies identify major shifts in the industrial structure of the U.S. economy since the 1970s as a leading explanation of persistent race and ethnic inequality in the labor market. These shifts have included a shrinking share of low-skilled manufacturing jobs (deindustrialization), an increase in demand for skills (skills mismatch), and a decline in the availability in low-skill jobs in the central city (spatial mismatch). Many scholars argue that these changes have combined with other processes maintaining racial stratification—including residential segregation, the concentration of poverty, increased competition for low-skill jobs from immigrants and other groups, and workplace discrimination—to intensify disadvantage among Latinos and African Americans (Moore and Pinderhughes 1993; Wilson 1987, 1996).

Economists contend that the industrial restructuring of the U.S. economy took at least two forms that contributed to rising inequality (Holzer and Vroman 1992). First, the types of jobs available changed as the economy moved from manufacturing to services. Second, there was an upgrading of skill requirements for jobs, and the returns to higher education increased (Juhn, Murphy, and Pierce 1993). Both of these processes were especially detrimental to African American and Latino men, who were more likely than white men to be employed in declining industries, to have low skills, and to reside in geographic areas undergoing the most rapid economic transitions (Holzer and Vroman 1992; Ortíz 1996). There is some evidence that industrial restructuring also undermined the wage and employment prospects of Latinas and African American women. Although men and women are employed in different industries and jobs, within their respective race or ethnic group they tend to have similar levels of education and to reside in the same locales.

Deindustrialization did not occur evenly across the United States. In the cities of the Northeast and Midwest, manufacturing jobs disappeared as companies moved their operations to the West and South (the "Sunbelt") or overseas. The cities of the Sunbelt actually added manufacturing jobs to their total employment and benefited from the largest relative job growth overall within the nation. However, in every region, services became a greater share of total employment while the share of manufacturing declined (Kasarda 1995).

Substantial evidence indicates that declining labor market opportunities associated with deindustrialization played an important role in the rise in black male joblessness in the 1980s (Holzer and Vroman 1992; Juhn 1992; but see Krugman 1996). The effects of deindustrialization may be largely relevant to men, however. A much larger proportion of women than men are employed in the service sector, so that the shifts away from manufacturing toward service industries may actually have boosted female employment and wages. Between 1970 and 1980, three-fourths of the increase in women's nonagricultural jobs occurred in service industries (Tienda, Ortíz, and Smith 1987). Although there is little evidence from studies of national trends that women's employment or wages suffered as a result of deindustrialization (Browne 1997), within services women remained disadvantaged relative to men. Industrial restructuring redrew the boundaries of the sex-based segregation of occupations, so that women continued to earn less than coethnic men (Tienda, Ortíz, and Smith 1987).

The loss of manufacturing jobs may have hurt women within particular local labor markets. Factories within some metropolitan areas employ a large proportion of women, the majority of whom are racial or ethnic minorities. For instance, in Los Angeles, 75 percent of operatives in apparel firms in 1980 were women of Mexican origin (Fernandez-Kelly and Garcia 1990).

In addition, there is a debate about the extent to which the increase in services represented a shift from "good" jobs to "bad" jobs (Meisenheimer 1998). Traditionally, factory workers with few years of schooling could still acquire upward mobility and move into positions that offered security and relatively high pay. Harrison and Bluestone (1988) claim that the "middle-level" jobs have disappeared. What remains are high-paying jobs that demand high levels of technical expertise and low-paying, "dead-end" jobs that require minimal education.

The skills mismatch thesis posits that there has been an upgrading of the skill requirements for low-skill jobs, so that opportunities for the least-skilled workers are fewer and fewer (Holzer 1995). Those groups with the lowest levels of education, such as African Americans, Mexicans, and Puerto Ricans, should be especially vulnerable to lost opportunities arising from skills mismatch.

There is some evidence that Latinas and African American women are affected by a skills mismatch. In his study of jobs requiring a high school degree or less, Holzer (1995) finds that jobs entailing reading and writing, arithmetic, or computer skills are less likely to go to African American than to white women. Latinas are less likely than white women to be hired for jobs involving daily interaction with customers or computers. White women's relative advantage in hiring for these jobs could be due either to actual differences in skill levels among white women, Latinas, and African American women or to negative employer biases regarding the skills of the latter two groups (Dovidio et al. 1992; Kirschenman and Neckerman 1992).

Residential segregation by race and ethnicity compounds the difficulties that Latinas and African American women encounter as they navigate through a restructuring economy. Proponents of the spatial mismatch thesis suggest that deindustrialization was especially pronounced in large metropolitan areas, as low-skill jobs in manufacturing left the central cities and moved to the suburbs or overseas (Holzer and Vroman 1992; Ihlanfeldt and Sjoquist 1989). As they followed the jobs, the move of many central-city residents into the suburban hinterlands precipitated a decline in the demand for services, further reducing the number of low-skill employment opportunities in the central city (Kasarda 1995). Competition for a smaller number of jobs decreased wages for those positions that did remain. Low-skilled African Americans were especially hard-hit by the departing jobs; they were more likely to reside in the inner city compared to similar white families and were restricted by persistent residential segregation from following jobs to the suburbs (Zax and Kain 1996).

Spatial mismatch may be less relevant to poor families of Mexican and Puerto Rican origin. Moore and Pinderhughes (1993) suggest that only some Puerto Rican communities resemble African American communities in the concentration of poor residents within the inner city. Housing discrimination is less severe for Latinos and Latinas than for African Americans, and even segregated Latino neighborhoods experience continual inflows and outflows of families through immigration. Discrimination by employers may also operate in favor of some Latinos and Latinas; even within the central city, employers may hire Mexican immigrants before they hire native-born African Americans residing in adjacent neighborhoods (Moore and Vigil 1993).

Human Capital

The restructuring of the U.S. economy appears to have increased the prominence of individual "skill" in determining a worker's lifetime chances in the market, as disparities between the requirements for low-skill and high-skill positions stretch farther apart and the availability of "middle-level" jobs shrinks (Bluestone and Harrison 1982). Without additional training, it is difficult for low-skilled workers to advance into higher-paying jobs and approach a middle-class standard of living for themselves and their children. Education is one of the foremost indicators of skill for employers and for researchers (Becker 1964). On average, Latinas and African Americans possess fewer years of education than whites do (Robles 1997).

Although there is agreement that these intergroup differences in skill contribute to economic inequality, debates abound over how important the skill differences are—that is, to what extent does skill explain labor market stratification by race and gender?—and what causes the differences in educational attainment—specifically, are the differences the result of individual choices or structural constraints? (Cancio, Evans, and Maume 1996; England 1992; Farkas and Vicknair 1996; Tam 1997). These debates are important for policy; if most of the wage gap between whites and other races or ethnic groups arises from skill differences, then interventions should be geared toward training and supplemental education programs. If skill is just one facet of the problem of inequality, and individuals with equal skill encounter different chances in the labor market because of employer practices and discrimination, then policy must address the demand-side aspects of the labor market.

Adherents of orthodox human capital theory would counter that antidiscrimination policy attempts to ameliorate skill discrepancies would be unwarranted. According to that theory, individuals make choices about the amount of time they want to invest in developing their human capital (Becker 1964). Thus, labor market stratification does not reflect any systematic biases against women or racial or ethnic minorities but is the result of individual choice and the impersonal forces of supply and demand. And although some studies find that African Americans and Latinos and Latinas receive lower returns to education than whites do (Cotton 1988), this discrepancy is interpreted within the human capital tradition as the result of differences in "unmeasured skills" and school quality rather than of discrimination (Smith 1984).

The human capital perspective is challenged by scholars who claim that skill differences are actually an outcome, rather than a cause, of racial or ethnic and class stratification (that is, that skills are "endogenous") (Roscigno 1995). For instance, residential segregation creates disadvantages that are more often the result of structural constraints than of individual decisions; Latinos and Latinas and African Americans dwelling in segregated urban neighborhoods often attend schools of poor quality (Farkas and Vicknair 1996; Orfield 1992; Bean and Tienda 1987). In addition, scholastic achievement may drop when there is little expectation that efforts will be rewarded in the labor market (Baker and Jones 1993).

Disarticulation

Wilson (1987) contends that residential segregation and concentrated poverty have not simply depleted resources for inner-city schools but rather have led to a breakdown, or "disarticulation," in the social processes linking low-skilled blacks to the labor market (Browne 1997). For Wilson (1987), industrial restructuring fueled the exodus of middle-class residents and middle-class institutions from black neighborhoods in the central city, leaving behind the "truly disadvantaged." His thesis turned the debates on race and inequality toward impoverished blacks who were concentrated in inner-city neighborhoods where deindustrialization was eliminating the low-skill manufacturing jobs in which residents were traditionally employed. High-poverty neighborhoods further separated residents from the labor market by isolating them from the institutions and social networks that could provide the information and role models necessary to secure a job (Wacquant and Wilson 1993). African American women were indirectly affected by the lack of viable employment opportunities. Fewer employed black males reduced the pool of potential marriage partners for black women. Women thus had to become state welfare recipients to support themselves and their children.

In contrast to Wilson's view, theorists such as Murray (1984) posit that welfare is a cause rather than a consequence of lower employment for black males. According to Murray, the availability of welfare to single mothers provides a disincentive for men to seek paid work, marry, and become the head of a family. Welfare not only erodes the Protestant work ethic, it also rewards poor teenaged mothers for having babies out of wedlock.

In Murray's formulation, the disincentive to work among the poor is characterized as a rational response to the choice between welfare and low-wage work. Others argue that the poor are motivated by a value system in which premarital sex, out-of-wedlock births, and welfare dependency are normative for young women (Anderson 1991). According to Lewis, "One can speak of the culture of the poor, for it has its own modalities and distinctive social and psychological consequences for its members" (1962, 2). In his ethnography of five Mexican families, he describes one family as especially typifying the "culture of poverty": "In this family there is almost complete absence of the middle-class values which are beginning to spread throughout the lower strata of Mexican society. The parents show little drive to improve their standard of living and do not place high value on education, clothing, or cleanliness for themselves or their children" (1962, 15). While Lewis's studies focused on low-income Mexican and Puerto Ricans in the 1950s and 1960s, more recent adaptations of the culture-of-poverty thesis have centered on impoverished inner-city African Americans—the "underclass"—and their dependency on welfare (Auletta 1982; Banfield 1974).

Neither the "structural" (Wilson's) version nor the "cultural" (Lewis's) version of the disarticulation thesis considers the direct relationship between women's labor market activity and their reliance on public assistance. Yet it seems reasonable that if employment opportunities in the inner city are dwindling and wages for low-skilled workers are falling, then poor Latinas and African American women may be pushed out of the labor market and onto the welfare rolls out of economic necessity. The evidence suggests that, in general, women are not opting for welfare as a "lifestyle" in an effort to avoid paid work, as the culture-of-poverty thesis would suggest. Over half of welfare recipients exit the program within two years (Bane and Ellwood 1986). Many long-term recipients actually cycle between spells of being employed and receiving aid to families with dependent children (AFDC), since the level of benefits that women receive from welfare is insufficient to sustain a family (Spalter-Roth, Hartmann, and Andrews 1994; Edin and Lein 1997; Harris 1993). In fact, the majority of women on AFDC engage in some form of additional income-generating activity—either through formal employment or in the informal economy (Edin and Lein 1997). African American, Mexican, and Puerto Rican women are more likely to receive welfare than non-Hispanic white women are, and the literature indicates that social class factors rather than race account for this difference (Harris 1993).

The AFDC program has been replaced by the much more restrictive temporary assistance to needy families (TANF). With a five-year lifetime limit on benefits, many poor women will be forced to seek alternate means of supporting their families and should enter the labor market. If Murray (1984) and the culture-of-poverty theorists are correct that welfare recipients simply do not want to work, then the elimination of support through federal transfers should induce former beneficiaries to get jobs. However, if industrial restructuring has limited the employment opportunities for low-skilled workers, then single mothers with few skills will be unable to find jobs, and poverty will rise (Burtless 1995). Mexican-origin, Puerto Rican, and African American women, who most often serve as the single head of a family and have the lowest levels of education, will be in the most precarious labor market position.

Discrimination

Theories of disarticulation focus on impoverished African Americans and Latinos living in blighted urban centers (Moore and Pinderhughes 1993). Yet labor market inequality by race (and gender) is not just the province of the poor. Even among those with the highest levels of education, inequality between the wages of blacks and whites is increasing, and there is a gender gap in pay (Blau and Beller 1992; Levy and Murnane 1992).

Theories of labor market discrimination posit that ongoing labor market disadvantage among Latinas and African American women cuts across social class lines (although discrimination may be articulated differently for each class) (Feagin and Sikes 1994). Discrimination can appear in many guises, including the use of group averages as proxies for human capital attributes of job applicants ("statistical discrimination"), insidious biases in the evaluation of skill and performance by employers and managers, and more blatant prejudice against individuals based on their gender and race (Becker 1957; England 1992; Feagin and Sikes 1994). Since discriminatory practices in the workplace are illegal, it is difficult to cull direct evidence that employers, workers, and customers favor some groups, especially white males, over other groups. Audit studies provide one test of the extent of employer discrimination in hiring. In typical audit studies of employment, individuals with identical résumés apply for jobs. These studies reveal that whites are more likely to be hired than "equally qualified" African Americans and that men are more likely to be hired than "equally qualified" women (see Fix and Struyk 1993). In-depth interviews with employers and personnel managers also reveal that many employers hold negative stereotypes of African American workers, particularly young African American males (Kirschenman and Neckerman 1992).

If discrimination is implicated in the growing labor market disadvantage of African American and Latino and Latina workers, then it would have had to increase during the 1980s. A reduction in the enforcement of affirmative action guidelines appears to be one avenue through which this increase could have occurred (Bound and Freeman 1992). Leonard (1994) argues that improvements in the labor market status of blacks in the 1970s were due to the enforcement of affirmative action guidelines. With the en-

/ 17

try of the Reagan administration in the 1980s, this enforcement slackened, reversing African Americans' earlier progress. In a recent study of employers, Holzer (1995) also finds that minorities and women are generally more likely to be hired in firms that have affirmative action policies in place.

Studies of employees and job seekers also provide evidence for the continued presence of discrimination in the labor market. Many workers of African American and Latino descent report that they have been passed over in hiring, raises, and promotions because of their race or ethnicity (Bobo and Suh 1996; Feagin and Sikes 1994; Segura 1992; Suh 1996).

Women of all backgrounds also perceive that they are facing gender discrimination at the workplace, as evidenced by the large number of Title VII suits brought before the Equal Employment Opportunity Commission (Goldin 1990, 203). Researchers are only beginning to consider how Latinas and African American women face the combination of racial or ethnic and gender discrimination. What they are finding is that discrimination occurs along the entire continuum of occupation and skill levels—from blue-collar work to professional employment (Tallichet 1995; Segura 1992; Higginbotham 1997; Zavella 1987). In fact, there is some evidence that racial or ethnic and gender discrimination is most prevalent within those jobs that bring the greatest amount of interaction with white or male coworkers, supervisors, and customers (Suh 1996).

NEW INSIGHTS

The literature suggests that the labor market experiences of Latinas and African American women over the past twenty years have been molded by the substantial upheavals within economic and social institutions in the United States. The growing racial and ethnic diversity within the U.S. population has created a more richly textured society while increasing the potential for conflict over resources and jobs (Laslett 1996); the changing industrial structure has fostered remarkable technological expertise while depressing wages among the low-skilled (Holzer and Vroman 1992); and the relaxation of traditional gender roles has opened new opportunities for women in the public arena while shifting onto their shoulders a greater share of the financial responsibility for their families (Danziger and Gottschalk 1993).

Yet the answer to the question of how these changes in social institutions are affecting the labor market experiences of Latinas and African American women remains incomplete, and the available knowledge is piecemeal. Written by scholars from a variety of disciplines using a range of methodologies, the chapters in this volume fill some of the gaps and bring fresh, innovative perspectives to bear on the issues.

The chapters in part I systematically examine and compare the contours of labor market outcomes among Latinas and African American women, exploring the extent of inequality between these women and white women, white men, and coethnic men. The contributions reveal the wide range of experiences and outcomes within populations of Latinas and African American women and demonstrate the need for theories that can take into account the processes that lead to inequality among women within particular races or ethnic groups as well as across genders and races or ethnic groups.

Mary Corcoran (chapter 1) addresses the question of whether the labor market fortunes of African American women have improved or deteriorated since 1970. Focusing on the young, a group whose experiences particularly capture the effects of industrial restructuring, the author describes trends in employment and wages among African American women from 1970 through 1990. She finds that the general picture of absolute economic progress among African American women pertains only to those who are well educated. A growing disparity between black and white women is quite pronounced among the young; wages for African American women under the age of thirty-five declined in the 1980s, while wages among young white women increased. Corcoran emphasizes that the extent and pace of black-white inequality are great among the young; these trends are missed in investigations that focus on the entire population and do not take age into account.

In analyses that complement the findings of Corcoran, John Bound and Laura Dresser (chapter 2) assess the underlying causes of the erosion in the wages and employment of young African American women relative to white women from 1973 to 1989. The authors uncover the distinctive ways that industrial restructuring has undermined economic progress among young black women both nationally and within particular regions of the country. When the authors focus on regional patterns, they discover that black women in the Midwest actually suffered wage losses with the decline of manufacturing employment. In all regions, young black women have been entering those sectors of the economy in which opportunities are shrinking. In fact, it is among the college-educated that the wage gap has eroded the most rapidly. Bound and Dresser trace this pattern to the influx of African American women into low-paying occupations; about one-third of African American women with college degrees are employed in clerical occupations. Other factors associated with industrial restructuring, namely, declining unionization and a reduction in the real wage, have contributed to the widening black-white wage gap among women.

In chapter 3, Mary Corcoran, Colleen M. Heflin, and Belinda L. Reyes follow trends in employment and earnings for young Mexican and Puerto Rican women and offer analyses that parallel Corcoran's examination of African American women. They also reveal the relative advantages that white women enjoy but that are hidden within trends for the total population. The authors show that the economic fortunes of Mexican-origin women deteriorated between 1970 and 1990 while those of Puerto Rican women improved. Both these groups, however, continue to lag behind white women in terms of employment and wages. Similar to the case of African American women, individual Mexican-origin and Puerto Rican women vary markedly in their labor market profiles, with marital status, education, geographic location, and nativity creating divergent pathways toward a bettering or a worsening of their labor market position. In particular, wage inequality between those with low levels of schooling and those with high levels of schooling has increased for both Mexican-origin and Puerto Rican women. These groups diverge, however, in the predominant issues that define their labor market disadvantage in the 1990s; for young Mexican-origin women, low levels of schooling and high immigration rates are shaping wages and opportunities. The economic condition of young Puerto Rican women, in contrast, is characterized by relatively low employment and high unemployment.

Employment and earnings differences across groups of African American, Latina, and white women are explored by Paula England, Karen Christopher, and Lori L. Reid (chapter 4) and Barbara F. Reskin (chapter 5). England, Christopher, and Reid focus specifically on wage inequality and probe the "intersection" of gender and race or ethnicity in the labor market. They ask whether the determinants of the gender gap in wages differ for African American, Latino and Latina, and white workers in the United States and whether the determinants of the race- or ethnicity-based gap in wages differ for women and men. They find that the answer to these questions depends on the particular labor market influence being considered. On the one hand, men's higher earnings within all ethnic groups are strongly related to the segregation of occupations and industries by sex. On the other hand, experience and seniority differences between men and women contribute to the gender gap in pay among whites much more than among African Americans or Latinos and Latinas. The pay gap between various ethnic groups is primarily driven by "human capital" for both men and women, although the strength of the effect varies by gender. In particular, a combination of education and cognitive skills appears to explain more of the difference in earnings among white women, African American women, and Latinas than between races or ethnic groups of men.

The segregation of jobs into male- and female-dominated positions is one of the main avenues through which the gender gap in wages is maintained (Reskin 1993). As Reskin notes, comparatively little is known about occupational segregation based on race and ethnicity beyond black-white distinctions. In chapter 5, Reskin explores current patterns of occupational segregation by race or ethnicity and gender to describe the labor market position of Latinas and African American women in the United States. She demonstrates that occupational segregation occurs along at least two important axes; women are allocated into positions on the basis of their race and ethnicity as well as their gender. The segregation of occupations by race and gender contributes to earnings inequality. The implications of Reskin's descriptive findings are that Latinas and African American women face dual constraints on their opportunities representing dual forces that push their wages downward: they are segregated into the lower-paying "female-dominated" positions, and they are further drawn into occupations that are heavily represented by coethnics (see also Browne, Tigges, and Press forthcoming).

The chapters in part I, which provide a context for understanding the labor market fortunes of Latinas and African American women, miss important distinctions among races or ethnic groups of women. The chapters in part II use an array of methodological tools to understand specific groups and theoretical issues to delve into the processes that underlie the national trends.

Aixa N. Cintrón-Vélez (chapter 6) recounts the narratives of Puerto Rican women in New York City to follow the avenues through which industrial restructuring affects their labor market status. She casts employment as a dynamic process in which women enter and exit jobs as they face changing opportunities, family situations, and personal needs, abilities, and expectations. The oral histories reveal the myriad strategies that Puerto Rican women devise to cope with constricting market opportunities in New York and demonstrate how these strategies are contingent; the pursuit of one path, such as migration, opens new options and closes others. Despite the multifaceted nature of the personal accounts of Cintrón-Vélez's respondents, two clear patterns shape employment among Puerto Rican women in New York City: the importance of the birth and migration cohort and the salience of a woman's family situation. The women's response to the dramatic shift in New York's economy away from manufacturing industries depended upon the age and year at which they entered the labor market, the jobs they initially took, and the responsibilities they carried for maintaining their households.

Susan González Baker (chapter 7) takes on the controversial question of the potential economic problems that arise from the recent influx of immigrants into the United States. She investigates whether the earnings prospects of Mexican-origin, African American, and white women in the Southwest have been hurt by the increasing immigration of women from Mexico. Her chapter speaks to the debate over whether immigrants are directly competing with native workers for jobs and thus pushing wages down, or whether immigrants are actually contributing to economic growth and filling positions that native workers do not want. She finds evidence for both sides of the debate. In 1980—but not in 1990—an increase in Mexican-origin women reduced wages among Mexican American women. The chapter's descriptive evidence provides a ready interpretation for the shift: between 1980 and 1990 the disparity between the individual, family, and labor market characteristics of Mexican-origin women and Mexican American women increased. In contrast to the experiences of Mexican American women, non-Hispanic white women actually benefited from the growth in the population of employed Mexican-origin women in 1980 and 1990.

Kathryn Edin and Kathleen Mullan Harris (chapter 8) grapple with the important policy issue of how women who leave welfare programs for a job cope financially and stay off the welfare rolls. Combining survey data from a national sample with interviews with former welfare recipients in four cities, the authors uncover striking differences in white and black women's ability to resist cycling back from employment to welfare. Although black and white women who leave welfare for paid work earn equal wages, black women are more likely to return to the welfare rolls. The authors find that this difference is the result of the greater social resources available to white women, which help to keep them economically afloat. For all women with low skills, employment is not a sufficient source of income. However, white women can avail themselves of wider and more ample financial assistance from ex-partners and relatives than can black women.

Edin and Harris's study suggests that social class differences translate into more restricted opportunities for black women with low skills. In chapter 9, Irene Browne and Ivy Kennelly provide evidence that race itself may also play a role in reducing opportunities for black women through processes related to discrimination in the workplace. In their study of in-depth interviews with employers in Atlanta, Browne and Kennelly find that employers speak of black women in low-skill jobs using common stereotypes. One of the most prevalent stereotypes that employers invoke to describe black women is the single mother whose child-care responsibilities often inhibit her ability to perform her job. Data from surveys of employed Atlantans support the authors' contention that, rather than simply describing their workforce, employers are attending to partial information that is consistent with common stereotypes. The survey data reveal that although employed black women are more likely than white women to be single mothers, the majority of black women in the labor force do not have any children living at home. In addition, employed white women are as likely as black women to report conflicts between child-care responsibilities and their jobs.

In their chapter on professional women (chapter 10), Elizabeth Higginbotham and Lynn Weber discern that race- and gender-based discrimination is also common within the middle class and investigate how discrimination is linked to perceived opportunities and career plans. African American women in professional and managerial occupations reported instances of racial discrimination that ranged from blatant to subtle. They also endured gender discrimination—as did white female professionals. Even when they did not personally experience direct incidents of discrimination, the women in the sample perceived group discrimination; the majority of African Americans believed that they were treated differently in the workplace because of their race. These perceptions influenced the women's career plans. The authors emphasize that striving toward career success is a central concern among professional women and that decisions about career paths are strongly influenced by where the women perceive the best opportunities to lie. White women were much more likely than black women to be content with their current place of employment and sought to move up within the organization. Black women anticipated moving to a new firm to advance their careers. Although all of the women possessed professional degrees, black women were much more prone than white women to perceive the need for further education in order to advance their careers.

The contributions in the first two parts of the volume raise the questions of what more needs to be known and what needs to be done to improve the economic prospects of Latinas and African American women. The chapters in the part III respond to these queries, drawing out the implications of the empirical results for theory, method, social action, and policy making.

For Delores P. Aldridge, the changes in the industrial structure of the United States spur a call to action for African American leaders and citizens. In chapter 11, Aldridge emphasizes the need for African American women—and men—to prepare themselves for the technological advancements of the future. Aldridge claims that the development of scientific and technological expertise will not only enable African American women to become fully incorporated into the labor market but will also strengthen the political and economic leverage of black communities and thus pose a challenge to current systems of racial inequality. This perspective moves past the narrow confines of the skills mismatch thesis and draws upon Afrocentric and Africana womanist theories to craft an agenda for self-empowerment within the African American community. Aldridge constructs a heuristic model that stresses "historical-cultural experiences, equity, and action for the labor market" (HEAL). The HEAL model fuses theory and action, outlining a strategy through which African Americans can effectively take control of their own economic destinies.

In "Now You See 'Em, Now You Don't" (chapter 12), Barbara Reskin and Camille Charles interrogate the common methodological practices in studies of Latinas and African American women. They uncover important pitfalls in current research on women of color in the labor market and discuss how blind spots can frequently distort or inhibit knowledge. One problem is the separation of the literature on gender on the one hand from the literature on race and ethnicity on the other hand, with little connection between them. This leads to theoretical models that focus mainly on one axis of inequality, such as gender, while ignoring other axes, such as race. The unique constellation of opportunities and outcomes that arise from the intersection of gender, race, and ethnicity are sidestepped. The authors identify five problems that these incomplete models can create. For instance, limiting the study to the dominant social groups—such as men or whites—precludes generalizing to the omitted groups. In addition, the failure to consider how gender and race may jointly determine labor market outcomes casts doubt on the accuracy of standard labor market analyses based on a single group (the problem of specification error). Of more sweeping import, the authors emphasize that the groups that benefit most from labor market stratification control the institutions that regulate that stratification. Scholars must more directly integrate the issue of power into theoretical models of the labor market in order to develop adequate understandings of labor markets and design effective policies to meet the needs of Latinas and African American women in the labor market.

Joya Misra (chapter 13) deftly synthesizes the empirical results from the chapters to reflect upon the public policies that could alleviate the persistent disadvantage that Latinas and African American women encounter in the U.S. labor market. Policies must be multifaceted, taking into account the great diversity in experiences, needs, and labor market outcomes *among* races or ethnic groups of women. Misra discusses the possible benefits of specific policy efforts such as skill and education enhancement, comparable worth, desegregation, wage and tax legislation, day care, and welfare. She engages arguments against these approaches, drawing upon the successful experiences of western European policies that intervene in the economy by regulating wage and employment practices or that directly provide funds to poor women and their households. Improving the labor market prospects of Latinas and African American women is imperative for reducing poverty in the United States.

As an increasing number of Latino and Latina and African American families are raised by single mothers, these women need the resources that will allow them to sustain their households. In addition, enforcing policies such as antidiscrimination legislation aimed at eliminating disadvantage based on race, ethnicity, and gender throughout social institutions will reduce inequities along the entire class spectrum. The chapters in this volume provide new and vital information that will facilitate policy making and planning in the public arena and within local communities. They suggest that while Latinas and African American women have gained ground in some corners of the labor market, they have lost ground in others.

Amidst these changes, racial and ethnic inequality is strongly embedded within the processes distinguishing women's life chances. Many white women are advancing in the labor market at a rapid pace, creating greater inequality between themselves and Latinas and African American women. What is needed are theories that more adequately explain the position of Latinas and African American women in the U.S. labor market. The contributions to this volume should aid scholars in articulating how race, ethnicity, and gender intersect in social institutions to create or restrict economic opportunities for Latinas and African American women.

A NOTE ON LANGUAGE

Although the main focus of this book concerns the dynamics of race and gender as they are played-out in the labor market, it should be noted that there are debates over how the discourse about these processes can itself be a source of inequality. The concepts of "race," "ethnicity," and "gender" are contested and politically-charged. Debates over whether or not to capitalize the word "black" are especially relevant to this volume. The editorial guidelines used by the Russell Sage Foundation and many other major publishers specifies that as an adjective or a noun, "black" should appear in lower-case letters. Some scholars disagree, arguing that "Black" designates a social group that has claimed its own identity. Rejecting the appellations that white people have historically created and imposed, many African Americans have chosen the moniker of "Black" when referring to a racial-ethnic group. The authors in this volume hold a range of views on this issue. In accordance with Russell Sage Foundation policy to maintain consistency throughout the book, "black" appears in lower-case in all of the chapters.

I extend my gratitude to the Russell Sage Foundation, which afforded me the time and resources to conduct the preliminary work for this chapter during my residence as a Visiting Scholar at the Foundation. The Foundation also awarded me a grant to hold a conference in preparation for this volume. I would like to thank Paula England and Mary Corcoran for their assistance with all phases of the project, and Barbara Reskin, Joya Misra, Jerry Jacobs, and an anonymous reviewer for their comments on the manuscript.

NOTES

1. Native American women are also among those with the highest adult poverty rates.

2. Some excellent comparative analyses do exist, but they use data from the 1980s and before. For instance, see Amott and Matthaei (1991) and Tienda, Ortíz, and Smith (1987).

3. Yearly data from the Current Population Survey (CPS) show that wages among African American women dropped between 1979 and 1985 and that African

American women still earned lower wages in 1986 than they did in 1976. Earnings among white women and Latinas rose steadily after the recession at the beginning of the 1980s (England and Browne 1992).

4. Yearly data from the CPS show that wages among white and African American men actually fell slightly during the first half of the 1980s and then rose slowly in the latter part of the decade (England and Browne 1992).

5. According to Yinger (1985), an "ethnic group" is "a segment of a larger society whose members are thought, by themselves and/or others, to have a common origin, share important segments of a common culture, and . . . participate in common activities in which the common origin and culture are significant ingredients" (cited in Bean and Tienda 1987, 8B9).

REFERENCES

Amott, Teresa L., and Julie A. Matthaei. 1991. *Race, Gender, and Work: A Multicultural Economic History of Women in the United States.* Boston: South End Press.

Anderson, Elijah. 1991. *Streetwise: Race, Class and Change in an Urban Community.* Chicago: University of Chicago Press.

Auletta, Ken. 1982. *The Underclass.* New York: Random House.

Baca Zinn, Maxine, and Bonnie Thornton Dill. 1996. "Theorizing Difference from Multiracial Feminism." *Feminist Studies* 22(2): 321–31.

Baker, David P., and Deborah Perkins Jones. 1993. "Creating Gender Equality: Cross-National Gender Stratification and Mathematical Performance." *Sociology of Education* 66(2): 91–103.

Bane, Mary Jo, and David Ellwood. 1986. "Slipping into and out of Poverty: The Dynamics of Spells." *Journal of Human Resources* 21(1): 2–23.

Banfield, Edward C. 1974. *The Unheavenly City Revisited.* Boston: Little, Brown and Co.

Bean, Frank, and Marta Tienda. 1987. *The Hispanic Population of the United States.* New York: Russell Sage Foundation.

Beasley, Chris. 1994. *Sexual Economyths: Conceiving a Feminist Economics.* New York: St. Martin's Press.

Becker, Gary. 1957. *Discrimination.* New York: Basic Books.

———. 1964. *Human Capital.* New York: Columbia University Press.

Blau, Francine, and Beller, Andrea. 1992. "Black-White Earnings over the 1970s and 1980s: Gender Differences in Trends." *Review of Economics and Statistics* 74(2): 276–86.

Bluestone, Barry, and Bennet Harrison. 1982. *Plant Closings, Community Abandonment, and the Dismantling of Basic Industry.* New York: Basic Books.

Bluestone, Barry, Mary Stevenson, and Chris Tilly. 1992. "An Assessment of the Impact of 'Deindustrialization' and Spatial Mismatch on the Labor Market Outcomes of Young White, Black and Latino Men and Women Who Have Limited Schooling." Working paper. University of Massachusetts, Boston, John W. McCormack Institute of Public Affairs.

Bobo, Lawrence, and Susan Suh. 1996. "Surveying Racial Discrimination: Analyses from a Multiethnic Labor Market." Working paper. New York: Russell Sage Foundation.

Bound, John, and Richard Freeman. 1992. "What Went Wrong? The Erosion of Relative Earnings and Employment among Young Black Men in the 1980s." *Quarterly Journal of Economics* 107(1): 201–32.

Browne, Irene. 1997. "Explaining the Black-White Gap in Labor Force Participation among Women Heading Households." *American Sociological Review* 62(2): 236–52.

Browne, Irene, Leann Tigges, and Julie Press. Forthcoming. "Inequality Through Labor Markets, Firms, and Families: The Intersection of Gender and Race in Three Cities." In *The Multi-City Study of Urban Inequality*, edited by Alice O'Connor, Chris Tilly, and Lawrence Bobo. New York: Russell Sage Foundation.

Burtless, Gary. 1995. "Employment Prospects of Welfare Recipients." In *The Work Alternative: Welfare Reform and the Realities of the Job Market*, edited by Demetra Smith Nightingale and Robert H. Haveman. Washington, D.C.: Urban Institute Press.

Cancio, A. Silvia, T. David Evans, and David J. Maume, Jr. 1996. "Reconsidering the Declining Significance of Race: Racial Differences in Early Career Wages." *American Sociological Review* 61(4): 541–56.

Clayton, Obie, Jr. 1996. *An American Dilemma Revisited: Race Relations in a Changing World*. New York: Russell Sage Foundation.

Collins, Patricia Hill. 1990. *Black Feminist Thought: Knowledge, Consciousness and the Politics of Empowerment*. London: HarperCollins.

Corcoran, Mary, and Sharon Parrott. 1992. "Black Women's Economic Progress." Unpublished manuscript. Institute for Policy Research. Ann Arbor, Mich.: University of Michigan.

Cotton, Jeremy. 1988. "Discrimination and Favoritism in the U.S. Labor Market: The Cost to a Wage Earner of Being Female and Black and the Benefit of Being Male and White." *American Journal of Economics and Sociology* 47(1): 15–27.

Danziger, Sheldon, and Peter Gottschalk, eds. 1993. *Uneven Tides: Rising Inequality in America*. New York: Russell Sage Foundation.

Day, Jennifer Cheeseman. 1996. "Population Projections of the United States by Age, Sex, Race, and Hispanic Origin: 1995–2050." *Current Population Reports*, series P25, no. 1130. Washington: U.S. Government Printing Office for U.S. Bureau of the Census.

Dovidio, John F., Samuel L. Gaertner, Phyllis A. Anastasio, and Rasyid Sanitioso. 1992. "Cognitive and Motivational Bases of Bias: Implications of Aversive Racism for Attitudes Towards Hispanics." In *Hispanics in the Workplace*, edited by Stephen B. Knouse, Paul Rosenfeld, and Amy L. Culbertson. Newbury Park, Calif.: Sage Publications.

Edin, Kathryn, and Laura Lein. 1997. *Making Ends Meet: How Single Mothers Survive Welfare and Low-Wage Work*. New York: Russell Sage Foundation.

England, Paula. 1992. *Comparable Worth: Theories and Evidence*. New York: Aldine de Gruyter.

England, Paula, and Irene Browne. 1992. "Trends in Women's Economic Status." *Sociological Perspectives* 35(1): 17–52.

England, Paula, and Barbara Stanek Kilbourne. 1990. "Feminist Critiques of the Separative Self Model of Self: Implications for Rational Choice Theory." *Rationality and Society* 2(2): 156–72.

Farkas, George, and Kevin Vicknair. 1996. "Appropriate Tests of Racial Wage Discrimination Require Controls for Cognitive Skill: Comment on Cancio, Evans and Maume." *American Sociological Review* 61(4): 557–60.

Feagin, Joe, and Melvin Sikes. 1994. *Living with Racism*. Boston: Beacon Press.

Fernandez-Kelly, M. Patricia, and Anna M. Garcia. 1990. "Power Surrendered, Power Restored: The Politics of Work and Family among Hispanic Garment Workers in California and Florida." In *Women, Politics and Change*, edited by Louise A. Tilly and Patricia Gurin. New York: Russell Sage Foundation.

Fix, Michael, and Raymond Struyk, eds. 1993. *Clear and Convincing Evidence: Measurement of Discrimination in America*. Washington D.C.: Urban Institute Press.

Glenn, Evelyn Nakano. 1985. "Racial Ethnic Women's Labor: The Intersection of Race, Gender and Class Oppression." *Review of Radical Political Economics* 17(3): 86–108.

Goldin, Claudia. 1990. *Understanding the Gender Gap: An Economic History of American Women*. New York: Oxford University Press.

Harris, Kathleen Mullan. 1993. "Work and Welfare among Single Mothers in Poverty." *American Journal of Sociology* 99(2): 317–52.

Harrison, Bennett, and Barry Bluestone. 1988. *The Great U-turn: Corporate Restructuring and the Polarizing of America*. New York: Basic Books.

Higginbotham, Elizabeth. 1997. "Black Professional Women: Job Ceilings and Employment Sectors." In *Workplace/Women's Place: An Anthology*, edited by Dana Dunn. Los Angeles, Calif.: Roxbury.

Hochschild, Arlie. 1983. *The Managed Heart: Commercialization of Human Feeling*. Berkeley: University of California Press.

Holzer, Harry. 1991. "The Spatial Mismatch Hypothesis: What Has the Evidence Shown?" *Urban Studies* 28(1): 105–22.

———. 1995. "Employer Hiring Decisions and Antidiscrimination Policy." Working Paper 86. New York: Russell Sage Foundation.

Holzer, Harry, and Wayne Vroman. 1992. "Mismatches and the Urban Labor Market." In *Urban Labor Markets and Job Opportunities*, edited by George E. Peterson and Wayne Vroman. Washington, D.C.: Urban Institute.

Hondagneu-Sotelo, Pierrette. 1994. *Gendered Transitions: Mexican Experiences of Immigration*. Berkeley: University of California Press.

———. 1997. "Working 'without Papers' in the United States: Toward the Integration of Legal Status in Frameworks of Race, Class, and Gender." In *Women and Work: Exploring Race, Ethnicity, and Class*, edited by Elizabeth Higginbotham and Mary Romero. Newbury Park, Calif.: Sage Publications.

Ihlanfeldt, Keith, and David Sjoquist. 1989. "The Impact of Job Decentralization on the Economic Welfare of Central City Blacks." *Journal of Urban Economics* 26(1): 110–30.

Jennings, James, ed. 1992. *Race, Politics, and Economic Development: Community Perspectives*. London: Verso.

Juhn, Chinhui. 1992. "Decline of Male Labor Market Participation: The Role of Declining Market Opportunities." *The Quarterly Journal of Economics* 107(1): 79–121.

Juhn, Chinhui, Kevin Murphy, and Brooks Pierce. 1993. "Wage Inequality and the Rise in Returns to Skill." *Journal of Political Economy* 101(3): 410–42.

Karoly, Lynn A. 1993. "The Trend in Inequality Among Families, Individuals and Workers in the United States: A Twenty-Five Year Perspective." In *Uneven Tides:*

Rising Inequality in America, edited by Sheldon Danziger and Peter Gottschalk. New York: Russell Sage Foundation.

Kasarda, John D. 1995. "Industrial Restructuring and the Changing Location of Jobs." In *State of the Union: America in the 1990s. Volume One: Economic Trends*, edited by Reynolds Farley. New York: Russell Sage Foundation.

Kilbourne, Barbara Stanek, Paula England, and Kurt Beron. 1994. "Effects of Individual, Occupational, and Industrial Characteristics on Earnings: Intersections of Race and Gender." *Social Forces* 72(4): 1149B76.

King, Deborah. 1988. "Multiple Jeopardy, Multiple Consciousness: The Context of Black Feminist Ideology." *Signs* 14(1): 42–72.

King, Mary C. 1993. "Black Women's Breakthrough into Clerical Work: An Occupational Tipping Model." *Journal of Economic Issues* 27(4): 1097–1125.

Kirschenman, Joleen, and Katheryn Neckerman. 1992. "We'd Love to Hire Them, But . . . : The Meaning of Race for Employers." In *The Urban Underclass*, edited by Christopher Jencks and Paul E. Peterson. Washington, D.C.: Brookings Institution.

Knouse, Stephen B., Paul Rosenfeld, and Amy L. Culbertson. 1992. *Hispanics in the Workplace*. Newbury Park, Calif.: Sage Publications.

Krugman, Paul. 1996. "Domestic Distortions and the Deindustrialization Hypothesis." NBER Working Paper 5473. Cambridge, Mass.: National Bureau of Economic Research.

Laslett, John H. 1996. "Historical Perspectives: Immigration and the Rise of a Distinctive Urban Region, 1900–1970." In *Ethnic Los Angeles*, edited by Roger Waldinger and Mehdi Bozorgmehr.

Leonard, Jonathan. 1994. "Employment and Occupational Advance Under Affirmative Action." *Review of Economics and Statistics* 66(3): 377–85.

Levy, Frank, and Richard Murnane. 1992. "U.S. Earnings Levels and Earnings Inequality: A Review of Recent Trends and Proposed Explanations." *Journal of Economic Literature* 30(3): 1333–81.

Lewis, Oscar. 1962. *Five Families: Mexican Case Studies in the Culture of Poverty*. New York: Random House.

Massey, Douglas S., and Nancy A. Denton. 1993. *American Apartheid: Segregation and the Making of the Underclass*. Cambridge, Mass.: Harvard University Press.

Mead, Lawrence. 1992. *The New Politics of Poverty: The Nonworking Poor in America*. New York: Basic Books.

Meisenheimer, Joseph II. 1998. "The Services Industry in the 'Good' Versus 'Bad' Jobs Debate." *Monthly Labor Review* 121(4): 22–47.

Moore, Joan, and James Diego Vigil. 1993. "Barrios in Transition." In *In the Barrios: Latinos and the Underclass Debate*, edited by Joan Moore and Racquel Pinderhughes. New York: Russell Sage Foundation.

Moore, Joan, and Racquel Pinderhughes, eds. 1993. *In the Barrios: Latinos and the Underclass Debate*. New York: Russell Sage Foundation.

Morris, Martina, Annette D. Bernhardt, and Mark S. Handcock. 1994. "Economic Inequality: New Methods for New Trends." *American Sociological Review* 59(2): 205–19.

Murray, Charles. 1984. *Losing Ground: American Social Policy, 1950–1980*. New York: Basic Books.

Myrdal, Gunnar. 1944. *An American Dilemma: The Negro Problem and Modern Democracy*. New York: Harper and Brothers.

Nelson, Candace, and Marta Tienda. 1985. "The Structuring of Hispanic Ethnicity: Historical and Contemporary Perspectives." *Ethnic and Racial Studies* 8(1): 49–74.

O'Neill, June. 1985. "The Trend in the Male-Female Wage Gap in the United States." *Journal of Labor Economics* 3(1): S91–S116.

Orfield, Daniel. 1992. "Urban Schooling and the Perpetuation of Job Inequality in Metropolitan Chicago." In *Urban Labor Markets and Job Opportunities*, edited by George Peterson and Wayne Vroman. Washington, D.C.: Urban Institute Press.

Ortíz, Vilma. 1996. "The Mexican Origin Population: Permanent Working Class or Emerging Middle Class." In *Ethnic Los Angeles*, edited by Roger Waldinger and Mehdi Bozorgmehr. New York: Russell Sage Foundation.

Portes, Alejandro, and Robert L. Bach. 1985. *Latin Journey: Cuban and Mexican Immigrants in the United States*. Berkeley, Calif.: University of California Press.

Reskin, Barbara. 1993. "Sex Segregation in the Workplace." *Annual Review of Sociology* 19: 241–70.

Reskin, Barbara, and Irene Padavic. 1993. *Women and Men at Work*. Thousand Oaks, Calif.: Pine Forge Press.

Robles, Barbara J. 1997. "An Economic Profile of Women in the United States." In *Women and Work: Exploring Race, Ethnicity, and Class*, edited by Elizabeth Higginbotham and Mary Romero. Newbury Park, Calif.: Sage Publications.

Rollins, Judith. 1985. *Between Women: Domestics and Their Employers*. Philadelphia: Temple Press.

Romero, Mary. 1992. *Maid in the U.S.A.* New York: Routledge.

Roscigno, Vincent J. 1995. "The Social Embeddedness of Racial Educational Inequality: The Black-White Gap and the Impact of Racial and Local Political-Economic Contexts." *Research in Social Stratification and Mobility* 14: 137–68.

Scott, Allen. 1996. "The Manufacturing Economy: Ethnic and Gender Divisions of Labor." In *Ethnic Los Angeles*, edited by Roger Waldinger and Mehdi Bozorgmehr. New York: Russell Sage Foundation.

Segura, Denise. 1992. "Chicanas in White Collar Jobs: 'You Have to Prove Yourself More.'" *Sociological Perspectives* 35(1): 163–82.

Smith, James P. 1984. "Race and Human Capital." *American Economic Review* 74(4): 685–98.

Spalter-Roth, Roberta, Heidi Hartmann, and Linda Andrews. 1994. "Mothers, Children and Low-Wage Work: The Ability to Earn a Family Wage." In *Sociology and the Public Agenda*, edited by William J. Wilson. Newbury Park, Calif.: Sage Publications.

Stromberg, Ann Helton, and Shirley Harkess. 1988. *Women Working*. Mountain View, Calif.: Mayfield.

Suh, Susan. 1996. "Impacts of Gender and Race: Perceived Discriminatory Workplace Experiences of Women Workers." University of California, Los Angeles. Unpublished paper.

Tallichet, Suzanne. 1995. "Gendered Relations in the Mines and the Division of Labor Underground." *Gender and Society* 9(6): 697–711.

Tam, Tony. 1997. "Sex Segregation and Occupational Gender Inequality in the United States: Devaluation or Specialized Training?" *American Journal of Sociology* 102(6): 1652–92.

Tienda, Marta, Katherine Donato, and Hector Cordero-Guzmán. 1992. "Schooling, Color and the Labor Force Activity of Women." *Social Forces* 71(2): 365–96.

Tienda, Marta, Vilma Ortíz, and Shelley Smith. 1987. "Industrial Restructuring, Gender Segregation, and Sex Differences in Earnings." *American Sociological Review* 52(2): 195–210.

Tomaskovic-Devey, Donald. 1993. *Gender and Race Inequality at Work: The Sources and Consequences of Job Segregation.* Ithaca, N.Y.: ILR Press.

U.S. Department of Commerce. U.S. Bureau of the Census. 1992. *Census of Population and Housing: Public Use Microdata Sample.* Washington: U.S. Government Printing Office.

———. 1997. *Poverty in the United States: 1996.* Current Population Reports P60–198. Washington: Government Printing Office.

———. 1998a. *Current Population Survey–March 1997.* Washington: Government Printing Office.

———. 1998b. *Hispanic Population of the United States: Current Population Survey–March 1997. Detailed Tables.* Table 1. Washington: Government Printing Office.

U.S. Department of Labor. U.S. Bureau of Labor Statistics. 1980. *Employment and Earnings* (January). Washington: U.S. Government Printing Office.

———. 1990. *Employment and Earnings.* Washington: U.S. Government Printing Office (January).

———. 1996. *Employment and Earnings.* Washington: U.S. Government Printing Office (January).

———. 1997. "Historical Income—Persons." *Current Population Survey.* Washington: U.S. Government Printing Office (March).

Wacquant, Loic, and William Julius Wilson. 1993. "The Cost of Racial and Class Exclusion in the Inner City." In *The Ghetto Underclass: Social Science Perspectives,* edited by William J. Wilson. Newbury Park, Calif.: Sage Publications.

Williams, Christine. 1992. "The Glass Escalator: Hidden Advantages for Men in the 'Female' Professions." *Social Problems* 39(3): 253–67.

Wilson, William Julius. 1978. *The Declining Significance of Race.* Chicago: University of Chicago Press.

———. 1987. *The Truly Disadvantaged.* Chicago: University of Chicago Press.

———. 1996. *When Work Disappears: The World of the New Urban Poor.* New York: Random House.

Yinger, Milton. 1985. "Emergent Ethnicity: A Review and Reformulation." *Annual Review of Sociology* 11: 151–80.

Zavella, Patricia. 1987. *Women's Work and Chicano Families: Cannery Workers of the Santa Clara Valley.* Ithaca, N.Y.: Cornell University Press.

Zax, Jeffrey, and John Kain. 1996. "Moving to the Suburbs: Do Relocating Companies Leave Their Black Employees Behind?" *Journal of Labor Economics* 14(3): 472–504.

Zsembik, Barbara A., and Chuck W. Peek. 1994. "The Effect of Economic Restructuring on Puerto Rican Women's Labor Force Participation in the Formal Sector." *Gender and Society* 8(4): 525–40.

Part I

EMPLOYMENT AND EARNINGS AMONG LATINAS AND AFRICAN AMERICAN WOMEN

Chapter 1

The Economic Progress of African American Women

Mary Corcoran

Researchers have extensively documented, theorized about, and studied the decline in African American men's earnings and employment in the 1970s and 1980s (see Moss and Tilly 1991; Levy and Murnane 1992; and Holzer 1993 for reviews of this prolific literature). But surprisingly little published theoretical or empirical research has focused directly on African American women's economic outcomes, seriously limiting both the poverty and the economic inequality literatures. African American women have historically earned much less than white men, and the incidence of poverty in households headed by African American women is high.

In the poverty literature, for example, many discussions of poverty, especially persistent ghetto poverty, emphasize the joblessness of African American men and the illegitimate births and welfare use of African American women (see, for example, Wilson 1987, 1996; Mead 1986, 1992; Murray 1984). Many analysts argue that male joblessness, illegitimate births, and welfare use are interdependent problems and that finding jobs for young African American men is the best way to solve these problems. This formulation often ignores young African American women's labor market behavior, employment outcomes, and employment opportunities. Did young African American women's economic prospects deteriorate in the 1970s and 1980s as did young men's economic prospects? That is, are young African American women, especially inner-city women, working less and, when they do work, earning less than they did in the past? If not, then the story of an underclass created by diminishing economic opportunities for inner-city youth may either not hold or be less relevant for young African American women living in inner cities than for young African American men. If African American women's employment and wages did diminish, what were the causes: changes in overall demand, changes in demand for workers in particular occupations or industries, the movement of "good" jobs from the central city to the suburbs, the influx of white women and immigrants into the labor force, a deemphasis of the enforcement of equal opportunity laws, or changes in African American women's qualifications? The poverty literature rarely raises and never answers these questions as they pertain to women.

Like the poverty literature, the theoretical and empirical literatures on employment and wage inequality typically discuss African American women only in passing, focusing instead on African American men and on white women (see, for instance, England 1992; Goldin 1990; and Marini 1989 for reviews of research on women's employment; and Holzer 1993; Moss and Tilly 1991; Levy and Murnane 1992; and Welch 1990 for reviews of research on African American men's employment). Neoclassical theories about African American men typically focus on their low levels of schooling, poor health, and supposedly low motivation. Structural theories focus on the loss of highly paid manufacturing jobs and on discrimination in access to well-paid blue-collar jobs.

The key issue in neoclassical economic theories of women's wages is how husbands' higher earnings and sex-role socialization lead to a sex-based division of labor within the home whereby women interrupt their careers to stay home and raise children. This interruption in turn lowers women's employment and work experience, which results in lower wages for women. The key issues in structural theories of women's wages are the causes and consequences of occupational segregation of the sexes and labor market segmentation (Sorensen 1989; Reskin and Roos 1990; England 1992, Jacobs 1989). Structuralists sometimes raise the issue that the "female" labor market sector may be further stratified by race, but they usually stop there.

These standard poverty and wage models offer few insights into African American women's work experiences. An example is neoclassical theories of women's wages. Historically, few African American women had husbands who earned enough themselves to support a family; African American women were less likely than white women to be married; and African American women participated in the labor force at much higher rates than white women did. Thus, the sex-based division of labor in the home and low labor force participation rates were unlikely to account for African American women's low wages. Furthermore, because African American female workers had more years of schooling than African American male workers did and were more committed to the labor force than white women were, the skills and motivation stories offered by neoclassical economists to explain African American men's low wages are unlikely to be able to explain African American women's low wages. And since African American women often work in service or white-collar occupations, the decline in highly paid manufacturing jobs may be less relevant to understanding trends in their employment, wages, and opportunities than to understanding trends in African American men's employment, wages, and opportunities. Finally, the literature on occupational segregation by sex implicitly assumes either that occupational segregation by sex affects African American and white women in similar ways or that the African American female experience can be described by combining models developed for African American men and models developed for white women (Jackson 1990).

Criticizing past researchers for ignoring or slighting African American women in their research is relatively easy. What is less easy is to develop and test new theories and models appropriate for African American women, particularly since the way wages and employment are changing for different groups of African American women is far from clear. In this chapter, I delineate trends in African American women's employment, wages, unemployment, and occupational segregation; estimate trends separately by education, region, and marital status; compare trends for African American women with those for white women; and map out an agenda for the study of African American women and work. My discussion of trends draws on three bodies of research: my analyses of trends in African American and white women's employment and unemployment; John Bound and Laura Dresser's analyses of trends in African American women's wages relative to those of white women (chapter 2 of this volume); and King's (1992) analyses of trends in race-based occupational segregation.

I begin by describing our data, samples, and variables. Next, I report on trends in African American women's wages, employment, unemployment, and occupational segregation. To conclude, I summarize my results and propose an agenda for research on African American women and work.

DATA, SAMPLE, AND VARIABLES

Many analysts compare the median annual earnings of full-time, full-year workers when estimating trends in earnings or in sex-based and race-based earnings ratios, a practice that ignores the earnings of part-time and part-year workers. In contrast, I report trends in the average hourly wages of all employed women.

A second difference between my analyses and those of other researchers is that I estimate trends in employment and unemployment separately rather than focusing on trends in women's labor participation rate (the sum of employment and the unemployment rates). An increase in African American women's labor force participation could be due to an increase in their employment rate, in their unemployment rate, or in both rates. These three potential causes of increases in labor force participation would lead to quite different assessments of how African American women are faring in the labor market. Thus I look at employment and unemployment separately for young African American women.

Finally, following the lead of Bound and Freeman (1992) and Bound and Dresser (chapter 2), I concentrate on young African American women because their employment and wages reflect changing economic conditions and constraints better than the labor market outcomes of older African American women do. This choice of age range is important. If one looks at all African American women, the successes or failures of older cohorts of African American women may dominate estimated trends and mask changes in opportunities, employment, and wages faced by labor market entrants.

The reports of trends in hourly wages are based on tables compiled by Bound and Dresser from the 1973 to 1978 March Current Population Survey (CPS) and the Monthly Outgoing CPS Rotation Groups of 1979 to 1991.[1] We estimated hourly wage as last week's wages in (1991 dollars) divided by last week's hours worked. The sample consisted of African American and white women aged eighteen years and older who were employed at the time of the survey, who were not in school, and whose potential experience (age minus education minus six) was less than ten years. Self-employed workers were eliminated from the sample.

My analyses of employment and unemployment are based on data from the 1970, 1975, 1980, 1983, 1988, 1990, and 1992 March CPS. The years 1970, 1980, 1988, and 1990 were chosen to represent peak years; the years 1975, 1983, and 1992 were chosen to represent trough years. My CPS samples include African American and white women aged eighteen years and older for whom potential experience was less than ten years. Women who defined their work status as "in school" were excluded from the sample.

I defined women as employed if they reported nonzero work hours in years prior to the survey.[2] Full-time workers were those who reported working thirty-five or more hours per week. Full-year workers were those working fifty or more weeks per year. A woman was defined as unemployed if at the time of the survey she was not working, but had looked for work in the previous four weeks.

TRENDS IN REAL WAGES

The conventional wisdom in the late 1970s and early 1980s was that African American women's economic fortunes had improved greatly in recent years both in absolute terms and relative to other groups (Smith and Welch 1989). This was certainly true for African American women's wages in the 1960s and throughout much of the 1970s. African American women's real hourly wages grew 57.5 percent from 1959 to 1969 and 21.0 percent from 1969 to 1979, and the ratio of African American women's to white women's hourly wages rose from .64 in 1959 to .99 in 1979 (Zalokar 1990, 18). But since then the picture has been mixed. On some dimensions African American women are still faring well, but on others they appear to be losing ground. In contrast, African American men's wages and employment have consistently declined since 1973 both in absolute terms and relative to those of white men.

For young women earning wages or a salary, wage growth differed widely by race between 1973 and 1991 (see figure 1.1). The hourly wages of young African American women workers were stable in the mid- to late

Figure 1.1 / Women Workers' Mean Hourly Wages, 1973 to 1991 (1991 Dollars)

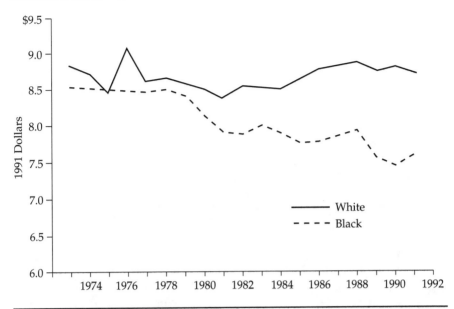

Sources: Current Population Survey (March, 1993 to 1978; Monthly Outgoing CPS Rotation Groups, 1979 to 1991).
Notes: African American and white female workers, aged eighteen and older, not in school, and not self-employed, whose potential experience (age − education − 6) is zero to nine years. Earnings are last week's wages divided by hours worked.

1970s and then declined slowly in the early and late 1980s.[3] The hourly wages of young white women workers, however, declined slightly in the mid- to late 1970s, rose in 1981 to 1987, and then remained stable. The wages of young African American women were close to those of young white women throughout most of the 1970s, but starting in 1979 the race-based wage gap widened steadily among young women workers. By 1991, young African American women's average wages were 14 percent lower than those of young white women (see chapter 2).

The trends in African American and white women's real wages show some similarities when plotted separately by level of schooling (see figure 1.2). Wage growth was flat in the 1970s for all women except college graduates. The mean wages of both African American and white women college graduates dropped from 1973 to 1979, although the drop was steeper for African American women's wages.

Wage growth in the 1980s varied in similar ways for African American and white women with the same level of schooling. The average wages of women with twelve or fewer years of schooling declined slowly through out the 1980s; the average wages of women with some college education

/ 39

Figure 1.2 / African American and White Women's Mean Hourly Wages, by Level of Schooling, 1973 to 1991 (1991 Dollars)

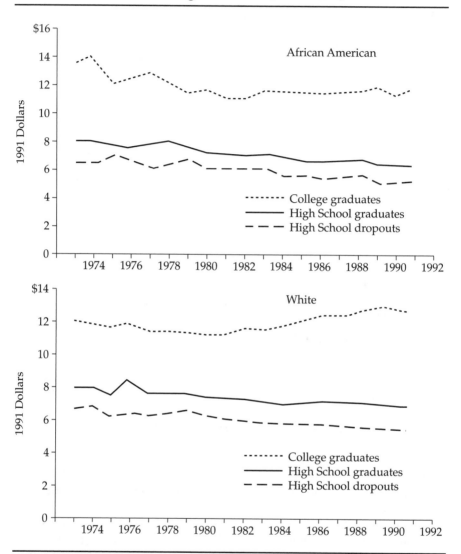

Sources: Current Population Survey (March, 1993 to 1978; Monthly Outgoing CPS Rotation Groups, 1979 to 1991).

Notes: African American and white female workers, aged eighteen and older, not in school, and not self-employed, whose potential experience (age − education − 6) is zero to nine years. Earnings are last week's wages divided by hours worked.

dropped in the early 1980s and then were stable, and the average wages of women college graduates grew slightly in the 1980s.

Although the growth trends in the wages of women with the same level of education were similar for white and African American women, the pace of these trends varied markedly. The wages of African American women college graduates decreased faster in the 1970s and increased more slowly in the 1980s than did the wages of white women college graduates. The ratio of African American women college graduates' mean wage relative to that of white women college graduates fell steadily over time, from 1.12 in 1973, to 1.00 in 1979, to 0.93 in 1991—an overall drop of 0.19. Among high school graduates and high school dropouts, mean wages fell more quickly in the 1980s for African American women than for white women, and as a result race-based wage gaps for high school graduates and high school dropouts were stable in the 1970s and widened moderately in the 1980s (see chapter 2).

Looking at levels of wages rather than at relative wages leads to a very different picture of wage growth among African American women. Based on the level of African American women's wages, college graduates fared better than high school dropouts did, since the wages of college graduates increased in the 1980s while the wages of high school dropouts decreased. Based on relative wages, college graduates fared worse: the gap between the wages of African American and white women college graduates widened faster in the 1980s than did the gap between the wages of African American and white high school dropouts.

Trends in wages and in relative wages also differed for women living in different parts of the United States (see figure 1.3). I discuss regional results only for women with twelve or fewer years of schooling since these women are most likely to be affected by regional economic conditions. In the Midwest, women's mean wages dropped sharply in the 1980s, while in the Northeast they did so in the 1970s. These patterns are not surprising given that recessions hit the Northeast in the 1970s and the Midwest in the 1980s. In both regions, wage declines were steeper among African American women than among white women.

Because African American women's wages respond more acutely to economic slowdowns than do white women's wages, race-based wage gaps widen during slowdowns. The gap for women living in the Northeast widened in the 1970s, when there was an economic downturn, and stabilized in the 1980s, when the economy improved. In the Midwest, the wage gap widened in the mid- to late 1980s, when the Midwest experienced an economic downturn (see chapter 2).

EMPLOYMENT TRENDS

I investigated trends in African American women's employment using March CPS data on weeks worked for 1969, 1974, 1979, 1982, 1987, 1989,

Figure 1.3 / African American and White Women's Mean Hourly Wages, by Region, 1973 to 1991 (1991 Dollars)

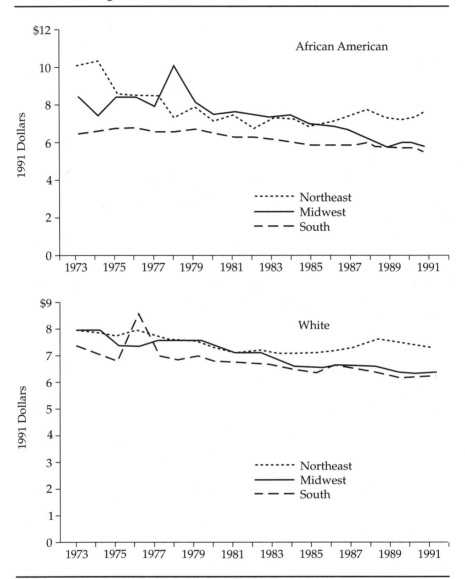

Sources: Current Population Survey (March, 1993 to 1978; Monthly Outgoing CPS Rotation Groups, 1979 to 1991).

Notes: African American and white female workers, aged eighteen and older, not in school, and not self-employed, whose potential experience (age − education − 6) is zero to nine years. Earnings are last week's wages divided by hours worked.

and 1991—four peak years and three trough years. I examined the weeks a woman had worked in the past year rather than whether she had worked during the survey week in order to pick up trends in part-time and part-year work.[4] I begin by describing the trends for all women with zero to nine years' potential experience and then estimate employment trends separately by marital status, education, and region.

The trends in the probability of having worked in the year before the survey differed markedly for African American and white women (tables 1.1 and 1.2; figure 1.4). Roughly equal proportions of African American and white women with zero to nine years' potential experience reported having worked in 1969—about 70 percent.[5] Young African American women's rate of employment varied little over the 1970s and 1980s, averaging 67 to 73 percent per year. Young white women's employment rate, on the other hand, grew rapidly from 1969 (71 percent) to 1987 (87 percent) and then stabilized: about 13 percent more young white women than

Table 1.1 / **Annual Employment Rate for African American Women, by Marital Status, Residency, Years of Education, and Region, 1969 to 1991 (Percent)**

	1969	1974	1979	1982	1987	1989	1991
All	72.5	67.7	68.1	66.6	72.5	72.9	73.1
Marital Status							
Married	72.1	70.2	73.2	77.0	79.0	81.3	81.3
Single	73.0	66.3	65.9	63.3	70.2	69.9	70.9
Single mother	69.6	58.4	58.0	48.4	56.5	58.8	61.9
Residency							
Center city	73.5	66.6	66.4	63.9	71.0	69.2	68.0
Suburb	66.4	69.0	73.9	74.6	78.4	83.1	84.3
Rural	73.8	69.9	64.9	63.6	66.8	60.9	70.4
Education							
< 12 years	57.8	49.8	43.1	38.8	38.0	39.9	40.9
12 years	76.3	68.7	70.3	64.2	72.1	71.0	72.1
13 to 15 years	82.4	81.8	77.2	80.3	89.3	86.6	85.2
16 years or more	96.4	88.8	90.1	92.5	89.2	94.3	93.0
Region							
Northeast	66.9	50.6	50.5	57.9	63.4	60.6	52.8
North Central	65.0	59.2	58.5	47.3	60.1	56.0	58.9
South	73.0	68.4	63.5	60.0	64.3	65.1	71.1
West	70.6	54.2	74.0	59.4	60.7	72.9	55.9
Northeast center city	65.5	47.6	50.3	57.6	61.2	50.1	46.2
North Central center city	64.6	59.3	55.5	49.2	60.9	49.7	53.0

Sources: Current Population Survey, March (1970, 1975, 1980, 1983, 1988, 1990, and 1992).
Note: Women aged eighteen years or older whose potential experience (age − education − 6) is zero to nine years.

Table 1.2 / Annual Employment Rate for White Women, by Marital Status, Residency, Years of Education, and Region, 1969 to 1991 (Percent)

	1969	1974	1979	1982	1987	1989	1991
All	71.2	76.4	83.5	82.9	87.2	86.7	85.6
Marital Status							
Married	61.8	68.6	76.5	76.0	81.1	82.9	82.4
Single	89.4	88.4	91.3	89.5	92.6	90.9	88.9
Single mother	73.5	69.7	74.2	66.7	72.6	74.3	68.2
Residency							
Center City	74.8	78.6	85.9	84.5	89.3	88.3	87.9
Suburb	69.8	75.8	83.8	85.6	88.9	87.3	86.4
Rural	69.7	75.1	80.7	78.0	81.3	83.0	83.1
Education							
< 12 years	56.6	59.5	65.4	61.9	68.2	61.4	57.1
12 years	72.5	75.6	82.7	78.1	85.9	85.3	81.0
13–15 years	76.7	82.9	88.5	90.3	90.9	88.9	89.1
16 years or more	75.8	83.5	89.8	92.8	91.9	88.9	93.7
Region							
Northeast	67.0	71.9	80.3	77.3	83.3	81.4	74.8
North Central	69.0	73.2	80.0	76.2	83.7	83.6	80.4
South	67.4	73.4	77.2	75.5	80.6	80.5	77.3
West	67.6	68.2	79.8	77.0	82.8	79.2	73.8

Sources: Current Population Survey, March (1970, 1975, 1980, 1983, 1988, 1990, and 1992).
Note: Women aged eighteen years or older whose potential experience (age − education − 6) is zero to nine years.

young African American women reported having worked in 1991 (86 percent and 73 percent, respectively).

While the proportions of young African American women who worked in 1969 and 1991 were roughly equal, the proportion of young African American women who worked full time for the full year increased from 1969 to 1991. Only about one-third of the young African American women who were employed in 1969 worked full time, full year, but half of young African American women who worked in 1991 did so.

The apparent stability in the proportion of young African American women who worked over time masks considerable changes in the employment behavior of particular subgroups of African American women. Trends in young African American women's employment varied systematically by marital status, education, region, and city residence.

Marital Status

In 1969, employment among young African American women did not vary by marital status: equal proportions—about 70 to 73 percent—of married

Figure 1.4 / Annual Employment Rates for African American and White Women, 1969 to 1991 (Percent)

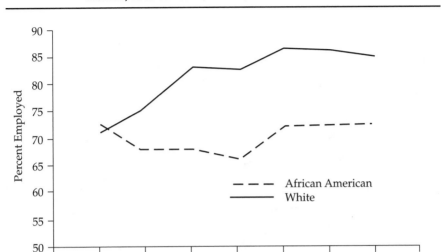

Sources: Current Population Survey, March (1970, 1975, 1980, 1983, 1988, 1990, and 1992).
Notes: Women aged eighteen years or older whose potential experience (age − education − 6) is zero to nine years. A woman was defined as employed if she reported working one or more weeks in the year before the survey.

women, single women, and single (currently unmarried) mothers worked. Marital status did predict employment for white women. Young, white married women (62 percent) were much less likely to have worked in 1969 than were either white single women (89 percent) or white single mothers (74 percent).

By 1991, the association between marital status and employment had changed dramatically for African American women (figure 1.5). Among young African Americans, the employment rate for married women increased steadily over the 1970s and 1980s, while that of African American single mothers fell sharply in the 1970s and early 1980s and picked up a bit in the 1987 recovery and thereafter. Because of these opposing trends, married women's employment rate (81 percent) greatly exceeded that of single mothers (62 percent) and single women (71 percent) among African Americans in 1991. In 1991, marital status predicted young African American women's employment: married women worked more.

For young white women, the relationship between marital status and employment actually reversed in the 1970s and 1980s, largely because of a dramatic increase in the employment of married white women (figure 1.5). In 1969 white married women were much less likely to work (62 percent) than either white single women (89 percent) or white single mothers (74

Figure 1.5 / Annual Employment Rates for African American and White Women, by Marital Status, 1969 to 1981 (Percent)

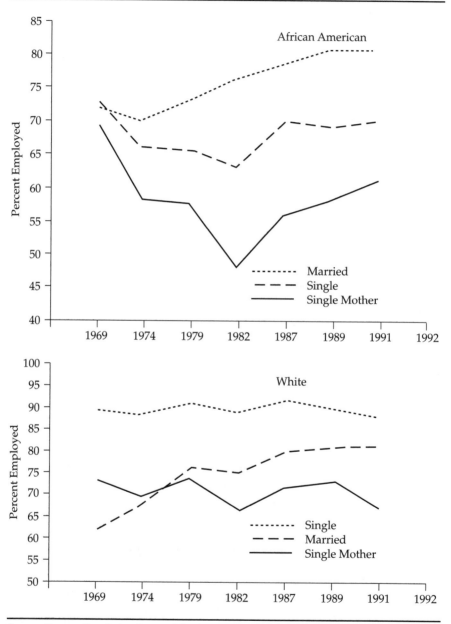

Sources: Current Population Survey, March (1970, 1975, 1980, 1983, 1988, 1990, and 1992).
Notes: Women aged eighteen years or older whose potential experience (age − education − 6) is zero to nine years. A woman was defined as employed if she reported working one or more weeks in the year before the survey.

percent). In 1991, married white women were slightly less likely to work (82 percent) than were single white women (89 percent) and more likely to work than were single white mothers (68 percent).

Education

In 1969, at every level of schooling, the employment rate for African American women exceeded the rate for white women—with the biggest gap at the college level. By 1991, this pattern had reversed itself. White employment had increased 12 percentage points for all education groups, while African American employment had increased only for women with some college education and had declined for other groups (figure 1.6). The change was particularly dramatic for high school dropouts. Between 1969 and 1991 the employment rate of young African American women high school dropouts fell 17 percentage points, from 58 to 41 percent, while employment for white high school dropouts was roughly the same in both 1969 and 1991—about 57 percent, resulting in a 16 percent employment gap between white and African American dropouts.

Region

The underclass argument emphasizes the importance of spatial mismatch to employment trends. I investigated how the employment rate of young women with twelve or fewer years of schooling varied by center-city residence, by region, and for center-city residents in the Northeast and Midwest. The trends in African American women's employment did vary somewhat by location, but the magnitude of these differences was smaller than those reported for marital status and education.

As predicted by Wilson's (1987, 1996) and Kasarda's (1989) spatial mismatch models, the employment of young African American women residing in the center city declined somewhat from 1969 to 1982, while the employment of suburban African American women rose steadily over the same period (figure 1.7). This pattern could be due to young urban African American women's moving to the suburbs when they found good jobs (Jencks and Mayer 1991). For white young women, living in the suburbs offered no advantage; the employment rate of both suburban and urban white women grew at the same rate from 1969 to 1991 (figure 1.7).

Three regional patterns are interesting. First, trends in employment did not vary systematically across the four regions for white young women (figure 1.8). In all regions, the employment rate among young white women increased rapidly from 1969 to 1979, dropped slightly in the 1982 recession, picked up in the 1987 recovery, and declined in the 1991 recession.

Second, trends in African American women's employment, unlike those of white women, varied by region, and African American women's em-

Figure 1.6 / Annual Employment Rates for African American and White Women, by Years of Schooling, 1969 to 1991 (Percent)

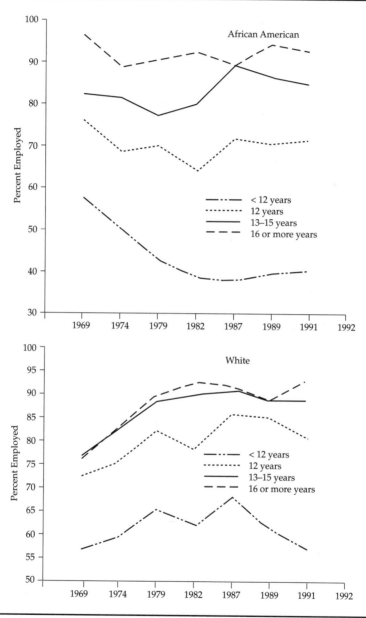

Sources: Current Population Survey, March (1970, 1975, 1980, 1983, 1988, 1990, and 1992).
Notes: Women aged eighteen years or older whose potential experience (age − education − 6) is zero to nine years. A woman was defined as employed if she reported working one or more weeks in the year before the survey.

Figure 1.7 / Annual Employment Rates for African American and White Women, by Residency Status, 1969 to 1991 (Percent)

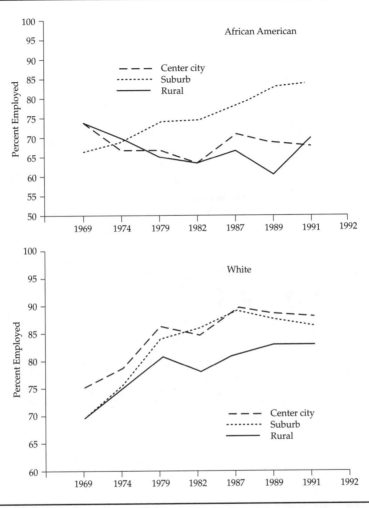

Sources: Current Population Survey, March (1970, 1975, 1980, 1983, 1988, 1990, and 1992).
Notes: Women aged eighteen years or older whose potential experience (age − education − 6) is zero to nine years. A woman was defined as employed if she reported working one or more weeks in the year before the survey.

ployment appears to have responded more to economic conditions than the employment of white women did (figure 1.8). For example, the employment rate of African American women in each region dropped sharply during the 1974 recession. During the 1982 recession, the employment rate dropped for young African American women in the Midwest and South but rose for young African American women in the Northeast and in

Figure 1.8 / Annual Employment Rates for African American and White Women with Twelve Years of Education or Less, 1969 to 1991 (Percent)

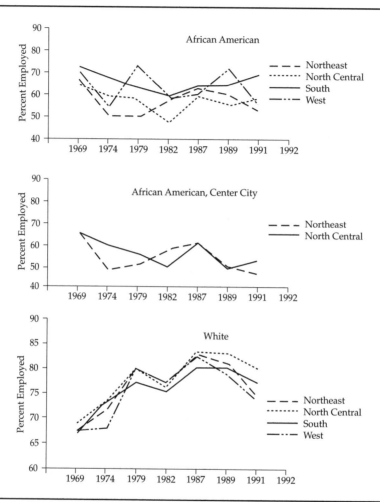

Sources: Current Population Survey, March (1970, 1975, 1980, 1983, 1988, 1990, and 1992).
Notes: Women aged eighteen years or older whose potential experience (age − education − 6) is zero to nine years. A woman was defined as employed if she reported working one or more weeks in the year before the survey.

northeastern city centers, which were experiencing a period of economic expansion. Then, when economic growth in the Northeast stalled and reversed in the late 1980s, employment dropped sharply for young African American women there.

The third notable pattern is that white women's and African American women's employment within regions was roughly equal in 1969. By 1991 that had changed; in each region, more white women than African American women reported being employed. This racial disparity was largest in the Northeast and Midwest—the two regions hit hardest by recessions.

Summary

The apparent stability in young African American women's employment from 1969 to 1991 is a result of considerable diversity in employment trends for particular subpopulations. Employment declined dramatically for young African American high school dropouts and for African American single mothers. African American women's employment responded dramatically to national and regional labor market conditions—falling in recessions and rising in periods of growth. The only subgroups of African American women for whom employment rose were married women and suburban women.

At the same time, young white women's employment increased rapidly overall—for every education group and in every region—so that the relative employment gap between African American women and white women widened in the 1970s and 1980s. By 1991, white women's employment levels were higher (sometimes much higher) than those of African American women of every marital status, at every level of education, and in every region.

SEX-BASED DIFFERENCES IN EMPLOYMENT TRENDS

The patterns of overall change in employment trends among young African men and women are quite different. Young African American men's rate of employment dropped between the mid-1970s and mid-1980s (Bound and Freeman 1992). Young African American women's employment held roughly steady after 1974, and among employed young African American women the incidence of full-time, full-year work actually increased over time. The employment of African American young men declined in every education group after 1973, and declines were especially steep for high school dropouts and college graduates (Bound and Freeman 1992). Employment also fell sharply for young African American women high school dropouts, but at other levels of schooling young African American women's employment was roughly constant from 1974 on. The major similarity here is that, among young African American high school dropouts, both men and women reported very low employment in the 1980s.

Trends in relative employment by race also differed for young men and women. Young white women's employment increased dramatically from 1969 to 1991, and as a result the percentage gap between the employment rates of African American and white women and the ratio of white women's employment to African American women's employment both in-

Figure 1.9 / Annual Unemployment Rates for African American and White Women, 1970 to 1992

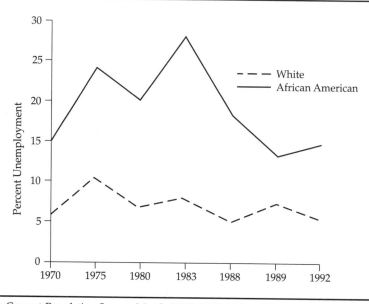

Sources: Current Population Survey, March (1970, 1975, 1980, 1983, 1988, 1990, and 1992).
Notes: Women aged eighteen years or older whose potential experience (age − education − 6) is zero to nine years. A woman was defined as employed if she reported working one or more weeks in the year before the survey.

creased sharply from 1969 to 1991. Young white men's employment rates, on the other hand, dropped from 1973 to 1989, so that the ratio of African American men's employment to white men's employment was roughly constant, although the percentage drop in employment was greater for African American than for white men (Bound and Freeman 1992).

TRENDS IN UNEMPLOYMENT

Both the wages and the employment of African American women relative to white women have declined in recent years. Badgett (1994) claims that another way in which African American women's relative disadvantages in the labor market have increased is that their unemployment rates have climbed both in absolute terms and relative to the unemployment rates of white women in recent years.

I examined unemployment among African American and white women with zero to nine years' potential experience using March CPS data for 1970, 1975, 1980, 1983, 1988, 1990, and 1992 (figure 1.9). In each of these years unemployment among young African American women greatly exceeded

Figure 1.10 / Annual Unemployment Rates for African American and White Women, High School Dropouts and High School Graduates, 1970 to 1992 (Percent)

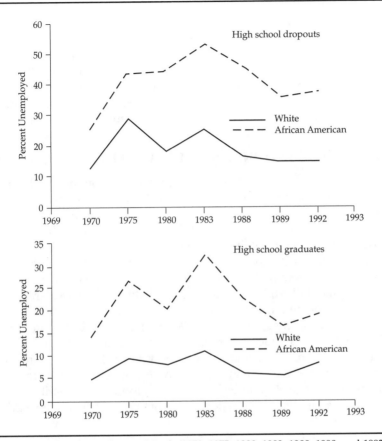

Sources: Current Population Survey, March (1970, 1975, 1980, 1983, 1988, 1990, and 1992).
Notes: Women aged eighteen years or older whose potential experience (age − education − 6) is zero to nine years. A woman was defined as employed if she reported working one or more weeks in the year before the survey.

unemployment among young white women, and the absolute gap between young African American and white women's unemployment expanded over time. African American women's unemployment rates went up much faster during recession years than did white women's unemployment rates, so that the racial gap in unemployment widened during recessions.

I also estimated young women's unemployment rate separately at each level of schooling. Perhaps the most dramatic finding here is how very high unemployment rates were for young African American women with low levels of schooling. For young African American females who were high school dropouts, unemployment rates ranged from 36 percent to 53 percent in the 1970s, 1980s, and early 1990s (figure 1.10). For young African American high school graduates, unemployment rates ranged from 17 percent to 33 percent in the 1970s, 1980s, and early 1990s (figure 1.10). Among young African Americans, unemployment rates for high school dropouts and graduates rose sharply in the mid-1970s recession, stabilized at rates much higher than the 1970 rate, and then rose sharply again during the recession in the early 1980s. At every education level and in every year (with the single exception of college graduates in 1970), African American women's unemployment rates were much higher than white women were. This white advantage grew over time and was especially large during recessions.

TRENDS IN OCCUPATIONAL SEGREGATION BY RACE AND SEX

Many authors argue that occupational segregation doubly disadvantages African American women because they tend to work in fields that are segregated both by race and by sex (Marini 1989; Jackson 1990; Reskin and Roos 1990; Zalokar 1990; Bergmann 1974). It is well established that sex-based occupational segregation is associated with lower wages for women (see Sorensen 1989 for a good review of these studies), and Zalokar (1990) has shown that differential allocations of women workers by race among occupations and industries is a strong predictor of historical race-based differences in women's wages.

King (1992) uses census data from 1940 to 1980 and data from the 1988 Annual CPS Income Extract to estimate the Duncan dissimilarity indices by sex and race for census occupation over the years 1940 to 1988. This index measures the proportion of either of the two groups being compared that would have to change occupations for the two groups to be distributed identically across occupations. She reports than between 1940 and 1960 African American and white women worked at very different occupations; the dissimilarity index is about .55 to .65 for African American and white women. She then shows that the level of occupational segregation between African American and white women fell steadily to about .30 between 1960 and 1980 and stayed roughly constant from 1980 to 1988. In the 1980s about 30 percent of white or African American women would have had to change occupations to eliminate occupational segregation by race among women.

King also reports on trends in occupational segregation by sex. In 1960, depending on the groups compared, between 65 percent and 81 percent of men or women would have had to change occupations to eliminate occupational segregation by sex. Like racial segregation, sex-based occupational segregation declined from 1960 to 1980 and remained steady in the 1980s, but the level of sex-based segregation remained high. In 1988, 57 to 66 percent of men or women would have had to change occupations to eliminate sex-based occupational segregation.

SUMMARY OF RESULTS

The overall trends in young African American women's employment and wages signal both good and bad news. The good news is that work commitment among young African American women shows no signs of a decline. Their employment remained steady after 1974, and the proportion of women who worked full time, full year increased steadily after 1973. This trend stands in sharp contrast to trends for young African American men and young white men, whose rate of employment dropped after 1973. The bad news is that the real wages of young African American women stagnated in the 1970s and declined in the 1980s.

But these overall trends do not hold for particular subgroups of young African American women. For instance, among young African Americans, employment dropped sharply for unmarried mothers and increased for married women after 1970. The association between marital status and employment thus changed for young African American women. In 1969, there were no differences in employment by marital status, but in 1991 young African American married women were more likely to work than were either single women or unmarried mothers.

Trends vary considerably by schooling. Employment among young, African American women high school dropouts declined substantially in the 1970s and 1980s, while the employment of women in other education groups remained constant. Mean wages dropped among young African American women with a high school diploma or less education during the 1980s but climbed for African American women college graduates.

Employment and wages have worsened in recent years for young African American women with twelve or fewer years of schooling. Evidence on the declining wages and employment of African American men and on falling rates of marriage among young African American women suggests that marriage opportunities are also diminishing for young African American women, especially those with low levels of schooling. In addition, the real value of welfare benefits has fallen steadily since 1973 (Moffitt 1992; Acs 1995). These declines in the real value of marriage and welfare alternatives would suggest that high school dropouts and single mothers should have more, not fewer, incentives to seek employment. Despite this, employment has dropped for young African American women high school dropouts and single mothers. The high rates of unemployment for black women with twelve or fewer years of schooling suggest that many of these women were seeking but were not able to find work. Marriage, welfare, and employment opportunities all diminished for young African American women with low levels of schooling in the 1970s and 1980s.

The Employment and Wage Gaps

The news about African American women's employment outcomes relative to those of white women is mostly bad. The 1970s and 1980s saw a slowdown and reversal of African American women's economic progress relative to that of white women. Among young women, the gap between the employment and unemployment rates of whites and African Americans expanded throughout the 1970s and 1980s, and the ratio of young African American women's mean wage to that of young white women decreased in the 1980s. On the other hand, occupational segregation by race declined sharply in the 1960s and 1970s but remained constant in the 1980s. In the mid-1970s, it looked like race was no longer going to predict women's economic fortunes (Jencks 1983; Smith and Welch 1989). This has changed; race is now an important predictor of women's employment, wages, and unemployment.

The Prospects of Low-Skilled African American Women

The news that low-skilled African American women have fared poorly in recent years is not surprising given the economic restructuring that occurred in the 1980s. The globalization of markets, the shift from a manufacturing to a service economy, and technological upgrading (for example, computerization) have reduced the demand for low-skilled labor (Levy and Murnane 1992, Danziger and Gottschalk 1996, Holzer 1996). Wilson (1996) argues that the movement of manufacturing jobs from inner cities to the suburbs has further reduced job opportunities for low-skilled, inner-city minority residents. Some recent evidence suggests that this restructuring has hurt African American women more than it has white women (see chapter 2; McCall 1996; Iceland and Smock 1997).

The rapid influx of young white women into the labor market may be contributing to widening racial employment, unemployment, and wage gaps. King's (1992) results show that African American and white women's occupational distributions grew more similar in the 1970s but that occupational segregation by sex was very high in the 1980s. To the extent that African American and white women compete for the same set of jobs, the rapid increase in the numbers of white women entering the labor market will expand the pool of women workers. If the supply of women workers rises faster than the demand for women workers, the result could be higher unemployment and lower employment.[6]

The second factor contributing to the gaps in employment, unemployment, and wages is that as white women have entered and remained in the market, the skills of young white women workers relative to those of young African American women may have increased. Bound and Dresser (chapter 2) report that about one-sixth of the trend in higher racial wage differentials among young women is due to increases in the level of white women's schooling vis-à-vis that of African American women.

A major result of the increases in women's labor force participation has been a rise in women's work experience. Wellington (1990), using data from the Panel Study of Income Dynamics, shows that for workers aged twenty-five to sixty-four years, the gap between African American women's and white women's work experience narrowed from 2.1 years in 1975 to 1.4 years in 1984. Jaynes and Williams (1989) estimate that changes in relative employment and unemployment by race among women will greatly reduce and eventually reverse racial differences in time spent employed over the lifetime. Since experience is a strong predictor of earnings, such changes could be driving some of the widening of the racial wage gaps among women. Changes in experience might be especially relevant to the dramatic widening of the race-based wage gap among women college graduates. African American women college graduates have always worked at very high rates, but white women college graduates have greatly increased their rate of employment in recent years. Thus, the change in relative experience is likely to be large for college graduates. Further, returns to work experience are much higher for college graduates than for women with less schooling (Mincer and Polachek 1974; Corcoran 1978).

The change in white women's employment could also alter employers' expectations about job applicants' potential productivity in ways advantageous to white women. In the past, employers might have assumed that African American women applicants were more likely to remain in the labor force than were white women applicants. Changes in employers' assumptions about African American and white women's future labor force attachment could reduce African American women's relative chances of being hired. That is, statistical discrimination may favor white women more now than in the past.

Another possibility is that increases in the numbers of white women workers may make it easier for employers to indulge in pure discrimination. As more white women enter the labor market, the pool of workers available for employers to choose from expands and so reduces the cost of favoring white women over equally qualified African American women.

There is fairly strong agreement that the demand for low-skilled labor has dropped. Bound and Johnson (1992) and Katz and Murphy (1992) both report that wage differentials by education have increased for both men and women. In chapter 2, Bound and Dresser report that increasing returns to schooling account for about one-sixth of the widening of the race-based wage gap among young women workers in the 1980s. Part of the reason for the widening gap between the wages of white and African American women might be that returns to skills other than education (for example, test scores or work experience) also rose in the 1980s and that employed white women had relatively more of the relevant skills. The decrease in relative demand for less-skilled labor might also explain the sharp drop in employment for African American women high school dropouts. If this explanation holds, however, it is hard to explain why the employment rate of white women high school dropouts was stable and even rose at the same time employment fell for African American high school dropouts.

NEEDED: MODELS SPECIFIC TO AFRICAN AMERICAN WOMEN

I began this chapter with the claim that African American women's labor market experiences have been relatively unstudied. I end by calling for new theory and research that focus directly on African American women and work. Simply borrowing from models originally developed for African American men or white women will not be enough. The experiences of African American women in the labor market are very different from those of African American men or white women. African American women need and deserve their own models.

I would like to thank John Bound, Marshall Cummings and Laura Dresser for providing us with computer runs for the means of African American and white women's wages from the CPS data. We also thank John Bound, Irene Browne, Paul Courant, Sheldon Danziger, Sharron Parrott, Gary Solon, and two anonymous reviewers for their advice and comments.

NOTES

1. Bound and Dresser provided me with computer runs done by Marshall Cummings calculating the annual mean and median both of hourly wages (in 1991 dollars) and of the natural log of hourly wages by race and sex, education, and region for the years 1973 to 1991.

2. In this way my analyses differ from those of Bound and Dresser (chapter 2), who define employment as whether a respondent worked in the week prior to being interviewed.

3. The picture would be different if we looked at trends in wages for all African American women. Corcoran and Parrott (1992) report that average wages for African American women aged sixteen to fifty-four years grew from 1973 to 1977, declined slightly in the late 1970s, and then grew steadily throughout the 1980s. The successes of older cohorts of African American women here mask the decline in opportunities for African American women labor market entrants.

4. I also estimated trends using the dependent variable of whether a woman had worked in the week prior to the survey. The trends were quite similar, but the estimated proportion of women working in the week prior to the survey was typically 10 to 20 percentage points lower than the proportion of women who had worked in the previous year.

5. This result seems to contradict the well-known fact that labor force participation rates were higher for African American women than for white women in the 1970s. This apparent contradiction has two causes. First, labor force participation rates are the sum of employment and unemployment rates, and African American women typically report much more unemployment than do white women. Second, my analysis includes only young women. Among women aged eighteen

to fifty-four years in 1970, 70 percent of African Americans and 61 percent of whites reported working in 1969.

6. There are two reasons to suspect that the demand for women workers is increasing. First, Katz and Murphy (1992) show that the demand is shifted toward women's fields. Second, there was a reduction in sex-based occupational segregation in the 1970s.

REFERENCES

Acs, Gregory. 1995. "Do Welfare Benefits Promote Out-of-Wedlock Child-Bearing?" In *Welfare Reform: An Analysis of the Issues*, edited by Isabel Sawhill. Washington, D.C.: Urban Institute Press.

Badgett, Lee. 1994. "Rising Black Unemployment: Changes in Job Stability or in Employability." *Review of Black Political Economy* 22(3): 55–75.

Bergmann, Barbara. 1974. "Occupational Segregation, Wages, and Profits When Employers Discriminate by Race or Sex." *Eastern Economic Journal* 1(2): 103–10.

Bound, John, and Richard Freeman. 1992. "What Went Wrong? The Erosion of Relative Earnings and Employment among Young Black Men in the 1980s." *Quarterly Journal of Economics* 107(1): 201–32.

Bound, John, and George Johnson. 1992. "Change in the Structure of Wages in the 1980s: An Evaluation of Alternative Explanations." *American Economic Review* 82(3): 371–92.

Corcoran, Mary. 1978. "The Structure of Female Wages." *American Economic Review* 68(2): 165–70.

Corcoran, Mary, and Sharon Parrott. 1992. "Black Women's Economic Progress." University of Michigan, Ann Arbor. Unpublished paper.

Danziger, Sheldon, and Peter Gottschalk. 1996. *America Unequal*. Cambridge, Mass.: Harvard University Press.

England, Paula. 1992. *Comparable Worth: Theories and Evidence*. New York: Aldine de Gruyter.

Goldin, Claudia. 1990. *Understanding the Gender Gap: An Economic History of American Women*. New York: Oxford University Press.

Holzer, Harry. 1993. "Black Employment Problems: New Evidence, Old Questions." Michigan State University. Unpublished paper.

———. 1996. *What Employers Want: Job Prospects for Less-Educated Workers*. New York: Russell Sage Foundation.

Iceland, John, and Pamela Smock. 1997. "The Impact of Industrial Shifts in Employment on the Earnings of African-American and White Women." University of Michigan, Center for Population Studies. Unpublished paper.

Jackson, Monica. 1990. "And Still We Rise: African-American Women and the U.S. Labor Market." *Feminist Issues* 10(2): 55–63.

Jacobs, Jerry A. 1989. *Revolving Doors: Sex Segregation and Women's Careers*. Palo Alto, Calif.: Stanford University Press.

Jaynes, Gerald David, and Robin M. Williams, Jr. 1989. *A Common Destiny: Blacks and American Society*. Washington, D.C.: National Academy Press.

Jencks, Christopher, and Susan Mayer. 1991. "The Social Consequences of Growing

Up in a Poor Neighborhood: A Review." Northwestern University, Center for Urban Affairs and Policy Research. Unpublished paper.

Kasarda, John D. 1989. "Urban Industrial Transition and the Underclass." *Annals of the American Academy of Political and Social Science* 501: 26–47.

Katz, Lawrence F., and Kevin M. Murphy. 1992. "Changes in Relative Wages, 1963–1987: Supply and Demand Factors." *Quarterly Journal of Economics* 107(1): 35–78.

King, Mary C. 1992. "Occupational Segregation by Race and Sex, 1940–88." *Monthly Labor Review* 115(4): 30–37.

Levy, Frank, and Richard Murnane. 1992. "U.S. Earnings Levels and Earnings Inequality: A Review of Recent Trends and Proposed Explanations." *Journal of Economic Literature* 30(3): 1333–81.

Marini, Margaret. 1989. "Sex Differences in Earnings in the United States." *Annual Review of Sociology* 15: 343–80.

McCall, L. 1996. "Restructuring and Inequality by Race, Class, Origin, and Gender in the U.S.A." Rutgers University. Unpublished paper.

Mead, Lawrence. 1986. *Beyond Entitlement: The Social Obligations of Citizenship.* New York: Free Press.

———. 1992. *The New Politics of Poverty: The Nonworking Poor in America.* New York: Basic Books.

Mincer, Jacob, and Solomon Polachek. 1974, "Family Investments in Human Capital: Earnings of Women." *Journal of Political Economy* 82(2, pt. 2): S76–S108.

Moffitt, Robert. 1992. "Incentive Effects of the U.S. Welfare System: A Review." *Journal of Economic Literature* 30(1): 1–61.

Moss, Philip, and Chris Tilly. 1991. *Why Black Men Are Doing Worse in the Labor Market.* Monograph. New York: Social Science Research Council.

Murray, Charles. 1984. *Losing Ground: American Social Policy, 1950–1980.* New York: Basic Books.

Reskin, Barbara, and Roos, P. 1990. *Job Queues, Gender Queues.* Philadelphia: Temple University Press.

Smith, James P., and Finis Welch. 1989. "Black Economic Progress after Myrdal." *Journal of Economic Literature* 27(2): 504–19.

Sorensen, Elaine. 1989. "The Wage Effects of Occupational Sex Segregation: A Review and New Findings." In *Comparable Worth: Analyses and Evidence,* edited by M. Anne Hill and Mark Killingsworth. Ithaca, N.Y.: ILR Press.

Welch, Finis. 1990. "The Employment of Black Men." *Journal of Labor Economics* 8(1, pt. 2): 526–74.

Wellington, Allison. 1990. "Employment Effects of the Minimum Wage on Youths and Changes in the Wage Gap by Gender and Race 1976–1985." Master's thesis, University of Michigan.

Wilson, William Julius. 1987. *The Truly Disadvantaged: The Inner City, the Underclass.* Chicago: University of Chicago Press.

———. 1996. *When Work Disappears: The World of the New Urban Poor.* New York: Alfred A. Knopf.

Zalokar, Nadja. 1990. *The Economic Status of Black Women: An Explanatory Investigation.* Washington: U.S. Government Printing Office for U.S. Commission on Civil Rights.

Chapter 2

Losing Ground: The Erosion of the Relative Earnings of African American Women During the 1980s

John Bound and Laura Dresser

A reasonably large literature examines the erosion of the relative wages of African American men and the increasing relative wages of white women during the 1980s, but the position of African American women in the labor market has received less attention. The historical importance of the contributions of African American women to family income and the increasing proportion of African American families that are headed by single women are just two reasons to develop a more detailed understanding of the relative position of African American women and the reason for its erosion (Simms and Malveaux 1986). In this chapter we document the distinctive experiences of African American women in the labor market, paying attention not only to race and gender but also to the important differences among African American women's experiences based on education and geography. We also look at key contributors to the increasing disparity in the wages of African American women and their white counterparts.

Following earlier work by Bound and Freeman (1992), which examined relative wage erosion of African American men, we examine trends in the wages of younger African American women relative to younger white women. The news for African American women, once heralded as an equal opportunity success story for their near wage parity with white women, is not good. After advancing to a fairly small wage disadvantage (4 percent) relative to young white women in the mid-1970s, the wage disadvantage for African American women more than tripled over the next fifteen years. By 1991, African American women's wages lagged 14 percent behind white women's wages. Documenting that trend is one thing; understanding why relative wages fell so significantly is quite another. Separate trends for African American women in distinct education and geographic groups suggest that no single factor will explain the decline. Changes in work experience, education, occupational and industrial structure, the minimum wage, and unions all have important effects on wages. In this chapter we document their effect on the decline in the relative wages of African American women.

Significantly, in this investigation we focus on young workers in an attempt to bring to light the forces that shape the U.S. workforce in the late 1990s. One reason that we look to the experience of young workers is that the experience of young African American women is likely to be a harbinger of future economic achievements of all African American women. In part, this is because seniority and experience do not guard the position of younger women, as they do for more experienced workers. The effects of economic change will be seen first among the youngest workers. Moreover, considering only young workers helps to minimize the influence of cohort effects in results. For example, relative to white working women, cohorts of African American women who entered the labor market during the 1960s and 1970s had substantially higher wages than did African American women who entered the labor market in the 1940s and 1950s. As the later cohorts have replaced earlier ones in the workforce, the earnings differential has tended to fall even when progress has ceased among new entrants. The emerging reality is more clearly demonstrated among young workers.

Our analysis places the labor market developments for African American women within the context of current labor market change. In the 1970s and 1980s, the labor market position of white women improved considerably in terms of both labor force participation and real wages. Women's increasing workforce attachment and shifts in the composition of the demand for different kinds of skill both contributed to a dramatic narrowing of the earnings differential between men and women during the 1980s (O'Neill and Polachek 1993; Wellington 1993; Blau and Kahn 1992; Katz and Murphy 1992). Additionally, the value of education and cognitive skills rose dramatically in the 1980s (Bound and Johnson 1991; Katz and Murphy 1992; Murnane, Willett, and Levy 1995).

As for the historical context, from 1940 to 1975 the economic performance of African American women advanced substantially (Cunningham and Zalokar 1992). In 1940, more than three-fourths of African American women were employed as either farm or domestic laborers (King 1992). From 1939 to 1969, the earnings of African American women high school graduates tripled, while the earnings of similar white women doubled (Badgett and Williams 1994). In the same period, African American women shifted from farm and domestic labor to clerical occupations (King 1992). The striking occupational advances of African American women and the near equality of the wages of white and African American women in the mid-1970s led to a premature conclusion that African American women were the success story of equal opportunity (see chapter 1). The recent decline in relative wages is especially remarkable in the context of the strong advances of previous periods.

It is now clear that this success story came to a close sometime in the 1970s. Cotton (1989) points to a range of indicators on economic well-being that show African Americans falling behind. With selected years of Current Population Survey (CPS) data, Blau and Beller (1992) showed that, while the relative wages of all African American women rose slightly from 1981 to 1988, the relative wages of young African American women declined in the 1980s.[1] The occupational distribution of African American women, which had advanced rapidly until 1980, remained roughly stagnant from 1980 to 1988 (King 1992). In the 1970s, the unemployment of African American women increased relative to white women's, especially among those with lower levels of education (Badgett and Williams 1994).

For this chapter, we draw on nineteen years of CPS data, using yearly information from 1973 to 1991. Earlier studies of the changes in the relative wages of African American women have used data from the National Longitudinal Survey (NLS) (McCrate and Leete 1994) or the Panel Study of Income Dynamics (PSID) (Sorensen 1991), but to our knowledge no one has used the full range of CPS data. While using PSID and NLS data carries important advantages, most notably the detailed work history data they contain, the CPS has the advantage of making large sample sizes available at yearly intervals. Drawing on this strength, we document trends more thoroughly than has been done before and seek to explain these trends.

OVERVIEW OF RESULTS

Our study documents the declining position of African American women in the 1970s and 1980s and shows that the relative wages of young African American women fell by almost 10 percent from 1976 to 1991.[2] Relative wage declines were especially significant among college graduates; in the early 1970s African American women with college degrees maintained a slight wage advantage over white women but by 1991 earned 10 percent less than white women did. African American women in the Midwest appear to have been especially hard hit as well.

Our decomposition of the wage erosion suggests that many sources contributed to the decline in the relative position of African American women. Changes in the educational distribution and the payoff to education both worked against wage parity over this period. The educational attainment of African American women rose over the 1970s and 1980s, but the educational attainment of employed white women rose even more rapidly, especially in the 1980s. These trends resulted in a widening gap in educational attainment. That gap, together with the widening gap in workforce attachment, explains some of the growing earnings differential between white and African American women. The wage payoff to the educational differential (that is, the widely noted increase in returns to education reaped by relatively highly educated white women over this period) grew as well, which is an equally important contributor to the decline in the relative wages of African American women.

The decomposition also shows that many of the forces that lowered the relative earnings of African American men also worked against African American women. For example, our evidence suggests that the economic decline of city centers, the loss of manufacturing jobs, declines in union density, and the declining value of the minimum wage all contributed to the erosion of the relative earnings of African American women with no more than a high school education, particularly those in the Midwest. Turning our attention to shifting demand in the economy, we also find that African American women, especially college-educated African American women, were concentrated in declining sectors of the economy.

EARNINGS TRENDS

The Current Population Survey

This research is based on the CPS questions regarding usual weekly earnings and weekly hours for each year from 1973 to 1991. Data limitations lie behind the choice of this time period. The CPS first collected usable data on weekly earnings in 1973. Between 1991 and 1992 the focus of the question regarding educational attainment was changed significantly, from years of schooling completed to degrees, making results from before and after the break not comparable (Jaeger 1997; Frazis and Stewart 1996). From 1973 to 1978, only the May CPS included questions on usual earnings and hours. In the following years, the earnings and hours questions were answered by outgoing rotation groups in all months, leading to much larger sample sizes from 1979 to 1991 than in the earlier period.

Our sample consists of young women with earnings data. "Young women" are those who we estimate had between zero and ten years of (postschooling) potential labor market experience.[3] The sample sizes ranged between 5,000 and 7,000 for the 1973 to 1978 period and between 22,000 and 28,000 for the 1979 to 1991 period. We use the usual weekly data rather than the March CPS annual earnings data for two reasons: starting in 1979 the former contains roughly three times as many individuals and thus allows for better estimation of wage differentials, and it links personal characteristics with current pay as opposed to the previous year's earnings, as in the March survey. All our tabulations have been weighted using the weights provided on the CPS and, subject to the caveats expressed below, can be interpreted as representative of the African American and white U.S. populations.[4]

While these data offer large samples for each year, the information they provide carries some limitations. Most importantly, the data contain no direct measure of work experience. We use information on schooling and age to derive potential labor market experience. However, this measure is crude, especially for women, because it cannot account for the increasing labor force attachment of women that has occurred in recent decades. In addition, the CPS has no so-called skill measures, such as standardized test scores. However, the data sets that do contain direct measures of work experience, such as the NLS, the PSID, or data sets that contain information on cognitive skills, are substantially smaller in size than the CPS and do not allow for extensive disaggregation.

The CPS shares additional data limitations with other commonly used surveys. First, the CPS likely underrepresents disadvantaged African Americans because they are undercounted in the census. However, since the census undercount is much less severe for women than it is for men (estimates suggest that the undercount represents about 3 percent of young African American and 1 percent of young white women; Fay, Passell, and Robinson 1988), we suspect that the undercount does not materially alter our conclusions. More problematic is the fact that women working in the underground economy (for example, day-care providers) are unlikely to report such earnings (Edin and Lein 1997). For this reason, our results should probably be interpreted as reflecting what African American and white women earn in the above-ground economy.

Earning Differentials

We document trends in relative earnings first for all African American women and then for African American women in specific educational and regional groups. To show trends in the wages of African American women relative to white women, we regressed the natural log of hourly earnings (usual weekly earnings/usual weekly hours) on a dummy variable for race and dummy variables for each year of potential labor market experience. This regression produced a racial wage gap for each year between 1973 and 1991, which accounts for the small differences in the age distribution of the white and African American populations. These log differentials can be loosely interpreted as the percentage gap in average earnings between African American and white women, and we refer to them as such throughout the remainder of the chapter.[5]

The relative earnings of African American women declined substantially beginning in the mid-1970s and continuing throughout the 1980s (figure 2.1). Between 1979 and 1991 the overall gap in hourly earnings between

Figure 2.1 / Hourly Earnings Differential, African American Relative to White Women, 1973 to 1991

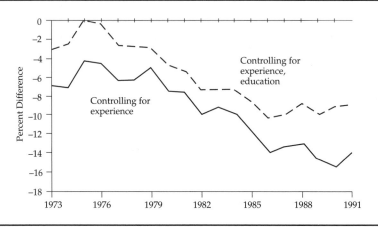

Source: Current Population Survey, 1973 to 1991.
Note: Data are for women with zero to ten years of potential experience.

young African American and white women widened a little less than 1 percentage point per year, dropping from −5 percent in 1979 to −14 percent in 1991. A regression of these differentials on a linear time trend shows the differential widening by 0.63 (0.06) percentage points per year from 1973 to 1991 and by 0.82 (0.08) percentage points per year for the period from 1979 to 1991. This relative decline is somewhat larger in magnitude than the relative wage erosion of African American men for a comparably defined sample (−0.35 [0.09] percentage points per year over the 1973 to 1989 period).

Relative wages can be measured many ways—women relative to men, African Americans relative to whites, African American women relative to white women. In fact, two contrary trends relate to the experience of African American women. The first is the significant wage gains of women relative to men over the 1970s and 1980s. The second is increasing wage inequality on the basis of race. These changes affected the earnings of African American women relative to white men over the period studied (figure 2.2). Between 1979 and 1991, the wage differential between young white men and women narrowed by 15 percentage points, from 25 percent to 10 percent. Over the same period the earnings gap between young African American women and white men narrowed from 30 percent to 24 percent. This is the broader context of the declining relative wages of young African American women: in the 1980s, young white women made significant wage advances relative to white men; the wages of young African American women did not keep pace with those advances.

Figure 2.2 / Hourly Earnings Differential, African American Men, African American Women, and White Women Relative to White Men, 1973 to 1991

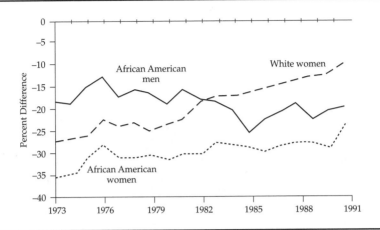

Source: Current Population Survey, 1973 to 1991.
Note: Data are for women with zero to ten years of potential experience.

Educational and Regional Differences in Relative Wage Decline

The erosion of the relative wages of African American women followed distinct paths for African American women in different regions and with different educational levels. Here we estimate trends in earnings differentials for African American and white women in three education groups—high school dropouts, high school graduates, and college graduates—and for women in the three regions with significant African American populations—the Midwest (the East North Central census division); the Northeast (New England and the Mid-Atlantic states); and the South (the South Atlantic, East South Central, and West South Central divisions). To determine regional trends, we restricted the sample to women with high school degrees or less education, because labor markets are relatively local for these women. The market for college graduates is less geographically constrained. As before, in these analyses we controlled for individual years of potential labor market experience.

Among the distinct educational groups, African American college-educated women clearly experienced the most precipitous decline in relative wages (see figure 2.3). These highly educated African American women earned substantially more than their white counterparts did until the late 1970s. Presumably, at least a part of the wage advantage that college-educated African American women maintained at this time represented re-

Figure 2.3 / Hourly Earnings Differential, African American Relative to White Women, by Education Level, 1973 to 1991

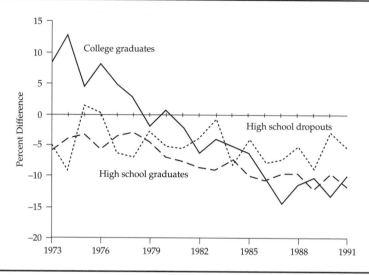

Source: Current Population Survey, 1973 to 1991.
Note: Data are for women with zero to ten years of potential experience.

turns to their relatively stronger labor force attachment in this period. The wage advantage of college-educated African American women had eroded completely by 1980. In 1991, college-educated African American women were at a 10 percent relative wage disadvantage. The relative wages of African American high school graduates fell more slowly, but the decline from 1979 to 1991 is apparent. In 1991, the relative wage disadvantage of African American college graduates was comparable to the disadvantage of African American high school graduates.[6] Although African American high school dropouts earned less than their white counterparts did, over time the wage differential hovered around 5 percent and showed little erosion.

Trends in African American women's relative wages were distinct for regional categories (see figure 2.4). Relative declines in African American women's earnings occurred in the Northeast in the 1970s, but relative wages improved there in the early 1980s. In the Midwest, relative wages declined significantly in the late 1980s. Until 1985 African American women in the Midwest maintained a wage advantage over white women, but by 1991 African American women earned 10 percent less than white women in the Midwest did. This differential is comparable to the racial earnings gap in the South. The wage gap in the South was consistently large, growing only slightly over time.

Figure 2.4 / Hourly Earnings Differential, African American Women Relative to White Women, by Region, for Women with no more than a High School Education, 1973 to 1991

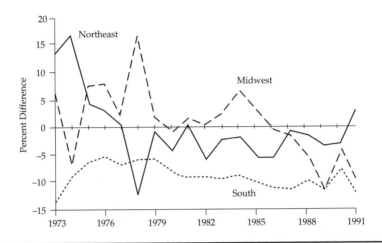

Source: Current Population Survey, 1973 to 1991.
Note: Data are for women with zero to ten years of potential experience.

These patterns are similar to trends found for African American men by Bound and Freeman (1992). As women did, African American men in the Midwest and African American male college graduates experienced the largest relative earnings erosion. The relative wages of African American college graduates, both men and women, follow a similar pattern. College-educated African American women and men maintained slight wage advantages in the early 1970s but earned considerably less than whites did at the end of the 1980s. In the Midwest, however, the erosion of African American men's relative wages began in the early 1980s and was much more severe than for African American women.

Following Bound and Freeman (1992), we investigated the causes of the trends detailed above with two analytic tools. In the first we developed regression decompositions that revealed the contribution of various explanatory variables to the erosion of the relative wages of African American women. The contribution of potential explanatory variables, such as education or industrial structure, to relative wage erosion was further decomposed into "price" and "quantity" components. For education, for example, the price effect is the contribution to the wage erosion of changing returns to education. The education quantity effect is the contribution to the wage gap of changes in the educational distribution of African American and white women. In the second analysis, we developed a decomposition that revealed sectoral shifts in the composition of the workforce. This approach

Table 2.1 / Educational Attainment of African American and White Women, 1973 to 1989

Education (Years)	1973			1979			1989		
	White	African American	Diff.	White	African American	Diff.	White	African American	Diff.
All women									
<12	19.2	33.9	-14.7	14.9	24.7	-9.8	13.0	18.6	-5.6
12	48.6	43.9	4.7	44.2	43.7	0.5	38.7	44.6	-5.9
13+	32.2	22.2	10.0	40.8	31.6	9.2	48.3	36.7	11.6
13–15	16.9	14.1	2.8	21.2	20.7	0.5	23.4	23.3	0.1
16+	15.3	8.1	7.2	19.6	10.9	8.7	24.9	13.4	11.5
Employed women									
<12	12.4	21.4	-9.0	9.4	12.5	-3.1	7.5	7.7	-0.2
12	49.4	47.2	2.2	44.7	43.8	0.9	37.7	43.0	-5.3
13+	38.2	31.4	6.8	46.0	43.7	2.3	54.8	49.2	5.6
13–15	19.0	18.4	0.6	23.4	26.9	-3.5	25.7	29.8	-4.1
16+	19.2	13.0	6.2	22.6	16.8	5.8	29.1	19.4	9.7

Source: Current Population Survey, 1973 to 1989.
Note: Data are for women with zero to ten years of potential labor market experience.

shows the extent to which white and African American women were employed in declining sectors of the economy.

DECOMPOSING THE WIDENING GAP

Numerous factors partially explain the relative erosion of African American women's wages. Our decomposition analysis estimates the effect of changes in education, location, employment structure, and institutional factors on the relative wages of African American women. Educational change is solely the result of changes in educational attainment, but location, employment structure, and institutional changes each have two facets to investigate. Location changes include both changes in the regional effects on wages and changes in metropolitan residence.[7] The changes in employment structure are changes in occupation and industry.[8] Institutional changes include the effects of declining unionization and of the falling minimum wage.

The effect of education in our analysis illustrates our methodology. Trends in education and wages over time could affect the relative wage gap in two ways. One is that the one group could become more educated relative to another group, which would have a quantity effect on wages. Though African American women raised their level of education from 1973 to 1991, their level of education relative to white women changed little over these years (table 2.1). In this same period, the educational level of white women, especially working white women, increased at least as significantly as that of African American women. From 1973 to 1989, the fraction of young African American women with a college education rose 65 percent (from 8.1 percent to 13.4 percent), while the fraction with less than a high school education dropped by 45 percent.[9] However, the educational attainment of working white women grew just as significantly over the period. In spite of African American advances, then, the racial gap in educational attachment did not narrow by any substantial amount. Thus among working women the racial gap in education changed little from 1973 to 1991, so one would expect the "quantity" effects of education to have been small.

In addition to quantity shifts, price changes can affect the relative wage gap over time. In education, the price effect is the payoff to a given gap in educational attainment. Over the 1980s, the returns to education increased; that is, the wage advantage for more educated individuals grew. As returns to education grow, so does the disparity between those with less and more education, even when the gap in education does not change. Because African American women had less education than white women, wage disparity should have grown as returns to education increased. This effect we identify as the "price" effect. Throughout this decomposition analysis, we break down the contribution of each factor (such as education) to

/ 71

wage disparity into these price and quantity effects (see the appendix for details).

The results of our decomposition are summarized in table 2.2. The first row of the table shows the estimated trend in the differential between the earnings of white and of African American women ($\bar{\gamma}_t$ from equation [2A.3] in the appendix) when the only controls are for potential experience (the trend represented by the line labeled "controlling for experience" in figure 2.1). The first entry in the table shows a trend of -0.625, a decline in relative earnings of young African American women of more than six-tenths of a percentage point per year over the period. Subsequent rows (5, 12, 16, 20, and 25) represent the trend in the earnings differential when education; education and location variables; and education, location, and industry and occupation variables, respectively, are included along with the controls for potential experience. Row 14 represents the trend in the differential after institutional factors (unionization rates and the level of the minimum wage) have also been controlled for. Comparisons between rows show how much of the initial trend can be accounted for by the various factors included in the regressions, which we further decompose into price and quantity effects.

Education

The relative earnings of young African American women declined somewhat under six-tenths of a percentage point per year after controlling for education (a total trend of -0.559; table 2.2, row 5). Thus a combination of the widening gap in educational attainment and the rising value of education can explain about 10 percent (0.066/0.625) of the widening earnings gap between young white and African American women. This effect was primarily accounted for by the increase in the returns to education; price changes accounted for 0.053 of the 0.066 effect of education. The relative education of African American women also declined, but this quantity effect accounted for only 0.013 of the 0.066 effect of education on the relative wage gap. The relative education of African American and white women changed little over the 1973 to 1991 period, but the penalty to the existing difference in education grew, and the wage gap widened between young white and African American women.

Reproducing these calculations for the years 1979 to 1991 shows that education explains a much larger part of the negative trend in the 1980s. The gap between the earnings of white and African American women widened at a rate of 0.816 percentage points per year when experience is controlled. With controls for education, this gap fell to 0.499 percentage points per year. Thus education explains almost 40 percent of the erosion in the 1980s. This 0.317 percentage point decline had to do almost equally with a widening gap in educational attainment (0.171 percentage points) and increasing returns to education (0.149 percentage points).

Table 2.2 / Contribution of Factors to the Average Annual Percentage Point Trend in the Erosion of African American Women's Relative Wages

		Education Level			Region[a]		
Trend and Factor	All	College Graduates	High School Graduates	High School Dropouts	Midwest	Northeast	South
Initial trend	-0.625	-1.330	-0.442	-0.125	-0.714	-0.558	-0.165
Education level	-0.066	-0.001	—	0.040	0.049	-0.014	0.133
Quantities	-0.013	-0.011	—	0.039	0.044	-0.004	0.121
Prices	-0.053	0.013	—	0.001	0.005	-0.010	0.008
Net of education level	-0.559	-1.329	-0.442	-0.165	-0.763	-0.544	-0.298
Location							
Region	0.002	-0.029	0.004	0.065	—	-0.132	0.019
Quantities	0.024	0.046	0.000	0.062	—	0.003	0.002
Prices	-0.022	-0.075	0.004	0.003	—	-0.134	0.017
Metropolitan residence	-0.021	-0.015	-0.036	-0.019	-0.045	-0.044	-0.045
Quantities	-0.003	0.003	-0.023	0.014	-0.020	0.015	-0.036
Prices	-0.018	-0.018	-0.013	-0.033	-0.025	-0.059	-0.009

(Table continues on p. 74.)

Table 2.2 / *Continued*

	Education Level				Region[a]		
Trend and Factor	All	College Graduates	High School Graduates	High School Dropouts	Midwest	Northeast	South
Net of location	−0.540	−1.285	−0.410	−0.211	−0.718	−0.368	−0.272
Employment structure							
Industry	−0.038	−0.015	−0.113	0.153	−0.356	−0.076	0.054
Quantities	−0.006	0.073	−0.084	0.070	−0.383	−0.094	0.038
Prices	−0.033	−0.088	−0.030	0.083	0.027	0.018	0.018
Net of industry	−0.502	−1.270	−0.297	−0.364	−0.362	−0.292	−0.326
Occupation	−0.026	−0.242	−0.001	−0.011	−0.024	−0.003	−0.005
Quantities	−0.008	−0.300	0.037	−0.009	0.020	0.003	0.032
Prices	−0.018	0.058	−0.038	−0.003	−0.044	−0.006	−0.037
Net of employment structure	−0.476	−1.028	−0.296	−0.353	−0.338	−0.289	−0.321
Institutional change							
Unionization	−0.064	−0.104	−0.053	−0.069	−0.145	−0.016	−0.053
Quantities	−0.031	−0.038	−0.055	−0.046	−0.146	0.015	−0.050
Prices	−0.032	−0.067	0.002	−0.023	0.001	−0.030	−0.003
Minimum wage	−0.065	−0.017	−0.092	−0.101	−0.075	0.006	−0.117
Net of institutional change	−0.347	−0.907	−0.151	−0183	−0.098	−0.279	−0.151
Total trend explained	44	32	66		86	50	8

Source: Current Population Survey, 1973 to 1991.
Note: Data are for women with zero to ten years of potential labor market experience.
[a]Women with a high school education or less.

In the Midwest and South, changes in the educational attainment of the workforce actually served to narrow earnings differentials between white and African American women, as a result of large declines in the fraction of African American workers with less than a high school education. However, the regional decompositions included only high school graduates and those with less than a high school education. If workers with education beyond high school had been included in regional tabulations, the regional results would look much more like the results for the United States as a whole.

Location

For the total population, racial differences in regional distribution appear to have had little effect on the declining relative wages of African American women. Regional differences did not account for the trends of the educational groups and the South (we made no regional correction for the Midwest because it is a single region). However, in the Northeast, the decline of wages in the Mid-Atlantic states (relative to the wages in New England) combined with the concentration of northeastern African Americans in that division explained a part of the increasing wage gap. The shift was almost completely accounted for by changes in prices (rising relative wages in New England), not by a shift in the distribution of the African American population. Metropolitan residence accounted for -0.021 of the downward trend of relative African American wages, and most of this shift came from the falling relative pay for jobs held by central-city workers. In each of the regions, metropolitan residence explained around -0.045 of the trend. In the South, the decline was the result of changes in quantities; the distribution of the African American population shifted disproportionately to city centers. In the Northeast, metropolitan residence explained some of the erosion of African American women's wages because of changes in prices, that is, the relative decline in wages paid to central-city workers. In the Midwest, the effects of price and quantity both contributed to the diminishing relative wages of African American women. This result for the Midwest contrasts considerably with the result for men in Bound and Freeman's (1992) decomposition. For midwestern men, metropolitan status accounted for a much larger share of the overall decline in relative wages (0.188 of 1.42), a decline that was completely attributable to a decrease in the wages paid to central-city residents.

Industry and Occupation

Overall, controlling for industry had a moderate effect on the racial differential in relative wages, explaining 0.038 of the erosion of African American women's relative wage. This effect was the result of changes in prices, not quantities; the racial wage gap increased within industries, but African American women did not find themselves increasingly concentrated in low-wage industries (the quantity effect is -0.006 while the price effect is -0.033). Industrial concentration was a more powerful consideration for women without any college education, especially in the Midwest. In this region, the addition of the industry dummies explained 0.356 of the 0.714 decline in the relative wages of African American women. Thus changes in industry explained half of the negative trend in African American women's wages in the Midwest, and quantity effects dominated; in this region, African American women were increasingly employed in low-wage industries. The decline in manufacturing in the Midwest hit African American women particularly hard. As of 1973, 29 percent of white women and 28 percent of African American women were employed in manufacturing. By 1989, the share of white women in manufacturing had dropped 10 percentage points, while the share of African American women in manufacturing had dropped almost 20 percentage points (see the appendix, table 2A.1).

While occupation had a muted effect on the total population, changes in occupational distribution contributed dramatically to the falling relative wages of college-educated women. For the total population, the addition of occupation dummy variables to the log earnings equation explained 0.026 of the 0.625 trend. For college graduates, occupation proved to be much more important; of the -1.33 trend, 0.242 (or 18 percent) was due to occupation. The quantity effects dominated, showing that African American college graduates were increasingly concentrated in relatively low-wage occupations (table 2A.2). This shift is especially apparent in the clerical occupations. In 1973, white and African American college graduates were equally likely to hold clerical jobs. By 1989, the proportion of white college graduates in clerical work was similar to the proportion in 1973 (14.5 percent in 1989, 13.4 percent in 1973). Over that period, the proportion of African American college graduates in clerical jobs had more than doubled. In 1989, nearly one-third of college-educated African American women (29.5 percent) held clerical jobs. This increase represents a relative shift into low-paying occupations, which contributed to the relative earnings erosion of African American college graduates.

Based on a fairly crude measure of occupational difference (eleven occupational categories), changes in occupation played an important role in increasing the racial wage gap, especially among college graduates. To check on the validity of the inferences we draw with basic occupational categories, we matched information on the earnings and wage distributions from the 1970 and 1980 U.S. Census with the occupational distributions derived from each year of CPS data. This allowed us to analyze occupational shifts at the more detailed three-digit occupational category level.[10] In contrast to the occupational downgrading that appears in the shift to clerical work, this more detailed investigation shows that African American college graduates upgraded their occupations over the period studied. The decline in the professional category represents, among other things, the diminishing representation of women in traditionally female professional jobs, such as teaching. However, this more nuanced analysis shows substantially more upgrading for white women than for African American women. The pace of occupational advancement among white women was much more rapid than that of African American women, and that advancement increased the wage disparity between the two groups.

Institutional Factors

Falling rates of unionization and the declining value of the minimum wage are two alterations in institutional structures that may have affected the relative wages of African American and white women. We completed the decomposition by investigating the effect of these institutional changes.

Young African American women were relatively more unionized in both private and public sector unions in the early 1970s, but this advantage had mostly disappeared by the end of the 1980s. The relative erosion was particularly severe among college-educated women and for Midwestern women with twelve or fewer years of education. As of 1973, with controls for industry and occupation, African American college-educated women were overrepresented in public sector unions by 10 percentage points. In 1973, African American women in the Midwest were overrepresented in private sector unions by 9 percentage points and in public sector unions by 5 percentage points. As union density fell over the next two decades, African American and white unionization rates converged, and by 1989 the unionization rates of African American and white women were equal.

Because African American women had been disproportionate beneficiaries of the union wage advantage, the decline in union membership contributed to the increase in the racial wage gap. We quantified the effect of declining union membership on relative earnings by estimating the racial earnings gap after controlling for union membership. Three dummy variables express union status: one each for being employed in the public sector, for being employed in private sector unions, and for being employed in public sector unions.[11] For the total population, declining unionization reduced the relative earnings of young African American women by 0.064 percentage points per year—a little over 10 percent of the overall trend. The effect was larger in groups of African American women that had maintained the largest union advantages in the 1970s and experienced the most significant wage decline—college-educated women and those living in the Midwest. Declining unionization explained 13 percent (0.104/1.33) of college graduates' relative wage decline and 20 percent (0.145/0.714) of the erosion of relative wages in the Midwest.

Because African American women are disproportionately employed in the lowest-wage jobs, the decline in the real value of the minimum wage may also contribute to the relative wage gap. Between 1981 and 1989, the minimum wage was frozen at $3.35 per hour. It was raised to $3.80 on April 1, 1990, and then to $4.25 a year later. Even at $4.25 per hour the minimum wage was, in real terms, much lower than it had been in 1981. In the mid-1970s, white and African American women had similar wage distributions, but over the 1980s African American women's relative position eroded considerably. This erosion implies that the value of the minimum wage became increasingly important to African American women's wages and that its decline contributed to the relative wage loss of African American women.

To calculate the extent to which a fixed real minimum wage would have mitigated the erosion of African American women's relative wages, we created a 1991 wage distribution holding the minimum wage constant at the 1981 level ($3.35 per hour). If the real minimum wage had been maintained, it would have been $5.06 per hour in 1991. For the simulated wage distribution, workers who earned the minimum wage in 1991 were assigned a new wage of $5.06 per hour. Workers who earned more than the minimum wage, but less than $5.06 per hour, were also assigned a simulated wage of $5.06. For workers who earned a fraction of the minimum wage in 1991, the new wage was calculated as the same fraction of the new minimum wage.[12] Then, controlling for all explanatory variables, we estimated the African American–white earnings differential for both the actual and the simulated wages of women. The minimum wage effect is the difference between the coefficient on the race dummy in these two estimations.

With a fixed real minimum wage, the relative differential of African American women's earnings would have been 1.04 percentage points less than it was in 1991 if the minimum wage had retained its 1981 value.[13] Annualized over the study period, this effect translates into a decline of 0.065 percentage points per year, which accounts for 10 percent of the relative erosion of African American women's wages. For high school graduates, if the value of the minimum wage had not declined, African American women would have suffered 20 percent less relative erosion of earnings. Constant real minimum wages apparently would have mitigated more than half of the relative decline for African American women in the South. In the Midwest, 13 percent of the relative erosion in wages would have been avoided if the real minimum wage had kept pace with inflation.

Taken together, the factors considered—education, location, employment structure, and institutional change—account for 44 percent of the relative erosion of young African American women's wages. Changes in relative education, deunionization, and the declining real value of the minimum wage appear to have been the most powerful explanatory variables for the total population. Among education and regional groups, the decomposition model does the best job of describing the relative declines in the Midwest, explaining 86 percent of the relative wage decline of African American women there. In that region, industrial shifts and declining unionization explain more than half of the negative trend of African American women's wages. However, the decomposition analysis explains only one-third of the erosion in wages of college graduates—the group that experienced the most significant earnings decline.

The Growing Gap in Labor Market Experience

Over the 1973 to 1991 period, not only the earnings but also the employment rates of young African American and white women became increasingly disparate (chapter 1; Bound and Dresser 1996). Tabulations using the CPS samples show that in 1973 young white and African American women were almost equally likely to be employed. But over the 1970s and 1980s the employment rate of white women rose faster than that of African American women, leading to a significant racial difference in employment rates by the end of the 1980s. Fifty-six percent of young white women and 52.8 percent of young African American women were employed in 1973. By 1991, almost three-quarters of young white women (72.7 percent) were working, compared with 56.8 percent of young African American women.

While relative to white women African American women in all educational groups were less likely to be employed in 1991 than in 1973, the nature of the change varied by level of education. College-educated African American women were much more likely to work in 1973 than their white counterparts were (86.7 percent and 69.8 percent, respectively). By 1991, African American and white college graduates were almost equally likely to work (86 percent and 85 percent, respectively). Thus, among college graduates, the decline in the relative odds of employment for African American women was due to the increasing employment of white women. For all groups other than college graduates, the employment rate of white women was higher than that of African American women in 1973, and the difference grew over the 1973 to 1991 period.

The rise in the workforce attachment of white women likely reflects changes in labor market opportunities for these women but is also likely to have contributed to the growing gap between the earnings of African American and of white women. Our decomposition analysis cannot control for actual experience of workers because the CPS data permit only an accounting for potential experience. However, the increasing relative participation of white women (as seen in the employment figures) implies that relative real experience changed significantly over this period, even though relative potential experience did not. Though CPS data are inadequate to account for these changes, McCrate and Leete (1994) use data from the National Longitudinal Survey of Youth (NLSY) and the NLSY–Women to show that young white women gained about one year of real experience relative to African American women over the 1977 to 1986 period. They estimate that the growing gap in work experience between African American and white women added between 3.2 and 3.4 percentage points to the earnings gap between these women, or roughly 0.3 percentage points per year, close to half of the overall trend we found.

With the CPS data we employed two methods to investigate the importance of relative increases in the ratio of real to potential labor market experience for white women. First, we examined trends in African American women's relative wages, limiting the sample to women with zero years of potential labor market experience. For these women, there can be no gap between real and actual experience. Second, we examined trends in returns to labor market experience for white and African American women separately. If the ratio of real to potential experience advanced for white women, we would expect that returns to potential labor market experience would also have risen more rapidly for white women.

These investigations suggest that the increasing labor force participation of white women contributed to the erosion of African American women's relative wages. When evaluated at zero years of potential experience, the decline in relative wages of African American women was about one-third the decline calculated for the sample of young women with ten years or less of potential experience. Regressions including the interaction of race and labor market experience show that returns to potential experience rose more rapidly for white than for African American women. For all educational and regional groups, the inclusion of the race-experience interaction significantly reduced the coefficient on the race dummy variable. However, this reduction was smallest for women in the Midwest and for college-educated women—the groups experiencing the greatest decline in relative earnings. These CPS investigations, and the work cited, suggest that declining relative experience contributed to the erosion of African American women's relative wages but cannot be considered the sole source of that erosion.

CHANGES IN INDUSTRIAL STRUCTURE

On its own, the decomposition cannot completely determine the reasons for the decline of African American women's wages. In fact, the importance of changes in industrial structure and the limitations on how the decomposition treats those changes warrant a second approach. The decomposition quantifies the negative earnings effect of relative population shifts out of well-paying industries; at the same time, the decomposition considers population shifts out of low-paying industries to be a positive change. However, it is easy to imagine that industrial decline could lead to wage erosion, even if the industries in decline are not high-paying ones.

For example, over the past few decades the education industry has declined precipitously. This shift has disproportionately affected college-educated women, both African American and white. Though teaching was never a highly paid profession for college graduates, the decline in the industry may well have had a negative effect on the wages of women college graduates. Therefore, we include a second analysis designed to show the effect of supply and demand shifts in industry on the wage disparity between young black and white women.

When industries decline, workers' wages may fall not only because their industry of employment is in decline, but also because they are pushed out and into less desirable jobs in other industries. Theoretically, we expect that industrial shifts will negatively affect workers concentrated in declining industries.[14] Job displacement and the search for new work are a difficult process, and the new job that replaces the old is rarely a better opportunity. In part, the difficulty with industrial decline is that workers have some "comparative advantage" in the declining industry, or else they might not have been concentrated in the industry originally. Given the constraints they face, workers choose jobs in particular industries that represent the best option available to them. Industrial decline pushes these workers into other, nonpreferred sectors. Thus industrial decline could be expected to diminish the relative wages of the types of workers concentrated in declining industries. Importantly, differences in industry mix are not simply the result of the comparative advantage of individual workers. Racial differences in the distribution of workers across industries also reflect such factors as the location of industries and patterns of industrial recruitment, factors that have been and continue to be influenced by racial discrimination. Whether comparative advantage or institutional history is at work in an existing distribution of workers across industries, workers are likely to suffer wage decline when the sectors in which they are concentrated decline.

To bring better focus to change in industrial composition and its effect on wage disparity, we investigated the extent to which industrial shifts differentially affected white and African American women. In this endeavor, we distinguished between changes that occurred between and those that occurred within sectors or industries (Murphy and Welch 1993). By "between" we mean shifts in the overall distribution of workers in the economy, for example, a decline in manufacturing or education. The "within" effects represent shifts in a specific population's share of employment in an industry, for example, a decline in the share of the total public administration jobs held by African American women. In this analysis, the portion of such shifts that occurred between sectors represents the portion that is predictable on the basis of the sector shifts occurring in the economy, while the portion occurring within sectors represents the residual. To reiterate, the "between effect" can be used to measure the effect that the decline of the education industry would have had on the employment of

African American women had industry employment fractions stayed constant. The "within effect" would then be a measure of the importance of changes over time in the fraction of employment accounted for by African American women within the education industry.

More formally, let K_{it} represent the share of the overall workforce in industry i as of year t. Thus $\Sigma_i K_{it} = 1$. Let R_{ijt} represent the fraction of the workforce in industry i that is from demographic group j as of year t. Thus $\Sigma_j R_{ijt} = 1$. For example, R_{ijt} might represent the fraction of the workforce in industry i represented by African American female college graduates. The fraction of the j_{th} demographic group in the overall workforce, R_{jt}, is a weighted average of the fractions in each industry, $R_{jt} = \Sigma_i K_{it} R_{ijt}$.

The change in the fraction of the workforce in demographic group j between two periods, t and $t + 1$, can then be decomposed into "between-factor" and "within-sector" components:

$$(2.1) \qquad R_{jt+1} - R_{jt} = \Sigma_i (K_{it+1} - K_{it}) R_{ijt} + \Sigma_i K_{it+1} (R_{ijt+1} - R_{ijt}).$$

The first component of this sum represents the change that would have occurred had the fraction of the workforce in each industry represented by demographic group j stayed constant. This "between-industry" component will be positive if the industrial composition of the workforce is shifting toward industries that employ a disproportionate share of the j_{th} demographic group and will be negative if the opposite is true. This component can be interpreted as representing a labor demand shift toward or away from the j_{th} demographic group (Freeman 1977; Bound and Freeman 1992). The "within-sector" component of the sum represents the average rise in the fraction of each industry's workforce represented by the j_{th} demographic group "necessitated" by the rise in the overall fraction of the workforce accounted by demographic group j.

To implement this decomposition, we calculated the share of the young workforce for each of eighteen distinct industries (see note 8). The base period was 1973 to 1978; the destination period, 1989 to 1991. In both periods, we averaged across years to increase the reliability of our results. To ease the interpretation of the results, we divide both the overall change in the fraction of the workforce accounted for by a demographic group, $R_{jt+1} - R_{jt}$, and all the components by the base line fraction, R_{jt}. As a result, the reported quantities represent percent changes. Along with the components of the decomposition, we also report the fraction of each industry's workforce comprising African American or white college graduates, high school graduates, or high school dropouts (table 2.3). As for our regression decomposition results, we also focus on African American and white women in the Midwest, Northeast, and South with no more than a high school education (table 2.4).

(Text continues on p. 87.)

Table 2.3 / Demand Shift Analysis for Young African American and White Women, by Education Level, 1979 to 1989

	Industrial Distribution of the Workforce				African American Women			White Women		
	African American Women		White Women		Between Effect	Within Effect	Total Effect	Between Effect	Within Effect	Total Effect
	1979	1989	1979	1989						
College graduates										
Manufacturing	6.0	8.5	6.1	10.7	-1.5	8.3	6.8	-1.5	11.7	10.2
Trade	4.9	8.8	7.6	11.9	1.3	7.0	8.3	1.8	8.5	10.3
FIRE[a]	3.9	12.3	5.3	10.7	0.8	14.0	14.8	1.1	9.7	10.8
Miscellaneous services	7.7	16.5	9.8	21.1	4.2	13.1	17.3	6.2	15.8	22.0
Health	8.0	15.6	13.1	16.0	0.2	15.3	15.6	0.4	10.5	10.9
Education	57.8	20.1	50.4	20.7	-23.6	-3.6	-27.2	-20.6	1.5	-19.2
Public administration	8.4	13.2	4.1	4.4	-0.9	12.5	11.6	-0.5	3.0	2.6
Other	3.4	5.0	3.7	4.4	-1.1	5.3	4.1	-1.1	4.1	3.0
Total	100.0	100.0	100.0	100.0	-20.5	71.9	51.4	-14.1	64.8	50.7
High school graduates										
Manufacturing	28.4	18.8	21.8	15.4	-7.0	-2.4	-9.4	-5.5	-3.8	-9.3
Trade	14.6	27.7	24.4	33.3	4.2	9.2	13.4	6.3	-3.7	2.5
FIRE[a]	9.0	7.8	13.0	12.1	1.9	-3.0	-1.1	2.7	-5.9	-3.2
Miscellaneous services	9.4	17.1	12.9	18.4	5.7	2.2	7.9	8.3	-6.3	2.0

(Table continues on p. 84.)

Table 2.3 / *Continued*

| | Industrial Distribution of the Workforce | | | | African American Women | | | White Women | | |
| | African American Women | | White Women | | | | | | | |
	1979	1989	1979	1989	Between Effect	Within Effect	Total Effect	Between Effect	Within Effect	Total Effect
Health	15.3	16.2	13.1	10.5	0.5	0.6	1.1	0.4	−5.0	−4.6
Education	6.0	3.4	3.4	1.9	−2.4	−0.1	−2.5	−1.4	−0.4	−1.8
Public administration	6.7	4.8	4.3	2.9	−0.7	−1.1	−1.8	−0.5	−1.4	−1.9
Other	10.5	4.0	7.3	5.5	−4.5	−1.9	−6.4	−2.7	−0.3	−2.9
Total	100.0	100.0	100.0	100.0	−2.5	3.7	1.2	7.6	−26.9	−19.3
High school dropouts										
Manufacturing	32.4	14.5	36.0	20.3	−7.8	−16.5	−24.2	−8.8	−15.8	−24.7
Trade	21.4	39.0	32.2	41.8	6.0	−5.2	0.8	9.2	−13.2	−4.0
FIRE[a]	3.3	2.8	3.0	3.0	0.7	−2.4	−1.7	0.6	−1.9	−1.3
Miscellaneous services	17.6	23.1	12.8	20.7	10.7	−15.3	−4.5	8.0	−7.0	1.0
Health	13.7	14.3	8.7	7.7	0.4	−6.0	−5.6	0.3	−4.2	−4.0
Education	3.5	1.5	2.1	1.3	−1.4	−1.2	−2.6	−0.9	−0.4	−1.3
Public administration	2.8	1.9	0.6	0.8	−0.3	−1.4	−1.7	−0.1	0.1	0.0
Other	5.3	2.9	4.4	4.5	−0.5	−3.1	−3.7	−0.5	−0.8	−1.2
Total	100.0	100.0	100.0	100.0	7.7	−51.0	−43.3	7.9	−43.3	−35.4

Source: Current Population Survey, 1973 to 1991.
Notes: Original analysis conducted with an eighteen-industry breakdown. Results reported are aggregations of that more detailed analysis.
[a] Finance, insurance, and real estate.

Table 2.4 / Demand Shift Analysis for Young African American and White Women, by Region, 1979 to 1989

	Industrial Distribution of the Workforce				African American Women			White Women		
	African American Women		White Women		Between Effect	Within Effect	Total Effect	Between Effect	Within Effect	Total Effect
	1979	1989	1979	1989						
Northeast										
Manufacturing	15.6	7.4	18.7	13.2	-4.8	-0.2	-5.0	-5.6	0.3	-5.4
Trade	7.3	11.6	17.2	21.7	1.6	7.7	9.3	3.8	0.9	4.6
FIRE[a]	14.8	18.9	12.5	15.6	4.8	7.4	12.3	4.1	-0.9	3.2
Miscellaneous services	13.5	23.9	12.1	21.2	8.6	12.1	20.7	8.3	0.9	9.2
Health	13.1	20.2	17.5	15.0	-0.3	16.1	15.9	-0.4	-2.0	-2.3
Education	21.9	8.4	13.5	6.0	-10.8	0.9	-9.9	-6.7	-0.8	-7.5
Public administration	4.3	6.0	3.3	2.9	0.0	4.3	4.3	0.0	-0.4	-0.3
Other	9.4	3.8	5.1	4.4	-4.2	0.2	-4.0	-1.8	1.1	-0.6
Total	100.0	100.0	100.0	100.0	-5.0	48.6	43.6	1.7	-0.8	0.9
Midwest										
Manufacturing	19.2	8.7	20.0	15.5	-5.0	-2.5	-7.5	-5.3	1.6	-3.7
Trade	10.8	21.7	21.5	25.2	3.0	15.3	18.4	5.6	-0.6	5.0
FIRE[a]	8.3	12.4	9.7	13.1	3.3	5.1	8.4	3.9	0.2	4.1
Miscellaneous services	11.7	21.0	11.2	18.9	8.7	7.9	16.6	7.8	0.9	8.7

(Table continues on p. 86.)

Table 2.4 / Continued

	Industrial Distribution of the Workforce				African American Women			White Women		
	African American Women		White Women		Between Effect	Within Effect	Total Effect	Between Effect	Within Effect	Total Effect
	1979	1989	1979	1989						
Health	14.8	18.1	15.3	14.5	1.9	7.7	9.6	1.9	-2.0	-0.1
Education	19.6	10.1	14.7	6.2	-8.9	2.8	-6.1	-6.7	-1.5	-8.2
Public administration	5.4	4.5	2.3	2.4	-0.3	0.9	0.6	-0.1	0.4	0.3
Other	10.2	3.5	5.3	4.2	-4.4	-1.0	-5.4	-1.6	0.7	-0.9
Total	100.0	100.0	100.0	100.0	-1.7	36.3	34.5	5.5	-0.3	5.2
South										
Manufacturing	22.6	15.7	16.3	11.5	-5.9	0.8	-5.1	-4.2	-0.2	-4.4
Trade	13.3	21.1	20.1	26.0	4.5	5.7	10.2	6.2	0.5	6.7
FIRE[a]	5.7	7.8	12.1	12.4	0.4	2.6	2.9	0.8	-0.2	0.6
Miscellaneous services	10.4	17.0	13.1	19.9	5.9	2.7	8.5	7.9	-0.5	7.4
Health	13.7	15.4	12.4	13.1	1.7	1.7	3.4	1.6	-0.4	1.1
Education	20.3	11.4	13.6	7.5	-6.7	-1.0	-7.7	-4.5	-1.4	-5.8
Public administration	7.7	7.8	5.6	4.4	-0.9	1.8	1.0	-0.6	-0.5	-1.1
Other	6.3	3.9	6.8	5.2	-2.4	0.4	-2.0	-2.2	0.7	-1.5
Total	100.0	100.0	100.0	100.0	-3.3	14.7	11.4	4.9	-1.9	3.0

Source: Current Population Survey, 1973 to 1991.
Notes: Original analysis conducted with an eighteen-industry breakdown. Results reported are aggregations of that more detailed analysis.
[a]Finance, insurance, and real estate.

This industrial structure analysis for college-educated women clearly shows the importance of the education and public administration sectors to women, especially to African American women. During the 1970s over half (57.8 percent) of African American college graduates were employed in the education sector. Two-thirds (66.2 percent) were employed in either education or public administration. By 1990 this fraction had dropped by half, to one-third. As of the 1970s, white women were also concentrated in these two sectors, but to a somewhat smaller extent. The decompositions show that these shifts out of education and public administration were driven by the overall decline in these two industries. In fact, over the period studied, the fraction of the workforce in the two industries accounted for by African American and white women actually rose.

Between the 1970s and 1990, the representation of college-educated African American and white women in the workforce rose just over 50 percent (for African American women, 51.4 percent—from 0.71 percent to 1.07 percent; for white women, 50.7 percent—from 8.0 percent to 12.1 percent). Had the fraction of the workforce in each industry represented by African American and white women stayed constant, the employment of African American women would have declined 21 percent and the employment of white women would have declined somewhat less (14 percent). A 72 percent rise in the "within-industry" fraction for African American women and a somewhat smaller, 65 percent rise for white women had to accommodate the roughly 50 percent increase in the fraction of the college-educated workforce accounted for by African American and white women. These shifts would have tended to exert a downward pressure on both African American and white women's wages, with the magnitude of the effect depending on the ease with which these groups could find employment in sectors of the economy outside of education and public administration. To the extent that African American women were more concentrated in education and public administration, and to the extent that they may have faced more barriers to employment in other sectors than white women did, the downward pressure on the wages of African American women should have been greater than the downward pressure on the wages of white women. In this analysis, then, industrial shifts were responsible for some of the relative decline in the wages of college-educated African American women, even though "industry" played a small role in explaining declining wages in the regression decomposition analysis.

Which industries accommodated the 50 percent increase in the college-educated African American and white workforce? For college-educated African American women, more than 50 percent ([15.6 + 11.6]/51.40) of the increase went into health and public administration (table 2.3, total effect column). The increases for white women were more evenly distributed, with less than 30 percent ([10.9 + 2.6]/50.66) going into health and public administration. The public sector continued to play an important role for college-educated women and to play a more important role for African American than for white women.

As for the other educational and regional groups, with the exception of the high school dropouts, the industrial composition of employment shifted against African American (compared with white) women while the share of the workforce accounted for by African American women rose more rapidly than that accounted for by white women (tables 2.3 and 2.4). If the sum of the within-sector shifts serves as the best indicator of the extent of the pressure on wages, there is some indication that supply and demand shifts did have negative effects on the wages of African American women. In both the Northeast and the Midwest, where the relative wages of African American women fell dramatically, the within-sector increases in the employment of African American women were also particularly large. In the South, where wage trends were less pronounced, the within-sector increases for African American women were also less pronounced.

While this demand shift analysis provides insight into sources for relative wage trends, perhaps especially among college-educated women, it also reveals something of a paradox. A comparison of demand indexes calculated for white men and white women shows that in most cases negative shifts were more pronounced for women than they were for men. This is especially true for college graduates, a group in which the number of white women increased dramatically. Yet over the period studied the wages of white women—even those of college-educated white women—rose relative to men's wages. Apparently white women were more successful than African American women were in making the transition out of traditionally female industries and occupations.

While we do not have the data to test directly these ideas, there are a number of plausible explanations why African American women may have been less successful than white women in shifting out of the sectors that have typically employed them. First, employers in sectors that have not traditionally employed African American women may be reluctant to do so, either because of their own prejudice or because of fears regarding the reactions of coworkers or customers (Kirschenman and Neckerman 1991; Holzer 1996). Second, African American women may be less connected than white women to the informal networks that are often critical for finding employment (Holzer 1987). Third, the real or perceived gap in cognitive skills that continues to exist between African American and white women may have made it more difficult for African American women to shift into some sectors of the economy (see chapter 3; Neal and Johnson 1996; Holzer 1996). Fourth, the likelihood that expanding industries will locate in the suburbs rather than in city centers, also differentially affects African American women (Holzer 1991). Finally, the sectors in decline— public administration and education especially—may well be those that most systematically enforce equal opportunity rules. Loss of employment in these sectors pushes African American women into sectors with fewer rules and regulations regarding hiring and promotion.

CONCLUSION

Since the mid-1970s, the economic position of young African American women, measured in terms of both earnings and employment, has declined relative to that of white women. This erosion occurred in all regions and for all educational groups but is most pronounced among college graduates and, to a lesser degree, among women in the Midwest with a high school diploma or less education. The first decomposition analysis shows the significant contribution, first, of changes in the distribution of and the relative payoff to education and, second, of changes in employment structure to the erosion of African American women's relative earnings. Declines in institutional factors—union membership and the minimum wage—also stand out for their disproportionate effect on African American women, regardless of region or level of education. For college-educated African American women, occupational distribution and declining unionization appear to have been the greatest contributors to the decline in earnings, although the decomposition explains only one-third of the relative declines for this group. In the Midwest, African American women's increasing concentration in low-paying industries and declining unionization taken together explain more than half of the relative decline. The decomposition is most successful in explaining the declining wages in the Midwest; it reveals the source of 86 percent of the erosion of African American women's earnings.

The analysis of changes in the industrial composition of employment away from sectors that have traditionally employed African American women offers an additional perspective on the relative earnings and employment declines. This approach emphasizes the differential effect that broad trends in supply and demand will have on different populations. In each of the disaggregated groups, African American women, especially college graduates, were disproportionately represented in declining industries, implying that they were disproportionately required to find new employment in the 1980s.

Taken together, these analyses show that, especially in the Midwest, African American women suffered as a result of industrial shifts. The effect of the decline in manufacturing, while smaller for African American women than for African American men, was still large. Additionally, deunionization significantly contributed to the relative decline of African American women's earnings. Clearly, deindustrialization and deunionization are not only the problems of male workers.

Investigations of this sort can never fully document and account for all the changes that may have contributed to increasing wage disparity. For example, declining federal budgets and support for enforcement of affirmative action and shifting attitudes of employers could also have been substantial contributing factors. And the fact that so much of the rise in the wage gap remains unexplained by forces that are commonly proposed— education, location, industry—suggests that important social and institutional factors remain unmeasured.

Although the CPS offers no measures of real experience, we expect that white women's increasing relative experience over the period also explains a considerable part of the growth in the earnings differential. However, declining relative experience was likely not only a cause but also an effect of declining economic opportunity for African American women. Employment data show that, in the Northeast in the 1980s, the relative odds of employment for African American women actually improved slightly. This region and period were the only ones for which relative earnings did not decline. This pattern is suggestive of the two-way relationship between labor market demand and the supply of African American women.

Situating the relative earnings declines of African American women in the context of the relative wage advances experienced by white women brings up important questions that this study only begins to answer. Which advances for white women did not equally benefit African American women? Young white women upgraded their occupations more rapidly than African American women did, and returns to education have clearly grown more quickly among white than among African American women. Neither the decompositions nor the fixed-factor analysis allows insight into changes in relative returns to education for white and African American women. Thus an important avenue for investigation is the earnings advances of white women relative to white men and the extent to which white women experienced advances that African American women did not.

While this study makes clear that all African American women, regardless of education or region, suffered relative earnings and employment declines from 1973 to 1991, the experiences of different groups of women appear to have been diverse. Thus future research should be informed by an appreciation for the ways in which the experiences of African American women differ from those of white women and of African American men and for the diversity of experience among African American women.

APPENDIX: DECOMPOSING TRENDS IN RELATIVE EARNINGS

While it differs in detail, in spirit the decomposition we use is very similar to the familiar Oxaca decomposition. The standard Oxaca decomposition starts with estimates of a wage equation,

(2A.1)
$$\ln(w_{rt}) = X'_{rt}\,\beta_{rt} + \epsilon_{rt},$$

where (w_{rt}) represents the natural logarithm of hourly earnings; X, a vector of observed characteristics; ϵ, unobserved characteristics; and β, a vector of coefficients. We imagine that equation (2A.1) is estimated separately by race (r) and time period (t). At any point in time the racial differential in average outcomes, $\Delta\overline{\ln(w_t)} = \overline{\ln(w_{wt})} - \overline{\ln(w_{at})}$, can be decomposed into a difference due to observed characteristics and a residual, unexplained difference:

(2A.2)
$$\Delta\overline{\ln(w_t)} = \Delta\overline{X}'_t\,\beta_{wt} + Rt.$$

We have presented this decomposition evaluating the mean differences in observed characteristics by using the white coefficients (β_{wt}) but could have as easily used the African American coefficients (β_{at}) or, for that matter, an average of the two. Using equation (2A.2) shows that changes over time in the racial differential in outcomes, $\Delta\overline{\ln(w_t)}$, can be accounted for either by changes over time in the mean racial differential in observed characteristics $(\Delta\overline{X}_t)$, by the changes in the value of these characteristics (β_{wt}), or by changes in the residual. We call the first of these components the *quantity effect*, the second the *price effect*, and the third the *residual* or *unexplained change*.

The decomposition begins with a wage equation estimated on both whites and African Americans:

(2A.3)
$$ln(w_{ij_t}) = \hat{\gamma}_t b_{ij_t} + X'_{ij_t}\hat{\Pi},$$

where i indexes the individual, j the race, and t the time period. The variable b_{ijt} is a dummy that is 1 if the individual is African American and 0 if she is white. X_{ijt} represents controls for experience. The $\hat{\gamma}_t$ are plotted on the solid line of figure 2.1.

Next we augment equation (2A.3) with controls for education:

(2A.4)
$$ln(w_{ij_t}) = \hat{\gamma}b_{ij_t} + \beta_t Ed_{ij_t} + X'_{ij_t}\hat{\Pi}',$$

where $\hat{\gamma}'_t$ represents the racial differential after controlling for education. These numbers are plotted on the dotted line in figure 2.1. Notice that the higher educational attainment of white women "explains" some of the wage gap; the racial earnings differential is smaller after accounting for differences in education. In defining $\hat{\delta}_t = \hat{\gamma}_t - \hat{\gamma}'_t$, the difference, $\hat{\delta}_t$, represents the effect of the gap in educational attainment on relative earnings. Because there is a racial gap in educational attainment (white women have more education than African American women do), we expect to find $\hat{\delta}_t < 0$. In figure 2.1, $\hat{\delta}_t$ is represented by the vertical distance between the solid and dotted lines.

At least during the 1980s, $\hat{\delta}_t$ grew in magnitude over time—the impact of education on the earnings differential between white and African American women increased in the 1980s (see figure 2.1). Thus the racial gap in earnings widens less rapidly over time once one accounts for changes in education.

The effect of the gap in educational attainment on earnings differentials, $\hat{\delta}_t$, is a function both of the educational attainment gap and of the value of education. In particular, in running the auxiliary regression equation

$$(2A.5) \qquad\qquad Ed_{ij_t} = \hat{\lambda}_t b_{ij_t} + X_{ij_t}\hat{\theta},$$

$\hat{\lambda}_t$ represents the racial gap in educational attainment controlling for as of time t. Then $\hat{\delta}_t = \hat{\lambda}_t\hat{\beta}_t$.[15] $\hat{\delta}_t$ can change over time either because of changes in $\hat{\beta}_t$—the value of education—or because of changes in $\hat{\lambda}_t$—the gap in educational attainment.

Next we decompose changes over time into constitutive price and quantity elements. To do this, many researchers use base- and end-period estimates. However, we follow a somewhat different strategy to try to minimize the influence of the choice of a base year on estimates. In particular, we can decompose into predicted and residual components:

$$(2A.6) \qquad\qquad \hat{\delta}_t = \overline{\beta}\hat{\lambda}_t + \hat{v}_t,$$

where $\overline{\beta} = \frac{1}{T}\Sigma\hat{\beta}_t\beta_t$, is the average value of education over the nineteen-year period. Equation (2A.6) decomposes $\hat{\delta}_t$ into a component predicted on the basis of the value of education averaged over the 1973 to 1991 period and the gap in educational attainment as of time t. For each year, this procedure yields an estimate of the impact of the gap in education on earnings, $\hat{\delta}_t$; an estimate of this gap evaluated at a constant set of prices, $\overline{\beta}\hat{\lambda}_t$ (the quantity effect); and an estimate of the importance of the average gap evaluated at varying prices, v_t (the price effect). We summarize these numbers by running regression lines through them.

Our decompositions differ from more traditional ones that typically involve four terms. By constraining slope coefficients to be the same across the races, we eliminate the term in the traditional decomposition that involves interactions between changes in means and differences in coefficients.[16] The differences in estimate coefficients are often neither large nor well estimated and are difficult to interpret.[17] We also reduce the within-component of the decomposition to a single term, but since the decomposition of this component into separate terms is arbitrary (Jones 1983), this hardly represents a loss.

(Text continues on p. 101.)

Table 2A.1 / Industrial Distribution of African American and White Women, 1973 to 1989

Group and Industry of Occupation	1973			1979			1989		
	White	African American	Difference	White	African American	Difference	White	African American	Difference
All									
Agriculture, mining, construction	1.7	1.6	0.1	2.2	1.6	0.6	2.6	1.4	1.2
Durable goods	10.0	9.9	0.1	9.1	8.9	0.2	7.2	5.7	1.5
Nondurable goods	10.0	15.0	−5.0	8.3	10.4	−2.1	7.5	10.0	−2.5
Transportation	1.8	3.0	−1.2	2.1	3.0	−0.9	2.5	3.3	−0.8
Communication	3.1	5.6	−2.5	2.5	4.8	−2.3	1.8	3.3	−1.5
Wholesale trade	2.6	1.4	1.2	2.9	1.5	1.4	3.2	1.8	1.4
Retail trade	16.8	11.8	5.0	20.5	12.8	7.7	26.1	23.7	2.4
FIRE[a]	10.4	5.8	4.6	10.6	10.6	0.0	12.7	11.9	0.8
Business	2.3	2.4	−0.1	2.6	2.7	−0.1	6.2	6.8	−0.6
Repair	0.3	0.6	−0.3	0.3	0.2	0.1	0.6	0.6	0.0
Personal service	4.0	5.1	−1.1	3.7	3.7	0.0	5.2	6.2	−1.0
Entertainment	0.7	0.2	0.5	1.1	0.7	0.4	1.2	1.2	0.0
Health	13.9	13.6	0.3	14.1	15.4	−1.3	12.5	13.1	−0.6
Education	14.6	14.5	0.1	11.5	11.2	0.3	2.2	1.5	0.7
Other professional	4.5	3.3	1.2	4.8	5.7	−0.9	7.3	5.9	1.4
Public administration	3.2	6.2	−3.0	3.8	6.7	−2.9	1.1	3.6	−2.5
By education level									
College graduates									
Agriculture, mining, construction	1.0	1.3	−0.3	1.5	0.5	1.0	1.8	0.8	1.0
Durable goods	1.7	1.4	0.3	2.8	2.5	0.3	5.4	4.2	1.2
Nondurable goods	2.9	5.4	−2.5	4.2	4.1	0.1	5.2	4.8	0.4

(Table continues on p. 94.)

Table 2A.1 / *Continued*

Group and Industry of Occupation	1973 White	1973 African American	1973 Difference	1979 White	1979 African American	1979 Difference	1989 White	1989 African American	1989 Difference
Transportation, communication	2.7	1.4	1.3	3.9	5.0	−1.1	4.4	9.4	−5.0
Wholesale trade	0.9	0.0	0.9	1.7	2.6	−0.9	2.8	2.2	0.6
Retail trade	5.2	2.7	2.5	7.7	4.9	2.8	9.2	5.3	3.9
FIRE[a]	4.0	2.7	1.3	7.0	8.0	−1.0	10.8	10.5	0.3
Business	2.4	1.3	1.1	2.7	2.6	0.1	7.0	4.9	2.1
Personal service, repair, entertainment	0.6	0.0	0.6	2.2	2.1	0.1	2.9	2.7	0.2
Health	12.3	7.2	5.1	16.4	14.4	2.0	15.5	12.8	2.7
Education	57.0	70.0	−13.0	36.9	34.8	2.1	19.9	21.4	−1.5
Other professional	6.2	2.8	3.4	8.0	9.1	−1.1	10.6	8.2	2.4
Public administration	2.9	3.9	−1.0	4.9	9.3	−4.4	4.4	12.8	−8.4
High school graduates									
Agriculture, mining, construction	1.5	1.1	0.4	2.5	1.7	0.8	2.5	0.8	1.7
Durable goods	12.6	12.3	0.3	11.7	10.7	1.0	7.3	6.0	1.3
Nondurable goods	10.6	17.2	−6.6	9.3	12.3	−3.0	7.9	11.2	−3.3
Transportation	1.7	4.4	−2.7	2.0	3.1	−1.1	2.7	2.0	0.7
Comunication	4.3	6.4	−2.1	3.0	5.1	−2.1	1.4	1.9	−0.5
Wholesale trade	3.7	1.4	2.3	3.5	1.2	2.3	2.9	1.6	1.3
Retail trade	19.4	14.2	5.2	25.2	15.5	9.7	31.1	25.4	5.7
FIRE[a]	13.7	7.3	6.4	13.2	11.3	1.9	12.7	8.7	4.0
Business	2.0	2.9	−0.9	2.5	2.9	−0.4	4.5	5.5	−1.0
Repair	0.4	0.4	0.0	0.4	0.1	0.3	0.7	0.9	−0.2

Personal service	5.0	4.9	0.1	4.6	4.2	0.4	6.2	7.2	-1.0
Entertainment	0.9	0.0	0.9	0.9	0.8	0.1	1.2	1.2	0.0
Health	12.8	13.5	-0.7	10.5	14.6	-4.1	9.3	14.5	-5.2
Education	3.7	5.3	-1.6	3.5	6.5	-3.0	2.1	2.6	-0.5
Other professional	4.1	3.5	0.6	3.4	4.2	-0.8	4.8	5.0	-0.2
Public administration	3.8	5.1	-1.3	3.8	6.0	-2.2	2.7	5.4	2.7
High school dropouts									
Agriculture, mining, construction	2.3	4.1	-1.8	2.9	3.1	-0.2	3.1	3.5	-0.4
Durable goods	18.2	12.4	5.8	17.3	11.2	6.1	9.6	4.2	5.4
Nondurable goods	23.9	23.7	0.2	20.3	20.5	-0.2	13.3	14.1	-0.8
Transportation, communication	2.1	4.1	-2.0	1.9	3.0	-1.1	1.4	0.0	1.4
Wholesale trade	2.1	1.9	0.2	2.1	1.3	0.8	2.6	1.0	1.6
Retail trade	26.4	16.9	9.5	29.3	20.5	8.8	37.8	33.0	4.8
FIRE,[a] business	4.8	3.7	1.1	6.3	5.2	1.1	8.0	10.5	-2.5
Personal service, repair, entertainment	9.4	13.8	-4.4	8.7	10.8	-2.1	12.0	14.7	-2.7
Health	6.9	13.8	-6.9	7.0	14.7	-7.7	6.1	10.0	-3.9
Education	2.9	2.1	0.8	2.0	4.8	-2.8	1.5	3.6	-2.1
Other professional, public administration	1.0	3.5	-2.5	2.3	5.0	-2.7	4.7	5.4	-0.7
By region[b]									
Northeast									
Agriculture, mining, construction	1.0	0.0	1.0	1.6	0.5	1.1	2.0	2.2	-0.2
Durable goods	15.1	17.5	-2.4	14.8	11.3	3.5	8.6	3.7	4.9
Nondurable goods	14.0	5.6	8.4	11.7	11.2	0.5	9.9	5.9	4.0

(Table continues on p. 96.)

Table 2A.1 / *Continued*

Group and Industry of Occupation	1973 White	1973 African American	1973 Difference	1979 White	1979 African American	1979 Difference	1989 White	1989 African American	1989 Difference
Transportation	1.3	4.7	−3.4	1.6	3.1	−1.5	2.4	3.9	−1.5
Communication	4.8	14.1	−9.3	2.4	3.6	−1.2	1.5	1.5	0.0
Wholesale	2.9	3.8	−0.9	3.2	2.2	1.0	2.9	3.5	−0.6
Retail	19.0	6.4	12.6	22.3	8.1	14.2	27.4	16.6	10.8
FIRE[a]	12.4	13.2	−0.8	14.1	23.1	−9.0	13.7	18.1	−4.4
Business	2.7	3.3	−0.6	3.4	0.9	2.5	5.4	8.1	−2.7
Personal service, repair, entertainment	4.9	1.6	3.3	5.2	5.3	−0.1	8.8	5.1	3.7
Health	14.0	15.0	−1.0	10.3	17.5	−7.2	9.2	16.8	−7.6
Education	1.9	1.7	0.2	2.8	4.7	−1.9	1.7	1.9	−0.2
Other professional	3.2	5.2	−2.0	3.6	5.5	−1.9	4.1	8.9	−4.8
Public administration.	2.9	7.9	−5.0	3.0	2.8	0.2	2.5	4.0	−1.5
Midwest									
Agriculture, mining, construction	1.1	1.7	−0.6	1.4	0.4	1.0	2.1	0.0	2.1
Durable	20.4	17.5	2.9	14.8	18.5	−3.7	9.7	4.7	5.0
Nondurable goods	8.7	10.5	−1.8	9.1	6.3	2.8	9.1	4.3	4.8
Transportation	1.2	6.4	−5.2	1.6	3.3	−1.7	2.9	1.2	1.7
Communication	3.5	6.1	−2.6	2.4	6.4	−4.0	0.9	0.8	0.1
Wholesale	3.3	0.0	3.3	3.4	2.0	1.4	3.0	1.8	1.2
Retail	20.7	24.1	−3.4	26.1	16.5	9.6	34.2	31.9	2.3
FIRE[a]	10.7	3.7	7.0	10.8	8.6	2.2	9.5	9.9	−0.4
Business	1.9	5.4	−3.5	2.7	1.7	1.0	4.4	6.1	−1.7
Personal service, repair, entertainment	7.5	10.3	−2.8	6.7	2.6	4.1	7.2	9.0	−1.8

Health	12.7	9.1	3.6	12.4	15.5	-3.1	9.2	18.0	-8.8
Education	3.2	0.0	3.2	2.8	8.0	-5.2	1.6	2.0	-0.4
Other professional	3.1	3.9	-0.8	3.4	4.8	-1.4	4.3	6.1	-1.8
Public administration	2.2	1.4	0.8	2.2	5.3	-3.1	1.8	4.2	-2.4
South									
Agriculture, mining, construction	2.4	2.5	-0.1	3.0	3.1	-0.1	2.9	1.0	1.9
Durable goods	9.8	9.0	.08	9.7	8.2	1.5	6.3	6.1	0.2
Nondurable goods	17.3	26.9	-9.6	14.7	19.3	-4.6	10.1	15.8	-5.7
Transportation	2.5	2.0	0.5	2.3	2.1	0.2	2.2	1.1	1.1
Communication	3.7	3.4	0.3	2.7	3.3	-0.6	1.3	1.5	-0.2
Wholesale trade	3.4	1.2	2.2	3.2	0.5	2.7	2.9	0.8	2.1
Retail trade	20.4	15.3	5.1	27.8	19.7	8.1	33.1	28.9	4.2
FIRE[a]	11.0	3.7	7.3	9.5	4.7	4.8	10.7	4.5	6.2
Business	1.9	1.6	0.3	2.1	3.3	-1.2	4.5	5.0	-0.5
Personal service, repair, entertainment	6.9	9.7	-2.8	6.0	7.9	-1.9	8.7	10.4	-1.7
Health	8.4	14.6	-6.2	8.7	13.0	-4.3	7.3	12.6	-5.3
Education	4.4	5.4	-1.0	3.5	6.7	-3.2	2.6	3.4	-0.8
Other professional	3.5	0.8	2.7	2.8	3.1	-0.3	4.6	4.2	0.4
Public admin.	4.3	3.8	0.5	4.1	5.3	-1.2	2.9	4.4	-1.5

Source: Current Population Survey, 1973 to 1991.
Note: Data are for women with zero to ten years of potential labor market experience.
[a]Finance and real estate.
[b]Women with a high school education or less.

Table 2A.2 / Occupational Distribution of African American and White Women, 1973 to 1989

Group and Occupation	1973			1979			1989		
	White	African American	Difference	White	African American	Difference	White	African American	Difference
All									
Management	3.9	2.8	1.1	7.0	4.5	2.5	11.8	7.0	4.8
Professional	17.4	12.3	5.1	16.6	12.1	4.5	11.4	5.4	6.0
Technical	2.9	1.7	1.2	3.6	2.1	1.5	4.1	3.0	1.1
Sales	7.8	4.9	2.9	9.9	7.0	2.9	16.8	17.3	-0.5
Clerical	40.1	33.4	6.7	35.2	38.2	-3.0	29.6	31.7	-2.1
Service	13.8	19.6	-5.8	14.1	18.2	-4.1	15.8	20.1	-4.3
Craft	1.0	1.2	-0.2	1.4	0.8	0.6	2.0	2.6	-0.6
Operative	10.7	18.2	-7.5	8.7	12.7	-4.0	5.4	9.6	-4.2
Transportation, labor, farm	2.4	5.8	-3.4	3.5	4.3	-0.8	3.1	3.3	-0.2
By education									
College graduates									
Management	6.8	7.4	-0.6	12.9	12.8	0.1	20.6	15.9	4.7
Professional	69.3	72.8	-3.5	55.9	48.8	7.1	42.6	31.6	11.0
Technical	3.9	1.1	2.8	4.2	2.1	2.1	6.1	7.3	-1.2
Sales	3.0	2.4	0.6	4.6	4.4	0.2	10.2	9.2	1.0
Clerical	13.4	13.6	-0.2	16.7	25.8	-9.1	14.5	29.5	-15.0
Service	2.6	2.7	-0.1	3.8	4.6	-0.8	4.0	4.3	-0.3
Other	1.0	0.0	1.0	1.8	1.5	0.3	1.9	2.1	-0.2
High school graduates									
Management	2.0	1.8	0.2	4.6	2.1	2.5	6.4	3.4	3.0
Professional	3.7	3.1	0.6	2.6	3.0	-0.4	2.3	2.0	0.3
Technical	2.4	2.2	0.2	2.5	1.4	1.1	2.0	2.4	-0.4
Sales	8.9	6.2	2.7	12.0	8.6	3.4	17.7	18.0	-0.3
Clerical	51.8	28.8	23.0	45.2	40.4	4.8	37.0	27.4	9.6

Service	15.4	21.1	-5.7	16.3	21.2	-4.9	20.4	26.9	-6.5
Craft	1.2	0.9	0.3	1.3	1.0	0.3	2.5	3.6	-1.1
Operative	11.8	21.8	-10.0	10.9	17.2	-6.3	7.4	12.6	-5.2
Transportation, labor, farm	2.9	4.0	-1.1	4.3	5.0	-0.7	3.8	3.8	0.0
High school dropouts									
Management, professional, technical	2.9	0.0	2.9	3.7	3.0	0.7	5.1	3.0	2.1
Sales	10.4	4.3	6.1	11.5	6.3	5.2	18.4	17.7	0.7
Clerical	13.4	13.7	-0.3	14.1	13.8	0.3	14.1	8.3	5.8
Service	28.8	32.8	-4.0	27.8	38.2	-10.4	32.4	43.9	-11.5
Craft	2.2	2.3	-0.1	2.9	1.4	1.5	3.8	4.4	-0.6
Operative	35.4	39.7	-4.3	30.9	26.3	4.6	18.1	15.9	2.2
Transportation, labor, farm	7.0	17.2	-10.2	9.1	11.1	-2.0	8.2	6.7	1.5
By region[a]									
Northeast									
Management	1.9	1.6	0.3	3.5	3.2	0.3	6.5	6.1	0.4
Professional	3.6	6.4	-2.8	3.2	3.6	-0.4	2.9	2.3	0.6
Technical	2.9	1.7	1.2	1.8	1.7	0.1	1.9	4.5	-2.6
Sales	9.6	5.4	4.2	11.4	4.0	7.4	15.7	11.5	4.2
Clerical	46.3	53.5	-7.2	44.4	48.9	-4.5	37.4	39.6	-2.2
Service	15.3	13.0	2.3	16.4	17.1	-0.7	20.1	27.3	-7.2
Craft	1.4	0.0	1.4	1.4	0.0	1.4	2.2	1.1	1.1
Operative	16.2	13.7	2.5	13.9	16.7	-2.8	8.9	6.2	2.7
Transportation, labor, farm	2.8	4.7	-1.9	4.0	4.8	-0.8	4.4	1.2	3.2
Midwest									
Management	1.0	0.0	1.0	3.5	1.5	2.0	5.0	1.8	3.2
Professional	3.4	3.3	0.1	2.3	3.1	-0.8	1.8	0.0	1.8
Technical	1.8	1.6	0.2	1.9	1.4	0.5	1.7	0.6	1.1

(Table continues on p. 100.)

Table 2A.2 / Continued

Group and Occupation	1973 White	1973 African American	1973 Difference	1979 White	1979 African American	1979 Difference	1989 White	1989 African American	1989 Difference
Sales	8.1	7.1	1.0	11.7	9.8	1.9	17.7	25.3	-7.6
Clerical	44.9	40.2	4.7	38.0	45.3	-7.3	31.9	28.4	3.5
Service	19.3	23.3	-4.0	21.5	18.2	3.3	23.4	31.6	-8.2
Craft	1.1	4.1	-3.0	1.5	0.0	1.5	2.6	0.0	2.6
Operative	16.1	8.7	7.4	13.5	15.6	-2.1	11.2	9.7	1.5
Transportation, labor, farm	4.3	11.8	-7.5	6.1	5.0	1.1	4.6	2.5	2.1
South									
Management	2.4	1.7	0.7	4.2	0.9	3.3	5.9	2.3	3.6
Professional	2.3	0.7	2.5	2.1	2.6	-0.5	2.4	1.9	0.5
Technical	1.7	1.7	0.0	2.5	0.9	1.6	1.9	1.5	0.4
Sales	9.5	5.7	3.8	13.4	8.7	4.7	19.3	18.2	1.1
Clerical	45.5	19.7	25.8	38.9	25.1	13.8	33.0	17.8	15.2
Service	14.9	28.0	-13.1	16.2	30.0	-13.8	20.1	31.3	-11.2
Craft	1.6	1.2	0.4	2.3	1.9	0.4	2.8	5.4	-2.6
Operative	18.4	32.4	-14.0	15.7	22.4	-6.7	10.0	16.9	-6.9
Transportation, labor, farm	2.7	9.1	-6.4	4.5	7.5	-3.0	4.8	4.7	0.1

Source: Current Population Survey, 1973 to 1991.
Note: Data are for women with zero to ten years of potential labor market experience.
[a]Finance and real estate.
[b]Women with a high school education or less.

An earlier version of this chapter was presented at the 1993 meetings of the Population Association of America. We have benefited from comments by seminar participants and by two anonymous referees. The support of the Russell Sage Foundation is gratefully acknowledged. We thank Marshall Cummings for programming assistance and Sandra Crump for editorial assistance.

NOTES

1. Blau and Kahn (1992) report similar results.

2. See also chapter 1.

3. Years of potential labor market experience is defined as the years an individual has been out of school. For those with no more than a high school degree, we calculated potential experience by subtracting eighteen from their age. For those with post-high school education, potential experience was calculated by subtracting (years of education plus six) from their age.

4. We did not eliminate Hispanics from either the African American or the white samples. Since relatively few Hispanics identify themselves as either white or African American (U.S. Department of Commerce 1992), it seems unlikely that this choice materially affects our results.

5. The sample was restricted to those whose major activity was working as wage and salary workers (thus eliminating most full-time students as well as the non-employed) with zero to ten years of potential work experience. Individuals whose imputed hourly pay was greater than $100 or less than $1 in 1983 dollars were excluded.

6. African American female college graduates lost ground not only relative to college-educated white women but also relative to college-educated white men. In the mid-1970s, young college-educated African American women earned about 10 percent less than comparably educated white men did; by the late 1990s the gap had widened to 20 percent.

7. We distinguish between those who live in the central city, the suburbs, and nonmetropolitan areas.

8. We distinguish eighteen major industries (agriculture, mining, construction, durable goods, nondurable goods, transportation, communication, retail trade, wholesale trade, finance and real estate, business, repair, personal service, entertainment, health, education, professional services, and public administration) and eleven major occupations following the 1980 census definitions (managerial, professional, technical, sales, clerical, service, craft, operative, transportation, laborer, and farm worker).

9. We use 1989 rather than 1991 because 1989 represented a business cycle peak.

10. In particular, for each three-digit occupation represented in the 1980 census, we calculated the average log hourly earnings among white women working full-

time, full-year. Then, for each year of CPS data for which the 1980 occupational codes were used (1983 to 1991), we calculated log wages for white and African American women using the share of each group in the employed workforce. In particular, let w_i represent the average log wage for white women in the ith occupation and s_{ibt} represent the share of African American women in the ith occupation as of year t. Then the predicted wage for African American women in year t is $\Sigma_i s_{ibt} w_i$. Essentially, this is the wage that African American women would earn in year t if their wages matched those of white women. The difference between the predicted wage and the real wage shows the importance of the different occupational distributions of white and African American women. The average wages of white workers from the three-digit census categories were used as a standard yardstick; the rate of improvement in occupational opportunity over time can be measured as predicted wages increase with new distributions across occupations observed in the CPS data. We investigated occupational upgrading for white women in a similar manner, calculating separately for college graduates, high school graduates, and high school dropouts.

11. The inclusion of the government sector dummy (over and above the industry dummies) alone has very little effect on the estimated racial wage gap. Thus, it is appropriate to think of these estimates as "unionization" effects.

12. Since the minimum did not go up to $4.25 until April, we used $3.80 for observations from the first three months of the year.

13. The effect of the declining minimum wage is even larger if calculated for 1989, before the minimum was raised.

14. By *industrial decline* we mean declines in sectoral output and employment associated with declines in the demand for the output of a sector. Employment in a sector can decline not only because the demand for the output of the sector declines but also because better alternatives arise for the workforce in the sector. Employment shifts due to such "supply-side" factors are likely to have a very different effect on compensation than the "demand-side" factors that we envision are currently driving the changing sectoral composition of the workforce. To be concrete, unlike the decline in the education sector, the historical decline in personal service was primarily a result of better alternatives opening up for African American women (King 1992). As a result, such developments should have had a positive effect on the wages of African American women, not only because they were moving out of poorly paying jobs but also because the exodus could have been expected to drive up the wages of those who continued to work in the sector.

15. This is, of course, just the left-out variable bias formula.

16. Since there are many more white than African American women in the samples we analyzed, the estimated slope coefficients are essentially the ones one would estimate if the sample were limited to whites.

17. Note that, by disaggregating by educational level and region, we are implicitly allowing for interactions along these particular dimensions.

REFERENCES

Badgett, M. V. Lee, and Rhonda Williams. 1994. "The Changing Contours of Discrimination: Race, Gender, and Structural Economic Change." In *Understanding American Economic Decline*, edited by Michael A. Bernstein and David E. Adler. New York: Cambridge University Press.

Blau, Francine D., and Andrea H. Beller. 1992. "Black-White Earnings over the 1970s and 1980s: Gender Differences in Trends." *Review of Economics and Statistics* 74(2): 276–86.

Blau, Francine D., and Lawrence M. Kahn. 1992. "Race and Gender Pay Differentials." In *Research Frontiers in Industrial Relations*, edited by David Lewin, Olivia Mitchell, and Peter Sherer. Madison, Wis.: Industrial Relations Research Association.

Bound, John, and Laura Dresser, 1996. "The Erosion of the Relative Earnings and Employment of Young African American Women during the 1980s." Research Report No. 96-367. Ann Arbor: University of Michigan, Population Studies Center.

Bound, John, and Richard Freeman. 1992. "What Went Wrong? The Erosion of Relative Earnings and Employment among Young Black Men in the 1980s." *Quarterly Journal of Economics* 107(1): 201–32.

Bound, John, and George Johnson. 1991. "Changes in the Structure of Wages in the 1980s: An Evaluation of Alternative Explanations." *American Economic Review* 82(3): 371–92.

Cotton, Jeremiah. 1989. "Opening the Gap: The Decline in African American Economic Indicators in the 1980s." *Social Science Quarterly* 70(4): 803–35.

Cunningham, James S., and Nadja Zalokar. 1992. "The Economic Progress of Black Women, 1940–1980: Occupational Distribution and Relative Wages." *Industrial Labor Relations Review* 33(3): 540–55.

Edin, Katherine, and Laura Lein. 1997. *Making Ends Meet: How Single Mothers Survive Low-Wage Work*. New York: Russell Sage Foundation.

Fay, Robert E., Jeffrey. Passell, and J. Gregory Robinson. 1988. "The Coverage of Population in the 1980 Census." U.S. Census of Population Document PHC-80-E4. Washington: U.S. Government Printing Office for U.S. Bureau of the Census.

Freeman, Richard B. 1977. "Manpower Requirements and Substitution Analysis of Labor Skills: A Synthesis." In *Research in Labor Economics*, Vol. 1, edited by Ronald Ehrenberg. Greenwich, Ct.: JAI Press.

Frazis, Harley, and Jay Stewart. 1996. "Tracking the Returns to Education in the Nineties: Bridging the Gap between the New and Old CPS Education Items." BLS Working Paper 288. Washington, D.C.: U.S. Government Printing Office for U.S. Bureau of Labor Statistics.

Holzer, Harry J. 1987. "Informal Job Search and Black Youth Unemployment." *American Economic Review* 77(3): 446–52.

———. 1991. "The Spatial Mismatch Hypothesis: What Has the Evidence Shown?" *Urban Studies* 28(1): 105–22.

———. 1996. *What Employers Want: Job Prospects for Less-Educated Workers*. New York: Russell Sage Foundation.

Jaeger, David A. 1997. "Reconciling the Old and New Census Bureau Questions: Recommendations for Researchers." *Journal of Business and Economic Statistics* 15(3): 300–09.

Jones, F. L. 1983. "On Decomposing the Wage Gap: A Critical Comment on Blinder's Method." *Journal of Human Resources* 18(1): 126–30.

Katz, Lawrence F., and Kevin M. Murphy. 1992. "Changes in Relative Wages, 1963–1987: Supply and Demand Factors." *Quarterly Journal of Economics* 107(1): 35–78.

King, Mary C. 1992. "Occupational Segregation by Race and Sex, 1940–88." *Monthly Labor Review* (4): 30–37.

Kirschenman, Joleen, and Kathryn M. Neckerman. 1991. "'We'd Love to Hire Them, But . . .' The Meaning of Race for Employers." In *The Urban Underclass*, edited by Christopher Jencks and Paul E. Peterson. Washington, D.C.: Brookings Institution.

McCrate, Elaine, and Laura Leete. 1994. "Black-White Wage Differences among Young Women, 1977–86." *Industrial Relations* 33(2): 168–83.

Murnane, Richard J., John B. Willett, and Frank Levy. 1995. "The Growing Importance of Cognitive Skills in Wage Determination." *Review of Economics and Statistics* 77(2): 251–66.

Murphy, Kevin M., and Finis Welch. 1993, "Industrial Change and the Rising Importance of Skill." In *Uneven Tides: Rising Inequality in America*, edited by Sheldon Danziger and Peter Gottschalk. New York: Russell Sage Foundation.

Neal, Derek A., and William R. Johnson. 1996. "The Role of Pre-Market Forces in Black-White Wage Differences." *Journal of Political Economy* 104(5): 869–95.

O'Neill, June, and Solomon Polachek. 1993. "Why the Gender Gap in Wages Narrowed in the 1980s." *Journal of Labor Economics* 11(1): 205–28.

Simms, Margaret C., and Julianne Malveaux. 1986. *Slipping through the Cracks: The Status of African American Women*. New Brunswick, N.J.: Transaction Books.

Sorensen, Elaine. 1991. "Gender and Racial Pay Gaps in the 1980s: Accounting for Different Trends." Urban Institute. Unpublished paper.

Wellington, Allison. 1993. "Changes in the Male/Female Wage Gap: 1976–1985." *Journal of Human Resources* 28(2): 383–411.

U.S. Department of Commerce. U.S. Bureau of the Census. 1992. *1990 Census of Population and Housing*. CPH-1-1. Washington: U.S. Government Printing Office (March).

Chapter 3

The Economic Progress of Mexican and Puerto Rican Women

Mary Corcoran, Colleen M. Heflin, and Belinda L. Reyes

In 1990, one in four Latinos and Latinas lived below the poverty line, with a significant portion living in extreme poverty (Enchautegi 1995). This fact implies a set of important policy issues, as Latinos and Latinas are the fastest-growing racial or ethnic group in the United States. Their demographic growth rate from 1980 to 1990 was nearly ten times that of non-Hispanic whites and more than five times that of African Americans (Morales and Bonilla 1993). Predictions are that Latinos and Latinas will be 15.5 percent of the U.S. population by 2020 (Edmonton and Passel 1992). They are geographically concentrated and are becoming a substantial share of the population of many states. In 1990, they made up 26 percent of the population of Texas and California and a third of the population of the Los Angeles and Houston metropolitan statistical areas (U.S. Department of Commerce 1991a). Latinos and Latinas represent a growing portion of the U.S. workforce, and they are a youthful population in an aging society. Nevertheless, they are often overlooked in poverty research, partly because many impoverished Latinos and Latinas work, and most of the current poverty policy debate centers around the nonworking poor (Enchautegi 1995). In addition, although 65 percent of Latinos and Latinas living in the United States were born there, policy makers often view them as immigrants, and hence they are generally ignored in the poverty policy debate.

A number of studies have examined the economic fortunes of Latinos and Latinas (Bean and Tienda 1987; Waters and Esbach 1995; Harrison and Bennett 1995; Portes and Trulove 1987; Reimers 1985), and a few examine the economic experience of Latinas (Carnoy, Daley, and Ojeda 1993; Reimers 1985; Abowd and Killingsworth 1985; Enchautegi 1995; Tienda and Guhleman; Cintrón 1994). However, little has been written about the trends in Latinas' employment rates and earnings in the 1980s.[1]

The largest groups of Latinos and Latinas differ so much among themselves that each group must be studied on its own (Reimers 1985). Puerto and Mexicans are the largest Latino groups in the United States and groups most readily analyzed using quantitative methods. In 1993, 64 percent of the Latinos and Latinas in the mainland United States were Mexican, and 11 percent were Puerto Rican (Enchautegi 1995). Mexicans were one of the fastest-growing immigrant groups. The Mexican-origin population increased by 52 percent during the 1980s, and the Puerto Rican population grew by 35 percent in the same period (Morales and Bonilla 1993; Rivera-Batiz and Santiago 1994). Mexicans and Puerto Ricans are also two of the poorest Latino and Latina groups in the United States. Close to a third of Mexican and Puerto Rican families were living below the poverty line in 1992 (Enchautegi 1995). Only Dominicans had lower poverty rates in 1990 (Rivera-Batiz and Santiago 1994, 41).

In this chapter we document trends in Puerto Rican and Mexican women's wages, employment, and unemployment from 1970 to 1990. We address three questions:

1. Did the economic fortunes of Puerto Rican women and Mexican women improve or deteriorate during that period?
2. Did the trends in economic attainment vary within subgroups of Puerto Rican and Mexican women (that is, by education level, marital status, residence, or nativity)?
3. Did the gaps between the labor market outcomes of white women and those of Puerto Rican women, and between the outcomes of white and of Mexican women, increase over that period?

LITERATURE REVIEW

A common theme in the research literature on Latinos' and Latinas' economic fortunes is the heterogeneity of the various Latino and Latina subgroups (Bean and Tienda 1987; Tienda, Donato, and Cordero-Guzmán 1992; Waters and Esbach 1995; Harrison and Bennett 1995; Portes and Trulove 1987; Reimers 1985). Portes and Trulove (1987, 360–61) note that "nationality does not simply stand for geographic places of birth; rather it serves as a code word for the very distinct history of each major immigrant flow, a history which molded, in turn, its patterns of entry and adaptation to American society." Tienda (1983) and Bean and Tienda (1987) argue that each Latino and Latina subpopulation has a very different "mode of incorporation" into the U.S. economy and that these modes of incorporation shape the subsequent labor market trajectories of each group.

Analysts further note that Puerto Ricans fare the worst economically among the Latino and Latina subgroups and that Mexicans fare somewhat better than Puerto Ricans and African Americans but worse than non-Hispanic whites and Cubans (Bean and Tienda 1987; Tienda and Jensen 1988; Portes and Trulove 1987; Waters and Esbach 1995). This fact puzzles many analysts, given that Puerto Ricans have the advantage of being citiz are better educated than are Mexicans. Portes and Trulove (1987) arg. this difference is partly the result of collective bargaining. They argu. Puerto Ricans initially worked in highly unionized industries in the N. east and therefore have a history of collective bargaining for employee rights whereas Mexican illegal immigrants can be deported. This difference makes Puerto Ricans appear more costly to potential employers.

One question in the literature has been the causes of the low earnings of Puerto Ricans and Mexicans relative to those of whites. Research on the relative wages of Latino men finds mixed results. All studies find that human capital differences (years of schooling, language proficiency, time since immigration, nativity) explain a large part of the relative wage gaps. Some studies find no residual effects of ethnicity (DeFreitas 1985, 1991; Reimers 1985; Abowd and Killingsworth 1985; Carnoy, Daley, and Ojeda 1993; Harrison and Bennett 1995). Studies of the wages of Latinas relative to those of white women typically find small or no wage differences once schooling is controlled (Carnoy, Daley, and Ojeda 1993; Reimers 1985; Abowd and Killingsworth 1985; Enchautegi 1995). However, Tienda and Guhleman (1985) find that the average differences in human capital account for only 27 percent of the gap between Mexican and white women's occupational status and 57 percent of the gap between Puerto Rican and white women's occupational status.

A key puzzle in past research on Latinas has been the low labor force participation rates and high unemployment rates of Puerto Rican women (Tienda, Donato, and Cordero-Guzmán 1992; Cintrón 1994; Tienda and Jensen 1988). In 1960, Puerto Rican women living in the mainland United States had much higher labor force participation rates than did Mexican, African American, and non-Hispanic white women. Between 1960 and 1970, however, the labor force participation rates of Puerto Rican women dropped 9 percentage points, reversing the situation. At the same time, the participation rates of Mexican, African American, and non-Hispanic white women increased, with the result that in 1970 Puerto Rican women had lower participation rates than did Mexican, African American, or white women (Bean and Tienda 1987; Cintrón 1994). This pattern of lower participation rates for Puerto Rican women continued throughout the 1970s and early 1980s (Bean and Tienda 1987; Tienda, Donato, and Cordero-Guzmán 1992).

According to Cintrón (1994, 4–20), the explanations for Puerto Rican women's disadvantaged labor market status fall into three categories: demand-side, supply-side, and institutional. Demand-side explanations include the shift away from manufacturing to service jobs, the increasing demand for high-skilled workers (skills mismatch), and spatial mismatch— that is, a movement of jobs away from the Northeast (where many Puerto Ricans live). Supply-side arguments focus on competition from other groups of migrants, changes in skills over time (for example, schooling and English proficiency), a decline in the quality of migrants, and increases in female-headed families. Institutional explanations focus on the decline in unionization, the declining enforcement of equal opportunity policies (hence increased discrimination), and changes in the welfare system.

Cintrón further argues that these explanations are "biased towards the male experience" (1994, 3). She claims that theoretical models need to recognize that women face different choices than do men, that immigrant status may affect women differently than it does men, and that Latinos and Latinas do not always work in the same occupations and industries. For example, Latinas may be discriminated against on the basis of sex as well as ethnicity, and marital status and children shape work choices and opportunities differently for Latinas than for Latinos.

Most of the research reviewed above is based on 1970 or 1980 census data or on Current Population Survey data. A major exception is Rivera-Batiz and Santiago (1994), who use 1990 census data to analyze the economic and demographic changes for mainland Puerto Ricans from 1980 to 1990. Their results present a picture of increased prosperity for Puerto Ricans. In the 1980s, labor force participation rates and annual earnings increased substantially for mainland Puerto Rican women, and the gaps in labor force participation between Puerto Rican women and Mexican women and between Puerto Rican and non-Hispanic white women narrowed.

WAGES AND EMPLOYMENT AMONG PUERTO RICAN AND MEXICAN WOMEN

Our analyses expand on past research, especially that of Rivera-Batiz and Santiago (1994). We outline trends in young Puerto Rican and Mexican women's wages from 1979 to 1989 and in their employment and unemployment from 1969 to 1989, and we compare these trends with those for white women. We estimate trends separately by schooling, language proficiency, nativity, immigration status, residential location, and marital status.

Our analyses differ from those of previous researchers in four ways. First, following the example of Bound and Freeman (1992) and of John Bound and Laura Dresser in chapter 2, we restrict our analysis to young women because their employment and wages best reflect the effects of changing economic conditions and constraints on labor market entrants. Second, instead of focusing on women's labor force participation, we analyze both employment and unemployment. The labor force participation rate is the sum of the employment and unemployment rates, and labor force participation would increase through either a rise in employment or a drop in unemployment. Third, we look at employment in the year before the survey rather than in the week before, since many Latinas may work only a part of a given year.[2]

Fourth, we explore the increasing economic polarization among Puerto Rican women and among Mexican women by estimating trends in economic outcomes separately by schooling, nativity, residential location, immigration status, and marital status. Chapters 1 and 2 of this volume, Bound and Freeman (1992), and Danziger and Gottschalk (1995) all report that trends in white and African American men's and women's employment rates and wages vary by schooling and by region and that, as a result, inequality within each of these four race-sex groups is increasing. Morales and Bonilla (1993) also find that income inequality is increasing within Latino and Latina populations between immigrants and nonimmigrants and between those with different levels of schooling.[3]

DATA, SAMPLE, AND MEASURES

We use the 1970 1/100 (5 percent) census file, the 1980 5/100 census file, and the 1990 5/100 census file for our analyses. Our samples for each year include Puerto Rican, Mexican, and non-Hispanic white women aged eighteen to thirty-seven years who were not in school or in the military and either whose potential work experience (age minus education minus six) did not exceed ten years or, if years of education were less than twelve, who were between eighteen and twenty-eight years of age.

We define a woman as employed if she reported nonzero work hours in the year prior to the survey and as unemployed if at the time of the survey she was not working and either was temporarily laid off or had looked for work in the four weeks prior to the survey. Hourly wage is wage earnings plus farm earnings plus self-employment income in the year prior to the survey, divided by the product of weeks worked times usual hours worked per week.[4]

A key theme in the economics and sociology literature is that returns to skills increased in the 1980s (Bound and Johnson 1992; Morales and Bonilla 1993, Katz and Murphy 1990). We construct four measures of skills typically used in analyses of Latina employment rates and wages: how many years of schooling the woman had; what the woman's English language proficiency level was; for Puerto Ricans, whether a woman was island-born or born in the mainland United States; and, for Mexicans, whether a woman was born in the United States, was a recent immigrant (in the United States for ten years or less), or was a long-term immigrant (in the United States more than ten years). The nativity and immigration measures were constructed on the assumption that Latinas born and raised in mainland United States are better socialized and trained to compete in the U.S. labor markets and that it takes immigrants about ten years to become fully assimilated into the U.S. labor market (Bean and Tienda 1987; Chiswick 1978, 1979, 1986; Borjas and Tienda 1985; LaLonde and Topel 1991). Bean and Tienda note that the language proficiency, nativity, and recentness of immigration measures may pick up the effects of employer discrimination as well as the effects of skills. Kenney and Wissoker's (1994) analysis of the Urban Institute's employer audit study provides some evidence for this hypothesis: they find that employers discriminate on the basis of Hispanic names.

Chapters 1 and 2 report that trends in women's employment rates vary by region. Latinos and Latinas tend to be concentrated in a few geographic areas. The vast majority of Mexicans live in Texas or California; the majority of Puerto Ricans live in New York and New Jersey. For the purposes of this study, we divide Mexicans into those that live in three geographic areas—Texas, California, and elsewhere—and characterize Puerto Ricans as living in New York and New Jersey versus all other areas.

A key concern in the literature on Puerto Rican women is the increasing numbers of female-headed families and the very low employment rate of female heads of families (Cintrón 1994; Enchautegi 1995). Cintrón finds that the rate of employment among married Puerto Rican women but not among Puerto Rican single female heads of household increased in the 1970s. We estimate trends in rates of employment for three groups of women: those who were married at time of the survey; those who were not married at the time of the survey (never married, separated, divorced, or widowed), and those who were not married and who had at least one child.

FINDINGS

Puerto Rican women began the period of our analysis substantially behind both Mexican and white women in terms of employment. By 1989, Puerto Rican women had caught up to Mexican women in the labor queue, and their wages far exceeded those of Mexican women. In general, the trends in wages and employment rates demonstrate substantial improvement in the 1980s for Puerto Rican women but stagnation and decline for Mexican women. However, both Puerto Rican and Mexican young women still lagged substantially behind their white counterparts. We also find substantial within-group variation, further complicating any traditional labor market explanations for these populations.

Puerto Rican and Mexican young women's economic trends displayed two similarities. The employment rate among married women rose sharply in the 1970s and 1980s, altering the traditional relationship between marital status and employment in both groups. Wages declined for women with low levels of schooling, and wage inequalities by schooling increased in the

1980s. These same trends occurred among young white and African American women (see chapters 1 and 2).

We next present our analyses of trends in Puerto Rican women's economic attainments, followed by a discussion of the analyses for Mexican women. We conclude by summarizing and discussing our major findings.

Puerto Rican Women

Demographic Trends   Between 1969 and 1989 the demographic profile of young Puerto Rican women living in the United States changed dramatically: U.S. nativity, skills, and geographic dispersion within the United States increased, and marriage decreased (table 3.1). In 1970, only 21 percent of young Puerto Rican women were born in the United States; by 1990, the proportion was 63 percent. During the 1970s and until the early 1980s, Puerto Ricans were concentrated in regions with declining economies. In 1970, three out of four Puerto Rican women living in the United States lived in either the New York or the New Jersey area; by 1990 this ratio had dropped to one out of two. In 1970, 63 percent of young Puerto Rican women did not have a high school diploma, and 31 percent had not even started high school. By 1990, these percentages had dropped to 29 percent and 13 percent, respectively. Between 1970 and 1990, the percentage of young Puerto Rican women who were married declined substantially—from 60 percent in 1970 to 39 percent in 1990. The percentage of Puerto Rican women who were single mothers increased from 19 percent in 1970 to 33 percent in 1990.

Although Puerto Rican women became more geographically dispersed and their educational attainment and English proficiency increased greatly, Puerto Rican women still differed a great deal from white women. In 1970, there was a vast gap in schooling between Puerto Rican and white women. This gap narrowed considerably in the 1970s and 1980s but was still sizable in 1990. In 1990, Puerto Rican women were almost three times more likely to be high school dropouts than were white women and were less than half as likely to be college graduates. They were three times as likely to be single mothers, and they were still more geographically concentrated than white women were.

Trends in Real Wages   The mean wages of Puerto Rican women increased from $8.81 per hour in 1979 to $9.29 per hour in 1989 (table 3.2). Although these wages had become roughly equal to those of white women, this apparent parity disappears in a comparison of Puerto Rican and white women's wages within geographic areas (figure 3.1). Two patterns stand out. First, wages were higher for women residing in the New York–New Jersey area than for women residing elsewhere in the United States. Sec-

Table 3.1 / Demographic Characteristics of Mexican, Puerto Rican, and White Women, 1970, 1980, 1990 (Percent)

Characteristic	1970			1980			1990		
	Puerto Rican	Mexican	White	Puerto Rican	Mexican	White	Puerto Rican	Mexican	White
Marital status									
Married	60.2	62.6	70.3	45.4	60.5	59.8	39.0	52.8	54.1
Unmarried (separated, divorced, widowed)	39.8	37.4	29.7	54.6	39.5	40.2	61.0	47.2	45.9
Unmarried with children	18.5	9.6	5.7	29.5	14.0	7.7	32.8	19.4	10.5
Schooling									
0–8 years	31.4	30.3	5.3	22.1	28.8	3.7	12.6	27.9	3.6
9–11 years	31.9	25.2	15.1	20.5	15.3	8.2	16.0	13.0	6.1
12 years	29.4	34.7	49.6	35.4	37.0	44.1	35.3	34.3	34.0
13–15 years	5.1	7.5	16.2	15.7	14.0	22.3	24.3	18.6	28.4
Bachelor's degree or higher	2.2	2.3	13.8	6.3	4.9	21.6	11.8	6.2	27.9

Residence									
New York and New Jersey	75.4	—	11.6	60.5	—	9.7	49.1	—	10.1
All other states	25.5	—	88.4	39.5	—	90.3	50.9	—	89.9
Texas	—	37.7	4.8	—	30.4	5.5	—	28.1	5.6
California	—	43.2	9.7	—	43.9	8.8	—	46.6	9.0
All other states	—	22.1	85.5	—	25.8	85.7	—	25.3	85.4
Nativity									
Mainland-born	20.5	—	—	51.4	—	—	62.9	—	—
Island-born	79.5	—	—	48.6	—	—	37.1	—	—
U.S.-born	—	77.5	—	—	67.5	—	—	55.3	—
Recent Immigrant <11yrs	—	14.8	—	—	23.9	—	—	30.9	—
Past Immigrant >10 yrs	—	7.7	—	—	8.5	—	—	13.8	—
English proficiency									
Proficient speaker	—	—	—	84.5	78.4	—	90.1	74.3	—
Non-English speaker	—	—	—	15.5	21.6	—	9.9	25.7	—
Total	1,441	3,645	125,100	9,349	41,262	771,315	9,552	52,514	636,955

Sources: U.S. Bureau of the Census, 1980 and 1990 Census.
Note: Data are for women aged eighteen to thirty-five years whose potential experience is less than or equal to ten years.

Table 3.2 / Mean Hourly Wages of Puerto Rican and White Women, 1980, 1990 (1989 Dollars)

Group	1980 Puerto Rican	White	Ratio	1990 Puerto Rican	White	Ratio
All	8.81	8.76	1.006	9.29	9.39	0.989
Marital status						
Married	8.90	9.06	0.982	10.25	9.81	1.045
Unmarried (separated,						
divorced, widowed)	8.71	8.38	1.039	8.52	8.93	0.954
Unmarried with children	8.01	8.13	0.985	7.69	7.40	1.039
Schooling						
0 to 8 years	6.57	6.50	1.011	5.73	5.80	0.988
9 to 11 years	8.10	6.63	1.222	6.24	5.92	1.054
12 years	8.25	7.41	1.113	8.19	6.94	1.180
13 to 15 years	8.74	8.61	1.015	9.51	8.79	1.082
Bachelor's degree or higher	13.16	11.98	1.098	13.50	13.16	1.026
Residence						
New York and New Jersey	9.22	9.78	0.943	10.05	11.78	0.853
All other states	8.31	8.65	0.961	8.68	9.13	0.951
Nativity						
U.S.-born	8.69	—	—	9.48	—	—
Island-born	8.99	—	—	8.86	—	—
English proficiency						
Proficient speaker	8.97	—	—	9.37	—	—
Non–English speaker	6.62	—	—	7.37	—	—

Sources: U.S. Bureau of the Census, 1980 and 1990 Census.
Notes: Data are for the year before the survey. Data are for women aged eighteen to thirty-five years whose potential experience is less than or equal to ten years.

ond, young Puerto Rican women earned less than young white women in the New York–New Jersey area did, and this gap grew between 1979 to 1989. Outside that area young Puerto Rican women earned only slightly less than white women in both 1979 and 1989.

The Puerto Rican–white wage differential across locations in New York and New Jersey may be due to differences in skills. With controls for schooling and location, Puerto Rican women and white women earned roughly equal wages (table 3.3).

As for trends in wage growth by education level, the mean wages of women with less than twelve years of schooling declined sharply between 1979 and 1989, while mean wages increased for women with some college

Figure 3.1 / Mean Hourly Wages of Puerto Rican and White Women, by Residence, 1979 to 1989

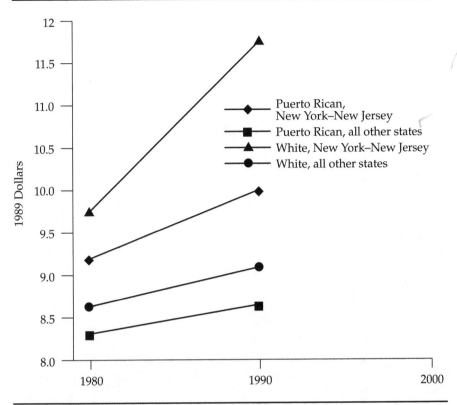

Source: U.S. Bureau of the Census, 1980 and 1990 Census.
Note: Data are for women aged eighteen to thirty-five years for whom potential work experience is less than or equal to ten years.

or with a college degree (figure 3.2). Returns to schooling clearly increased for young Puerto Rican women workers in the 1980s.

The pattern of increasing gaps between the wages of groups of Puerto Rican women workers holds with respect to U.S. nativity. The returns to U.S. birth increased dramatically during the 1980s. While in 1979 U.S.-born Puerto Rican women earned $8.69 per hour to the island-born Puerto Rican women's $8.99, by 1989 their earnings were $9.48 per hour and $8.86 per hour, respectively (table 3.2).

Wage disparities between married and single Puerto Rican women and between married Puerto Rican women and single Puerto Rican mothers also increased in the 1980s. In 1979, the average wages of employed married and employed single Puerto Rican women were roughly equal, and

Table 3.3 / Mean Hourly Wages of Puerto Rican and White Women, by Level of Schooling, 1980, 1990 (1989 Dollars)

	1980						1990					
	New York and New Jersey			Other U.S. Locations			New York and New Jersey			Other U.S. Locations		
Schooling	Puerto Rican	White	Ratio	Puerto Rican	White	Ratio	Puerto Rican	White	Ratio	Puerto Rican	White	Ratio
0 to 8 years	6.59	6.48	1.017	6.55	6.50	0.936	6.32	6.46	0.978	5.27	5.76	0.91
9 to 11 years	8.76	6.53	1.342	7.23	6.64	1.033	6.65	6.91	0.962	5.96	5.87	1.02
12 years	8.80	7.57	1.162	7.59	7.37	1.084	8.89	8.25	1.078	7.60	6.82	1.11
13 to 15 years	9.20	9.07	1.014	8.15	8.56	1.164	10.36	9.92	1.044	8.81	8.68	1.01
Bachelor's degree or higher	13..39	13.11	1.021	12.95	11.81	1.85	14.89	15.78	0.944	12.58	12.77	0.99

Sources: U.S. Bureau of the Census, 1980 and 1990 Census.
Notes: Data are for the year before the survey. Data are for women aged eighteen to thirty-five years whose potential experience is less than or equal to ten years.

Figure 3.2 / Mean Hourly Wages of Puerto Rican Women, 1979, 1989, by Years of Schooling

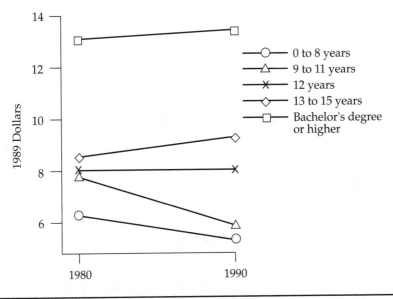

Source: U.S. Bureau of the Census, 1980 and 1990 Census.
Note: Data are for women aged eighteen to thirty-five years for whom potential work experience is less than or equal to ten years.

married women earned 11 percent ($0.70) more per hour than did single mothers. Between 1979 and 1989, married women's average hourly wage increased substantially, while single women's and single mother's average hourly wages declined. By 1989, employed married women earned 20 percent ($1.73) more per hour than employed single women and 33 percent ($2.56) more per hour than employed single mothers.

Employment Trends As mentioned in our review of research on Latinas, a major puzzle is the sharp drop in the labor force participation of Puerto Rican women between 1960 and 1970 (Bean and Tienda 1987; Cintrón 1994). This trend, which is inconsistent with trends exhibited by other groups of women who increasingly entered the labor force in the 1960s was reversed in the 1970s and 1980s (table 3.4). The employment rate among young Puerto Rican women grew sharply over those two decades, from 42.2 percent in 1969, to 48.5 percent in 1979, to 62.3 percent in 1989 (figure 3.3). In fact, employment among Puerto Rican women increased at a faster

Table 3.4 / Annual Employment Rate of Puerto Rican and White Women, 1970, 1980, 1990 (Percent)

Characteristic	1970			1980			1990		
	Puerto Rican	White	Ratio	Puerto Rican	White	Ratio	Puerto Rican	White	Ratio
All	42.2	66.1	0.638	48.5	78.1	0.621	62.3	84.4	0.738
Marital status									
Married	39.2	58.1	0.675	51.4	70.8	0.726	68.9	80.5	0.856
Unmarried (separated, divorced, widowed)	46.8	85.2	0.549	46.0	88.8	0.518	58.0	89.0	0.652
Unmarried with children	24.4	74.6	0.327	26.6	74.5	0.357	40.2	74.2	0.542
Schooling									
0 to 8 years	27.4	43.7	0.627	24.2	50.6	0.478	27.6	52.6	0.525
9 to 11 years	35.5	52.8	0.672	32.2	59.8	0.538	40.6	63.6	0.638
12 years	58.0	67.0	0.866	57.9	77.3	0.749	62.5	81.0	0.772
13 to 15 years	68.5	71.5	0.958	70.7	83.0	0.852	81.3	89.0	0.913
Bachelor's degree or higher	75.0	76.6	0.979	82.0	86.8	0.945	88.9	92.6	0.960
Residence									
New York and New Jersey	38.8	65.9	0.589	44.3	78.0	0.568	59.3	84.9	0.698
All other states	52.2	66.2	0.789	54.8	78.1	0.702	65.2	84.4	0.773
Nativity									
U.S.-born	54.4	—	—	56.6	—	—	67.1	—	—
Island-born	39.0	—	—	39.8	—	—	54.0	—	—
English proficiency									
Proficient speaker	—	—	—	52.7	—	—	65.0	—	—
Non–English speaker	—	—	—	25.4	—	—	37.1	—	—

Sources: U.S. Bureau of the Census, 1980 and 1990 Census.
Notes: Data are for the year before the survey. Data are for women aged eighteen to thirty-five years whose potential experience is less than ten years.

Figure 3.3 / Annual Employment Rate of Puerto Rican and White Women, 1969, 1979, 1989

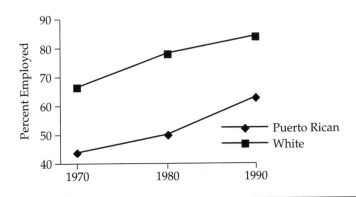

Source: U.S. Bureau of the Census, 1980 and 1990 Census.
Note: Data are for women aged eighteen to thirty-five years for whom potential work experience is less than or equal to ten years.

rate in the 1980s than did the employment of white women, narrowing the gap between Puerto Rican and white women's rates of employment.

Despite this, Puerto Rican women's employment rate still lagged behind that of white women. About 84 percent of young white women reported working in 1989, but only 62 percent of young Puerto Rican women did. Some of this differential may have been due to Puerto Rican women's greater difficulty in obtaining jobs and to their activity in the informal labor market. In both 1980 and 1990, the percentage of young Puerto Rican women who were unemployed averaged in the mid-teens, more than double the unemployment rates of young white women (table 3.5).

In the 1970s, the employment rate dropped for Puerto Rican women with less than twelve years of schooling but increased for Puerto Rican women with schooling beyond high school (figure 3.4). In contrast, the rate of employment for white women at every level of schooling increased in the 1970s and increased faster than that of Puerto Rican women at all levels of schooling above eight years. Thus in the 1970s the gap between the employment rates of white and Puerto Rican women widened at every level of schooling above eight years (see table 3.4).

The 1980s, however, were a period of improvement in employment for Puerto Rican women at every level of schooling, and the gaps between Puerto Rican and white women's rates of employment narrowed at every level of schooling. Despite this faster growth in employment, young Puerto Rican women were still less likely to be employed in 1989 than were young white women with comparable schooling. The differentials were small for

Table 3.5 / Annual Unemployment Rate of Puerto Rican and White Women, 1970, 1980, 1990 (Percent)

Characteristic	1970			1980			1990		
	Puerto Rican	White	Ratio	Puerto Rican	White	Ratio	Puerto Rican	White	Ratio
All	10.6	6.1	1.738	15.1	6.8	2.221	14.7	6.1	2.410
Marital status									
Married	9.5	6.5	1.462	14.0	6.4	2.188	11.3	5.2	2.173
Unmarried (separated, divorced, widowed)	11.6	5.6	2.071	16.1	7.2	2.236	17.1	6.9	2.478
Unmarried with children	16.4	7.7	2.130	25.0	12.0	2.083	26.4	13.5	1.956
Schooling									
0 to 8 years	15.5	11.4	1.360	25.1	19.0	1.321	37.9	21.2	1.788
9 to 11 years	13.5	12.2	1.107	24.9	17.7	1.407	27.0	19.7	1.371
12 years	7.5	6.1	1.230	13.9	8.2	1.695	16.7	8.3	2.012
13 to 15 years	6.8	4.4	1.545	10.3	4.8	2.146	9.8	4.5	2.178
Bachelor's degree or higher	5.0	2.8	1.786	6.0	2.9	2.069	4.5	2.4	1.875
Residence									
New York and New Jersey	11.3	4.8	2.354	16.0	7.2	2.222	14.5	5.5	2.636
All other states	8.9	6.3	1.413	14.0	6.8	2.059	14.9	6.1	2.443
Nativity									
U.S.-born Puerto Rican	7.9	—	—	16.8	—	—	17.4	—	—
Island-born Puerto Rican	11.6	—	—	14.0	—	—	13.5	—	—
English proficiency									
Proficient Speaker	—	—	—	14.2	—	—	14.0	—	—
Non-English speaker	—	—	—	24.9	—	—	26.8	—	—

Sources: U.S. Bureau of the Census, 1980 and 1990 Census.
Notes: Data are for the year before the survey. Data are for women aged eighteen to thirty-five years whose potential experience is less than or equal to ten years.

Figure 3.4 / Annual Employment Rate of Puerto Rican Women, by Years of Schooling, 1969, 1979, 1989

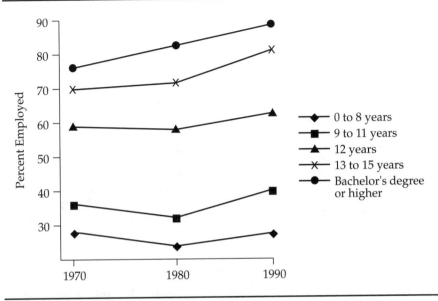

Source: U.S. Bureau of the Census, 1980 and 1990 Census.
Note: Data are for women aged eighteen to thirty-five years for whom potential work experience is less than or equal to ten years.

women with schooling beyond high school, large for high school graduates, and very large for women with less than twelve years of schooling.

In support of Cintrón's (1994) findings on Puerto Rican women's employment, we find that the employment rate of young, married Puerto Rican women increased substantially—by about 75 percent—in the 1970s and 1980s (figure 3.5). Single Puerto Rican women were more likely than married women to work in 1969. However, this relationship reversed in 1979 and 1989, as married women's employment rate increased at a faster rate than that of single women.

Bean and Tienda (1987), Cooney and Ortíz (1983), and Cintrón (1994) note the remarkably low rate of employment of Puerto Rican single mothers and the lack of growth in their rate of employment in the 1970s. Our results confirm their findings: only one in four young Puerto Rican single mothers reported working in 1969 and 1979. However, in the 1980s young Puerto Rican single mothers experienced sizable increases in their employment. Despite this increase, 60 percent of Puerto Rican single mothers did not work in 1989, their unemployment rate was 26.4 percent, and their employment still significantly lagged behind that of young white or Mexican single mothers.

Figure 3.5 / Annual Employment Rate of Puerto Rican Women, by Marital Status, 1969, 1979, 1989

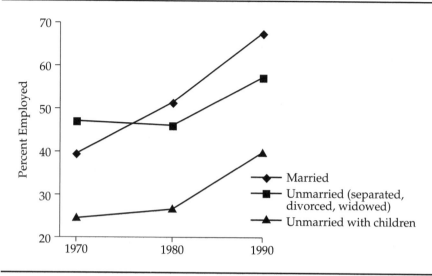

Source: U.S. Bureau of the Census, 1980 and 1990 Census.
Note: Data are for women aged eighteen to thirty-five years for whom potential work experience is less than or equal to ten years.

In 1969, young Puerto Rican women's employment rates differed according to their residential location: 38.8 percent of women residing in New York and New Jersey worked in 1969, compared with 52.2 percent of women residing elsewhere in the United States. Employment rates rose between 1969 and 1989 for Puerto Rican women living in both locations but increased more for women living in New York and New Jersey, so that by 1989 young Puerto Rican women living in New York or New Jersey were only slightly less likely to work than were those living elsewhere.

Unemployment Trends Although young Puerto Rican women's schooling and rate of employment improved considerably in the 1980s—both in absolute terms and relative to white women—this was not the case with unemployment. In both 1980 and 1990, young Puerto Rican women's unemployment rates averaged about 15 percent, and the ratio of their unemployment rate to that of white women grew from 2.2 in 1980 to 2.4 in 1990 (table 3.5; figure 3.6). A substantial minority of young Puerto Rican women were having trouble finding work.

The unemployment rates of young Puerto Rican women varied with their level of schooling. This relationship became stronger in the 1980s as unemployment rates increased for women with twelve or fewer years of

Figure 3.6 / Annual Unemployment Rate of Puerto Rican and White Women, 1969, 1979, 1989

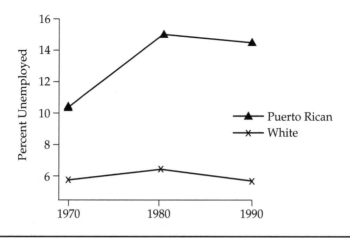

Source: U.S. Bureau of the Census, 1980 and 1990 Census.
Note: Data are for women aged eighteen to thirty-five years for whom potential work experience is less than or equal to ten years.

schooling and decreased for women with postsecondary schooling. In 1990, the unemployment rates of young Puerto Rican women with less than twelve years of schooling ranged from 27 percent to 38 percent; the rate for high school graduates was 17 percent. These unemployment rates were between 1.4 and 2.2 times as large as those of young white women with comparable schooling. At every level of schooling, Puerto Rican women were more likely to be unemployed than were white women.

The unemployment rates of young Puerto Rican women also varied according to their residential location, nativity, and marital status. In 1980, Puerto Rican women living in the New York–New Jersey area were more likely to be unemployed than were Puerto Rican women elsewhere, but in 1990 this pattern was reversed. In 1980, island-born Puerto Rican women were less likely to be unemployed than were U.S.-born Puerto Rican women, and this difference grew over time. In 1980 married women were less likely to be unemployed than were single women and single mothers; these gaps were also larger in 1990.

Mexican Women

Demographic Trends The most striking demographic characteristic of young Mexicans is their extremely low levels of schooling (table 3.1). In both 1970 and 1990, almost 30 percent of young Mexican women had completed less than nine years of schooling. In 1970 only 40 percent of the young Mexican women had completed high school. This percentage grew to 56 percent in 1980 and to 59 percent in 1980. Unlike among Puerto Rican women, there was little upgrading in years of schooling among young Mexican women between 1980 and 1990.

One reason for the continuing low levels of schooling among Mexicans is their high rate of immigration to the United States. In 1970, only 22.5 percent of young Mexican women were immigrants; in 1990 almost half were. In 1990, 58 percent of recent Mexican immigrants had less than nine years of schooling, compared with 11 percent of Mexican women who were born in the United States and 31 percent of long-term immigrants. The high rate of immigration is also likely to account for both the decrease in English proficiency in the 1980s and the continued geographic concentration of 75 percent of young Mexican women in the border states of Texas and California. This pattern of decreasing U.S. nativity, decreasing English proficiency, and continued geographic concentration contrasts sharply with the experiences of young Puerto Rican women, who were characterized by increasing U.S. nativity, increasing English proficiency, and increasing geographic dispersion over the same period.

Between 1970 and 1990, the proportion of Mexican women who were married and living with their husbands declined from 62.6 percent to 52.8 percent, and the proportion of Mexican women who were not married and were the parent of a child increased from 9.6 percent to 19.4 percent. These family structure changes are similar to those experienced by whites and Puerto Ricans.

Trends in Real Wages   The wages of young Mexican women were low in 1979 and dropped over the next decade (table 3.6). In 1979 the average young Mexican woman earned $7.77 per hour; by 1989 this wage had dropped to $7.32 per hour. Since white women's average wage increased in the 1980s, the gap between the wages of young white and young Mexican women widened (figure 3.7). In 1979 the average Mexican woman earned 89 percent as much per hour as did the average white woman. By 1989, this percentage had dropped to 78 percent.

Returns to schooling clearly increased for young Mexicans in the 1980s (figure 3.8). Average wages declined between 1979 and 1989 for women with little schooling and increased for women with college degrees. This same pattern held for white women, but the declines in wages for less educated women were steeper, and the increases in wages for more educated women were flatter for Mexican women than for white women.

Many researchers have argued that much of the differential in wages of white and Mexican women is due to differences in education. In 1979, either Mexican and white women's wages were close, or Mexican women held a wage advantage over white women with the same amount of

Table 3.6 / Mean Hourly Wages of Mexican and White Women, 1980, 1990
(1989 Dollars)

Characteristic	1980			1990		
	Mexican	White	Ratio	Mexican	White	Ratio
All	7.77	8.76	0.887	7.32	9.39	0.780
Marital status						
Married	7.78	9.06	0.859	7.61	9.81	0.776
Unmarried (separated, divorced, widowed)	7.77	8.38	0.927	7.05	8.93	0.789
Unmarried with children	8.19	8.13	1.007	6.75	7.40	0.912
Schooling						
0 to 8 years	6.82	6.50	1.049	5.96	5.80	1.028
9 to 11 years	7.27	6.63	1.097	6.12	5.92	1.034
12 years	7.50	7.41	1.012	6.64	6.94	0.957
13 to 15 years	8.38	8.61	0.973	8.15	8.79	0.927
Bachelor's degree or higher	11.56	11.98	0.965	11.96	13.16	0.909
Residence						
California	8.37	9.74	0.859	8.00	11.06	0.723
Texas	7.12	8.55	0.833	6.52	8.98	0.726
All other states	7.55	8.67	0.871	7.05	9.24	0.763
Nativity						
U.S.-born	7.89	—	—	7.73	—	—
Recent immigrant (< 11 years)	6.85	—	—	5.83	—	—
Past immigrant (> 10 years)	8.69	—	—	7.47	—	—
English proficiency						
Proficient speaker	7.95	—	—	7.65	—	—
Non–English speaker	6.74	—	—	5.61	—	—

Sources: U.S. Bureau of the Census, 1980 and 1990 Census.
Notes: Data are for the year before the survey. Data are for women aged eighteen to thirty-five years whose potential experience is less than or equal to ten years.

schooling (table 3.6). By 1990, the ratio of Mexican women's wages to white women's wages had dropped at every schooling level. Wages were about equal among women with less than twelve years of schooling, but at higher levels of schooling Mexican women earned less than white women. This pattern of decreasing wages relative to those of white women is similar to patterns reported for the relative wages of African American and white women (see chapter 2).

Figure 3.7 / Mean Hourly Wages of Mexican and White Women, 1979, 1989

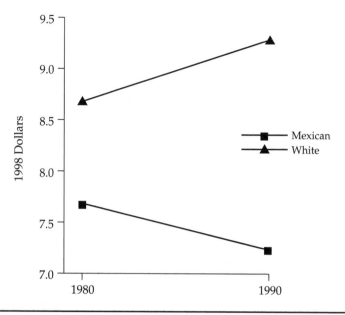

Source: U.S. Bureau of the Census, 1980 and 1990 Census.
Note: Data are for women aged eighteen to thirty-five years for whom potential work experience is less than or equal to ten years.

Another explanation for the decline in wages for Mexican women is the continuous immigration from Mexico. In 1980 Mexican women who were born in the United States earned a dollar more per hour than did Mexican women immigrants who had been in the United States for less than ten years (table 3.6). This wage advantage had grown to almost two dollars by 1990. Immigrants who had been in the United States for longer than ten years had wages at least as high as those of women of Mexican origin who were born in the United States. Furthermore, the wage advantage associated with English proficiency increased for young Mexican women during the 1980s. In 1980, Mexican women who spoke English well earned 18 percent more per hour than did Mexican women who spoke little or no English. By 1990, this advantage had climbed to 30 percent.

In the 1980s, wage disparities among young Mexican women changed sharply according to their marital status. In 1979, married and unmarried young Mexican women had roughly the same average hourly wage—$7.78—and the average hourly wage of single mothers—$8.19—exceeded that of married women. By 1989, married young Mexican women earned 8 percent more per hour than unmarried women did and 13 percent more per hour than single mothers did. Young, married women averaged an

Figure 3.8 / Mean Hourly Wages of Mexican and White Women, by Years of Schooling, 1979, 1989

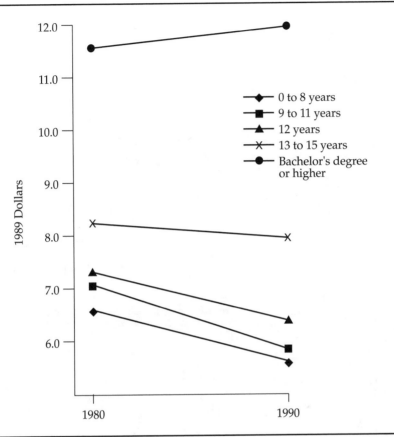

Source: U.S. Bureau of the Census, 1980 and 1990 Census.
Note: Data are for women aged eighteen to thirty-five years for whom potential work experience is less than or equal to ten years.

hourly wage of $7.61 in 1989, compared with $7.05 for unmarried women and $6.75 for single mothers.

Employment Trends The employment rate was flat during the 1980s for young Mexican women (table 3.7; figure 3.9). After an increase from 57.6 percent in 1969 to 63.7 percent in 1979, employment remained at about 64 percent in 1989. Since white women's employment rate grew steadily in the 1980s, the gap between young white women's and young Mexican women's rates of employment widened. About 84 percent of young white women but only about 64 percent of young Mexican women worked in 1989.

Table 3.7 / Annual Employment Rate, Mexican and White Women, 1970, 1980, 1990 (Percent), Age Eighteen to Thirty-Five with Zero to Ten Years Work Experience

Characteristic	1970 Mexican	1970 White	1970 Ratio	1980 Mexican	1980 White	1980 Ratio	1990 Mexican	1990 White	1990 Ratio
All	57.6	66.1	0.871	63.7	78.1	0.816	64.1	84.4	0.759
Marital status									
Married	48.6	58.1	0.836	58.0	70.8	0.819	59.3	80.5	0.737
Unmarried (separated, divorced, widowed)	72.6	85.2	0.852	72.4	88.8	0.815	69.5	89.0	0.781
Unmarried with children	64.3	74.6	0.862	60.4	74.5	0.811	57.7	74.2	0.778
Schooling									
0 to 8 years	44.7	43.7	1.023	48.3	50.6	0.955	45.8	52.6	0.871
9 to 11 years	49.4	52.8	0.936	53.9	59.8	0.901	51.8	63.6	0.814
12 years	69.8	67.0	1.042	71.4	77.3	0.924	69.2	81.0	0.854
13 to 15 years	74.1	71.5	1.036	81.4	83.0	0.981	83.1	89.0	0.934
Bachelor's degree or higher	77.3	76.6	1.009	85.5	86.8	0.985	86.8	92.6	0.937
Residence									
California	59.6	67.8	0.879	62.8	79.7	0.788	62.6	82.9	0.755
Texas	55.1	66.1	0.834	63.3	79.1	0.800	63.8	83.6	0.763
All other states	57.6	66.0	0.873	65.7	77.8	0.844	67.3	84.6	0.796
Nativity									
U.S.-born	59.9	—	—	68.2	—	—	72.7	—	—
Recent immigrant (< 11 years)	43.0	—	—	50.2	—	—	47.3	—	—
Past immigrant (> 10 years)	61.9	—	—	65.6	—	—	69.0	—	—
English proficiency									
Proficient speaker	—	—	—	68.0	—	—	70.3	—	—
Non-English speaker	—	—	—	48.0	—	—	46.3	—	—

Sources: U.S. Bureau of the Census, 1980 and 1990 Census.
Notes: Data are for the year before the survey. Data are for women aged eighteen to thirty-five years whose potential experience is less than or equal to ten years.

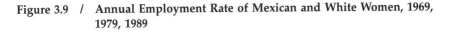

Figure 3.9 / Annual Employment Rate of Mexican and White Women, 1969,
1979, 1989

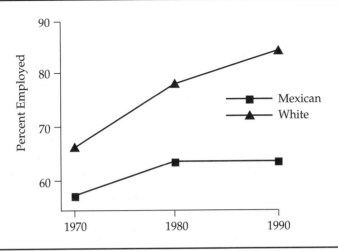

Mexican
White

Source: U.S. Bureau of the Census, 1980 and 1990 Census.
Note: Data are for women aged eighteen to thirty-five years for whom potential work experience is less than or equal to ten years.

Education is a good predictor of young Mexican women's employment: less than half of women with fewer than twelve years of schooling worked in 1969, while more than three out of four women college graduates did so. This relationship between schooling and employment became stronger over time. In the 1970s, the rate of employment grew slowly for young Mexican women at low levels of schooling and grew more rapidly for women with postsecondary schooling (figure 3.10). In the 1980s the employment rate declined among young Mexican women with less than a high school education and increased slightly among those with postsecondary schooling. As a result, gaps in employment by schooling widened slightly. In 1969, young Mexican women and white women with comparable years of schooling were equally likely to work. But in both the 1970s and the 1980s, the employment rate increased for white women at every level of schooling, and by 1989 white women's rate of employment had outstripped that of Mexican women at every level of schooling.

Some of this variation in employment was associated with nativity and immigration. Only half of all young Mexican women who had immigrated to the United States within the past ten years worked in 1979, while 66 percent of U.S.-born young Mexican women and 68 percent of young Mexican women who had immigrated to the United States more than ten years before worked in 1979. During the 1980s, employment dropped slightly among the more recent immigrants and increased slightly among U.S.-born Mexican women and the longer-term immigrants. The same pattern holds

Figure 3.10 / Annual Employment Rate of Mexican Women, by Years of Schooling, 1969, 1979, 1989

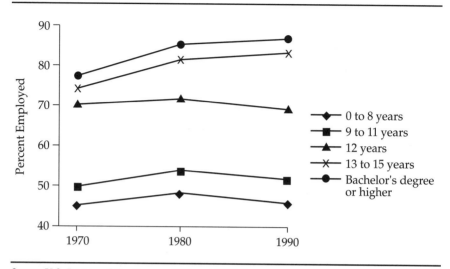

Source: U.S. Bureau of the Census, 1980 and 1990 Census.
Note: Data are for women aged eighteen to thirty-five years for whom potential work experience is less than or equal to ten years.

true for Mexican women who spoke little or no English as against Mexican women who spoke English well. As a result, gaps in employment rate by nativity status and by English language proficiency widened in the 1980s.

In terms of marital status, in 1969 young married Mexican women were less likely to work than were young unmarried women and young single mothers (figure 3.11). The gap between the employment rates of married and unmarried women dropped from 24 percentage points in 1969 to 10 percentage points in 1989. This change was due mostly to the large increase in the employment rate of young married Mexican women between 1969 and 1979.

Unemployment Trends The unemployment rate for young Mexican women grew from 11 percent in 1980 to 13 percent in 1990 (table 3.8). Unemployment rates grew for every segment of the population of young Mexican women analyzed: women at every level of schooling; women born in the United States and immigrants; women proficient and not proficient in English; women living in California, Texas, and elsewhere; and married women, single women, and single mothers. Unemployment increased the most among those with twelve or fewer years of schooling, recent immigrants, those not proficient in English, residents of Texas, and single mothers.

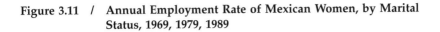

Figure 3.11 / Annual Employment Rate of Mexican Women, by Marital Status, 1969, 1979, 1989

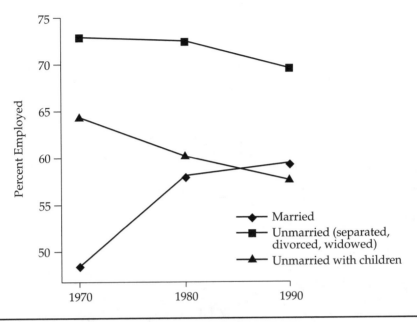

Source: U.S. Bureau of the Census, 1980 and 1990 Census.
Note: Data are for women aged eighteen to thirty-five years for whom potential work experience is less than or equal to ten years.

The unemployment rates for young Mexican women in 1980 and 1990 were about twice those for young white women (figure 3.12). Schooling differences were a major cause of this gap. In 1980 and 1990, about two of five young Mexican women had not completed high school, and their unemployment rates ranged from 16 percent to 22 percent. Mexican and white women with low levels of education had similar levels of unemployment.

Even though unemployment rates increased for young Mexican women, they had lower unemployment rates than did young Puerto Rican women in 1980 and 1990. This finding is surprising given that Puerto Rican women had completed more schooling than Mexican women had. Among women with less than twelve years of schooling, the 1990 unemployment rates of the two groups of Latinas evidence a large gap: Puerto Rican women's unemployment rates ranged from 27 percent to 38 percent, and Mexican women's unemployment rates were about 22 percent.

Table 3.8 / Annual Unemployment Rate of Mexican and White Women, 1970, 1980, 1990 (Percent)

Characteristic	1970			1980			1990		
	Mexican	White	Ratio	Mexican	White	Ratio	Mexican	White	Ratio
All	9.8	6.1	1.607	11.1	6.8	1.632	13.3	6.1	2.180
Marital status									
Married	8.3	6.5	1.277	11.2	6.4	1.750	13.0	5.2	2.500
Unmarried (separated, divorced, widowed)	11.0	5.6	1.964	11.1	7.2	1.542	13.5	6.9	1.957
Unmarried with children	14.6	7.7	1.896	15.0	12.0	1.250	19.3	13.8	1.399
Schooling									
0 to 8 years	10.1	11.4	0.886	15.8	19.0	0.832	21.9	21.2	1.033
9 to 11 years	11.6	12.2	0.951	17.8	17.7	1.006	21.9	19.7	1.112
12 years	10.6	6.1	1.738	9.9	8.2	1.207	12.2	8.3	1.470
13 to 15 years	6.0	4.4	1.364	6.5	4.8	1.354	6.9	4.5	1.533
Bachelor's degree or higher	3.3	2.8	1.179	3.3	2.9	1.138	4.3	2.4	1.792
Residence									
California	10.8	8.5	1.271	12.2	6.8	1.794	13.4	5.7	2.351
Texas	8.1	5.5	1.473	8.2	4.2	1.952	13.1	6.1	2.148
All other states	10.5	5.8	1.810	12.8	7.0	1.829	13.3	6.1	2.180
Nativity									
U.S.-born	10.0	—	—	10.0	—	—	11.3	—	—
Recent immigrant (< 11 years)	8.3	—	—	14.7	—	—	18.4	—	—
Past immigrant (> 10 years)	9.9	—	—	12.1	—	—	12.7	—	—
English proficiency									
Proficient speaker	—	—	—	10.3	—	—	11.7	—	—
Non-English speaker	—	—	—	15.4	—	—	19.7	—	—

Sources: U.S. Bureau of the Census, 1980 and 1990 Census.
Notes: Data are for the year before the survey. Data are for women aged eighteen to thirty-five years whose potential experience is less than or equal to ten years.

Figure 3.12 / Annual Unemployment Rate of Mexican Women, 1969, 1979, 1989

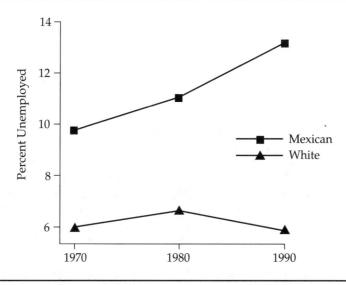

Source: U.S. Bureau of the Census, 1980 and 1990 Census.
Note: Data are for women aged eighteen to thirty-five years for whom potential work experience is less than or equal to ten years.

CONCLUSIONS

The results of our study strongly reinforce the conventional wisdom that Latina subpopulations need to be studied separately. Puerto Ricans and Mexicans reside in different parts of the United States, and the trends in their demographic characteristics and economic outcomes differ quite a lot. In the 1980s, young Puerto Rican women experienced progress on many fronts: their level of schooling, their wages, and their employment rate all improved. On the other hand, Mexican women's schooling grew very little, their employment rate remained stable, their wages declined, and their unemployment rate rose. Different forces are clearly shaping these divergent trends. Puerto Rican women and white women show similar trends in economic outcomes, while much of the negative trends in Mexican women's economic outcomes can be explained by continuous immigration, low levels of education, and high rates of residency in areas with depressed economies, such as Texas. More research is needed to elucidate the reasons for the trends in the wages and employment rates of Mexican and Puerto Rican women.

Trends in wages and employment rates relative to those of white women also differed for young Puerto Rican and Mexican women. In the 1980s the gap between young Puerto Rican and young white women's rate of employment narrowed. In contrast, the gaps between young Mexican women's and young white women's wages and rate of employment widened in that period. This finding is similar to the trends for African American women's wages and employment relative to those of white women (see chapter 2).

Perhaps our most significant finding was the diversity within the subpopulations of young Puerto Rican women and young Mexican women. Trends in economic outcomes varied considerably within each group by schooling, nativity, marital status, and residence. It is unlikely that any one explanation can account for this diversity in economic trends, which has increased within-group economic polarization for both young Puerto Rican and young Mexican women (see also Rivera-Batiz and Santiago 1994; Morales and Bonilla 1993). Economic differentials are widening between those with a great deal of schooling and those with a little, between women born inside and outside the United States, and between married women and single mothers. Similar diversity and similar increases in within-group inequality have also been reported among young white and African American women in the 1980s (see chapters 1 and 2).

Our results are consistent with the argument that Latinos' and Latinas' low level of education put them increasingly at risk as industrial restructuring shrank the wage and employment opportunities of low-skilled workers in the 1980s (Morales and Bonilla 1993). Between 1980 and 1990, real wages dropped sharply and unemployment rates increased for young Puerto Rican women with fewer than twelve years of schooling. Real wages dropped, employment dropped, and unemployment increased for young Mexican women with twelve or fewer years of schooling. These declines are similar to those experienced by young African American women high school dropouts in the 1980s (see chapter 1). Understanding how industrial restructuring has shaped young Mexicans' employment opportunities is the key to understanding their economic fortunes, since three-quarters of the young Mexican women we studied had had twelve or fewer years of schooling.

We began this chapter with the observation that, according to the conventional academic wisdom, Puerto Ricans are the most economically disadvantaged Latino and Latina subpopulation. Tienda and Jensen (1988, 53) argue that one cause of this disadvantage is the fact that "the labor market position of Puerto Rican women has not kept pace with that of other minority women." They argue that the key labor market problem in earlier decades was seen by many to be the low labor force participation rates of Puerto Rican men and women. Our results, like those of Rivera-Batiz and Santiago (1994), suggest that this pattern of Puerto Rican employment disadvantage relative to other minorities has begun to change. Young Puerto Rican women's employment rate increased by almost 50 percent between 1969 and 1989 and caught up to that of young Mexican women in 1989.

The gap between young Puerto Rican women's employment rate and that of young African American women narrowed by two-thirds between 1969 to 1989. About 42 percent of Puerto Rican women and 73 percent of African American women worked in 1969; in 1989, 62 percent of Puerto Rican women and 73 percent of African American women worked (see chapter 1).

Despite the overall improvement in young Puerto Rican women's employment levels, some groups of young Puerto Rican women suffered persistent disadvantages. Those with low levels of schooling and those who were single mothers worked at very low rates and had very high unemployment rates. Their employment outcomes were worse than those of young Mexican women with comparable schooling and of young Mexican or young African American single mothers.

The continuing high unemployment rates of Puerto Rican women in the 1980s present a puzzle. During that period, schooling increased sharply among Puerto Rican women. Employment also increased substantially, due partly to increases in Puerto Rican women's schooling and partly to increased employment among Puerto Rican women at every level of schooling. Both of these trends should have reduced unemployment rates.

Although trends in young Puerto Rican women's employment are positive, these women are far from achieving parity with white women. Only 62 percent of young Puerto Rican women worked in 1989; 84 percent of young white women did. The unemployment rate for Puerto Rican women was 14.7 percent in 1990, 2.4 times that of white women. Puerto Rican women were less likely to work and more likely to be unemployed than were white women with comparable schooling.

IMPLICATIONS FOR PUBLIC POLICY AND RESEARCH

As Latino and Latina populations begin to make up a greater share of the labor supply, understanding their economic outcomes becomes increasingly important. Public policies must address the relative labor market disadvantages Latinas face. To be successful, policies must target specific subpopulations by skill level, marital status, English proficiency, and nativity status. Interestingly, the geographic concentrations of Latinos and Latinas makes geographically targeted policies a good option. Alternatively, though, one state's hostile policies toward Latinos and Latinas could affect a large segment of the national Latino and Latina population.

We have told only part of the story here. Data and time limitations prevented us from analyzing other Latina populations More work is required to understand the changing roles of Latinas in the labor force. Our limited descriptive analysis shows that traditional labor market theories do not provide adequate explanations for Latinas' relationship to the formal labor market.

Our analysis provides some indicators for future research. First, the appropriate economic models will differ for Puerto Rican and Mexican women. The key issues for Puerto Rican women in the 1990s are low employment and high unemployment; for Mexican women the issues are the roles of low levels of schooling and high immigration rates in shaping wages and employment opportunities. Clearly, too, several models are needed to capture the diverse labor market experiences of different subgroups of Mexican or Puerto Rican women. College-educated women face different labor market problems than women with little schooling do. Disparities between immigrants' (or migrants') outcomes and those of native-born women are increasing over time. The relationships between marital status and the labor market are changing, as market outcomes are improving for married women and getting worse for single mothers. At the same time, marriage is declining and single motherhood is increasing among Puerto Rican and Mexican women.

Finally, our findings have important policy implications. Since Puerto Rican and Mexican young women tend to be geographically concentrated, their overall economic well-being is quite sensitive to changes in the regional economies and welfare benefit levels of a handful of states. Additionally, high unemployment rates among Latinas with low human capital suggest that finding jobs for similar welfare mothers will be difficult and could displace other Latinas searching for employment.

NOTES

1. A major exception is Rivera-Batiz and Santiago (1994).

2. This is the definition of employment used by Cintrón (1994), and Enchautegi (1995).

3. Enchautegi (1995) finds that earnings inequalities are widening for Puerto Rican men. Rivera-Batiz and Santiago (1994, viii) claim there are the "beginnings of a polarization within the Puerto Rican community in terms of economic opportunities and outcomes."

4. Wages are expressed in 1989 dollars. Since hours worked and weeks worked are bracketed in the 1970 census, we estimate only hourly wages for 1979 and 1989.

REFERENCES

Abowd, John M., and Mark R. Killingsworth. 1985. "Employment, Wages, and Earnings of Hispanics in the Federal and Non-federal Sectors: Methodological Issues and Their Empirical Consequences." In *Hispanics in the U.S. Economy*, edited by George J. Borjas and Marta Tienda. Orlando, Fla.: Academic Press.

Bean, Frank D., and Marta Tienda. 1987. *The Hispanic Population of the United States*. New York: Russell Sage Foundation.

Borjas, George J., and Marta Tienda, eds. 1985. *Hispanics in the U.S. Economy.* Orlando, Fla.: Academic Press.

Bound, John, and Richard Freeman. 1992. "What Went Wrong? The Erosion of Relative Earnings and Employment among Young Black Men in the 1980s." *Quarterly Journal of Economics* 107(1): 201–32.

Bound, John, and George Johnson. 1992. "Changes in the Structure of Wages in the 1980s: An Evaluation of Alternative Explanations." *American Economic Review* 82(3): 371–92.

Carnoy, Martin., Hugh M. Daley, and Raul H. Ojeda,, 1993. "The Changing Position of Latinos in the U.S. Labor Market since 1939." In *Latinos in a Changing U.S. Economy,* edited by Rebecca Morales and Frank Bonilla. Newbury Park, Calif.: Sage Publications.

Chiswick, Barry R. 1978. "The Effect of Americanization on the Earnings of Foreign-Born Men." *Journal of Political Economy* 86(5): 897–921.

———. 1979. "The Economic Progress of Immigrants: Some Apparently Universal Patterns." In *Contemporary Economic Problems,* edited by William Fellner. Washington, D.C.: American Enterprise Institute for Public Policy Research.

———. 1986. "Is the New Immigration Less Skilled Than the Old?" *Journal of Labor Economics* 4(2): 168–92.

Cintrón, Aixa. 1994. "Puerto Rican Women's Labor Force Participation." Master's thesis, University of Michigan, Ann Arbor.

Cooney, Rosemary S., and Vilma Ortíz. 1983. "Nativity, National Origin and Hispanic Female Participation in the Labor Force." *Social Science Quarterly* 64(3): 510–23.

Danziger, Sheldon, and Peter Gottschalk. 1995. *America Unequal.* New York: Russell Sage Foundation.

DeFreitas, Gregory. 1985. "Ethnic Differentials in Unemployment among Hispanic Americans." In *Hispanics in the U.S. Economy,* edited by George J. Borjas and Marta Tienda. Orlando, Fla.: Academic Press.

———. 1991. *Inequality at Work: Hispanics in the U.S. Labor Force.* New York: Oxford University Press.

Edmonston, Barry, and Jeffrey S. Passel. 1992. "Immunization and Immigrant Generations in Population Projections." *International Journal of Forecasting* 8(3): 459–76.

Enchautegi, M. 1995. "Education, Location and Labor Market Outcomes of Puerto Rican Men during the 1980's." *Eastern Economic Journal* 19(3): 295–308.

Harrison, Roderick J., and Claudette Bennett. 1995. "Racial and Ethnic Diversity." In *State of the Union: American in the 1990s,* edited by Reynolds Farley. Vol. 2, *Social Trends.* New York: Russell Sage Foundation.

Katz, Lawrence F., and Kevin M. Murphy. 1992. "Changes in Relative Wages, 1963–1987: Supply and Demand Factors." *Quarterly Journal of Economics* 107 (1): 35–78.

Kenney, Genevieve M., and Douglas A. Wissoker. 1994. "An Analysis of the Correlates of Discrimination Facing Young Hispanic Job Seekers." *American Economic Review* 84(3): 674–83.

LaLonde, Robert J., and Robert H. Topel. 1991. "Immigrants in the American Labor Market: Quality Assimilation and Distributional Effects." *American Economic Review* 81(2): 297–302.

Morales, Rebecca., and Frank Bonilla, eds. 1993. *Latinos in a Changing U.S. Economy.* Newbury Park, Calif.: Sage Publications.

Portes, Alejandro, and Cynthia Trulove. 1987. "Making Sense of Diversity: Recent Research on Hispanic Minorities in the United States." *Annual Review of Sociology* 13: 359–85.

Reimers, Cordelia W. 1985. "A Comparative Analysis of the Wages of Hispanics, Blacks, and Non-Hispanic Whites." In *Hispanics in the U.S. Economy*, edited by George J. Borjas and Marta Tienda. Orlando, Fla.: Academic Press.

Rivera-Batiz, Francisco L., and Carlos Santiago. 1994. *Puerto Ricans in the United States: A Changing Reality*. Washington, D.C.: National Puerto Rican Coalition.

Tienda, Marta. 1983. "Nationality and Income Attainment among Native and Immigrant Hispanic Men in the United States." *Sociological Quarterly* 24(2): 253–72.

Tienda, Marta, and Patricia Guhleman. 1985. "The Occupational Positions of Employed Hispanic Women." In *Hispanics in the U.S. Economy*, edited by George J. Borjas and Marta Tienda. London: Harcourt Brace.

Tienda, Marta, and Lief Jensen. 1988. "Poverty and Minorities: A Quarter-Century Profile of Color and Economic Disadvantage." In *Divided Opportunities: Minorities, Poverty and Social Policy*, edited by Gary D. Sandefur and Marta Tienda. New York: Plenum Press.

Tienda, Marta, Katherine Donato, and Hector Cordero-Guzmán. 1992. "Schooling, Color and the Labor Force Activity of Women." *Social Forces* 71(2): 365–96.

U.S. Bureau of the Census. 1983. *1980 Census of Population and Housing: Public Use Microdata Samples*. Technical documentation. Washington, D.C.: U.S. Department of Commerce.

———. 1992. *1990 Census of Population and Housing: Public Use Microdata Samples*. Technical documentation. Washington, D.C.: U.S. Department of Commerce.

U.S. Department of Commerce. 1991a. *1990 Census Population: General Population, Characteristics of Texas*. CP-1-45, Washington: U.S. Government Printing Office.

———. 1991b. *1990 Census Population: General Population, Characteristics of California*. CP-1-6, Washington: U.S. Government Printing Office.

Waters, Mary, and Karl Esbach. 1995. "Immigration and Racial Inequality in the United States." *Annual Review of Sociology* 21: 419–46.

Chapter 4

Gender, Race, Ethnicity, and Wages

Paula England, Karen Christopher, and Lori L. Reid

In the United States, discussions of race are often about the relative privilege of white men vis-à-vis African American men, and discussions of gender often tell the story of relations between white men and women. Thus knowledge about the situation of women of color is limited, and race is often seen as strictly a black-white issue, an anachronistic formulation at a time when Latinos and Latinas will soon outnumber African Americans. This chapter attends to racial or ethnic group and gender simultaneously and looks at how they affect the pay of two groups of women of color in the U.S.: African American women and Latinas.

Recent conceptual writings stress the importance of studying intersections of race and gender. Authors advocating "intersectionality analyses," many of them women of color, point out that the social position of women of color is distinct from that of either white women or men of color (hooks 1984; Crenshaw 1990; Collins 1990; Mohanty, Russo, and Torres 1991; Baca Zinn and Dill 1994; Hall 1995). Many of these writings use examples from historical, ethnographic, or textual analyses to illustrate the qualitative differences between the positions of these groups. Of course, racial or ethnic group and gender also intersect with other socially salient dimensions that a fuller analysis would attend to—class, sexual orientation, or nation of residence or birth, to name a few that critically affect life chances. Here we pursue the more modest goal of understanding intersections of ethnicity and gender for one outcome, pay.[1]

Given an outcome that can be quantified, what form should intersectionality analyses take? Following an approach suggested by Kilbourne, England, and Beron (1994), we focus on these questions:

1. What factors explain differences in pay between ethnic groups? Is the "ethnic inequality story" (of which factors explain how much of the differences in pay) basically the same for men and women? For example, if educational differences are important in ethnic inequality, are

ʃually important for ethnic inequality among women and among

⌐ctors explain differences in pay between men and women? Is ₍ɴɪs "gender inequality story" basically the same for the three ethnic groups? For example, if gender differences in seniority, or in placement in typically male versus female occupations, are important in explaining gender differences in pay, are they equally important for whites, African Americans, Latinos, and Latinas?

To answer these questions, we use the 1993 wave of the National Longitudinal Survey of Youth (NLSY), a national sample of young adults. We assess how individuals' characteristics and the characteristics of their jobs affect earnings and how these characteristics are relevant in explaining gender and ethnic gaps in earnings. We attend to whether and how much the factors explaining gender-based gaps vary by ethnicity and whether and how much factors explaining ethnicity-based gaps vary by sex.

The variables in our analysis fall into two categories, nonjob and job characteristics. In the first category are qualifications or other background characteristics of individuals. We consider years of education, employment experience, and seniority (that is, experience in the firm one currently works in), distinguishing between part- and full-time experience and seniority. Using a measure of cognitive skills, the Armed Forces Qualifying Test (AFQT), we determine whether the skills measured by such tests are rewarded, net of educational credentials. We also control for region of the country and residence in a rural or urban area. Differences between ethnic groups and between men and women that are unexplained by these factors are sometimes seen as a result of discrimination, defined as unequal treatment by current employers of persons with the same nonascriptive characteristics. This interpretation can be misleading, as it underestimates the total effect of a broader concept of discrimination; it excludes discrimination outside labor markets (for example, in housing markets, public policy, or informal interaction) and the effects of past labor market discrimination, both of which may affect group differences in experience, education, or cognitive skills or the extent to which these qualifications are rewarded. On the other hand, this interpretation may overestimate discrimination insofar as group differences in job qualifications are unmeasured in the analysis. Thus we do not claim to definitively measure how much of the ethnicity-based and gender-based gaps discrimination explains. Rather we measure how much group members' relative pay is affected by differences in their individual characteristics and the jobs they hold.[2] Because our analysis omits people who are not employed, our conclusions do not reveal the factors that explain ethnic or gender differences in employment; they pertain only to what affects wages among those who have a job.

We also consider various job characteristics to find which ones affect pay and to discover how much the job placement of lower-earning groups explains their lower pay. This reveals the dimensions along which desegregation of jobs would help reduce group differences in earnings. In this part of the analysis, we make no assumption about whether individuals got into the jobs they hold through demand-side discrimination, qualifications, or their aspirations.

If the "gender story" varies little by ethnicity and the "ethnicity story" varies little by sex, the conclusion will be that the dynamics affecting women of color in the labor market are an additive combination of the dynamics involved in ethnic inequality and those involved in gender inequality. If the factors explaining gender differences in pay vary importantly by ethnicity, and the factors explaining ethnic differences in pay vary importantly by sex, then a more complex, interactive model is needed. In that case, any description of ethnic inequality that is claimed to hold for both sexes but comes only from an analysis of one will be misleading, and any description of gender inequality that purports to be "generic" but comes from an analysis limited to (or statistically dominated by) whites (or any other single ethnic group) will be misleading.

To foreshadow our conclusions, the truth seems to be somewhere between these two views. For example, ethnic differences in some combination of education and cognitive skills explain sizable shares of ethnicity-based differences in pay for both men and women, although the effects vary somewhat in size for the two sexes. And, broadly speaking, gender inequality in pay is strongly affected by the segregation of occupations or industries by sex in all ethnic groups, although the more detailed picture varies somewhat by ethnic group. However, the role of experience and seniority in sex-based gaps in pays is much less important among African Americans than among Latinos and Latinas or whites.

PAST RESEARCH

To put our research in context, we review studies examining how individual or job characteristics affect earnings and affect group differences in earnings by ethnicity, sex, or both.

Education and Cognitive Skills

Blacks, Latinos, and Latinas have less education and lower levels of cognitive skill (at least as measured by standardized tests) compared with whites, and work in occupations with lower cognitive demands. Past research suggests that this cognitive dimension is relevant to ethnic pay gaps for both men and women (Corcoran and Duncan 1979; Kilbourne, England, and Beron 1994; Farkas et al. 1997; Cancio, Evans, and Maume 1997; O'Neill 1990). However, these factors explain little or none of the sex-based gap in pay for any ethnic group (Kilbourne, England, and Beron 1994; Kilbourne, England, Farkas, Beron, and Weir 1994; England 1992; England et al. 1994).

But what causes the ethnic differences in education and cognitive skills? Both are strongly affected by parents' education and parents' cognitive skills, and some evidence points to the effects of parental income and neighborhood and school characteristics net of these (Corcoran 1995; Neal and Johnson 1996). Thus any discrimination in labor or housing markets at one point in time adversely affects the education or cognitive skills of the next generation of people of color entering the labor market through its effects on their parents' income and residence. Hernnstein and Murray (1994) argue that racial or ethnic differences in cognitive skills are, at least in part, innate. Evidence that both heredity and environment affect within-race differences in cognitive skills comes, for example, from studies comparing twins or other siblings reared apart and together. But this research design cannot be used to study between-race differences, since twins rarely differ in race and identical twins never do. Thus, given that no credible evidence shows that such racial or ethnic differences are innate, that currently available methods could not demonstrate such effects, and that clear evidence of environmental influences exists, we interpret ethnic differences in cognitive skills as environmentally determined.

Experience and Seniority

Past research has found experience and seniority, together, to explain between a quarter and half of the sex-based gap in pay (Mincer and Polachek 1974; Corcoran and Duncan 1979; Wellington 1994; Kilbourne et al. 1994). Using slopes and means from Corcoran and Duncan's analysis to compute a decomposition, England (1992, 31) shows experience and seniority to be relevant to the sex-based gap in pay for blacks as well as whites. We know of no studies examining this for Latinos and Latinas. Given the increased joblessness experienced by black men and some subgroups of black women in recent decades, experience may be a factor in the gap between the pay of black males and that of white males as well, since periods of joblessness leave people with less experience (Browne 1997). Chapter 1 reports a historic reversal among women; young white women are now more likely to be employed than young black women are, while the opposite was true in the past and is still true in older cohorts. Thus experience may be increasingly relevant to race-based gaps in pay for women (see also chapter 2). Whether the employment and resulting experience gaps between ethnic groups result from labor market discrimination or other factors is not well understood, since few multivariate analyses have taken employment as a dependent variable (exceptions, all dealing with women, are Browne 1997; Reid 1997; Christopher 1996).

Job Segregation by Sex

Jobs are quite segregated by sex (Bielby and Baron 1984), although tion has declined since 1970 (Cotter et al. 1995). Segregation is linked to the sex-based gap in pay, with female-dominated jobs paying less (Petersen and Morgan 1995; Tomaskovic-Devey 1993). This link could arise because, through either discriminatory hiring or self-selection, women are concentrated in positions that pay less because of the type and amount of skill they require (Marini and Fan 1997). Also, jobs filled largely by women pay less than expected on the basis of their demands for skill, their disamenities (such as onerous working conditions), or the human capital of the workers. That is, the composition of jobs by sex has a net effect on the wages they pay. (Many studies are reviewed in Sorensen 1989, table 4.1; more recent analyses include England et al. 1988; Kilbourne, England, and Beron 1994; Kilbourne, England, Farkas, Beron, and Weir 1994; England 1992; Tomaskovic-Devey 1993; Jacobs 1995; Macpherson and Hirsch 1995; Jacobs and Steinberg 1990; Reid forthcoming; Aman 1996). Although the procedures used in studies of the effect of the sex composition of jobs have varied, most use either individuals or occupations as cases and enter controls for individual human capital, for various skill demands of the occupations, for difficult working conditions, and sometimes for industry. Studies find the percentage of females in an occupation has some net negative effect on the wages of both men and women. (For two exceptions, finding no effect, see Filer 1989; Tam 1997.) This negative effect of being in a more female occupation holds for blacks as well as whites (Kilbourne, England, and Beron 1994; Tomaskovic-Devey 1993; Reid forthcoming). Reid finds that the sex composition of Latinos' and Latinas' jobs has no effect on their starting wages in a firm. This finding may indicate a different process for Latinos and Latinas or may result from a small sample size.

Some skills are culturally linked to one sex. The best example is the association of nurturant or caregiving work with women because they care for children and others in their homes and in paid jobs. Is nurturant social skill devalued in wage systems because of its association with women? Several studies suggest so, finding that, net of other factors, people in occupations requiring nurturant social skill earn depressed wages (England 1992; England et al. 1994; Kilbourne, England, and Beron 1994; Kilbourne, England, Farkas, Beron, and Weir 1994). Kilbourne, England, and Beron (1994) show that the effect holds for blacks and whites. We know of no similar research for Latinos and Latinas.

Researchers interpret the net negative effects of the percentage of females in certain jobs and of the requirement of nurturant skill in various ways. We favor the interpretation underlying policy initiatives for comparable worth in wage setting, sometimes termed the *devaluation thesis*. The notion is that occupations filled largely by women are less valued because of their association with women and because of the devaluation of women in U.S. culture. Some types of skill are also more invisible and seen as less important if they are associated with women. The contribution of female-dominated jobs or the types of skills in them to organizations' goals is thus underestimated, so employers are willing to pay less for such jobs and the lower pay is perpetuated by institutional inertia. Thus we see the situation as a kind of wage discrimination, albeit one distinct from either hiring discrimination or lack of equal pay for work in the same job (England 1992). Most economists who accept the notion of discrimination in labor markets nonetheless reject the devaluation thesis in favor of the crowding thesis (Bergmann 1974, 1986). They reason that employers' discriminatory exclusion of women from jobs earmarked for men sends an artificially large supply of labor to the jobs for which employers will hire women, thus reducing the market wage in female jobs below what it would be otherwise. Unfortunately, we know of no way to adjudicate empirically between the crowding and devaluation perspectives with the data available.

An analogous question for race is, do jobs containing disproportionate members of minority groups have lower wages than would be predicted by the characteristics of the jobs? We do not include measures of ethnic composition of occupations because our work withn the NLSY has not found such effects, and most research has not, once controls for jobs' skill levels are introduced.[3]

Our analysis includes a measure of occupational demand for cognitive skill, which is an important predictor of earnings. We also include measures of occupations' demand for physical strength and the hazards they entail. The theory of compensating differentials suggests that requirements workers find onerous will enhance pay; increased pay is how employers get people to work in onerous jobs. But empirical support for this doctrine is not strong. Findings are mixed on whether physical skill has a payoff, and other physical disamenities are seldom found to boost pay (Kilbourne, England, Farkas, Beron, and Weir 1994; Jacobs and Steinberg 1990). Thus the fact that more men than women are in jobs with such requirements does not contribute to the higher pay of men (Kilbourne, England, Farkas, Beron, and Weir 1994; England 1992). We are unaware of analyses that examine the role of physical demands in ethnicity-based pay gaps or in sex-based gaps in pay among people of color, despite the fact that men of color are the most concentrated in jobs requiring physical strength and hazards.

Industry

Occupations are defined by task; industries are defined by the product or service sold. Industry as well as occupation affects wages, according to theories of industrial segmentation, which claim that some industries pay better because of their higher profit levels, resulting from oligopoly rents or the productivity provided by capital intensity. Unionization helps workers capture some of the increased profits. Advocates of the segmentation approach have drawn criticism by using wildly differing categorizations of industries or firms, although they generally find that industrial characteristics associated with core status predict higher wages (for a review, see Farkas, England, and Barton 1994). The efficiency wage thesis (part of the new neoclassical institutionalism within economics) offers another explanation for wage differences among industries: some, but not all, employers find it profitable to pay more than the market-clearing wage for workers at the level of human capital being hired. Higher wages can boost profits despite the cost increase if the wage affects workers' behavior in ways that boost productivity (Katz 1986; England 1992, 83–89).

Do women or people of color disproportionately work in peripheral industries or in industries that do not pay "efficiency wages," and does this help explain their lower pay (although not why they are concentrated in these industries)? The application of the efficiency wage perspective to sex- or race-based gaps has been more speculative than empirical. Other research findings are mixed. What seems fairly clear is that women work in lower-paying industries and that the different industrial locations of men and women thus explain some of the difference in their pay. (Fields and Wolff 1995 show the industry of employment to explain 15 to 19 percent of the male-female gap in 1988 data, using about twenty industry dummy variables.) Whether this finding relates to the categorizations of industries used in the dual economy literature is more open to debate. Two studies claim that peripheral placement explains a portion (5 to 15 percent) of the sex-based gap in pay (Hodson and England 1986; Coverdill 1988). Beck, Horan, and Tolbert (1980) show some relevance of sector (core-periphery) for gaps between the pay of men and women and between the pay of blacks and whites. However, two analyses show no significant effect of sector (measured in a core-periphery dichotomy) on women's wages (Maume 1985; Kilbourne, England, and Beron 1994). Kilbourne, England, and Beron (1994) show industry sector (again measured in a core-periphery dichotomy) to have no role in the black-white gap in pay among either men or women, because blacks are no more concentrated in peripheral industries than are whites of either sex.

DATA, VARIABLES, AND METHODS

Data

We analyzed data from the youth cohort of the NLSY, a national probability sample of individuals aged fourteen to twenty-one years in 1979 who have been interviewed each year since. We used the 1993 wave, when respondents were twenty-eight to thirty-five years old. All individuals classified as Hispanic by the NLSY were included as Latinos and Latinas (including the small number of Hispanic blacks). Those classified as non-Hispanic black were our African American sample. All respondents were placed in one of these two categories or in an "other" category based on a screener question used to determine eligibility for the sample. To form our white sample, we deleted from the category "other" those who reported a non-white ethnic identity, such as American Indian or Asian, when asked their first such identity. We limited the sample to those individuals employed (full- or part-time) in 1993.

Models and Variables

Means and standard deviations presented are weighted by the NLSY sample weights (see table 4.1), but regression analyses are unweighted. (See Winship and Radbill 1997 for a discussion of weighting.) Our regression analyses focused on two models, a reduced-form model that includes only the nonjob variables (education, test scores, seniority and experience, socioeconomic background, and residence; see table 4.2) and a full model that includes nonjob and job variables (see table 4.3). Both models have hourly wage as their dependent variable.

In preliminary analyses, we estimated these two ordinary least squares (OLS) regression equations for each of six ethnicity-gender groups: African American, white, and Latino and Latina men and women. However, to avoid presenting differing slopes for groups when the differences are not statistically significant, we employed the following strategy separately for the reduced-form and full models: a model pooling all six ethnicity-gender groups was run first. This model included five dummy variables representing the individual's ethnicity-gender group as well as interactions of these five ethnicity-gender dummies with each of the other variables.[4] "White male" was chosen as the dummy variable to omit, making this group the reference category. This group was chosen because it is the largest, so that its slopes have the least sampling error. Then, to achieve a more parsimonious model, we trimmed nonsignificant interactions from the models and reestimated them. We then used the resulting trimmed models to generate tables 4.2 and 4.3.

Tables 4.2 and 4.3 show the effect of each variable (other than ethnicity-gender dummies and interactions) from this pooled, trimmed model in the column labeled "Pooled." Other columns correspond to each of the ethnicity-gender groups other than white males. If no coefficient is given for a given group for a particular variable, the group's slope on this variable was

(Text continues on p. 150.)

Table 4.1 / Means and Standard Deviations for Key Variables

	Men			Women		
Variable	White	African American	Latino	White	African American	Latina
Education (years)	13.37	12.65	12.26	13.54	13.20	12.55
	(2.48)	(2.04)	(2.62)	(2.33)	(2.01)	(2.51)
	All but AF	All but LF	All but LF	All	All but WM	All but AM, LM
AFQT score (z score)	.49	−.62	−.26	.45	−.52	−.35
	(.93)	(.88)	(.99)	(.83)	(.79)	(.88)
	All but WF	All	All but LF	All but WM	All	All but LM
Full-time experience (years)	9.71	8.34	9.15	7.52	7.17	7.23
	(3.99)	(3.90)	(3.82)	(4.06)	(4.11)	(4.20)
	All but LM	All	All but WM	All but AF, LF	All but WF, LF	All but WF, AF
Full-time seniority (years)	4.36	3.21	3.80	3.24	3.76	3.46
	(4.17)	(3.50)	(3.82)	(3.73)	(3.85)	(3.72)
	All	All but WF, LF	All but AF, LF	All but AM, LF	All but LM, LF	WM
Part-time experience (years)	2.60	2.09	2.11	3.99	2.61	2.73
	(2.79)	(2.28)	(2.38)	(3.48)	(2.57)	(2.70)
	All but AF, LF	All but LM	All but AM	All	All but WM, LF	All but WM, AF
Part-time seniority (years)	.24	.24	.23	.80	.50	.48
	(.89)	(.87)	(.72)	(1.80)	(1.39)	(1.13)
	All but AM, LM	All but WM, LM	All but WM, AM	All	All but LF	All but AF
Parents' Education (years)	12.17	10.75	8.49	12.05	10.69	8.31
	(2.61)	(2.72)	(4.25)	(2.55)	(2.65)	(3.89)
	All	All but AF	All but LF	All	All but AM	All but LM
Parents' occupational prestige (scales, 0–100)	41.47	32.31	32.87	41.16	31.59	32.81
	(12.78)	(12.76)	(13.31)	(12.66)	(12.08)	(12.27)
	All but WF	WM, WF	WM, WF	All but WM	WM, WF	WM, WF

(Table continues on p. 148.)

Table 4.1 / *Continued*

	Men			Women		
Variable	White	African American	Latino	White	African American	Latina
Urban (dummy)	.76	.87	.93	.77	.88	.94
	(.43)	(.34)	(.26)	(.42)	(.33)	(.24)
	All but WF	WM, WF	WM, WF	All but WM	WM, WF	WM, WF
Northeast (dummy)	.19	.17	.14	.19	.15	.16
	(.40)	(.38)	(.35)	(.39)	(.36)	(.37)
	All but WF	WM, WF	WM, WF	All but WM, LF	WM, WF	WM
North Central (dummy)	.34	.17	.07	.30	.17	.07
	(.47)	(.38)	(.25)	(.46)	(.38)	(.26)
	All	All but AF	All but LF	All	All but AM	All but LM
South (dummy)	.30	.57	.34	.33	.61	.34
	(.46)	(.49)	(.47)	(.47)	(.49)	(.47)
	All but LM, LF	All but AF	AM, AF	All but LM, LF	All but AM	AM, AF
West (reference category of dummy)	.17	.08	.46	.18	.07	.42
	(.38)	(.28)	(.50)	(.39)	(.25)	(.49)
	All but WF	All but AF	All but LF	All but WM	All but AM	All but LM
Cognitive demands of occupation (z score)	.13	-.42	-.14	.24	-.09	.12
	(1.01)	(.91)	(.93)	(1.00)	(.97)	(.95)
	All but LF	All	All but AF	All but LF	All but LM	All but WM, WF
Authority (dummy based on occupation)	.18	.08	.16	.11	.07	.11
	(.39)	(.28)	(.36)	(.31)	(.25)	(.31)
	All but LM	WM, LM	AM, AF	WM, AF	All but AM	WM
Strength demands of occupation (z score)	.16	.51	.35	-.43	-.18	-.45
	(1.00)	(.96)	(.98)	(.86)	(.92)	(.83)
	All	All	All	All but LF	All	All but WF

	Col 1	Col 2	Col 3	Col 4	Col 5	Col 6
Hazards in occupation (z score)	.24 (1.14) All but LM	.29 (1.12) All but LM	.28 (1.14) All but WM, AM	−.35 (.64) All but LF	−.20 (.82) All but LF	−.34 (.67) All but WF, AF
Percentage of females in occupation (proportion)	.27 (.23) All but AM, LM	.29 (.24) All but WM, LM	.26 (.24) All but WM, AM	.65 (.26) All but AF, LF	.66 (.25) All but WF, LF	.67 (.25) All but WF, AF
Nurturance (dummy based on occupation)	.08 (.27) All but AM, LM	.09 (.28) All but WM, LM	.09 (.29) All but WM, AM	.32 (.46) All but LF	.25 (.43) All but LF	.31 (.46) All but EF, AF
Part-time (dummy)	.06 (.24) All but AM, LM	.08 (.28) All but WM, LM	.06 (.25) All but WM, AM	.29 (.45) All	.18 (.39) All but LF	.19 (.38) All but AF
Union (dummy)	.18 (.38) All but LM, LF	.28 (.45) All but LM, AF	.22 (.42) WF	.14 (.34) All	.26 (.44) All but AM, LM	.19 (.40) All but EM, LM
Establishment Size (ln no. of employees)	3.62 (2.30) AM, AF	3.97 (2.24) WM, AF	3.65 (2.34) AF	3.68 (2.30) AF	4.50 (2.19) All	3.86 (2.19) AF
Wage ($)	13.41 (7.04) All	10.00 (5.66) All but AF, LF	12.01 (6.60) All	10.65 (6.36) All but LF	9.04 (4.94) All but AM, LF	9.81 (5.62) EM, LM

Source: National Longitudinal Survey of Youth, 1993 wave.
Notes: Standard deviations are in parentheses. The third line in each cell indicates the groups that had means significantly different from this group ($p <$ .05, two-tailed). All computations for this table are weighted by sample weights. WM, AM, and LM are white males, African American males, and Latinos, respectively; WF, AF, and LF are white females, African American females, and Latinas, respectively.

Table 4.2 / Unstandardized Coefficients from OLS Regressions of Hourly Wages on Nonjob Variables (Reduced-Form Model)

| | | Men | | | Women | |
| | | African | | | African | |
Variable	Pooled[a]	American	Latino	White	American	Latina
Education (years)	0.78*	—	0.44	—	—	—
AFQT score (z score)	0.97*	—	—	—	—	—
Full-time experience (years)	0.19**	—	—	0.34	—	—
Full-time seniority (years)	0.25*	—	—	0.14	—	—
Part-time experience (years)	−0.14*	0.11	—	0.08	—	—
Part-time seniority (years)	.10	—	—	.24	—	—
Parents' education (years)	0.06+	—	—	—	—	—
Parents' occupational prestige	0.03*	—	—	—	—	—
Urban (dummy)	1.10*	0.08	—	—	—	—
Northeast (dummy)	1.41*	−0.54	—	—	—	—
North Central (dummy)	−0.83*	—	—	—	—	—
South (dummy)	−.66*	−2.00	−1.76	—	−0.90	—

Source: National Longitudinal Survey of Youth, 1993 wave.

Notes: Although the coefficients are not shown, models also contain five ethnicity/gender dummy variables (white males are the omitted reference category) and four dummy variables indicating whether the respondent had a missing score on mother's education, father's education, mother's occupational prestige, or father's occupational prestige. For regional dummies, the reference category is West.

[a]Coefficients from the pooled model apply to white males plus all groups for which this variable coefficient was not significantly different from the white male coefficient. Separate coefficients for other groups are present in the table when the group's slope on this variable is significantly different ($p < .05$, two-tailed) from that of white males. Significance tests not provided for slopes for individual groups. See text for details.

*$p < .05$ (two-tailed). +$p < .05$ (one-tailed)

not significantly different from the white male slope. Because we trimmed all nonsignificant interactions from the models and reestimated them, the pooled slope is not merely the white male slope (although because white men are the omitted reference category, they are always included in the

Table 4.3 / Unstandardized Coefficients from OLS Regressions of Hourly Wages on Job and Nonjob Variables (Full Model)

		Men		Women		
Variable	Pooled[a]	African American	Latino	White	African American	Latina
Education (years)	0.61*		0.38			
AFQT score (z score)	0.52*	0.54			0.54	
Full-time experience (years)	0.23*					
Full-time seniority (years)	0.19*			0.08		
Part-time experience (years)	−0.08*			0.02		
Part-time seniority (years)	0.15+					
Parents' education (years)	0.02					
Parents' occupational prestige	0.02*	0.05				
Urban (dummy)	0.82*					
Northeast (dummy)	1.23*	−0.13				
North Central (dummy)	−0.81*					
South (dummy)	−0.71*	−1.58	−1.12	−1.16		
Cognitive demands of occupation (z)	1.38*					
Authority (dummy based on occupation)	.73*					
Strength demands of occupation (z score)	−0.58*	0.40		0.37	1.44	1.08
Hazards in occupation (z score)	−0.06		−0.05			
Percentage of females in occupation (proportion)	−1.38*				0.01	

(Table continues on p. 152.)

Table 4.3 / *Continued*

		Men			Women	
		African			African	
Variable	Pooled[a]	American	Latino	White	American	Latina
Nurturance (dummy based onoccupa- tion)	−0.74*					
Part-time (dummy)	1.15*		2.29			
Union (dummy)	1.89*			0.40	−0.25	−0.29
Establishment size (ln)	0.31*					

Source: National Longitudinal Survey of Youth, 1993 wave.
Notes: Although the coefficients are not shown, models also contain five ethnicity/gender dummy variables; four dummy variables indicating whether the respondent was missing a score for mother's education, father's education, mother's occupational prestige, or father's occupational prestige; and nineteen dummies representing industry. For regional dummies, the reference category is West.
[a]Coefficients from the pooled model apply to white males plus all groups for which this variable coefficient was not significantly different from the white male coefficient. Separate coefficients for other groups are present in the table when the group's slope on this variable is significantly different ($p < .05$, two-tailed) from that of white males. Significance tests not provided for slopes for individual groups. See text for details.
*$p < .05$ (two-tailed). +$p < .05$ (one-tailed).

pooled estimate) but is the pooled slope for all groups except those for whom a separate slope is presented. When a separate estimate is not presented for a group, the pooled slope can be interpreted as an adequate estimate of the effect of the variable for that group.

Whenever the effect of a variable on a group significantly differed from its effect on white males, that effect, computed from the trimmed model, is found in the column for the indicated ethnicity-gender group to show that the pooled estimate is not accurate for this group.[5] For example, table 4.2 indicates that (male) Latinos are the only group whose returns to education differed significantly from the white male slope, so the leftmost column contains a pooled slope (from the trimmed model that excludes all interactions not significant in the original model) for education that applies to the five other groups, and the column for Latinos contains Latinos' significantly lower slope. Their return was calculated by adding the (pooled) coefficient for education to the coefficient for the interaction of the dummy for male Latinos with education from the trimmed model. We present significance tests only for the pooled slopes, not for the separate group slopes.[6]

AFQT is the Armed Forces Qualifying Test, administered to the entire sample in 1980. It is composed of four subtests covering arithmetic reasoning, math knowledge, word knowledge, and paragraph comprehension. Each of the subtest scores was converted to a Z score, these scores were averaged and equally weighted, and the average was converted to a Z score.[7] The resulting scale has a reliability (Cronbach's α) of .91. We chose the AFQT to measure cognitive skills because measures of very specific skills are inappropriate for predictions across the entire labor market. A general test of fairly basic skills, in contrast, could apply to diverse jobs. Given our commitment to work with the NLSY because of its recent data, employment histories, and oversampling of blacks and Hispanics, the AFQT was the only measure of general cognitive skills available.

Other independent variables include education, years of full-time and part-time experience from 1978 to 1993, and years of full-time or part-time seniority (that is, experience in the organization for which an individual currently works). These measures cover the entire life cycle except for jobs held before 1978 (when the youths were thirteen to twenty years old). Experience includes seniority in one's present establishment. These measures were computed from the NLSY work history file, with values in weeks; we then converted them to years.

Parents' education is the average of the years of school completed by the youth's mother and father. We wanted to use information on both parents. However, if we had used separate variables for fathers' and mothers' education, missing values would have forced us to eliminate the large number of respondents who did not grow up with their father and did not report on him. To avoid this, we averaged the education of the parents if information was present on both. If one parent had a missing value for education, we used the education value of the other parent. These respondents were assigned a value of 1 on a dummy variable (one for mothers and one for fathers) indicating whether information on one parent's education was missing, and these missing value indicators were entered as control variables. Our calculations of parents' (average) occupational prestige were analogous to those for parents' education. We used the Hodge-Siegel-Rossi prestige scale (National Opinion Research Center 1978), merging according to the detailed occupational categories for 1970 in which parents' occupations were coded. Missing value indicators for each parent's occupational prestige were also entered. (These missing value indicators never had significant coefficients.)

The urban dummy is 1 if an individual lived in a county with more than half of its population living in cities of over 50,000 people. The measures of region were dummy variables for North, North Central (often called "Midwest") and South, with a reference category of West.[8]

The first author created the measure of the cognitive demands of a respondent's occupation from a factor analysis of numerous items, mostly from the *Dictionary of Occupational Titles* (England 1992, 135). We merged the score onto the NLSY respondents' records according to their detailed

(1980) census occupational category in 1993 and converted them to Z scores.

Authority is a dummy variable for whether or not a respondent's occupation involved supervisory or managerial power over others. A score of 1 was given to all detailed census occupational categories with titles containing the words "management" or "supervisor." We measured whether an occupation involves nurturant social skill by means of a dummy variable that the first author coded 1 if, in her judgment, one of the major activities on which time is spent involves providing a face-to-face service to one or more clients or customers (not coworkers or managers). (See England 1992, 137–39, for occupations coded 1 on authority and nurturance. Examples are nurse, doctor, teacher, receptionist, sales worker, and barber.)

Measures of the physical strength and physical hazards faced in one's job were taken from the *Dictionary of Occupational Titles* (England 1992, chap. 3), merged onto these data, and converted to Z scores. The percentage of females in a detailed census occupation in 1990 was taken from U.S. Department of Commerce (1993). We merged these data according to the 1980 census occupational codes used in the 1993 NLSY wave; this was possible because of the nearly one-to-one match between the 1980 and 1990 codes.

We collapsed detailed (1980 census) industry categories into nineteen dummies representing twenty categories corresponding to two-digit census industry categories, except that a few categories had to be collapsed to generate enough cases to be used with our other dummy variables. Individuals were coded part-time workers if they worked fewer than thirty-five hours a week.[9] Union is a dummy variable for whether or not respondents reported that the wages earned in their job were set by collective bargaining. Size is the natural log of the number of employees who worked at the current job establishment, as reported by the respondent.

Decomposition

The key part of the analysis is the decomposition, a technique that can be used when two groups (here, pairs of the six ethnicity-gender groups) differ on a dependent variable (wages) and regression analysis is used to get slopes for each group. The difference between the mean wages of the two groups can be divided into portions that are due to group differences in means on each independent variable, group differences in slopes (returns) on each independent variable, the difference between the two groups' intercepts, and interactions between the slope and intercept terms (Jones and Kelley 1984). We present the portion of the decomposition showing how much group differences in means contribute to the pay gap.[10] Computing this for each independent variable involved multiplying the difference between the two groups' means (the mean for the higher-earning group minus the mean for the lower-earning group) by the slope and dividing this product by the pay gap in dollars. This procedure yielded the percentage of the pay gap explained by the groups' mean differences on this independent variable. When our trimming of nonsignificant interactions to arrive at the coefficients in tables 4.2 and 4.3 (discussed in the preceding section) showed that the pooled slope adequately represented both groups, we used that slope. When table 4.2 or 4.3 presents a slope distinct from the pooled slope for one or both of the groups involved in the decomposition, we include two estimates of the contribution of the mean difference, one for each group's slope. If a separate slope is not presented for one of the groups, indicating that it is adequately represented by the pooled slope, then we used the pooled slope for this group and the separate slope presented in table 4.2 or 4.3 for the other group. When we computed two estimates of the contribution of group differences in means to the gap between the pay of two groups, we present both estimates in tables 4.4 to 4.8. In both text and tables, we include the figure arrived at by using the higher-earning group's slope (or the pooled slope if the group is included in it) first, followed by a dash, and then the estimate arrived at by using the lower-earning group's slope (or the pooled slope if the group is included in it). Because of this ordering, the smaller number is not always on the left. For example, the statement that education explained 20 to 17 percent of a gap means that 20 percent is the estimate using the higher-earning group's slope and 17 percent is the estimate using the lower-earning group's slope.

We decomposed the gaps between the pay of whites and African Americans and between that of whites and Latinos and Latinas, each within each sex (table 4.4, nonjob variables; table 4.6, job variables). We also decomposed gaps between the pay of males and females within each ethnic group (table 4.5, nonjob variables; table 4.7, job variables). The results of all decompositions are summarized in table 4.8, which also contains a summary of decompositions (not shown elsewhere) for gaps between the pay of white men and that of women of color. The broad conclusions taken from table 4.8 are consistent with conclusions reached from decompositions based upon regressions using the natural log of wage as the dependent variable (not shown).

RESULTS

Differences in Pay Among Groups

How big were the gaps between the groups' pay? White men's average hourly earnings were the highest at $13.41, followed by the earnings of Latinos at $12.01, white women at $10.65, African American men at $10.00, Latinas at $9.81, and African American women at $9.04 (table 4.1). White women, however, did not earn more than African American men in older

Table 4.4 / Percentage of Ethnicity-Based Pay Gap Explained by Mean Differences on Nonjob Variables

	Percentage of Ethnicity-Based Gap Explained	
Groups and Variable	Men	Women
African-American and white		
Education	17	17
AFQT score	32	58
Full-time experience	8	7 − 4
Full-time seniority	8	−5 − −8
Part-time experience	−2 − 2	6 − −12
Part-time seniority	0	4 − 2
Parents' education	3	5
Parents' occupational prestige	7	16
Urban	−3 − −0	−8
Northeast	1 − 0	4
North Central	−4	−6
South	5 − 16	11 − 15
Total	Σ = 71 − 89	Σ = 111 − 88
Latino or Latina and white		
Education	62 − 35	93
AFQT score	52	92
Full-time experience	8	11 − 6
Full-time seniority	10	−4 − −7
Part-time experience	−5	12 − −20
Part-time seniority	0	9 − 4
Parents' education	17	28
Parents' occupational prestige	16	26
Urban	−13	−23
Northeast	5	5
North Central	−16	−22
South	2 − 4	1
Total	Σ = 139 − 114	Σ = 229 − 183

Source: National Longitudinal Survey of Youth, 1993 wave.
Notes: The percentage explained is the slope times the mean difference, divided by the gap between the two groups' mean hourly wage. The first number in the range is the percentage explained using the higher-earning group's slope; the number to the right was obtained using the lower-earning group's slope. Slopes are from table 4.2; means are from table 4.1. Sums at the bottom of each two-group decomposition include components for the variables indicating missing values for father's or mother's occupation and education, although these components are not listed.

Table 4.5 / Percentage of Sex-Related Gaps in Pay Explained by Mean Differences on Nonjob Variables

	Percentage of Sex Gap Explained		
Variable	Whites	African Americans	Latinos and Latinas
Education	-5	-45	-6 − -10
AFQT	1	-10	4
Full-time experience	15 − 27	24	17
Full-time seniority	10 − 6	-14	4
Part-time experience	7 − -4	-6 − -7	4
Part-time seniority	-2 − -5	-3	-1
Parents' education	0	0	1
Parents' occupational prestige	0	2	0
Urban	0	0 − -1	0
Northeast	0	-1 − 3	-1
North Central	-1	0	0
South	1	6 − 3	1 − 0
Total	$\Sigma = 27 − 20$	$\Sigma = -47 − -35$	$\Sigma = 21 − 16$

Source: National Longitudinal Survey of Youth, 1993 wave.
Notes: The percentage explained is the slope times the mean difference, divided by the gap between the two groups' mean hourly wage. The first number in the range is the percentage explained using the higher-earning group's slope; the number to the right was obtained using the lower-earning group's slope. Slopes are from table 4.2; means are from table 4.1. Sums at the bottom of each two-group decomposition include components for the variables indicating missing values for father's or mother's occupation and education, although these components are not listed.

cohorts did and did not earn more in earlier periods; the average hourly earnings reflect recent increases in white women's pay and a recent deterioration of the labor market position of African American men.

Effects of Nonjob Variables on Wages and Wage Gaps Between Groups

Education and Scores on Tests of Cognitive Skills The positive effect of AFQT score, net of education, indicates that individuals with higher scores on this test of basic cognitive skills had higher earnings even if they had the same education and socioeconomic background. A one-standard-deviation increase in AFQT score increased earnings by about a dollar an hour

Table 4.6 / Percentage of Ethnicity-Based Pay Gap Explained by Mean Differences on Job Variables

Groups and Variable	Percentage of Ethnicity-Based Gap Explained	
	Men	Women
African-American and white		
Cognitive demands	22	28
Authority	2	2
Strength	6 − −4	−6 − −23
Hazards	0	1
Percentage female	1	1 − 0
Nurturance	0	−3
Part-time	−1	8
Union	−6	−3 − 2
Size	−3	−16
Industry[a]	2	−5
Total	Σ = 24 − 14	Σ = 7 − −6
Latino or Latina and White		
Cognitive demands	26	19
Authority	2	0
Strength	7	1 − 3
Hazards	0 − 0	0
Percentage female	0	4
Nurturance	1	0
Part-time	0 − −1	14
Union	−6	−3 − 2
Size	−1	−7
Industry[a]	5	6
Total	Σ = 33 − 32	Σ = 33 − 41

Source: National Longitudinal Survey of Youth, 1993 wave.
Notes: The percentage explained is the slope times the mean difference, divided by the gap between the two groups' mean hourly wage. The first number in the range is the percentage explained using the higher-earning group's slope; the number to the right was obtained using the lower-earning group's slope. Slopes are from table 4.2; means are from table 4.1. Sums at the bottom of each two-group decomposition include components for the variables indicating missing values for father's or mother's occupation and education, although these components are not listed.
[a]Total for the group of industry dummies.

($.97), and all groups' returns were similar enough to be adequately represented by the pooled slope (table 4.2).

How do we interpret the positive effects of test scores on earnings, net of education, given that many employers did not even know the person's score? A number of mechanisms may have been at work. First, employers may have used tests that correlate with the AFQT to screen workers for

Table 4.7 / Percentage of Sex-Related Pay Gap Explained by Mean Differences on Job Variables

Variable	Percentage of Sex Gap Explained		
	Whites	African Americans	Latinos and Latinas
Cognitive demands	−6	−47	−16
Authority	2	1	2
Strength	−12 − 8	29 − 103	−21 − 40
Hazards	−1	−3	−1 − −2
Percentage female	19	53 − 0	26
Nurturance	6	13	7
Part-time	−10	−11	−13 − −7
Union	3 − 0	3 − 0	2 − 0
Size	−1	−17	−3
Industry[a]	20	42	24
Total	Σ = 21 − 38	Σ = 61 − 80	Σ = 6 − 71

Source: National Longitudinal Survey of Youth, 1993 wave.
Notes: The percentage explained is the slope times the mean difference, divided by the gap between the two groups' mean hourly wage. The first number in the range is the percentage explained using the higher-earning group's slope; the number to the right was obtained using the lower-earning group's slope. Slopes are from table 4.2; means are from table 4.1. Sums at the bottom of each two-group decomposition include components for the variables indicating missing values for father's or mother's occupation and education, although these components are not listed.
[a]Total for the group of industry dummies.

better-paying jobs. But we doubt that this was the major mechanism since most employers do not use such tests.[11] However, most employers require personal interviews before hire (Neckerman and Kirschenman 1991). Those who interview job candidates may assess their cognitive skills from cues like grammar or the logic of answers. If the assessments correlated with test scores, those scores would contribute to the effects shown here. Also, workers with better cognitive skills may conduct "smarter" job searches that yield higher-paying jobs. Finally, cognitive skills may affect a worker's productivity or supervisors' perceptions of it and thereby affect pay through raises or promotions.

Each year of education yielded a positive return of $.78 per hour (table 4.2). This pooled slope represents all groups adequately except for (male) Latinos, whose return was a lower $.44. These returns, in effect, apply to people whose AFQT scores were equivalent since the variable is controlled. Thus part of the effect may reflect pure credentialing; that is, employers

Table 4.8 / Percentage of Pay Gap Explained by Mean Differences on Selected Groups of Variables

Groups	Difference	Nonjob Variables[a]				Job Variables[b]			
		Education and AFQT Score	Experience and Seniority	Parental Education and Occupation	Total of All Nonjob Variables[c]	Cognitive Demands	Percentage Female and Nurturance	Industry	Total of All Job Variables[c]
African American and white men	Ethnicity	49	14 – 18	10	71 – 89	22	1	2	24 – 14
African American and white women	Ethnicity	75	12 – –14	21	111 – 88	28	–2 – –3	–5	7 – –6
Latinos and white men	Ethnicity	114 – 87	13	33	139 – 114	26	1	5	33 – 32
Latinas and white women	Ethnicity	185	28 – –17	54	229 – 183	19	4	6	33 – 41
White women and men	Sex	–4	30 – 24	0	27 – 20	–6	25	20	21 – 38

African American women and men	Sex	−55	1 – 14	2	−47 – −35	−47	66 – 13	42	61 – 80
Latinas and Latinos	Sex	−2 – −6	24	1	21 – 16	−16	33	24	6 – 71
African American women and white men	Ethnicity, sex	25	13	8	47 – 49	7	16 – 3	11	17 – 23
Latinas and white men	Ethnicity, sex	43	21	14	67	0	21	17	20 – 49

Source: National Longitudinal Survey of Youth, 1993 wave.

Note: Totals include portions explained by variables excluded from table (urban residence, region, and parental missing value indicators for nonjob variables; authority, strength demands, hazards, size, part-time status, and union status for job variables).

[a] Percents for nonjob variables are their total effects, including effects operating directly and those operating indirectly through job variables. (This follows from the fact that the slopes were taken from the model for nonjob variables.)

[b] Percents for job variables are the total explained by groups' differential placement across job variables whether or not the job placements were due to group differences on nonjob variables. (This follows from using unadjusted means for job characteristics; see text.)

[c] Includes portions explained by variables excluded from table (urban residence, region, and parental missing value indicators for nonjob variables; authority, strength demands, hazards, size, part-time status, and union status for job variables).

may have rewarded educational credentials despite no evidence that those with credentials were more productive. Some or all of the effects may have arisen from a weaker version of credentialing: employers may have used credentials rather than direct measures of cognitive skill to choose or reward workers, but they hired and retained more workers with higher cognitive skill on average by doing so. They may have used education as an imperfect proxy because it is expensive to measure cognitive skill directly (for example, by administering a test or letting the applicant work for a probation period). Education had some power to predict cognitive skills; its correlation with AFQT score was about .6 in these data. This positive correlation arose because individuals with better cognitive skills (whether attained through innate ability, past schooling, or extra-school environment) stay in school longer and because school imparts cognitive skills. If employers use education as a proxy for cognitive skills, it will produce the effect seen here—that among people with equal AFQT scores, those with more education earned more. School may also impart (or staying in school may select on) other cognitive and noncognitive qualities that employers want but that are not captured by the AFQT score, such as cultural capital, obedience to authority, or perseverance. We cannot tell how much each of these mechanisms explains the education coefficients.

How do education and AFQT score relate to group differences in wages? Based on the decompositions (tables 4.4 and 4.5; summarized in table 4.8), these factors are crucial to understanding gaps between the pay of whites and minorities but contributed nothing to sex-based differences within ethnic groups. The reason is that education and AFQT scores had positive returns, and minority groups had lower mean education and AFQT scores than whites, but women did not have significantly lower means on either variable within ethnic groups. In fact, since Latinas and black women had slightly higher means than men of their ethnic group on both variables and white women had higher means than white men on education, these factors "negatively contributed" to sex-based gaps—they would have been even larger if the means for men and women had converged on these variables.

Among these employed individuals, differences between the AFQT scores of whites and blacks were in the neighborhood of one standard deviation, while the difference between the scores of Latinos and Latinas and whites were about three-quarters of a standard deviation. Although the differences between the AFQT scores of whites and blacks were larger than those between the scores of whites and Latinos and Latinas, the reverse was true for education—for both sexes. For both Latinos and Latinas and blacks relative to whites, schooling differences were much smaller than the differences in AFQT scores were when expressed in standard deviation units (computed from table 4.1).

Given these ethnicity-based differences in education and AFQT scores and the positive returns of these variables, these two factors together are more than sufficient to explain the entire gap between the wages of Latinas and white women and to explain all or most (114 to 87 percent) of the pay gap between Latinos and white men (tables 4.4 and 4.8). Education and AFQT score together explain about half (49 percent) of the gap between the wages of white and black men and 75 percent of the gap for white and black women. Thus these factors were more important in wage gaps between whites and Latinos and Latinas than in wage gaps between blacks and whites but were very large factors in each.

Experience and Seniority Full-time experience and full-time seniority each had significant positive returns (table 4.2). The pooled slopes adequately describe all groups, except that white women had higher returns to full-time experience and slightly lower returns to full-time seniority.[12] Returns to each year of full-time seniority were $.25 per hour, and returns to each year of full-time experience were $.19 per hour for the pooled groups.

In contrast, part-time experience and seniority had little return. The pooled estimate of returns to part-time seniority was a nonsignificant $.10 per hour per year (table 4.2), but the return for white women was a larger $.24. Part-time experience actually had negative returns in the pooled model, which adequately represents all groups except African American men and white women, who had positive returns of $.11 and $.08, respectively. Since white women are the group that most often worked part-time (see table 4.1), it is interesting that they had higher returns than most other groups to both part-time experience and part-time seniority.

Differences in seniority or experience have been discussed as factors much more in male-female than in ethnicity-based gaps in pay, since women usually take responsibility for child rearing, which may lead to nonemployment, thus reducing experience and seniority. However, taken together, experience and seniority explain small to medium amounts of some gaps between ethnic groups but were not important in all groups' male-female wage gaps (table 4.8). Looking at ethnic gaps, experience, and seniority together explain 14 to18 percent of the gap between black males and white males and 13 percent of the gap between Latino and white males. This result reflects the fact that white men had more full-time experience and seniority, which had positive returns. Among women, whether experience and seniority contributed to ethnicity-based pay gaps is simply unclear. White women had a bit (but not significantly) more full-time experience than Latinas and African American women did, but African American women had more full-time seniority than either of the other groups of women did. Also, white women are not well represented by the pooled slopes; however, they had higher returns to full-time experience but lower returns to full-time seniority. Thus the estimates from the decomposition formula (depending on whose slope we used) range from positive to negative contributions to the gap.

Turning to sex-based gaps in pay, the ethnic group in which experience and seniority explain most of the sex-based gap is whites—30 to 24 percent. An intermediate 24 percent is explained for Latinos and Latinas. In the gap between black males and females, seniority and experience had either no role or a very small role (1 to 14 percent). The small role of seniority and experience in sex-based gaps among blacks stemmed from black women's higher full-time seniority relative to black men's, combined with the high returns to seniority. Black women's average seniority was higher than that of the other female groups and was not significantly different from that of (male) Latinos. Although black men had 1.17 more years of full-time experience than black women did, they had 0.55 year less full-time seniority (both differences are significant). The difference in experience helps explain the gap, but the seniority difference works the opposite way—the pay gap would have been even bigger without it. The high seniority but relatively low experience of black women suggests a pattern: they were often jobless, but if they got a decent job, they seldom changed employers.[13]

Region and Urban Residence   Place of residence is simply a control for our purposes here, so we do not discuss the findings in detail. The decompositions never reveal residence to be important to male-female differences within an ethnic group (table 4.5), because within ethnic groups the two sexes had nearly the same geographical distribution. The big differences in place of residence related to ethnicity, with Latinos the most urban, blacks more urban than whites, whites the most concentrated in the northeast and north central regions, and blacks the most southern (table 4.1). Yet, despite ethnic differences in residence, region and urban residence, taken together, never positively explain much of the gap between ethnic groups (tables 4.4 and 4.5). However, the greater concentration of blacks in the South explains 5 to 16 percent of the gaps between the pay of black and white men and 11 to 15 percent of the gap between black and white women.

Socioeconomic Background   The measures of socioeconomic background— parents' education and occupational prestige—were entered as control variables, primarily to make sure that the effects of education and AFQT score were not spurious, because of their endogeneity to social class background.[14] Some of the effects of socioeconomic status were indirect through education and AFQT score, but our coefficients on socioeconomic background exclude these indirect effects because we included education and AFQT score in the model. The direct and indirect effects of class background (many of the latter not captured in our coefficients) are important examples of how past discrimination by employers affects current race-based differences. The decompositions, also capturing only direct effects (not those operating indirectly, through education and AFQT score), show a clear pattern in which these variables affected ethnic, but not within-ethnic-group, sex-based differences (table 4.8). The parents of employed men and women from the same ethnic group had similar average levels of education and prestige; the big mean differences were between ethnic groups. These direct effects were more important in pay gaps between Latinos and Latinas and whites than between blacks and whites, because the parents of Latinos and Latinas had a lower level of education than the parents of blacks but about the same occupational prestige.

Effects of Job Variables on Wages and Wage Gaps Between Groups

Here we use the full models (table 4.3) to examine which attributes of jobs affected earnings, net of the qualifications of job incumbents. The decompositions (tables 4.6 and 4.7; summarized in table 4.8) show the extent to which differences in the jobs held by the gender-ethnicity groups affected pay gaps. Since differences in jobs held may have resulted from qualifications, background, or discrimination, the portions of the pay gaps explained by job characteristics should not be interpreted as indicating the cost of discriminatory placement. Rather, the portions explained by job characteristics reflect differences in the measured job characteristics, whether or not these differences are due to discrimination or to group differences in qualifications or aspirations. Even though the coefficients used in the decomposition come from a regression that controlled for human capital and other nonjob variables, the group differences in means on the job variables are raw—without such an adjustment. In the summary, which includes both job and nonjob variables (table 4.8), we do not add the percentages explained by job variables to those explained by nonjob variables; they are overlapping.[15]

Cognitive Demands of Occupations   Being in an occupation with higher demands for cognitive skill showed positive returns, with one pooled slope an adequate representation for all six groups. The effect of a standard deviation increase in the cognitive skill demand of the job was $1.38 per hour (table 4.3). Working in occupations with greater cognitive demands contributed to the wage gaps between whites and blacks and between whites and Latinos and Latinas (table 4.8), since, within each sex, blacks and Latinos and Latinas were in jobs with lower cognitive skill demands (table 4.1) and such demands had positive returns. This factor explains 22 percent of the pay gap between African Americans and whites among men and 28 percent of this ethnicity-based gap among women (table 4.8). It explains 26 percent of the gap between the wages of Latinos and white males and 19 percent of the gap between the wages of Latinas and white females. Differences in the amount of cognitive skill required by their occupations explain none of the gender-based gaps within ethnic groups, since within each ethnic group women were in jobs requiring more cognitive skill. In fact, Latinas' jobs required virtually the same cognitive skills as the jobs of white men did. Thus a job's requirement of cognitive skill explains little or none of the gap between white men and women of color (none for Latinas and 7 percent for black women); the generally higher female mean and generally lower minority mean placement cancel each other out (table 4.8).

Authority Being in jobs with managerial or supervisory authority had significant positive returns; the pooled slope, indicating that being in a job involving authority increased pay $.73 per hour, adequately represents all six ethnicity-gender groups. While a higher percentage of white and Latino men were in positions of authority than were women of their same race or ethnicity, this was not true for African Americans (table 4.1). Overall, the gaps in authority were small enough that, even with a fairly hefty return, authority never explains more than 2 percent of any of the pay gaps by ethnicity or sex (tables 4.6 to 4.7).[16]

Physical Strength and Hazardous Working Conditions Under the assumption that marginal workers find facing hazards and exerting strength a nonpecuniary disamenity (that is, they would prefer not to do so), the neoclassical economic theory of compensating differentials predicts a wage premium for these job characteristics. Our findings are mixed. A requirement of physical strength had a significant negative effect on the wages of Latinos and white men (the two groups to whom the pooled slope applied) but a positive effect on the other four groups' wages (table 4.3).[17] Table 4.1 shows that on average in each ethnic group more men than women are in jobs requiring more physical strength. All means for males on this variable are higher than all means for females. The group for whom the decomposition findings are most dramatic is African Americans: since both black men and women experienced positive returns to working in jobs requiring more strength, black men's greater representation in such jobs explains the 29 to 103 percent of the sex-based gap in pay among blacks (table 4.7). Among whites and Latinos, we get a positive contribution to the gap if we use women's positive slopes and negative contributions if we use men's negative slopes, so a clear conclusion is simply impossible. Thus there is warrant to conclude that women's concentration in jobs requiring less strength contributes to the sex-based gap in pay only among African Americans.

A similarly confusing picture emerges for the contribution of jobs requiring physical skill to ethnicity-based gaps. The one clear case is the gap between white males and Latinos: Latinos held jobs requiring more strength, and both groups earned less in such jobs, which explains 7 percent of the gap (table 4.6). But black-white differences among either men or women each yield one positive and one negative estimate, depending on whose slope is used.

Working in a job with physical hazards had no significant effect on wages in the pooled slope, which adequately represents all groups except (male) Latinos, who earned significantly more if they worked with hazards (table 4.3). Men were generally in jobs with more hazards than women were, but because this job characteristic yielded no returns for any group but Latinos, it did not affect any gaps except possibly that between Latinos and Latinas, to which its contribution was either negative or trivial (table 4.7). Thus, overall, physical hazards were not important in the pay gaps.

The Sex Composition of Occupations and Demands for Nurturant Social Skill As past research has found, the higher the percentage of females in an occupation, the more depressed the wages of the workers in that occupation. The pooled slope indicates that, net of other factors, the difference between the pay of an occupation that was 0 percent female and the pay of one that was 100 percent female was $1.38 per hour; this pooled slope adequately represents all groups except African American women, whose slope is near 0.

The sex composition of a worker's occupation was relevant to gender-based, not race-based, pay gaps, because the three ethnic groups of men were all, on average, in occupations that were 26 to 29 percent female; for three groups of women, the average was 65 to 67 percent female. Given the large differences by sex and the negative returns to being in an occupation with more females, this factor explains 19 percent of the male-female gap for whites and 26 percent for Latinos and Latinas. Its explanatory power is less clear for African Americans, since it explains 53 percent of the wage gap if we used the pooled negative return that applies to black men but none if we use the black women's slope of near 0.

Occupations involving nurturance paid $.74 per hour less, and this pooled slope is an adequate fit for all six groups (table 4.3). Women of all groups were much more likely than men of any group to be in nurturant occupations: 8 to 9 percent of each of the three male groups held such jobs whereas 25 percent of black women, 31 percent of Latinas, and 32 percent of white women did (table 4.1). Given the tiny within-sex ethnic differences in placement in nurturant jobs, this factor explains none of the ethnicity-based pay gaps (table 4.6); it is a gender story. Differences in men's and women's employment in nurturant jobs explain 13 percent of the sex-based gap in pay for African Americans, 7 percent among Latinos and Latinas, and 6 percent among whites.

Part-time Status We were surprised not to find that working part-time negatively affected hourly wage. Instead, part-time status had significant positive effects for all groups (the pooled slope adequately describes all groups except male Latinos, for whom the positive return was especially large; see table 4.3). However, this is one case in which analyses using the natural log of earnings as the dependent variable did not show similar results; effects were not significant for most of the groups. (Thus we put little stock in our decomposition findings for the part-time factor.) We expected to find significant negative effects, which neither the logged or non-logged analysis show. However, to put the lack of negative effects of working part-time in context, remember that for most groups past part-time experience had negative effects on pay and that, except for white women, past part-time seniority had effects that were not significant (table 4.2). Thus, while working part-time may not have hurt an individual's current wage, it did hurt wage growth over time for most groups.

Unionization, Firm Size, and Industry   Working in a job that had a union had large, significant positive effects on the wages of all groups of men, for whom a pooled slope of $1.89 fit, but had drastically smaller positive returns for white women and small negative slopes for women of color. This finding suggests that, if women earned more when they were in unions, it was because the jobs had characteristics that generally led to better pay even without unions. Being in a union never explains even 5 percent of any gap (tables 4.6 and 4.7). Part of the reason is that people of color were more, not less, likely to be unionized than whites were, probably because whites were less often in blue-collar jobs; thus among men unionization contributed negatively to white-minority pay gaps.

The size of the work establishment had significant positive effects on wages; one pooled slope adequately represents the returns for all six groups. Black women worked in the largest establishments, followed by black men. The values for other groups were quite close to each other. But this variable contributes nothing (or contributed negatively) to pay gaps between groups because it had positive returns for all. The lower-earning groups, however, consistently worked in larger establishments, so their placement in larger firms made the gap slightly smaller than it otherwise would have been (tables 4.6 and 4.7).

The coefficients on the nineteen industry dummies are not reported in table 4.3, although the variables were included. The decompositions in tables 4.6 to 4.8 show a sum of the components for all the dummies for industry. Industry made a sizable contribution to male-female gaps in pay, explaining 20 percent among whites, 42 percent among African Americans, and 24 percent among Latinos and Latinas. Two factors in the sex-based gaps were the high pay in the construction industry, which employs many more men than women, and women's tendency to work in service industries.[18] Industry contributes little, if anything, to the gap between the wages of blacks and whites but contributes a modest 5 percent and 6 percent, respectively, to the gap between Latinos and white males and Latinos and white females.

CONCLUSION

Here we review our findings, focusing on the summary in table 4.8, with an eye to implications for how ethnicity and gender intersect—whether the "ethnicity story" varies by gender and whether the "gender story" varies by ethnicity. We then discuss the implications of our findings for public policy.

Cognitive Skills, Education, Experience, and Seniority

Differences in cognitive skills and years of education are important in explaining pay gaps between ethnic groups but irrelevant to gaps between men's and women's pay. This aspect of the ethnicity story is extremely important for both sexes but explains a higher portion of ethnic inequality in pay for women than for men.

Differences in experience and seniority, taken together, explain some of the ethnicity-based pay gaps among men—14 to 18 percent for black-white gaps and 13 percent for gaps between Latinos and whites (table 4.8), but their role among women is unclear (contributions were positive or negative depending on whose slopes we used).

As for the role of seniority and experience in male-female gaps, they are most important among whites (explaining 30 to 24 percent) and are also important among Latinos and Latinas (explaining 24 percent), but whether they have any role among African Americans is unclear (1 to 14 percent). In these young cohorts, the estimates are all at or lower than the lower-bound estimates from earlier studies. Most important for intersectionality is that this "generic" account of gender-based differences does not well describe the situation of African Americans, in part as a result of the unusually high level of seniority among black women. Of the six groups, black women are the most likely to be single parents (Moore 1995). Their high rate of single parenthood is explained, in part, by their unique social location: the group of men who are their probable marriage partners have the lowest employment and wage rates, and many are simply not present in the community because of death by homicide or because of imprisonment. We suspect that black women's high rate of single parenthood partly explains the otherwise anomalous finding of their low experience but high seniority: Being a single parent means that, for employment to "pay," a job must offer a combination of pay and health benefits that, minus the costs of travel to work and child care, is better than that offered by welfare (which ofers little money but provides Medicaid). The fact that the employment available to black women often does not pay well, offer health insurance, or neither may lead to long periods of nonemployment. Yet black women's status as the sole support of children may explain why black women often stay with one firm when they find a viable job, gaining relatively high full-time seniority. Thus the perspective of intersectionality is important for understanding why neither an ethnicity story about experience and seniority taken from analyses of black and white males nor a gender story drawn from analyses of white males and females explains the situation of black women well.

The direct effects of socioeconomic background are important for ethnicity, not gender. They are much more important for the gaps between Latinos and Latinas and whites than for the gaps between blacks' and whites because Latinos and Latinas' parents have the lowest level of education—in part because some of the parents are immigrants from nations with less universal primary and secondary education. We consider only direct effects here, excluding the indirect effects of ethnic differences in socioeconomic background that operate by affecting the next generation's education and cognitive skill.

Job Types

How much of the pay gaps among members of the six groups is explained by differences among the types of jobs in which they worked? Our decomposition with job variables answers this question but remains silent on the extent to which discrimination explained placement in different jobs.

We find that large shares of pay gaps between ethnic groups, but none of the gaps between men and women, come from the extent to which group members' jobs demanded higher levels of cognitive skills. Some of this placement is explained by the lower cognitive skills and education levels of blacks and Latinos and Latinas. In every ethnic group, women were in jobs requiring more cognitive skill than the jobs held by men did, so this factor is irrelevant to gender gaps. Here the gender story (of the irrelevance of cognitive skill required) holds for all ethnic groups, and the ethnic story of the concentration of blacks and Latinos in jobs with lower cognitive demands holds for both sexes.

The gender-related dimensions of occupations that we examined were their sex composition and their requirement of nurturant social skill. Both the percentage of females in a job and its requirement of nurturant social skill depressed wages. Women of all ethnic groups were more likely than men to be in female-dominated occupations and in those requiring nurturant social skill. These two gender-related factors, taken together, explain some of the sex-based gap in pay among African Americans (66 to 13 percent), whites (25 percent), and Latinos and Latinas (33 percent).

Placement in firms of different sizes and unionized jobs are not important for any of the pay gaps. Unionization had no role in group differences, in part because blacks and Latinos were more unionized than whites were, and women received no returns to unionization. Working in a larger firm did help earnings but explains nothing of group differences in pay because lower-paid groups worked in larger firms. The industry people worked in contributed little to ethnicity-based gaps but substantially to sex-based gaps, with the effects especially large for African Americans (42 percent, compared with 20 percent for whites and 24 percent for Latinos and Latinas).

Implications for Public Policy

What are the implications of our analysis for policy? First, we offer two caveats. Our analysis was limited to a relatively young cohort; different factors may affect pay gaps among older cohorts. However, if this is true and any changes are cohort (rather than life-cycle) effects, then our analysis is instructive for policies that will help reduce gaps in the future. Second, our analysis included only employed persons; we cannot infer from our analysis whether the same policies that would close pay gaps between ethnic groups and between men and women would also help reduce joblessness in the ethnicity-gender groups in which it is disproportionate.

One major policy implication of our findings is that any steps that would reduce gaps in education and cognitive skills between ethnic groups would greatly reduce pay gaps. Latinos and Latinas have the lowest levels of schooling. While blacks have less education than whites do, the differences are not large and have narrowed dramatically over time. These data show a gap of less than a year between employed black and white men and of only one-third of a year between black and white women. By contrast, Jaynes and Williams (1989, 335) show a four- to five-year gap between the education levels of blacks and whites of both sexes in 1950. Thus a more alarming issue is the large gap between the cognitive skills of blacks and those of whites. The fact that gaps in test scores have narrowed in recent decades (Jaynes and Williams 1989, 349), but much less dramatically than the education gap, suggests a serious problem with the quality of education blacks are receiving in or out of school. We did not analyze the causes of ethnic differences in education or cognitive skills, but we draw some policy implications from other research. Schools are not doing what is needed to bring black and Latino and Latina students, particularly blacks, up to national norms on cognitive skills. Nonetheless, Entwisle and Alexander (1992) show that black and white grade-school children in even the poorest inner-city Baltimore neighborhoods improve their test scores during the school year, suggesting that schools contribute to the learning of even the most disadvantaged students. But they also show that middle-class children continue to move ahead during the summer, while poor children, black and white, fall back in scores, not just relatively but absolutely. Thus home and neighborhood environments contribute to how much children learn, and the kinds of environments poor children face are harmful to the types of learning relevant to test scores.

This conclusion is consistent with Corcoran's (1995) review of research showing the deleterious effects of growing up in poverty on children's learning and the disproportionate number of children of color that grow up in poverty. Thus income support for the poor is an investment in human capital, despite the recent determination of both major U.S. political parties to reduce such support. If neighborhood effects are also important, then residential segregation (Massey and Denton 1993) probably contributes to perpetuating the gap between blacks and whites—and the lesser segregation of Latinos and Latinas may be one reason the gap between their test scores and those of whites is smaller. Policies that attack residential segregation might reduce the skills gap, and anything done in schools to increase the test scores of students of color would reduce pay gaps between ethnic groups. A number of school enrichment programs have been found to benefit children starting out behind in cognitive skills (Farkas 1996). The returns to cognitive skills make policies aimed at reducing poverty and segregation and at improving education critical for communities of color, particularly for African Americans.

Would it benefit blacks and Latinos and Latinas if the criteria for pay in labor markets were changed to deemphasize education and cognitive skills? It is hard to say. The legal doctrine of "disparate impact," articulated in the 1971 U.S. Supreme Court case of *Griggs* v. *Duke Power* (Burstein and Pitchford 1990; England 1992, 230–32; Dobbin et al. 1993), provides a way to legally challenge hiring criteria as discriminatory even when they are applied uniformly to groups. After a Supreme Court decision that seemed to reverse the doctrine, Congress restored it with the Civil Rights Restoration Act of 1990. The disparate impact doctrine says that a screening device (such as a test) that disproportionately disqualifies members of any group protected by Title VII of the Civil Rights Act of 1964 is discriminatory unless the employer can show that the selection device is relevant to the job. Court challenges to the use of tests can be effective if a test is irrelevant to performance in the job for which it is given. However, because industrial psychologists have shown general tests of cognitive skills to be decent predictors of performance in many kinds of jobs, courts will generally allow employers to use tests even when they have a disparate impact if the test's predictive value has been documented in a validation study.[19] Even when court challenges to tests can be successful, whether eliminating tests helps people of color depends upon the selection criteria that replace them. For example, using education as a criterion may help blacks substantially but hurt Latinos and Latinas; using arrest records may particularly hurt black males; for blacks, increasing the role of informal networks may be as bad as or worse than giving tests, given blacks' high degree of residential segregation.

A good share of the return to AFQT score may not have arisen from employers' using formal tests in hiring, since the studies we reviewed showed no more than half of even large firms using them. We suspect that some of the return to cognitive skill came from interviewers' guessing about interviewees' cognitive skills and from cognitive skills affecting job performance, real and perceived, and thus affecting raises and promotions. This conclusion highlights again the importance to communities of color of formulating policies that decrease ethnic differences in cognitive skills, not just in years of education.

We also advocate vigilant enforcement of antidiscrimination legislation and affirmative action regarding sex, race, and ethnicity. The large shares of ethnicity-based gaps explained by variables tapping characteristics often treated as qualifications (education, test scores, experience, and seniority) in our analysis may be the cumulative effects of years of such legislation. And relatively small portions of the within-ethnic-group, male-female gaps, and only moderate portions of the gaps between women of color and white men, were explained by our nonjob variables tapping qualifications.[20] If the enforcement of equal opportunity laws is reduced, overt discrimination might well increase.

We also would welcome public policies directed at reducing the pay gaps between the best- and worst-paying jobs, regardless of who is holding them and whether or not qualifications explain who holds those jobs. The overall level of pay inequality in the United States has increased dramatically since 1980. Thus the slightly smaller gap between the cognitive skills of people of color and those of whites in the mid-1990s may explain more dollars of earning difference than a larger gap in skills did two decades before because returns to cognitive skills have risen (Murnane, Willett, and Levy 1995). We support political attempts to challenge the overall level of income inequality—whether through the wage system, the Earned Income Tax Credit, more progressive tax rates, or the meeting of some basic needs, such as child care and health care, publicly through taxation. Although these measures may not change the percentage of ethnicity- or gender-based gaps explained by individual characteristics, they will change the dollar amounts entailed in such gaps, helping both current adult and future generations of blacks and Latinos and Latinas.

Desegregating occupations and industries by sex, whether through the education of young women about the wage penalties associated with traditional choices, affirmative action, or other enforcement of antidiscrimination legislation, would help narrow the gender gap in pay. While the relative importance of these factors to the sex-based gap in pay was greater for African Americans than for other groups, the factors were important in each ethnic group's sex-based gap.

Gaps between the pay of men and women would also be reduced by comparable worth policies. The gender gap does not come from women's having less education or cognitive skill than men do or from women of any ethnic group's being concentrated in jobs requiring less cognitive skill than men's jobs do. The gap is the result of the lower pay of female-dominated jobs, nurturant jobs, or the industries in which most women are employed. Comparable worth policies could tackle differences caused by the devaluation of female and nurturant jobs within organizations; such policies would not reduce between-industry differences in pay since such policies would apply to a single employer's decisions. Current law does not require the use of comparable worth principles in setting between-job pay differences, however (England 1992).

Public provision of child care might well encourage women's employment and thus their experience and thereby decrease sex-based gaps in pay, especially among whites and Latinas. Any measures that promote the consideration of child care as equally the responsibility of men and women, such as a public persuasion campaign like that against smoking or drug use, might be effective. For many women rearing children alone, universal health care would make employment a more viable alternative to welfare; currently children often lose medical coverage when their mother gets a job since many of the jobs available to poor women do not include such coverage.

In sum, our findings show that the factors important in ethnicity-based pay gaps are not the same as those important in sex-based gaps. Related issues of cognitive skills, education, and access to jobs with high cognitive demands are important to ethnicity- and race-based gaps in pay. Gender gaps are determined more by experience and seniority (except among blacks) and by the segregation of occupations and industries by sex. At this broad level, the racial or ethnic story holds for both sexes, and the segregation part of the gender story holds for all three races and ethnic groups, but the importance of experience and seniority to gender gaps does not hold for blacks. Moreover, men and women differ in the proportion of ethnicity-based gaps explained by education and AFQT score (more is explained for women), and ethnic groups differ in the amount of male-female gaps in pay that are explained by occupational and industrial segregation by sex, with these factors especially important for African Americans.

We thank Jerry Jacobs and participants at the Russell Sage Foundation conference on this topic in April 1996 for useful comments. We thank Barry Hirsch for the program used to convert 1980 census occupational codes to 1990 codes.

NOTES

1. While whites, African Americans, Latinos, and Latinas span what are usually called race and ethnicity, for brevity we refer to them as "ethnic groups."

2. If we were confident that we could measure the amount of pay gaps between ethnic groups and between the sexes that arises from current discrimination by employers, then one obvious question for an intersectionality analysis would be whether the amount of pay (in dollars or percent) people of color lose to ethnic discrimination is equal for men and women and whether the amount women lose to sex discrimination is equal for all ethnic groups. If ethnic discrimination is equal in magnitude for men and women and sex discrimination is equal in magnitude for each ethnic group, the implication is that the discrimination experienced by women of color is simply an additive combination of ethnic and gender discrimination. If not, the implication is that ethnic and gender discrimination interact, in a statistical sense.

3. Dill, Cannon, and Vanneman (1987), using 1980 census data, show a negative relationship between the percentage of minority group members (and the percentage of women of color) in occupations and pay after controlling for the education and age of those in the occupations. Their analysis includes neither any measure of the skill or other demands of the occupations nor controls for industry. In an analysis using the NLSY, Reid (1998) examines the effects of the percentage of white females, the percentage of black females, the percentage of black males, the percentage of Latinos, and the percentage of Latinas in occupation-industry categories on individuals' wages. With controls for education, experience, industry, and job demands (taken from the *Dictionary of Occupational Titles*), she finds no effects of composition variables involving people of color. She also interacts these measures with the the percentage of blacks and the percentage of Latinos in the county to see if these effects only show up in local areas with a large percentage of people of color; there is no evidence for this. Jacobs (1995) also fails to find any net effects of the racial composition of occupations within standard metropolitan statistical areas. Tomaskovic-Devey (1993), using a North Carolina sample with the positive feature of measuring composition by sex and race at the firm-specific job level (by asking respondents the percentage of females and the percentage of blacks in their jobs), finds that most of the gross relationship between the percentage of blacks and pay disappears when job characteristics are entered. Moreover, the effect of the percentage of blacks is no longer significant in race-specific equations or when the race of the individual is controlled. If race-based differences in the wages of individuals within occupations are not controlled (either by using separate equations for each racial group or by controlling for race within a pooled equation), then significant effects of the percentage of blacks in jobs may be attributable to differences in the wages of blacks and whites within the same occupation rather than to the devaluing of wages for an entire occupation because of its association with blacks. Thus, Tomaskovic-Devey's results do not demonstrate an effect of racial composition. Two analyses from the New York State pay equity study (pertaining to public sector jobs) find no effects of the percent-

/ 175

age of minority group members (Steinberg et al. 1986; Jacobs and Steinberg 1990), although another analysis of the same data reports such an effect (Berheide, Chertos, and Steinberg 1987). Remick, Ginorio, and Britz (1987) find that the percentage of black males in an occupation has a net negative effect on wages in the Washington pay equity study. Our conclusion is that such effects will be found only in firm-specific studies or studies of local labor markets in which the measures of the racial composition of occupations are local, since only some local areas have enough blacks or Latinos that some jobs may come to be associated with a devalued group and thereby devalued. Such effects have not yet been demonstrated.

4. To avoid using excessive degrees of freedom, we did not interact the ethnicity-gender dummies with the industry dummies or the missing value indicators for parents' education and occupation.

5. In some cases, the effect for the group was not significantly different from the pooled estimate in the trimmed model, even though the earlier model with interactions (before trimming) showed it to be different from the slope for white males. In these cases, we still included the separate effect for the group.

6. Given this method of calculating whether slopes for groups differ significantly from the white male slope, a significance test for the slope for other groups when their slope differs significantly from that of white males is not easily obtained and thus is not presented. One way to get a significance test for an effect for one group is to make that group the omitted reference category of ethnicity-gender dummies; in this case the "additive" slope for variables involved in interactions (for example, the slope on education in a model including education interacted with ethnicity-gender dummies) is the effect for the reference group. However, that will not work here because trimming nonsignificant interactions means that these slopes virtually always pertain to two or more groups pooled.

7. Whenever we used variables in Z-score form (see table 4.1), we computed the means and standard deviations to create the Z scores from unweighted computation on the pooled sample of the six race-sex groups. The cases are the same ones found in the reduced-form model in table 4.2.

8. The regions are North: Maine, New Hampshire, Vermont, Massachusetts, Rhode Island, Connecticut, New York, New Jersey, Pennsylvania; North Central: Ohio, Indiana, Illinois, Michigan, Wisconsin, Minnesota, Iowa, Missouri, North Dakota, South Dakota, Nebraska, Kansas; South: Delaware, Maryland, District of Columbia, Virginia, North Carolina, South Carolina, Georgia, Florida, Kentucky, Tennessee, Alabama, Mississippi, Arkansas, Louisiana, Oklahoma, Texas; West: the remainder of the U.S. states.

9. To check whether our decision to include both part-time and full-time workers in the analysis was sound, we interacted the part-time dummy with all other variables in table 4.2, estimating separate models for the six ethnicity-gender groups. Of the seventy-two possible interaction effects, seventeen were significant, with no clear pattern by variable or group. A similar exercise for the model in table 4.3 (but omitting part-time X industry dummy interactions because empty cells made coefficients inestimable for some groups) showed

eleven significant interactions out of forty-eight possible interactions with job variables. We took the small number of interactions as evidence that the relationships were fairly consistent across full- and part-time status.

10. We omit the part of the decomposition that is due to slope and intercept differences because how much of a gap is attributed to intercept versus slopes is sensitive to the choice of metric for the variable, including fairly arbitrary choices such as which category of a series of dummies is omitted or whether a variable is converted to a Z score (Jones and Kelley 1984). However, the total contribution of differences in the intercept, all slopes, and their interaction is not affected by metric. This total is 100 percent of the gap minus the percentage explained by mean differences on all the independent variables.

11. Studies estimating the percentage of employers that use tests produce differing estimates but agree that most employers do not use tests. Neckerman and Kirschenman (1991) interviewed 185 employers in the Chicago area, with inner-city firms oversampled; about 40 percent of the employers used a skills test. Bishop (1988) reports on a 1987 survey of a probability sample of small- and medium-sized employers. Formal tests had only been used for 3 percent of the hiring decisions. Large firms undoubtedly use tests more than small firms, because their greater volume of hires would make the costs of developing or buying tests more worth paying and because they are more likely to hire personnel professionals. Dobbin et al. (1993) gathered a probability sample of large firms and report that in 1985 about 45 percent of them used tests for hiring. Holzer's (1996) sample of employers from the Multi-City Project, which implicitly weighted large firms more heavily, found that nonphysical tests were used in screening for about half of noncollege jobs.

12. Past research by Corcoran and Duncan (1979) and Wellington (1994) shows that white men receive higher returns to seniority at least in part because they are in jobs providing more formal or informal training. We have no good measure of such training in these data.

13. See Blau and Kahn (1981) for a finding of no differences between blacks and whites for men or women in quit rates and lower quit rates for blacks after an adjustment for personal and job characteristics.

14. One might be concerned that the measures of social class included were not adequate as controls. We did not add the measure of the income of the youth's family of origin in 1979 that is available on the NLSY because it has many missing values. A recent analysis by Korenman and Winship (1995) shows that incomplete measures of family background, while leading to underestimates of its effect, do not lead to overestimates of the effects of AFQT score on earnings in the NLSY. Since we included socioeconomic background simply as a control, this is reassuring.

15. We have not decomposed the nonjob variables using slopes from model 2 (if we did, the nonjob and job components could be added since the slopes on individual variables would not include indirect effects through job placement on measured variables). We believe that the effects of individual characteristics from the reduced-form model are more telling since their effects are evident through access to different jobs and through advancement within jobs together.

16. An interesting question is whether authority would have explained more of the sex- or race-based gaps if we had had more elaborate measures of authority, such as those used by Wright and Baxter (1995).

17. In separate regressions for each group, the positive returns for black and white women disappeared if wages were logged, however.

18. We suspect that employment in construction would explain less of annual pay gaps, however, since workers in the industry are often unemployed part of the year.

19. Hunter (1986) reviews many studies showing a correlation between cognitive test scores and performance in a variety of types of jobs (including managerial, clerical, service, craft, operative, and sales positions) whether the measure of job performance is relatively objective or consists of supervisors' ratings. Schmidt (1988) and Wigdor and Green (1991) review evidence that such tests predict job performance for both minorities and whites, albeit imperfectly. They also show that, while some tests show less predictive power for minorities, they do not generally underpredict the job performance of minorities relative to whites.

20. They are, however, affected by supply-side differences that we did not measure, such as sextyped job aspirations, shown by Marini and Fan (1997) to explain some but definitely not all of differences in men's and women's first job.

REFERENCES

Aman, Carolyn J. 1996. "Occupational Sex Composition and Wages: Using Panel Data to Assess Causal Order." University of Arizona. Unpublished paper.

Baca Zinn, Maxine, and Bonnie Thornton Dill. 1994. "Difference and Domination." In *Women of Color in U.S. Society.* Philadelphia: Temple University Press.

Beck, E. M., Patrick M. Horan, and Charles M. Tolbert. 1980. "Industrial Segmentation and Labor Market Discrimination." *Social Problems* 28(2): 113–30.

Bergmann, Barbara. 1974. "Occupational Segregation, Wages, and Profits When Employers Discriminate by Race or Sex." *Eastern Economic Journal* 1(2): 103–10.

———. 1986. *The Economic Emergence of Women.* New York: Basic Books.

Berheide, Catherine White, Cynthia H. Chertos, and Ronnie Steinberg. 1987. "Pay Equity for Blacks and Hispanics in New York State Employment." In *Pay Equity: An Issue of Race, Ethnicity, and Sex.* Washington, D.C.: National Committee on Pay Equity.

Bielby, William, and James Baron. 1984. "A Woman's Place Is with Other Women: Sex Segregation within Organizations." In *Sex Segregation in the Workplace: Trends, Explanations, Remedies,* edited by Barbara F. Reskin. Washington, D.C.: National Academy Press.

Bishop, John. 1988. "Employment Testing and Incentives to Learn." *Journal of Vocational Behavior* 33(3): 404–23.

Blau, Francine D., and Lawrence M. Kahn. 1981. "Race and Sex Differences in Quits by Young Workers." *Industrial and Labor Relations Review* 34(4): 563–77.

Browne, Irene. 1997. "Explaining the Black-White Gap in Labor Force Participation among Women Heading Households." *American Sociological Review* 62(2): 236–52.

Burstein, Paul, and Susan Pitchford. 1990. "Social-Scientific and Legal Challenges to Education and Test Requirements in Employment." *Social Problems* 37(2): 243–57.

Cancio, A. Silvia, T. David Evans, and David J. Maume, Jr. 1997. "The Declining Significance of Race Reconsidered: Racial Differences in Early Career Wages." *American Sociological Review* 61(4): 541–56.

Christopher, Karen. 1996. "Explaining the Recent Employment Gap Between Black and White Women." *Sociological Focus* 29(3): 263–80.

Collins, Patricia Hill. 1990. *Black Feminist Thought: Knowledge, Consciousness, and the Politics of Empowerment.* Boston: Unwin Hyman.

Corcoran, Mary. 1995. "Rags to Rags: Poverty and Mobility in the United States." *Annual Review of Sociology* 21: 237–67.

Corcoran, Mary, and Greg J. Duncan. 1979. "Work Experience, Job Segregation, and Wages." In *Sex Segregation in the Workplace: Trends, Explanations, Remedies,* edited by Barbara F. Reskin. Washington, D.C.: National Academy Press.

Cotter, David A., Joann M. DeFiore, Joan M. Hermsen, Brenda Marsteller Kowalewski, and Reeve Vanneman. 1995. "Occupational Gender Desegregation in the 1980s." *Work and Occupations* 22(1): 3–21.

Coverdill, James E. 1988. "The Dual Economy and Sex Differences in Earnings." *Social Forces* 66(4): 970–93.

Crenshaw, Kimberle. 1990. "A Black Feminist Critique of Antidiscrimination Law and Politics." In *The Politics of Law: A Progressive Critique* (2d ed.), edited by David Kairys. New York: Pantheon Books.

Dill, Bonnie T., Lynn W. Cannon, and Reeve Vanneman. 1987. "Race and Gender in Occupational Segregation." In *Pay Equity: An Issue of Race, Ethnicity, and Sex.* Washington, D.C.: National Committee on Pay Equity.

Dobbin, Frank, John R. Sutton, John W. Meyer, and W. Richard Scott. 1993. "Equal Opportunity Law and the Construction of Internal Labor Markets." *American Journal of Sociology* 99: 396–427.

England, Paula. 1992. *Comparable Worth: Theories and Evidence.* New York: Aldine de Gruyter.

England, Paula, George Farkas, Barbara S. Kilbourne, and Thomas Dou. 1988. "Explaining Occupational Sex Segregation and Wages: Findings from a Model with Fixed Effects." *American Sociological Review* 53(4): 544–58.

England, Paula, Melissa S. Herbert, Barbara Stanek Kilbourne, Lori L. Reid, and Lori M. Megdal. 1994. "The Gendered Valuation of Occupations and Skills: Earnings in 1980 Census Occupations." *Social Forces* 73(1): 65–99.

Entwisle, Doris R., and Karl L. Alexander. 1992. "Summer Setback: Race, Poverty, School Composition, and Mathematics Achievement in the First Two Years of School." *American Sociological Review* 57(1): 72–84.

Farkas, George. 1996. *Human Capital or Cultural Capital? Ethnicity and Poverty Groups in an Urban School District.* New York: Aldine de Gruyter.

Farkas, George, Paula England, and Margaret Barton. 1994. "Structural Effects on Wages: Sociological and Economic Views." In *Industries, Firms, and Jobs* (expanded ed.), edited by George Farkas and Paula England. New York: Aldine de Gruyter.

Farkas, George, Paula England, Keven Vicknair, and Barbara S. Kilbourne. 1997. "Cognitive Skill, Skill Demands of Jobs, and Earnings Among Young European-American, African American, and Mexican-American Workers." *Social Forces* 75(3): 913–40.

Fields, Judith, and Edward Wolff. 1995. "Interindustry Wage Differentials and the Gender Wage Gap." *Industrial and Labor Relations Review* 49(1): 105–20.

Filer, Randall. 1989. "Occupational Segregation, Compensating Differentials, and Comparable Worth." In *Pay Equity: Empirical Inquiries*, edited by Robert T. Michael, Heidi I. Hartmann, and Brigid O'Farrell. Washington, D.C.: National Academy Press.

Hall, Jacquelyn Dowd. 1995. "'The Mind That Bums in Each Body': Women, Rape, and Racial Violence," In *Race, Class, and Gender*, edited by Margaret L. Andersen and Patricia Hill Collins. Belmont, Calif.: Wadsworth.

Hernnstein, Richard, and Charles Murray. 1994. *The Bell Curve*. New York: Free Press.

Hodson, Randy, and Paula England. 1986. "Industrial Structure and Sex Differences in Earnings," *Industrial Relations* 25(1): 16–32.

Holzer, Harry. 1996. *What Employers Want: Job Prospects for Less-Educated Workers*. New York: Russell Sage Foundation.

hooks, bell. 1984. *Feminist Theory: From Margin to Center*. Boston: South End Press.

Hunter, John. 1986. "Cognitive Ability, Cognitive Aptitudes, Job Knowledge and Job Performance." *Journal of Vocational Behavior* 29(3): 340–62.

Jacobs, Jerry A. 1995. "Why Gender Composition But Not Racial Composition Reduces Occupational Earnings: An Analysis of Local Labor Markets." Paper presented at the annual meeting of the Society for the Advancement of Socioeconomics. Washington, D.C. (1995).

Jacobs, Jerry A., and Ronnie J. Steinberg. 1990. "Compensating Differentials and the Male-Female Wage Gap: Evidence from the New York State Comparable Worth Study." *Social Forces* 69(2): 439–68.

Jaynes, Gerald David, and Robin M. Williams, Jr. 1989. *A Common Destiny: Blacks and American Society*. Washington, D.C.: National Academy Press.

Jones, F. L., and Jonathan Kelley. 1984. "Decomposing Differences Between Groups: A Cautionary Note on Measuring Discrimination." *Sociological Methods and Research* 12(3): 323–43.

Katz, Lawrence. 1986. "Efficiency Wage Theories: A Partial Evaluation." In *NBER Macroeconomic Annual 1986*, edited by Stanley Fischer. Cambridge, Mass.: National Bureau of Economic Research.

Kilbourne, Barbara, Paula England, and Kurt Beron. 1994. "Effects of Individual and Occupational Characteristics on Earnings: Intersections of Race and Gender." *Social Forces* 72(4): 1149–76.

Kilbourne, Barbara, Paula England, George Farkas, Kurt Beron, and Dorothea Weir. 1994. "Returns to Skill, Compensating Differentials, and Gender Bias: Effects of Occupational Characteristics on the Wages of White Women and Men." *American Journal of Sociology* 100(3): 689–719.

Korenman, Sanders, and Christopher Winship. 1995. "A Reanalysis of the Bell Curve." Working Paper 5320. Cambridge, Mass.: National Bureau of Economic Research.

Macpherson, David, and Barry T. Hirsch. 1995. "Wages and Gender Composition: Why Do Women's Jobs Pay Less?" *Journal of Labor Economics* 13(3): 426–71.

Marini, Margaret M., and Pi-Ling Fan. 1997. "The Gender Gap in Earnings at Career Entry." *American Sociological Review*.

Massey, Douglas S., and Nancy A. Denton. 1993. *American Apartheid: Segregation and the Making of the Underclass*. Cambridge, Mass.: Harvard University Press.

Maume, David. 1985. "Government Participation in the Local Economy and Race- and Sex-Based Earnings Inequality." *Social Problems* 32(3): 285–89.

Mincer, Jacob, and Solomon Polachek. 1974. "Family Investments in Human Capital: Earnings of Women." *Journal of Human Resources* 13(2, pt. 2): 118–34.

Mohanty, Chandra Talpade, Ann Russo, and Lourdes Torres, eds. 1991. *Third World Women and the Politics of Feminism.* Bloomington: Indiana University Press.

Moore, Kristin A., ed. 1995. *Report to Congress on Out-of-Wedlock Childbearing.* Hyattsville, Md.: U.S. Department of Health and Human Services.

Murnane, Richard J., John B. Willett, and Frank Levy. 1995. "The Growing Importance of Cognitive Skills in Wage Determination." *Review of Economics and Statistics* 77(Spring): 251–65.

National Opinion Research Center. 1978. *General Social Surveys, 1972–1987: Cumulative Codebook.* Chicago: National Opinion Research Center.

Neal, Derek A., and William R. Johnson. 1996. "The Role of Pre-Market Factors in Black-White Wage Differences." *Journal of Political Economy* 104(5): 869–95.

Neckerman, Kathryn M., and Joleen Kirschenman. 1991. "Hiring Strategies, Racial Bias, and Inner-City Workers." *Social Problems* 38(4): 433–47.

O'Neill, June. 1990. "The Role of Human Capital in Earnings Differences between Black and White Men." *Journal of Economic Perspectives* 4(4): 25–46.

Petersen, Trond, and Laurie A. Morgan. 1995. "Separate and Unequal: Occupation Establishment Sex Segregation and the Gender Wage Gap." *American Journal of Sociology* 101(2): 329–65.

Reid, Lori L. 1997. "Race, Gender, and the Labor Market: Black and White Women's Employment." Ph.D. diss., University of Arizona.

———. 1998. "Processes of Devaluing Women and Minorities: The Effects of Race and Sex Composition of Occupation on Wage Levels." *Work and Occupations* 25(4): 511–36.

Remick, Helen, Angela B. Ginorio, and Patricia Britz. 1987. "A Case Study in Washington State." In *Pay Equity: An Issue of Race, Ethnicity, and Sex.* Washington, D.C.: National Committee on Pay Equity.

Schmidt, Frank L. 1988. "The Problem of Group Differences in Ability Test Scores in Employment Selection." *Journal of Vocational Behavior* 33(3): 272–92.

Sorensen, Elaine. 1989. "The Wage Effects of Occupational Sex Segregation: A Review and New Findings." In *Comparable Worth: Analyses and Evidence,* edited by M. Anne Hill and Mark Killingsworth. Ithaca, N.Y.: ILR Press.

Steinberg, Ronnie J., Lois Haignere, C. Possin, C. H. Chertos, and K. Treiman. 1986. *The New York State Pay Equity Study: A Research Report.* Albany, N.Y.: SUNY Press.

Tam, Tony. 1997. "Sex Segregation and Occupational Gender Inequality in the United States: Devaluation or Specialized Training?" *American Journal of Sociology* 102(6): 1652–92.

Tomaskovic-Devey, Donald. 1993. *Gender and Racial Inequality at Work: The Sources and Consequences of Job Segregation.* Ithaca, N.Y.: ILR Press.

U.S. Department of Commerce. U.S. Bureau of the Census. 1993. "Detailed Occupation and Other Characteristics from the EEO File for the United States." *1990 Census of Population Supplementary Reports.* Washington: U.S. Government Printing Office.

Wellington, Allison. 1994. "The Male/Female Wage Gap among Whites: 1976 and 1985." *American Sociological Review* 59(6): 839–48.

Wigdor, Alexandra, and Bert F. Green, Jr., eds. 1991. *Performance Assessment in the Workplace*. Vol. 1. Washington, D.C.: National Academy Press.

Winship, Christopher, and Larry Radbill. 1997. "Sampling Weights and Regression Analysis." Sociological Methods and Research 23(2): 230–57.

Wright, Erik Olin, and Janeen Baxter. 1995. "The Gender Gap in Workplace Authority: A Cross National Study." *American Sociological Review* 60(3): 407–35.

Chapter 5

Occupational Segregation by Race and Ethnicity Among Women Workers

Barbara F. Reskin

Segregation is a social mechanism that preserves inequality across groups (van den Berghe 1960; Reskin 1988; Massey and Denton 1993). Occupational segregation by sex, for example, contributes to the pay gap between the sexes and to sex-based differences in job prestige, promotion opportunities, working conditions, and other work rewards (England 1992; Reskin 1994). There is every reason to suspect that occupational segregation based on race and ethnicity plays a similar role in generating racial and ethnic disparities in workplace rewards. However, in contrast to occupational segregation by sex, little is known about occupational segregation based on race and ethnicity. Without knowledge of the extent of race- and ethnicity-based segregation, researchers can neither ascertain its role in race- and ethnicity-based economic inequality nor formulate effective ways to reduce that inequality.

Whether workers are white or black affects a variety of labor market outcomes, including labor force participation, occupation, earnings, job authority, chances of promotion, and risk of unemployment (Kluegel 1978; Becker 1980; Beller 1984; Farley 1984; Albelda 1986; Braddock and McPartlin 1987; Zalokar 1990; Kirschenman and Neckerman 1991; Lichter and Landry 1991; King 1992; McGuire and Reskin 1993; Tomaskovic-Devey 1993; Butler 1996; Browne 1997). Unfortunately, knowledge of the effects of race on labor market outcomes is largely limited to blacks and whites. In ignoring the occupational outcomes of Hispanics, Asians, and Native Americans, researchers implicitly assume that either (1) these groups' labor market experiences resemble those of blacks or those of whites or (2) these groups' labor market experiences may differ from those of blacks and whites, but they are not important enough to merit study. In the absence of research that compares the labor market outcomes of Hispanics, Native Americans, and Asians to those of blacks and non-Hispanic whites, the first assumption must be suspect. The second assumption is, of course, unwarranted. Although there were 13.5 million black workers in the U.S. labor force in 1990, there were also 9.6 million Hispanic, 3.2 million Asian, and 0.8 million Native American workers (U.S. Department of Commerce 1994; Harrison and Bennett 1995).

Ethnicity is an important basis of workplace inequality. Workers' ethnicity affects their labor force participation, unemployment rates, and earnings (Almquist 1987; Glenn and Tolbert 1987; Tienda and Lii 1987; Glass, Tienda, and Smith 1988; Smith and Tienda 1988; Lieberson and Waters 1990; Amott and Matthaei 1991; Harrison and Bennett 1995). However, little is known about the effect of workers' ethnic ancestry on their occupations (for exceptions, see Lieberson and Waters 1990, 129–34; and Reskin and Cassirer 1997).[1] Because occupations serve as a distributive mechanism for economic and social rewards, assessing occupational segregation by race and ethnic groups is essential for understanding racial and ethnic inequality in labor markets. This chapter enhances the understanding of occupational segregation in three ways. First, it shows that women workers are occupationally segregated based on their ethnicity as well as their race. While a few groups are almost perfectly integrated, others are almost as segregated as all women are from all men. Second, it shows that the structure of ethnic segregation is driven by two dimensions. On the first dimension, ethnic groups are ordered according to their race; on the second dimension, they are ordered in terms of compositional characteristics that are likely proxies for their qualifications. Third, it shows that occupational segregation by ethnicity—as captured by the two dimensions mentioned above—contributes to earnings inequality across ethnic groups.

METHODS

This analysis uses data from the 1990 census 5 percent *Public Use Microdata Sample* (PUMS) that have been weighted to make them representative of the U.S. population (U.S. Department of Commerce 1992, chap. 4). Like the other contributors to this volume, I focus on women workers. I analyze occupational segregation among female workers who were at least sixteen years old and were employed during 1990. The weighted sample size is 2,647,441 female workers.

Measuring Race, Hispanic Origin, and Ethnic Ancestry

One goal of this chapter is to estimate the effects of race and ethnicity on workers' allocation to occupations, so instead of dismissing some ethnic distinctions as unlikely to affect women's occupational outcomes, I examined as many detailed ethnic groups as the data permitted. Given a 5 percent sample of the labor force, I was able to distinguish twenty-six detailed groups based on women's ethnicity, Hispanic origin, and race. Below, I use the term "race" as a shorthand for the four broad groups in the U.S. labor force: non-Hispanic whites, blacks, Asians, and persons of Latin/Hispanic origin.

I used four census variables to classify workers into twenty-six mutually exclusive groups according to their race, Hispanic origin, ethnicity, and nativity (shown in italics below and listed in table 5.1). First, I used the race variable to categorize people as black, white, *Native American, Asian Indian, Chinese, Filipina, Japanese, Korean,* and *Southeast Asian.*[2] I then used "Hispanic origin" to categorize Hispanic whites as *Mexican, Puerto Rican, Cuban, Central American,* and *"other Hispanic"* (for example, non-black Dominicans or South Americans). I used "nativity" to distinguish blacks into two groups: *African Americans* (who were born in the United States) and *black immigrants* (who were born outside of the United States, usually in the West Indies or Africa). I used "ethnic ancestry" to classify non-Hispanic whites into twelve ancestry groups: *English, French, German, Irish, Italian, Polish, other Eastern European, Scandinavian, Scotch, other European ancestry, "North American,"* and a residual category, *"other non-Hispanic whites."*[3]

To measure occupational segregation by ethnicity, I used the segregation index (also known as the index of dissimilarity; Duncan and Duncan 1955).[4] The segregation index compares two groups' distributions across a set of categories—in this case, occupations. To assess segregation among multiple groups, I computed segregation indices among all possible pairs of groups. Among twenty-six racial-ethnic groups, 325 pairs and hence 325 segregation indices are possible. I assessed segregation across detailed occupations (of which there are 501 in the civilian labor force) for the same reason I used detailed racial and ethnic categories—because aggregated categories conceal segregation (Bielby and Baron 1986; Reskin 1993, 242). However, even detailed occupational categories involve considerable aggregation. Workers who share the same detailed occupation may perform it in different establishments (for example, secretary) or do very different jobs within the same establishment (for example, in a single hotel, the night manager of the coffee bar, the manager of the laundry service, and the hotel's general manager share the occupational title "manager, food serving and lodging establishments"), although their race or ethnicity may segregate them into different jobs. For this reason, the occupational segregation indices in this chapter underestimate the actual extent of ethnicity- and race-based segregation at work in the United States.

RESULTS

Occupational Segregation by Race and Ethnicity

The segregation indices for the twenty-six groups confirm the importance of women's ethnicity for their occupational outcomes. The average seg-

Table 5.1 / Size and Compositional Characteristics of Female Race-Ethnic Groups, 1990

Group	Mean Segregation Index with All Groups	Percent Post-1980 Immigrants	Percent Fluent	Percent Who Did Not Complete High School	Percent with B.A. Degree
British	.213	.6	99.5	9.2	29.7
German	.187	.3	99.2	10.3	22.3
Irish	.191	.3	99.5	11.7	22.9
Scottish	.226	.4	99.5	7.6	31.6
Italian	.213	.3	97.6	11.4	23.0
Polish	.195	2.0	96.7	10.3	25.3
Scandinavian	.210	.4	99.3	7.5	28.0
French	.191	.6	98.7	12.6	18.9
E. European	.241	1.8	96.7	7.4	37.4
Other European	.187	1.5	96.2	13.0	24.9
North American	.205	.3	99.3	20.9	12.6
Other white	.188	1.6	97.8	17.4	16.5
Native American	.219	.7	97.8	21.3	9.4
Mexican	.274	13.9	67.4	40.1	7.4
Central American	.390	55.8	35.3	51.2	7.9
Puerto Rican	.239	12.7	73.0	27.1	13.9
Cuban	.245	16.0	57.7	26.8	19.9
Other Hispanic	.225	22.9	66.2	26.0	15.3
African American	.275	0.0	99.0	20.5	15.1
Hispanic black	.288	25.6	65.9	33.9	12.9
Other black	.323	42.6	87.7	23.0	17.9
Chinese	.318	30.4	51.3	20.4	40.2
Filipina	.303	38.2	77.7	12.0	44.5
Japanese	.251	6.4	84.7	7.8	33.4
Asian Indian	.321	47.2	75.8	13.6	50.2
Korean	.342	38.4	45.9	20.0	25.7
S.E. Asian	.387	47.7	38.1	36.8	14.5

Source: Computed for women in the civilian labor force in PUMS 5–percent sample (weighted N = 2,647,441); U.S. Department of Commerce (1992).

Percent Managerial Occupations	Percent Service Occupation	Percent Self-Employed	Percent Prime Workers	Median Earnings ($1000s)	Size (1000s)
13.6	11.5	8.1	81.1	15.0	258
11.8	14.3	6.8	79.8	13.5	515
12.6	13.7	6.2	81.8	14.5	268
13.7	10.8	8.0	82.0	15.0	83
13.4	12.8	5.6	80.4	15.2	126
12.5	12.6	5.6	80.0	15.0	76
12.9	13.4	8.0	80.2	14.0	82
11.9	15.5	7.2	79.5	13.5	73
14.4	10.0	8.4	80.1	17.0	88
12.3	14.2	7.8	78.2	14.0	85
8.9	17.0	6.3	78.8	12.0	135
10.3	16.3	6.3	77.3	12.0	246
9.6	19.5	6.0	77.5	11.0	52
6.7	19.7	4.2	60.1	10.0	101
4.8	26.4	6.3	28.1	9.1	13
9.0	15.2	2.9	66.1	13.5	19
11.0	11.2	6.5	57.6	14.0	11
9.2	18.7	6.3	55.5	12.0	30
8.1	20.9	2.4	85.8	13.0	282
7.2	23.0	3.1	55.3	12.0	5
8.1	27.9	3.1	51.4	15.6	19
15.2	12.4	8.4	42.5	15.0	18
9.8	15.5	3.4	51.7	17.0	20
14.0	12.7	6.9	77.0	18.0	11
10.1	10.8	7.7	40.1	14.2	7
9.7	19.8	17.8	35.9	12.5	8
6.4	19.2	7.4	34.2	12.2	8

Table 5.2 / Indices of Occupational Segregation for Women, by Race and Ethnicity, Selected Pairs, 1990

Race and Ethnicity	Mean	Range	Number of Pairs
All pairs	24.6	3.5–48.6	325
Intraracial cross-ethnic pairs	15.2	3.5–40.0	92
Asian[a]	32.6	23.5–40.0	15
Hispanic[b]	23.1	14.6–36.8	10
European[c]	10.0	3.5–22.4	66
Black[d]	20.4	—	1
Interracial cross-ethnic pairs	29.1	8.1–48.6	220
Black and Hispanic	26.4	17.0–37.5	10
Asian and Hispanic	33.1	22.1–45.7	30
European and Hispanic	26.8	14.8–48.6	60
Black and Asian	35.1	24.3–43.9	12
European and Asian	31.0	16.6–46.8	72
Black and European	29.4	20.9–35.3	24
European and Native American	18.5	8.1–26.5	12

Source: U.S. Department of Commerce (1992).
Notes: Data are for women who were at least sixteen years old and were employed during 1990. Weighted sample size is 2,647,441.
[a]Women of Chinese, Filipino, Japanese, Korean, Southeast Asian, and Asian Indian descent.
[b]Women of Central American, Cuban, Mexican, Puerto Rican, or other Hispanic (including Spanish and South American) descent.
[c]Women of British, Eastern European, French, German, Irish, Italian, Polish, Scandinavian, or Scotch descent as well as non-Hispanic, nonblack North Americans and women who described their race as white or Anglo but did not report ethnic ancestry.
[d]African American women and black female immigrants to the United States from any country.

regation index for all 325 possible pairs is 24.6 (see table 5.2), and the indices for most of the pairs fall between 20.0 and 40.0 (for summaries, see table 5.2; detailed results not shown tabularly). Thus, to assess and explain occupational segregation accurately, researchers must take ethnicity into account.

Although ethnicity contributed to occupational segregation among women, the extent to which various pairs of ethnic groups were segregated from each other varied widely in 1990. The indices of ethnic segregation ranged from a low of 3.5 for British and Scottish women, indicating that they were almost identically distributed across occupations, to 48.6 for Central American and Eastern European women, indicating that almost half of either all Central American or all Eastern European women would have had to change to an occupation in which they were underrepresented for the groups to be identically distributed across detailed occupations. These two groups of women were only 4.5 points less segregated in 1990 than all women were from all men ($d = 53$; Reskin and Cassirer 1997).

Ethnic segregation within and across racial categories contributed to the variability in the women's indices of occupational segregation by ethnicity. A comparison of the minimum and maximum segregation indices for pairs of ethnic groups that share a common race (table 5.2, first panel) with those for pairs from different racial groups (table 5.2, second panel) shows that, of the 92 intraracial pairs, only one had a segregation index as high as 40 (Japanese and Southeast Asian women), while of the 228 interracial pairs, 25 had indices above 40. At the other extreme, three-fourths of the intraracial pairs had ethnic segregation indices below 20, whereas only 18 of the interracial pairs had indices below 20. Three phenomena account for most of these 18 relatively integrated cross-race pairs: (1) Japanese women and several European-ancestry ethnic groups were quite integrated; (2) Cuban women and a few non-Hispanic European-ancestry groups were quite integrated; and (3) African American women were as integrated with both Mexican women and Puerto Rican women as the latter two groups were with each other ($ds = 17, 19,$ and 18; results not shown tabularly). African American women's modest levels of segregation with Puerto Rican and Mexican women stem partly from regional specialization, in which African American, Mexican, and Puerto Rican women pursued the same occupations in different labor markets. Supplementary analyses for the three metropolitan areas with the largest civilian labor force in 1990 revealed that African American and Puerto Rican women were almost as integrated in New York ($d = 21.7$) as they were in the United States as a whole ($d = 17.0$), but they were considerably more segregated in Los Angeles ($d = 35.3$) and Chicago ($d = 30.3$). And in contrast to African American and Mexican women's segregation index of 19.0 in data for the United States, their index was 38.0 in Chicago, 35.3 in Los Angeles, and 53.0 in New York.[5]

In general, ethnic groups that belong to different races were more segregated than ethnic groups in the same racial category. The mean indices for same-race ethnic groups ranged from 10.0 to 32.6 (table 5.2, top panel), compared with means ranging from 26.4 to 35.1 for cross-race pairs (table 5.2, bottom panel. However, the extent to which race attenuated ethnic segregation differed across the four racial categories. Rearranging the mean segregation indices for groups belonging to the same and different racial categories so that the mean indices for same-race ethnic groups are arrayed on the main diagonal highlights the dependence of the effect of ethnicity on the racial categories of each pair of ethnic groups (see table 5.3). With one exception, the values of the mean indices of segregation for same-race ethnic groups are smaller than the off-diagonal means that summarize segregation between interracial ethnic groups. For example, the sixty-six pairs that are formed by the twelve non-Hispanic, white ethnic groups had a mean index of just 10.0, compared with 26.8 between white non-Hispanic and white Hispanic ethnic groups, 29.4 between white non-Hispanic and black ethnic groups, and 31.0 between white non-Hispanic and Asian eth-

Table 5.3 / Mean Indices of Women's Occupational Segregation, by Race and Ethnicity, 1990

Race or Ethnicity	European[a]	Hispanic[b]	Black[c]	Asian[d]
European	10.0	26.8	29.4	31.0
Hispanic	—	23.1	26.4	33.1
Black	—	—	20.4	35.1
Asian	—	—	—	32.6

Source: U.S. Department of Commerce (1992).
Notes: Data are for women who were at least sixteen years old and were employed during 1990. Weighted sample size is 2,647,441.
[a]Women of British, Eastern European, French, German, Irish, Italian, Polish, Scandinavian, or Scotch descent as well as non-Hispanic, nonblack North Americans and women who described their race as white or Anglo but did not report ethnic ancestry.
[b]Women of Central American, Cuban, Mexican, Puerto Rican, or other Hispanic (including Spanish and South American) descent.
[c]African American women and black female immigrants to the United States from any country.
[d]Women of Chinese, Filipino, Japanese, Korean, Southeast Asian, and Asian Indian descent.

nic groups. The two black ethnic groups—black women who were born in the United States and those who immigrated to the United States—were moderately integrated occupationally ($d = 20.0$), whereas their mean index with Asian ethnic groups was 35.1. Hispanic ethnic groups were considerably less segregated from each other (mean index, 23.1) than they were from Asian ethnic groups (mean index, 33.1). However, the small differences in the means in the fourth column of table 5.3 indicate that Asian female ethnic groups were only slightly less segregated from each other than they were from women from other racial categories.

The segregation indices summarized in tables 5.2 and 5.3 imply three conclusions. First, ethnicity plays a significant role in segregating women into different occupations. Beyond the sex-based division of labor that segregates the sexes into different occupations, American employers also use an ethnic division of labor to structure work. Second, although important exceptions exist, sharing a racial category is negatively associated with the level of ethnic segregation among women. Most intraracial ethnic segregation is low to moderate, whereas most of the interracial segregation is moderate. Third, the interactions between race and ethnicity mean that simply talking about the effect of race or the effect of ethnicity on occupational segregation is misleading. We cannot accurately portray occupational segregation without considering both race and ethnicity.

The Structure of Racial and Ethnic Segregation

In a multigroup context like the United States, although descriptive statistics can be used to summarize segregation indices computed for all possible groups, as in tables 5.2 and 5.3, the amount of information produced by more than three or four groups can make it difficult to identify important patterns. Highlighting the structure of occupational segregation by ethnicity requires a data-analytic technique that takes advantage of each data point. One such technique that is suitable for illuminating how and why race and ethnicity affect groups' occupational outcomes is multidimensional scaling (MDS).

MDS, like factor analysis, uncovers the structure in a set of data by revealing the dimensions that can best account for the similarity—or dissimilarity—in some characteristic across a set of groups (Kruskal and Wish 1978). By using information about the degrees of similarity in the occupational distributions of every pair of ethnic groups (as measured by their segregation indices), multidimensional scaling depicts the structure of racial and ethnic segregation.

In addition to identifying the dimensions underlying the degree of similarity in groups' segregation with other groups, MDS estimates each group's coordinates (or "loadings") on each of the dimensions it identifies. These loadings locate each group in a multidimensional space such that the distance between any pair of groups reflects both the similarity of their occupational distributions to each other (the closer the groups, the more occupationally integrated they are) and the similarity of their patterns of segregation with all other groups. As I show, one can use the loadings to interpret the meaning of the dimensions by regressing groups' scores on a dimension of hypothesized explanatory factors.

Figure 5.1 depicts the structure of occupational segregation among the twenty-six female ethnic groups in 1990, as revealed by the multidimensional scaling. Two dimensions account for 95 percent of the variation in the 325 segregation indices. The groups' positions in figure 5.1 reflect their location on those two dimensions, which appear on the horizontal and vertical axes. The pattern in figure 5.1 mirrors that observed in tables 5.2 and 5.3, of course, because it is based on the same data. Compare, for example, the distance between British and Scottish women, the most integrated pair (d = 3.5), with that between Central American and Eastern European women, the most segregated pair (d = 48.6).

Figure 5.1 also depicts the cross-race variation in ethnic segregation levels, summarized in the top panel of table 5.2. The figure shows the cross-race variation in the varying degrees of ethnic-group clustering across the four racial categories. Note, for instance, the substantial similarity in the occupational distributions of white, non-Hispanic women, particularly those of European ancestry, as seen in their cluster on the right side of the figure. This cluster of European-ancestry ethnic groups could reflect three distinct processes: (1) employers' indifference to ethnicity among white, non-Hispanic women combined with a propensity of differentiating the former from women of color, (2) any tendency for white

Figure 5.1 / Multidimensional Scaling of Segregation Indices for All Women Workers (Computed for Detailed Occupations, 1990)

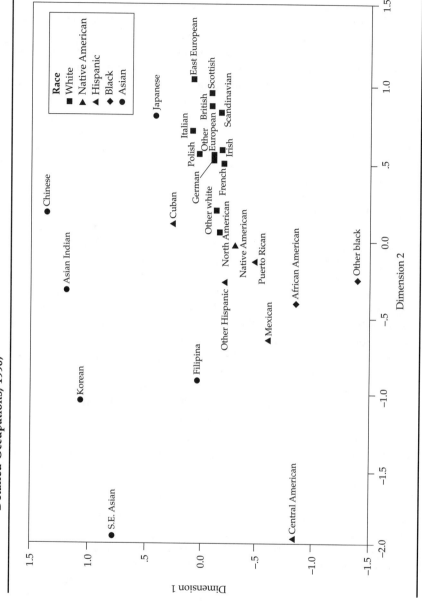

women to prefer or qualify for similar occupations that differ from those that women of color prefer or qualify for, and (3) the segregation of informal networks through which hiring occurs into networks that are composed of European-ancestry groups irrespective of ethnicity but that exclude women who are not of European ancestry.

In contrast to European-ancestry women, neither the Asian nor the Hispanic ethnic groups formed single clusters. Notice too that Japanese women are closer to European ancestry women than to other ethnic groups classified as Asian and that Cuban women are as similar to the European groups as to any other Hispanic group. The location of the cluster of North American and "other white" women is noteworthy. On the vertical dimension, these groups resemble the European-ancestry, white, non-Hispanic groups, but on the horizontal dimension they are closer to three other "new world" ethnic groups: Native Americans, Cubans, and Puerto Ricans (as well as Chinese women).[6]

MDS allows researchers to assess possible explanations for the structure of ethnic groups' patterns of segregation by investigating the factors that contribute to their loadings on the dimensions underlying their pattern of segregation. For example, one could test the possibility that groups' average number of generations in the United States is associated with the degree of similarity in patterns of segregation among groups by regressing the mean number of generations on a dimension that structured groups' segregation. Or, if skin color was suspected to structure intergroup segregation (and if each group's members' typical values on skin color gradient were measurable), one could assess the degree to which skin color contributes to the pattern of segregation among ethnic groups.

The racial clustering shown in figure 5.1, with the Asian ethnic groups concentrated at one end of the vertical dimension and the black and Hispanic groups at the other end, suggests that groups are ordered on this dimension partly on the basis of their race. To test this hypothesis, I regressed the ethnic groups' loadings on the vertical dimension on three dummy variables for their race. Three race dummies (black, Asian, and Hispanic) explained 73 percent of the variance in the vertical dimension. Relative to white, non-Hispanic women (the reference category), the effect of being Asian was in the opposite direction from the effect of being Hispanic or black, and the coefficient for blacks was triple that for Hispanics, reflecting Asians' extreme location at one end of the vertical dimension and blacks' at the other as well as Hispanics' intermediate position between non-Hispanic whites and blacks.[7] The size, direction, and significance of the coefficients for these race dummy variables are consistent with the vertical dimension tapping ethnic groups' ranking on a race-based labor queue.

The concentration of the white women on the far right side of the horizontal dimension suggests that this dimension may also involve race. To assess whether race figures into ethnic groups' location on the horizontal dimension, I regressed the groups' position on this dimension on the three dummy variables for race. The result was consistent with the horizontal dimension's also tapping a racial ordering of the labor queue for ethnic groups: the three race dummy variables explained 40 percent of the variance in ethnic groups' scores on the horizontal dimension. Although I cannot determine what gave rise to this race effect, the distribution of the ethnic groups on the horizontal dimension is consistent with ethnic-group differences in compositional characteristics that are linked with employability, affecting their occupational distributions and hence their levels of segregation from all other groups. According to queuing theory, employers rank groups of workers in occupational labor queues partly on the basis of their probable productivity (Thurow 1969, 48; Lieberson 1980; Reskin 1991). To explore whether the horizontal dimension measures characteristics that may signal productivity to employers, such as education and assimilation into United States work culture, I regressed the horizontal dimension on the proportion of each group that had completed college, spoke English fluently, had immigrated since 1980, was native born, and was under age twenty-three. (Table 5.1 shows each group's values on these variables.)

The results of regressing compositional characteristics of ethnic groups on the horizontal dimension support interpreting the dimension as expressing compositional characteristics that employers use in ranking ethnic groups within labor queues in terms of their probable productivity. The proportion of each ethnic group whose members had completed college, had come to the United States after 1979, and were under twenty-three years old—all proxies for ethnic groups' attractiveness to employers—jointly explained 87 percent of the variance in the horizontal dimension.[8] Net of these compositional characteristics, none of the dummy variables for race exerted a significant effect on ethnic groups' positions on the horizontal dimension.

Although investigating the bases for this ranking is beyond the scope of this chapter, I suspect that the ranking reflects employers' racial preferences and stereotypes with respect to incumbents of particular occupations. For example, the extreme ranking of Asian ethnic groups may have stemmed from stereotypes that they are conscientious, reliable, and the like, whereas stereotypes portray African Americans as lacking a work ethic or being unreliable (Kirschenman and Neckerman 1991; Sigelman and Tuch 1997; see chapter 9). The duties in the most common occupations for Japanese, Chinese, Filipina, and Asian Indian women are consistent with these stereotypes. These white-collar occupations (accountant, bookkeeper, secretary, elementary school teacher, nurse, doctor, sales supervisor, and cashier; see table 5.4) all involve responsibility, self-supervision, and trust.

If employers' racial preferences were based on accurate impressions

Table 5.4 / Top Three Occupations for Women, by Race and Ethnicity, 1990

Race or Ethnicity	Occupation
European	1. Secretary 2. Elementary teacher
Italian, Eastern European	3. Manager, not elsewhere classified
French	3. Cashier
British, German, Irish, Scotch, Polish, Scandinavian	3. Nurse
Native American	1. Secretary 2. Cashier 3. Nursing aide
African American	1. Nursing aide 2. Cashier 3. Secretary
Black immigrant	1. Nursing aide 2. Nurse 3. Secretary
Mexican	1. Secretary 2. Cashier 3. Janitor
Central American	1. Household cleaner 2. Janitor 3. Textile operative
Puerto Rican	1. Secretary 2. Cashier 3. Nursing aide
Cuban	1. Secretary 2. Textile operative 3. Bookkeeper
Southeast Asian	1. Assembler 2. Baker 3. Textile operative
Chinese	1. Textile operative 2. Accountant 3. Cashier
Filipina	1. Nurse 2. Nursing aide 3. Cashier

(Table continues on p. 196.)

Table 5.4 / *Continued*

Race or Ethnicity	Occupation
Japanese	1. Secretary
	2. Elementary teacher
	3. Bookkeeper
Asian Indian	1. Nurse
	2. Doctor
	3. Cashier
Korean	1. Cashier
	2. Sales supervisor
	3. Textile operative

Source: U.S. Department of Commerce (1992).
Notes: Data are for women who were at least sixteen years old and were employed during 1990. Weighted sample size is 2,647,441.

about group differences in productivity (in other words, if employers were practicing statistical discrimination; Phelps 1972), then the importance of race should be smaller in a subsample of workers who were more homogeneous on compositional characteristics that employers believed to be associated with productivity, such as English fluency or educational attainment. To create such a more homogeneous sample, I constructed a subsample of "prime" workers by excluding from the original sample women who had immigrated after 1980, who had not completed high school, who spoke English poorly, and who were under twenty-three years old. I also excluded unpaid family workers and the self-employed because their occupations are not a function of employers' actions. With this subsample of prime workers, which constituted 84 percent of the total sample, I replicated the MDS analysis. In general, the results for prime workers are substantially the same as those for all workers.[9] The only noteworthy difference is that African Americans rather than black immigrants to the United States are at one extreme of the dimension I interpret as employers' racial queue. Black immigrants were ranked above Central Americans and Mexicans. This implies that the low rank of African Americans is based on anti-black prejudice (in England's [1992, 55] terminology, "error discrimination").

In sum, ethnic segregation among women was structured by ethnic groups' compositional characteristics as well as their race. Compositional characteristics contributed to variation in ethnic segregation partly because these characteristics affected ethnic groups' differential attractiveness to employers. However, excluding from the analysis workers with characteristics likely to restrict their attractiveness to employers had little effect on the MDS results. The effect of race should reflect the fact that the networks through which employers recruit workers were structured partly by

Table 5.5 / Effect of Occupational Segregation on the Median Earnings of Women, by Race and Ethnicity

Race or Ethnicity	Equation 1	Equation 2	Equation 3
Vertical dimension	—	916[+] (534)	−1513 (797)
Horizontal dimension	—	481* (409)	2,647* (412)
Asian	837 (936)	—	5155* (1127)
Black	26 (1,440)	—	812 (1,158)
Hispanic	−2250* (998)	—	329 (746)
Summary statistics			
Constant	13,973 (529)	13,737* (325)	12,423* (402)
Adjusted R^2	16.1*	36.0*	70.0*
Number of cases	26	26	26

Source: U.S. Department of Commerce (1992).
Notes: Data are for women who were at least sixteen years old and were employed during 1990. Weighted sample size is 2,647,441. Standard errors are in parentheses.
*$p < .05$, one-tailed. + $p < .01$, one-tailed.

race as well as by racial biases and stereotypes that affected employers' hiring practices across occupations.

The Effects of Ethnic Segregation on Earnings

Occupational segregation based on group membership is problematic primarily because it links group membership to earnings. Although sex segregation translates ascriptive characteristics into unequal rewards by concentrating women in low-paying jobs or by driving down women's pay through crowding (Treiman and Hartmann 1981; Reskin and Hartmann 1986; England 1992), evidence that a similar process operates through ethnic segregation is lacking. However, the results of the multidimensional scaling make it possible to assess the effect of ethnic segregation on earnings. Assuming that the two dimensions that the MDS identified capture the structure of segregation among ethnic groups, I estimated the effect of ethnic segregation on variation in ethnic groups' median earnings by regressing each group's 1989 median earnings on its loadings on the two dimensions (see table 5.5).

Both the dimensions significantly affected ethnic groups' median earnings in 1989, according to the regression results. Of the two dimensions, the effect of the horizontal dimension that hypothetically taps compositional characteristics that employers used as proxies for groups' employability in an occupation is the stronger, with a beta of .58. The standardized coefficient for the vertical dimension that I have interpreted as race is .27. Together these two dimensions explain 36 percent of the variance for median earnings (see equation 2, table 5.5). Race alone explains only 16 percent of the variation across ethnic groups in median earnings (table 5.5, equation 1), but race along with ethnic segregation explains 70 percent of the variation (see equation 3). Thus, although additional research is needed on how and why ethnic segregation translates into ethnic-based earnings inequality, occupational segregation by ethnicity plays a nontrivial role.

CONCLUSIONS

Most research on occupational segregation compares just two groups—women and men—partly because the conventional measure of segregation—the segregation index—compares two groups' distributions across a set of occupations, and partly because researchers typically specialize in a single form of occupational segregation. This dyadic approach to segregation disregards the fact that more than one ascriptive status affects occupational outcomes. In this chapter, I have shown that both the race and the ethnicity of female workers are bases for their distribution across occupations.

The patterns of segregation in a multiracial, ethnically diverse society are part of a complex structure of advantage and disadvantage. To understand ethnic and racial segregation among women requires making this structure visible. Multidimensional scaling permitted me to depict the structure of ethnic segregation among women, and two dimensions sufficed to capture that structure. One of these dimensions is based primarily on race, which explained more than 70 percent of the variance in the twenty-six ethnic groups' positions on one of the dimensions. This finding suggests that ethnic segregation stems to an appreciable degree from racial differentiation. Ethnic groups' ordering on this racial dimension is black, Hispanic, non-Hispanic white, and Asian.

For white, non-Hispanic ethnic groups of European ancestry, race (and, of course, sex; Reskin 1993) virtually determines their most likely occupational outcomes. Comparing the top three occupations for the twenty-six ethnic groups illustrates this point (see table 5.4). For all nine of the European-ancestry ethnic groups, the modal occupation was secretary, and the second most common occupation was elementary school teacher. Of the other seventeen groups, only two—Japanese and "other white" women—shared these top two occupations. Only in their third most common occupation did the non-Hispanic white women show any diversity. For six of the nine, this occupation was nurse, but French-ancestry women's third most common occupation was cashier, and Italian and Eastern European women's third most common occupation was manager, not elsewhere classified. These small differences among European-ancestry women in their most common occupations mirror the low levels of occupational segregation among them. With the exception of women of Eastern European ancestry, employers were largely indifferent to ethnicity among white, non-Hispanic women. This indifference stems partly from the groups' similarity in their likelihood of having completed high school and college, having immigrated to the United States in the past ten years, and having a certain level of English fluency (see table 5.1), and partly from the erosion of stereotypes about European ethnic groups. Eastern European women differ from other European-ancestry women on these compositional measures, and, according to Kirschenman and Neckerman (1991, 210), employers perceive that they differ from other white, non-Hispanic groups in their work effort. With the decline of residential segregation among European-ancestry groups, I suspect that ethnicity is of little importance in the informal networks through which women find jobs. In sum, ethnicity was not an obstacle to occupational integration among European-ancestry non-Hispanic women in 1990.

Among Hispanic and Asian ethnic groups, however, ethnicity played an important role in occupational segregation in 1990. The horizontal dimension of segregation in figure 5.1 captures this within-race ethnic segregation. Ethnicity contributes to segregation in large part through compositional differences between same-race ethnic groups that prospective employers may treat as a signal of ethnic groups' potential productivity in particular occupations. Groups' compositional characteristics—that is, their typical educational attainments, nativity, time of immigration, and English fluency—accounted for 87 percent of the variance in their positions on this dimension. Thus, this dimension taps both occupational segregation among ethnic groups in the same broad racial category (for example, Japanese women's occupational segregation from other Asian women or Central American women's segregation from other Hispanics) as well as occupational dissimilarities across ethnic groups of different races (for example, non-European white women and African American, Native American, Puerto Rican, and Mexican women).

To summarize, my analysis indicates that most of the variation in the structure of ethnic segregation among female workers stemmed from ethnic groups' race and their compositional characteristics that may have been associated with their employability in some occupations. Ethnic segregation stems partly from how employers rank ethnic groups in labor queues on the basis both of their race and their compositional characteristics that employees may use to predict occupational performance.

Segregation by sex has been the linchpin of women's economic and social disadvantages. By relegating women to jobs that pay less than men's jobs and provide fewer benefits, fewer hours of work, and fewer opportunities for advancement, segregation helps to maintain women's subordinate position in the workplace, the family, and society. The analysis described here suggests that segregation by race and ethnicity similarly preserves racial and ethnic inequality both by maintaining the social distance between groups and by generating earnings disparities. Occupational segregation also renders women workers from different racial and ethnic groups differentially vulnerable to job loss. For example, during the 1990 to 1991 recession, black and Hispanic workers were 15 percent more likely than non-Hispanic whites were and 43 percent more likely than Asians were to lose a job. In part, this disparity stemmed from blacks' concentration in clerical and machine-operator jobs, jobs that had the second- and third-highest rates of worker displacement, according to the U.S. General Accounting Office (1994).

The racial and ethnic structuring of occupational access also has important implications for ethnic and racial conflict. Ethnic- and race-based occupational segregation reduces the likelihood that women from different groups will compete for the same job. While segregation might reduce intergroup conflict based on occupational competition, this does not necessarily reduce the perception of economic competition. Indeed, ethnic and racial segregation into different economic roles can be the source of intergroup conflict, as has sometimes been the case for African Americans and Asians, who interact less frequently as coworkers who might share common goals than they do as buyers and sellers whose interests are more likely to conflict. In Los Angeles, a city whose ethnic and racial conflict has frequently drawn national attention in recent years, Korean and African American women are quite occupationally segregated (44 percent of either group would have had to change to a different occupational category in 1990 for their occupational distributions to be identical), and job-level segregation is certainly far greater. Since, the modal occupation for Korean women is cashier, often in a family business, African American women are therefore probably more likely to encounter Korean women as proprietors in retail shops than as coworkers. High levels of work segregation among racial and ethnic groups reduce the likelihood that women from these groups will interact as equals. Thus, segregation hinders the opportunity for the kind of equal-status contact that can reduce stereotyping and antipathy between ethnic and racial groups.

Occupational segregation is an engine of social inequality that ensures that ascribed statuses become barriers to community and that facilitate and legitimate unequal workplace rewards. Efforts to reduce racial and ethnic inequality must address workers' segregation on the basis of their ethnicity as well as their race and sex.

I am particularly grateful to Lowell Hargens for a variety of help with this project and to Naomi Cassirer for painstaking assistance in data analysis and for her comments on earlier drafts of this chapter. I also appreciate the helpful suggestions of Irene Browne, Susan González-Baker, Jerry Jacobs, Robert Kaufman, Laurie Krivo, and Townsand Price-Spratlen. This project was supported by National Science Foundation grant SBR-9310867.

NOTES

1. Lieberson and Waters (1990, 129–34) used 1980 census data to assess occupational segregation based on detailed ethnicity among two Asian, three Hispanic, and several European ethnic groups.

2. I excluded a residual group of "other Asians" that comprises Polynesians, Micronesians, and other Pacific Islanders because the PUMS data include too few women of these ethnicities for meaningful analysis.

3. North Americans include 162,000 non-Hispanic white women who reported their ancestry as North American, American, or Canadian or gave a Canadian or U.S. regional or place-name identifier (for example, "Yankee," "Anglo," "Hoosier"). The category "other European" includes 79,000 non-Hispanic European women not elsewhere classified (for example, Greek, Welsh, Dutch, Austrian). A residual category of other non-Hispanic whites includes 218,000 white non-Hispanic women who reported a non-European ancestry (for example, African, Middle Eastern) as well as women who identified themselves as white and said that they were not Hispanic but did not report their ethnic ancestry.

4. The segregation index, which ranges from 0 to 100, indicates the proportion of either group that would have had to change from occupations in which they were overrepresented to occupations in which they were underrepresented for the two groups to have been identically distributed across occupations.

5. Although the national data understate ethnic and racial segregation within local labor markets, ethnic segregation at the national and local levels exhibited very similar structures to those described later in the chapter for the national data. Thus, one can draw valid conclusions from the national data regarding the structure, causes, and consequences of women's occupational segregation.

6. Cluster analysis (Hubbell 1965) confirmed the patterns in figure 5.1. In addition, it indicated that Asian ethnic groups formed two loose clusters: one of Korean and Southeast Asian women, and a second of Chinese and Asian Indian women.

7. The regression coefficients are 0.09 for Asian, -0.29 for Hispanic, and -1.03 for black women.

8. The standardized regression coefficients of -0.66 for the proportion who immigrated after 1980, -0.13 for the proportion under twenty-three years old, and 0.49 for the proportion who completed college suggest that ethnic groups with relatively large proportions of immigrants were particularly disadvantaged. The proportion of the group that immigrated after 1979 and the proportion that is

native born were highly correlated ($r = -.87$), so including the latter rather than the former in the equation yielded similar results.

9. The correlation between ethnic groups' scores on the vertical dimension among all workers and prime workers is .90.

REFERENCES

Albelda, Randy P. 1986. Occupational Sex Segregation by Race and Gender, 1958–1981. *Industrial Labor Relations Review* 39(3): 404–11.

Almquist, Elizabeth M. 1987. "Labor Market Gender Inequality in Minority Groups." *Gender and Society* 1(4): 400–14.

Amott, Teresa L., and Julie A. Matthaei. 1991. *Race, Gender, and Work: A Multicultural Economic History of Women in the United States.* Boston: South End Press.

Becker, Henry J. 1980. "Racial Segregation among Places of Employment." *Social Forces* 58(3): 761–76.

Beller, Andrea H. 1984. Trends in Occupational Segregation by Sex: 1960–1980. In *Sex Segregation in the Workplace: Trends, Explanations, Remedies,* edited by Barbara F. Reskin. Washington, D.C.: National Academy Press.

Bielby, William T., and James N. Baron. 1986. "Men and Women at Work: Sex Segregation and Statistical Discrimination." *American Journal of Sociology* 91(4): 759–99.

Braddock, Jomills Henry, and James M. McPartland. 1987. "How Minorities Continue to Be Excluded from Equal Employment Opportunities: Research on Labor Market and Institutional Barriers." *Journal of Social Issues* 43(1): 5–39.

Browne, Irene. 1997. "Explaining the Black-White Gap in Labor Force Participation among Women Heading Households." *American Sociological Review* 62(2): 236–52.

Butler, John Sibley. 1996. "Myrdal Revisited. The Negro in Business, the Professions, Public Service, and Other White Collar Occupations." In *An American Dilemma Revisited: Race Relations in a Changing World,* edited by Obie Clayton, Jr. New York: Russell Sage Foundation.

Duncan, Otis Dudley, and Beverly Duncan. 1955. "Residential Distribution and Occupational Stratification." *American Journal of Sociology* 60(5): 493–503.

England, Paula. 1992. *Comparable Worth: Theories and Evidence.* New York: Aldine de Gruyter.

Farley, Reynolds. 1984. *Blacks and Whites: Narrowing the Gap?* Cambridge, Mass.: Harvard University Press.

Glass, Jennifer, Marta Tienda, and Shelley A. Smith. 1988. "The Impact of Changing Employment Opportunity on Gender and Ethnic Earnings Inequality." *Social Science Research* 17(3): 252–76.

Glenn, Evelyn Nakano, and Charles M. Tolbert II. 1987. "Technology and Emerging Patterns of Stratification for Women of Color: Race and Gender Segregation in Computer Occupations." In *Women, Work, and Technology,* edited by Barbara Drygulsk Wright. Ann Arbor: University of Michigan Press.

Harrison, Roderick J., and Claudette E. Bennett. 1995. "Racial and Ethnic Diversity." In *State of the Union: America in the 1990s,* edited by Reynolds Farley. Vol. 2, *Social Trends.* New York: Russell Sage Foundation.

Hubbell, Charles H. 1965. "An Input-Output Approach to Clique Detection." *Sociometry* 28(1): 377–99.

King, Mary L. 1992. "Occupational Segregation by Race and Gender, 1940–1989." *Monthly Labor Review* 115 (April): 30–37.

Kirschenman, Joleen, and Kathryn M. Neckerman. 1991. "'We'd Love to Hire Them, But . . .' The Meaning of Race for Employers." In *The Urban Underclass*, edited by Christopher Jencks and Paul E. Peterson. Washington, D.C.: Brookings Institution.

Kluegel, James R. 1978. "The Causes and Costs of Racial Exclusion from Job Authority." *American Sociological Review* 43(June): 285–301.

Kruskal, Joseph B., and Myron Wish. 1978. *Multidimensional Scaling*. Beverly Hills, Calif.: Sage Publications.

Lichter, Daniel T., and David J. Landry. 1991. "Labor Force Transitions and Underemployment: The Stratification of Male and Female Workers." *Research in Stratification and Social Mobility* 10: 63–87.

Lieberson, Stanley. 1980. *A Piece of the Pie: Blacks and White Immigrants since 1880*. Berkeley: University of California Press.

Lieberson, Stanley, and Mary C. Waters. 1990. *From Many Strands: Ethnic and Racial Groups in Contemporary America*. New York: Russell Sage Foundation.

Massey, Douglas S., and Nancy A. Denton. 1993. *American Apartheid: Segregation and the Making of the Underclass*. Cambridge, Mass.: Harvard University Press.

McGuire, Gail M., and Barbara F. Reskin. 1993. "Authority Hierarchies at Work: The Impacts of Race and Sex." *Gender & Society* 7(4): 487–506.

Phelps, Edmund S. 1972. "The Statistical Theory of Racism and Sexism." *American Economic Review* 62(4): 659–61.

Reskin, Barbara F. 1988. "Bringing the Men Back In: Sex Differentiation and the Devaluation of Women's Work." *Gender & Society* 2(4): 58–81.

———. 1991. "Labor Markets as Queues: A Structural Approach to Changing Occupational Sex Composition." In *Macro-Micro Interrelationships in Sociology*, edited by Joan Huber. Newbury Park, Calif.: Sage Publications.

———. 1993. "Sex Segregation in the Workplace." *Annual Review of Sociology* 19: 241–70.

———. 1994. "Segregating Workers: Occupational Differences by Ethnicity, Race, and Sex." In *46th Annual Proceedings of the Industrial Relations Research Association*. Madison, Wisc.: Industrial Relations Research Association.

Reskin, Barbara F., and Naomi R. Cassirer. 1997. "Occupational Segregation by Gender, Race, and Ethnicity." *Sociological Focus* 29(3): 231–43.

Reskin, Barbara F., and Heidi Hartmann. 1986. *Women's Work, Men's Work: Sex Segregation on the Job*. Washington, D.C.: National Academy Press.

Sigelman, Lee, and Steven A. Tuch. 1997. "Metastereotypes: Blacks' Perceptions of Whites' Stereotypes of Blacks." *Public Opinion Quarterly* 61(1): 87–101.

Smith, Shelley A., and Marta Tienda. 1988. "The Doubly Disadvantaged: Women of Color in the U.S. Labor Force." In *Women Working*, edited by Ann H. Stromberg and Shirley Harkess. Mountain View, Calif.: Mayfield.

Thurow, Lester. 1969. *Poverty and Discrimination*. Washington, D.C.: Brookings Institution.

Tienda, Marta, and Ding-Tzann Lii. 1987. "Minority Concentration and Earnings Inequality: Blacks, Hispanics, and Asians." *American Journal of Sociology* 93(1): 141–65.

Tomaskovic-Devey, Donald. 1993. *Gender and Racial Inequality at Work: The Sources and Consequences of Job Segregation.* Ithaca, N.Y.: ILR Press.

Tomaskovic-Devey, Donald, Arne Kalleberg, and Peter V. Marsden. 1996. "Organizational Patterns of Gender Segregation." In *Organizations in America: Analyzing Their Structures and Human Resource Practices,* edited by Arne Kalleberg, David Knoke, Peter V. Marsden, and Joe L. Spaeth. Thousand Oaks, Calif.: Sage Publications.

Treiman, Donald J., and Heidi I. Hartmann. 1981. *Women, Work and Wages.* Washington, D.C.: National Academy Press.

U.S. Department of Commerce. U.S. Bureau of the Census. 1992. *1990 Census of Population and Housing: Public Use Microdata Sample Technical Documentation.* Washington, D.C.: U.S. Government Printing Office.

———. 1994. *Statistical Abstract of the United States.* Washington, D.C.: U.S. Government Printing Office.

U.S. General Accounting Office. 1994. *Equal Employment Opportunity, Displacement Rates, Unemployment Spells and Reemployment Wages by Race.* Washington, D.C.: U.S. Government Printing Office.

Van den Berghe, Pierre L. 1960. "Distance Mechanisms of Stratification." *Sociology and Social Research* (January/February): 155–63.

Zalokar, Nadja. 1990. *The Economic Status of Black Women: An Exploratory Investigation.* Washington, D.C.: U.S. Government Printing Office for U.S. Commission on Civil Rights.

Part II

THE DYNAMICS OF RACE AND GENDER IN THE LABOR MARKET

Chapter 6

Generational Paths into and out of Work: Personal Narratives of Puerto Rican Women in New York

Aixa N. Cintrón-Vélez

I never had much trouble finding a job. The reason is that there were "People Wanted" signs all over the place, for anything you'd like. If you didn't know how to sew, they would teach you. And once you were in the union, you could go to the union and they would give you referrals. But, now it is a different story. Now all there is is jobs to take care of the elderly. I think, I think that there are no more jobs in anything.

—Marta, age sixty-nine, retired garment worker

Sometimes I feel that it is not the government's fault, it is the people themselves, you know. Because, I guess, I look at myself: I came from one of those [public housing] buildings, and so did my friends, and look where we are. I mean, how much can you give them? How much do you have to do for these people? They have to do something for themselves.

—Elisa, age forty-four, part-time bookkeeper

Since the end of World War II and until recently, the economic fortunes of Puerto Ricans in the United States have been closely tied to the performance of the New York economy. Even before the world recession and oil price shocks of the early 1970s, this northern industrial city heralded the changes that were to alter urban economies in the United States (Bailey and Waldinger 1991). The movement away from primary-sector jobs in the goods-producing industries and the erosion of employment and earning opportunities for the less skilled resulted in economic hardship and increased inequality, particularly among those who were once just "the newcomers" in a changing metropolis and expected to move up the economic ladder (Handlin 1962; Glazer and Moynihan 1970).

Marta and Elisa, first- and second-generation Puerto Ricans respectively, capture the general terms of the debate over the reasons for the declining economic prospects of a significant group of individuals and families (like themselves). This chapter begins to outline a framework that will lead to a better understanding of Puerto Rican women's work and family strategies in a changing political and economic environment. Placing their individual experiences in the context of historical and contemporary forces allows the generation of more complete explanations of their perceived choices and courses of action within a climate of increasing constraints on the social and economic mobility of poor women and families.

In this chapter, I examine the paths into and out of work of three different cohorts of Puerto Rican women, defined by their place of birth and, for the Island-born, the time of their arrival in the United States. The next two sections situate Puerto Ricans in the context of the work, family, and poverty debate and of their migration to the United States and the changing employment structure in one of their traditional areas of settlement, New York City. This is followed by a presentation of findings from my 1993 qualitative study of a sample of Island-born and U.S.-born or -educated, poor or working-class Puerto Rican women. The chapter concludes with an assessment of the paths into and out of work for the different groups in an attempt to shed light onto the changing relationships between women's work and family lives and the local economy.

PUERTO RICAN WOMEN AND THE WORK, FAMILY, AND POVERTY DEBATE

In 1950, Puerto Rican women participated in the U.S. labor force at a higher rate than both non-Hispanic black and white women did. Yet by 1970 they showed the lowest rate of participation among all women. While participation among non-Hispanic white and black women was increasing, participation for Puerto Rican women slowed down and eventually declined. The marked drop in participation has been attributed to the relative decline in operative and laborer jobs and Puerto Ricans' concentration in those industries and areas of the country hardest hit by structural decline (DeFreitas 1985, 1991; Sassen-Koob 1985; Waldinger 1986). By 1980 participation had increased 8.8 percentage points from the 1970 low of 32.9 percent. The gains of that period, however, did not offset the decline or lack of growth in previous decades (Tienda, Donato, and Cordero-Guzmán 1990); the gap between Puerto Rican and other women remained.

Rapidly growing female-headship rates and increasing poverty have accompanied the disproportionately high rates of joblessness among Puerto Ricans in the United States in recent decades. From 1960 to 1980, the percentage of families headed by women more than doubled for Puerto Ricans, from 15.6 percent to 34.2 percent (Smith 1988), and the poverty rate reached 33.4 percent, the highest among all ethnic groups for which data were available (Bean and Tienda 1987). The observed trends generated a diversity of explanations, ranging from differences in human capital investment, to shifts in labor demand, to a recast of "culture-of-poverty" themes.

The conjunction of demographic trends, conservative politics, and industrial restructuring that transformed women's poverty into a major public policy issue also put Puerto Ricans at the center of the "underclass" debate (see, for example, Tienda 1989). The attempt to link changes in family structure with welfare dependence and persistent poverty gives the impression that poverty can be explained by changes in household structure rather than by changes in jobs and earnings, or both.

PUERTO RICAN WOMEN WORKERS IN A CHANGING LOCAL ECONOMY

Migration, a New York location, and garment manufacturing represent significant phenomena in the labor market experience of Puerto Rican women in the United States. They are crucially related to observed social and economic outcomes for the group, particularly before 1970.[1] While non-Hispanic white workers increasingly moved out of the most unstable operative and laborer jobs during the 1950s and 1960s, Puerto Rican men and women remained heavily concentrated in these occupations in those industries hardest hit by the restructuring. For example, in 1965, 46.7 percent of Puerto Rican women workers were employed as factory operators or laborers in the garment industry and represented a fourth of all such workers in that industry in the New York metropolitan area (Safa 1978).

But Puerto Ricans had entered an industry in decline. Puerto Rican workers found themselves vulnerable to layoffs and easily replaced by other unskilled labor. The erosion of garment industry jobs meant seasonal or uncertain employment, high turnover rates, a greater distance to work, and increasingly inadequate wages. A household that depended on pooled-income arrangements was very likely destabilized by these larger forces. In fact, throughout the 1970s many Puerto Ricans returned to the Island. It was not until the 1980s that net outmigration from the Island resumed.

In 1970, the majority of Puerto Ricans were Island-born, and 43.8 percent of all Puerto Ricans in the United States were under the age of eighteen. The increasing number of women and young people entering the labor force accounted for an excess supply of first-time workers at a time of diminishing demand for the less skilled or experienced. Large-scale job creation in the public sector represented a buffer, for example, for the African American population in New York City, but relatively lower levels of education and English language proficiency meant that Puerto Ricans were less likely to benefit from these measures. As the real earnings of less-skilled male workers dropped sharply, more married women from all groups (regardless of education) entered the labor force.

Despite earlier losses in jobs and income and the continued deterioration of less-skilled labor markets, Puerto Rican women in New York City experienced an increase in labor force participation over the 1980s. A report by the New York City Department of Planning (1993) shows that 42 percent of all Puerto Rican women aged sixteen years and over were employed or looking for work in 1990, compared with only 34 percent in 1980. In particular, U.S.-born Puerto Rican women displayed labor force participation rates at the level of all female New York City residents (53 percent and 54 percent, respectively). Island-born Puerto Rican women did not do as well as their U.S.-born counterparts, having a participation rate of only 41 percent.

According to the 1990 census, the occupational and industrial distribution of employed Puerto Rican New Yorkers changed significantly during the 1980s. The most remarkable change in the occupational distribution of Puerto Rican women workers was the consistent movement out of blue-collar jobs—specifically, the shift away from machine operator jobs, formerly the bastion of immigrant Puerto Rican women. In 1990, for the first time, more Puerto Rican women were employed in professional and service occupations than in blue-collar ones.

Contrary to the opinion that New York City is a welfare magnet for poor Puerto Rican families, city-level data reveal that more households on public assistance left than arrived there in 1990. Puerto Ricans moving into New York City from the Island were relatively younger and better educated than Puerto Ricans in New York and were otherwise similar in terms of ratio of men to women, household structure, and participation in public assistance. Nevertheless, Puerto Ricans in New York City continued to experience high levels of residential segregation and poverty. They were concentrated in community districts that were bypassed by a partial economic recovery that rested on the rapid growth of information-intensive professional service industries and an increase in higher-skill managerial and professional specialty occupations.

It is tempting to conclude that what was true for Puerto Ricans in the 1970s (that is, low levels of labor force participation, growing numbers of families headed by females, increasing poverty) did not hold in the 1980s. Research on young Puerto Rican women (that is, workers with less than ten years of experience or women between the ages of eighteen and thirty-eight years) reported in chapter 3 shows Puerto Ricans nationwide making improvements in schooling, English language proficiency, employment, and wages during the decade. But the gains were not evenly spread. Whereas women in all marital, nativity, and education groups experienced gains in participation, only those who were U.S.-born, were married, and had at least some college experienced wage growth. The group as a whole continued to experience alarmingly high rates of poverty and unemployment (38 percent and 14 percent, respectively, in New York City in 1990).

THE STUDY

A review of the literature on Puerto Rican women and work suggests that U.S.-born Puerto Rican women and the more recent arrivals face a different set of economic options than earlier Puerto Rican immigrants did.[2] In order to look more carefully at process and within-group differences in labor market outcomes, I gathered oral histories from a sample of primarily Is-land-born, low-income Puerto Rican women in New York City. The in-depth interviews sought to construct migration and employment histories and to elicit these women's views on work, welfare, and social opportunity. Women were also encouraged to contrast their own choices and options with those of their children, particularly their daughters.

The idea of a qualitative study was prompted by the fragmented stories that emerged from the analysis of cross-sectional data. For instance, since Puerto Ricans are U.S. citizens, most survey instruments do not inquire about their motives for migration, their date of arrival, or any returns to the Island.[3] Yet a significant segment of the U.S. Puerto Rican population consists of immigrants, and the timing of migration and their location deci-sion is closely related to later labor market outcomes. Retrospective life stories can also help determine the timing of transitions (for example, movements into and out of the labor force) and the factors that motivate these transitions (for example, household composition and resources, per-ceptions of trade-off).

Specifically, the qualitative study addresses the following questions about work, welfare, and social opportunity:

1. What is the nature of Puerto Rican women's experiences in the labor market? What are their expectations regarding paid employment? That is, how easy is it to find jobs, where do they find jobs, what would a "good job" be like, and how likely is it that someone with their charac-teristics will get a job like that?

2. What is the impact of job loss on Puerto Rican women and their fami-lies? Do the women interpret that experience as part of a unique or an individual history? Can they get new jobs? What kinds of jobs do they get? How do their options compare with those of men?

Data and Methods

The data upon which this chapter is based come largely from fieldwork conducted in New York City during 1993. Statements made about Puerto Rican women's experience at this location are based on unstructured inter-views with key informants as well as on casual conversations and observa-tions of participants in households, community settings, and social gather-ings over the same period. Depending on the interviewee's preference, the interviews were conducted in either English or Spanish, often in a combination of the two—as is common practice, particularly among members of the second generation. All interviews were taped and subsequently transcribed verbatim.

I generated a snowball sample consisting of (1) early migrants, arriving in the United States between 1940 and 1970; (2) recent migrants, arriving from 1970 to the early 1980s; and (3) second-generation (that is, U.S.-born or of a young age upon arrival and U.S.- educated) Puerto Rican women.[4] I secured initial contact with potential study participants primarily through referrals by individuals, although I also visited local agencies providing services to the Hispanic community and contacted organizations of garment workers and retirees. Because of time and financial constraints, I limited my sample to women still living in the New York metropolitan area.[5]

The data analysis is based upon a sample of twenty-two New York Puerto Rican women ranging in age between twenty-four and seventy-nine years (see table 6.1).[6] Almost 60 percent of the women were married at the time of the interview (compared with about 34 percent of the overall Puerto Rican population in New York City in 1990). Consistent with their age distribution, the majority were Island-born.[7] Most of the women in the sample had arrived in the United States before 1970 (only five of the Island-born women arrived after 1970). Six of the women were either born in the United States or had arrived before the age of fifteen.[8] Of those who were U.S.-born or who were at an early age upon arrival, one was a recent migrant who didn't significantly partake in the U.S. educational system; she dropped out of school after getting married at the age of fifteen.

Overall, both early migrants and recent migrants averaged less than an eighth-grade education. But early migrants, in particular, displayed a wider range of educational attainment, from no formal education to some college. In contrast, the U.S.-born or -educated women averaged fourteen years of education (the equivalent of some college). Among those twenty-five years old or older, 45.8 percent were high school graduates, compared with 46.0 percent of Puerto Ricans in New York City in 1990.

Of those aged twenty-five to sixty-four years, eight of seventeen, or 47.0 percent, were employed at the time of the interview; the corresponding figure for Puerto Ricans in New York City in 1990 was 42.4 percent. Of the twenty-two women in the total sample, eleven had at one point or another applied for and received some kind of public assistance. When interviewed, five of the women were on public assistance; one received Aid to Families with Dependent Children (AFDC), and four others received Home Relief.[9] All four Home Relief recipients stated that they combined work and welfare to make ends meet. Two of the women on Home Relief had multiple health-related problems, and one was awaiting determination of eligibility for disability insurance benefits.

(Text continues on p. 217.)

Table 6.1 / General Characteristics of Informants

Identification	Age in 1993	Marital and Household Situation (Age of Children)	Education (Years)	Year of Arrival (Age in Years)	Occupation in Puerto Rico	Occupation in the United States	Ever on Welfare?
Marina	79	Married, spouse present	8	1943 (28)	Sewing machine operator	Sewing machine operator; retired after 39 years when plant relocated to Queens	No
Estela	70	Married, spouse present	12	1944 (21)	Bilingual secretary	Wartime army recruit (office clerk), bilingual secretary	No
Marta	69	Divorced, remarried, widowed	8	1945 (22)	Sewing machine operator	Sewing machine operator; retired at 62 because of plant relocation to Florida	No
Elba	64	Divorced, remarried, spouse present	8	1947 (18)	Sewing machine operator	Sewing machine operator, sample maker	No
Luisa	71	Divorced, remarried, widowed; living with youngest son (51)	6	1948 (26)	Child labor (industrial homework)	Sewing machine operator	No
Teresa	73	Single, had been married twice in Puerto Rico; living with grandchild (18)	2	1953 (33)	Child labor (domestic), industrial homework	Domestic, floor worker and ironer at garment factory	Yes

(Table continues on p. 214.)

Table 6.1 / Continued

Identification	Age in 1993	Marital and Household Situation (Age of Children)	Education (Years)	Year of Arrival (Age in Years)	Occupation in Puerto Rico	Occupation in the United States	Ever on Welfare?
Nydia	72	Single, married and widowed three times; living with son, granddaughter, and great-grandchild	2	1950 (34)	Homemaker	Food service worker, machine operator	Yes
Celeste	59	Widowed	2	1957 (23)	Sewing machine operator	Factory laborer (laid off after 27 years of work because of plant relocation to Florida), domestic (combines work and welfare)	Yes
Solangel	73	Twice divorced; living with two grandchildren	0	1958 (38)	Child labor (sewing machine operator)	Sewing machine operator, hospital food service worker; retired	Yes
Francisca	61	Married, spouse present	11	1962 (32)	Homemaker	Laborer at electronics and toy factories, sorter at garment factory	Yes
Irene	42	Married, spouse present, two children (13, 20)	7	1965 (16)	—	Child-care worker, machine operator at a toy factory, laborer at women's clothing warehouse and distributor, laborer at mail/catalog company	No

Name	Age	Family status		Year (age)		Work history	
Dora	49	Married, spouse present, three children (15, 16, 18)	12	1966 (22)	Office clerk in public employment program	Child-care worker, laborer and machine operator in garment industry, worker in costume jewelry manufacturing	Yes
Gilda	45	Divorced, remarried, spouse present; living with two sons (17, 23; 23-year-old is handicapped and on SSI)	2	1968 (20)	Child labor (food service worker)	Machine operator and laborer at clothing and toy factory	Yes
Damaris	45	Married, spouse present, two children (15,18)	14	1968 (20)	—	Laborer at clothing and plastics manufacturing shops, machine operator at an electronics factory, bank office clerk, secretary	No
Mercedes	50	Twice divorced; living with partner	4	1971 (28)	Child labor (domestic)	Ironer/pieceworker at garment factory, food-service worker, home attendant; combines work and welfare	Yes
Carmín	45	Married, spouse present; raising a grandchild (4)	2	1976 (17)	Child labor (domestic)	Food-service worker, machine operator, home attendant; combines work and welfare	Yes

(Table continues on p. 216.)

Table 6.1 / *Continued*

Identification	Age in 1993	Marital and Household Situation (Age of Children)	Education (Years)	Year of Arrival (Age in Years)	Occupation in Puerto Rico	Occupation in the United States	Ever on Welfare?
Beatriz	24	Divorced; living with three children (3, 5, 7); expecting a child	9	1983 (14)	—	Laborer (assembly and packing) at toy factory, cleaner and housekeeper, floor worker at garment factory	Yes
Lida	64	Married, spouse present	14	U.S.-born	—	Administrator of social service agency, sewing machine operator	No
Elisa	44	Divorced	14	1953 (4)	—	Bookkeeper	No
Belén	45	Married, spouse present, three children (10, 17, 20)	12	1962 (14)	—	Secretary	No
Angela	44	Married, spouse present, three children (12, 19, 22)	16	1963 (14)	—	Licensed practical nurse, pharmacy intern	No
Zulma	26	Divorced, remarried, spouse present, three children (2, 4, 10)	15	1963 (.5)	—	Vocational counselor, unpaid family worker	Yes

FINDINGS

Women, Migration, and Wage Work

Puerto Rican in-migrants are a heterogeneous population. Differences in individual characteristics, motives for migration, and socioeconomic outcomes define their experience in U.S. society. Migration was but one strategy families and individuals adopted to meet the challenges of rapid economic transformation on the Island. To begin with, I consider the stories of Marina and Teresa, both of whom migrated in the postwar years.

Marina, seventy-nine years old, had retired after working for thirty-nine years in the New York garment industry. She had been married to Antonio, a retired carpenter, for fifty-three years, and they owned a home in a working-class section of the South Bronx. They had two daughters who were married and had grown children of their own—one lived in New York City, and the other, in Puerto Rico. Marina and Antonio's only son had been killed in Miami, Florida, in 1992. Antonio had left the Island first because he was discouraged with the inferior job prospects there in the early 1940s. Even though they had both worked for wages in Puerto Rico, they could barely make ends meet:

> Marina: First he left for California.[10] There he started working as a carpenter. I already had two kids, a boy and a girl, and I was pregnant. Since he was thinking of moving from California to New York, I told him: when you get to New York, I'll join you there. After I gave birth, when my youngest was about three and a half months old, I came over, bringing her along. I left the other two with my mother.

Marina left the Island when she was twenty-eight years old, like the average migrant. She was married and had children, and she had had previous work experience in manufacturing on the Island. She had a job and a social support network in Puerto Rico, but in this case the social mobility project took precedence:

> Marina: I wanted to leave the Island. One has to look around, you know? I must have been, probably about your age. Because there one could never make enough money. Carpenters . . . , how much did they make then? Whereas, here, carpenters . . . , girl! Here the carpenters' union is the best union there is. That was during the war . . . and everybody was coming over.

The oldest child of cigar makers, Marina was aware of work and workers' rights.[11] When she graduated from eighth grade, with vocational training, at the age of fourteen, she knew that she would be expected to work, and she did, all her life:

Marina: You retire when you want to, because I retired at sixty-six. And I retired because they closed the factory. . . . Because I can still work. I worked every day of my life and I would have continued working, even after retirement age, but they started closing factories.

Teresa was seventy-three years old and, in terms of age, a contemporary of Marina. She had arrived in New York City ten years after Marina, a time when the Puerto Rican population in the United States increased fourfold.[12] Unlike Marina, she had not come to New York City to reunite with family or to achieve a specific economic target. She had migrated to the United States seeking specialized health care for her youngest daughter. She opted to stay in New York City to escape marital discord and physical violence. When she first left the Island for New York City, she brought along just her youngest daughter—who would spend long periods of time hospitalized due to a disabling illness—and an older daughter, to help her get settled.

The third of four children, Teresa had been raised by her maternal grandmother and intermittently lived with her mother. Her mother was a cook; she had a small Creole food stand and also worked in family homes. Teresa had never finished more than the second grade at school and would often tag along with her mother to work. In Puerto Rico, Teresa had been married twice and had five children. She had held sporadic work as a lottery vendor and a pieceworker, but her most stable employment was as a housekeeper.

Teresa, like most immigrant Puerto Rican women at the time, got her first job in New York's garment industry, as a presser and floor worker. Her former employer on the Island had helped pay her way to New York and alerted her to employment opportunities in the garment industry:

Teresa: Don Luis told me everything that I needed to know. He told me: "When you get to New York, go to a factory to look for work. When they ask you if you know how to iron or if you've ever worked in garment before say yes." And I did just that.

A combination of personal circumstances and changing welfare policies forced her back into off-the-books domestic work, which she had done in Puerto Rico:

Teresa: I worked in a factory till the hospital told me to get out. I had to take care of my daughter. They forced me out of work—the social worker, that is. And that's how I got on welfare. They filled out the paperwork and everything; they helped with housing and clothing. But, since I was a good presser, I always had two or three days of work with the factory. Then I sent away for the boys. Yes, I kept working, you see, secretly. Because if they found out, they would take me off the aid. And when work at the factory got slow, I would do cleaning and ironing at a family's home.

She worked as a domestic until she was sixty-two, when she had to quit because of poor health.

At the time of the interview Teresa lived in public housing in Manhattan and often shared her limited space and resources with one or another grandchild or great-grandchild. She had three daughters and a son. All but one of the daughters lived in New York; her oldest daughter, from a previous marriage, lived in Ohio. The oldest son had died in an accident.

These two vignettes offer contrasting examples of employment outcomes by timing of migration and by personal and local labor market characteristics at the time of migration: a two-earner household with low-income but steady labor versus a single-earner household with low-income and wage work occasionally interspersed with informal work and welfare receipt. Although both Marina and Teresa were early immigrants, the first arrived at a time when job opportunities were plentiful and a welcoming climate greeted the few new arrivals. Teresa's status as a single female family head, the fact that she was black, and the government's social welfare practices of the time led her into a markedly different employment path. Their experiences suggest that integration into the labor force depends very much not only on whether the economy is expanding or contracting but on who else is in the household.

For well over half of the Puerto Rican population in the United States today, migration is a pivotal event. Marina at times seems to conform to the conventional image of the female migrant: a wife who migrates in order to follow or join her husband. She talked about a move in search of better opportunities for her husband, not for both her and her husband. Yet she was the behind-the-curtains orchestrator of a household strategy of economic mobility. Teresa's journey appears just as motivated by the economic constraints of a single, female head-of-household in Puerto Rico as by her stated motive for migration (that is, her child's health care needs).

For both Marina and Teresa, working for wages was a fact of life. It is practically the norm in working-poor households for women to be economically active. As a general rule, the further down the class structure one looks, the greater the proportion of household subsistence that women contribute (Blau and Ferber 1986; Blumberg 1991).[13] But only among families headed by married couples, or among economically active single adults living at home and pooling resources, does women's work contribute to alleviating poverty.

Marina and Antonio were not unemployed, marginalized workers from rural areas but urban dwellers with a stable history of employment in relatively skilled sectors of the urban economy. That Marina held a job both before and after marriage lessened the threat that her employment might have posed to marital stability upon migration. The nature of her employment is another factor worth noting. Although her income as a machine operator made a significant difference in total family income, it would not have been sufficient to support her and her children on the Island or in the United States. The success of Marina and Antonio's social mobility project was contingent upon their staying together. Teresa had to defer the American Dream for longer.

The Social Mobility Project in a Time of Economic Expansion

Puerto Rican women migrants like Marina, who arrived in the 1940s, entered an industry in decline. The full employment of the war economy to some extent masked longer-term trends in the regional economy. Employment in the garment industry started falling gradually as early as the 1930s, when manufacturers and contractors started abandoning New York for lower-cost, labor-surplus areas elsewhere in the Northeast. Though World War II temporarily boosted demand, the erosion of garment industry jobs resumed in the postwar era. The drive to cut labor costs and the desire to evade unionization continued until the mid-1970s, when the pace of decline seemed to level off (Bailey and Waldinger 1991). Yet early migrants' personal narratives tell of a period when work was still abundant and they could move from one shop to another. Analysts of the city's economic history suggest that this mobility might have been the result of white flight from New York rather than of an expansion in the number of jobs (Mollenkopf and Castells 1991).

Older Early Migrants   With the exception of Estela, the early migrants in the sample who were sixty-five years old or older at the time of the interview all had held jobs in the garment industry.[14] The highly competitive industry was heavily represented by Island-born Puerto Ricans, who at the time constituted the majority of Puerto Ricans in the United States. Despite the unstable nature of employment (downsizing, relocation, and closing were becoming commonplace), most had retired from their operative jobs. In all cases, years of experience were not appreciably rewarded with increases in wages or occupational mobility. For instance, Marina had been a machine operator for thirty-nine years, always doing piecework, as her sister Marta and Marta's friend, Luisa, had been.

Among retirees, particularly those with daughters of working age, there was a general cognizance that the job market in 1993 was very different. Marta had arrived in New York City in 1945, at age twenty-two. She had come only to escort her older sister's children, but a year and a half later she had married and was still living in New York City. Like her sister, Marina, she had an eighth-grade education, vocational training in the needle trades, and previous work experience in a factory.

In Marta's time, the job search worked primarily through informal and word-of-mouth recruitment into manufacturing and services:

Marta: When I got to this country, I went to live with my sister, with Marina. At the time, she worked at a factory that made women's slacks. She took me along but I didn't like it. I started to work there but I didn't like her friends; they were older and couldn't see beyond work in a factory.

I moved to work in a factory that made costume jewelry. It paid little but I was single. And it was enough to get to work, to eat, and even save a little. I would send money home, to my mother. I worked there, it was a unionized job, for fifteen years. But work was often slow, because they kept changing product lines.

So, when I moved to where I live now, a girl told me that they were looking for a machine operator on 125th, where they made window shades. I was the only operator. It wasn't unionized, because the carpenter's union didn't want us [her or the woman previously in that position] in. But I liked it; it paid well. When the owner died, they relocated to Miami. I retired then. It was 1981, I was sixty-two, and my husband was ill.

Marta did not recall ever having much trouble finding a job. But the work careers of her daughters had made her realize how different the labor market is today. Both her daughters had high school degrees. Her oldest was married, had four children, and lived in New York City. She had just been laid off after seven years working with the Trump casinos. The younger one, who was single, had moved to California, where she found a job with an insurance company. Marta acknowledged the increasing association between education and employment but was quick to point out that the connection is not always certain: "You see, eventually it will take two or three years of college to get any job. And, still, it will depend on what you studied. Because not everyone with a college education can get a job."

Luisa, Marta's neighbor and friend, was twenty-six years old when she arrived in New York City in 1948:

Luisa: I arrived in this country the 30th of August, Tuesday, at six in the afternoon, in a small bimotor plane. I got here with my son, the youngest. I got here and started working; then looked for a better job one day and another, until I settled in one place. My husband came first, he was already here when I arrived with my son. I left the other one with my godmother, the one who raised me, in Puerto Rico. He [the husband] was a cook at a hospital, and he made good money. But we started having problems, problems, problems. I sent for my other son. More problems still. I divorced him in '57. I raised them by myself and, in '66, I remarried.

The second of eleven children, Luisa was raised by her godmother, a single head of household, who did industrial homework, worked for the Bureau of the Census and for school lunchrooms, and eventually moved to New York herself. In the late 1940s and early 1950s, a good number of Puerto Ricans seemed to know of somebody else, often whole families, who had migrated to the states from the same Island town.

Luisa's job search was also typical. Another boarder in the house where she lived showed her the ropes. First, he took her over to a traditional service sector employer of Puerto Ricans, Mount Sinai Hospital, but Luisa did not like it. She kept looking. She went up and down the street looking for employee-wanted signs until she found a machine operator job at a garment factory:

> Luisa: The owner was Jewish, an old Jew, aha. But then he moved over to Tremont, there, he moved the factory there. And, once again, he had problems. They closed the factory and he moved to another place with a different name. We worked there until he died.
>
> The union found us new jobs, downtown. And we moved, moved, up until it moved to 27th Street, and that's when I retired. I was always a machine operator, always an operator, in women's housecoats, housecoats.

In this earlier period, the continued employment of women in the clothing and apparel industry, even at lower wages, meant that they could hold on to their pensions (Jensen and Davidson 1984; Rosen 1987):

> Luisa: And they [coworkers] would tell me, when I retired: Girl, wait, wait until you turn sixty-five. To wait three years, girl?! What if I die before and I don't get anything after all? So, I retired at sixty-two.
>
> You have to have worked for at least twenty years—I worked more with the union, but you had to be sixty-five, and I retired at sixty-two. If you retire at sixty-five, then you get the full amount; if at sixty-two, they look for the number of years you have worked, how much you earned and that. Then the union would give $125 full, that's what they give when you retire at sixty-five. I get 96, $96 every month and with that I live, with that and a little money that my husband left me.

Luisa had retired from her machine operator job nine years before, in 1984. At the time of the interview, she had been a widow for eight years. She was living on a small pension in a rent-controlled apartment in the Upper West Side, and she received Medicare. Her oldest son, a high school graduate, was married and worked as a building contractor in Massachusetts. The younger one, who had dropped out of high school, was divorced, was unemployed, and lived at home.

Within the same migrant cohort, work experiences in the industry were qualitatively different depending on a woman's marital and parental status. Teresa and women with similar backgrounds, like Solangel and Nydia, having gone through marital disruption and become solely responsible for their children, had few options when work became slow or a factory closed. They could not afford to wait to be called back; they had to resort either to public assistance, to changing jobs, or to both. For example, when the hospital social worker demanded that Teresa quit her job and sign up for welfare so that she would be able to look after her sick child, Teresa did as she was told. She took on piecework from the factory and worked as an off-the-books domestic to make ends meet. And faced with successive work slowdowns and factory relocations, Solangel, through an acquaintance, found a food-service job at Mount Sinai Hospital. But Nydia was not as lucky. After being laid off from work during a slowdown, she became very ill and spent almost a year in the hospital. She had lost her apartment and was unable to send remittances home to Puerto Rico for her children. In the absence of family or friends, a hospital administrator and his wife, who had grown fond of her, assisted Nydia in applying for welfare. In the absence of kin support networks, public assistance became a complement to uncertain paid employment.

Younger Early Migrants   Younger postwar migrants[15] had had somewhat different experiences in the labor market. They were still concentrated in blue-collar occupations, but they did not identify themselves first as working class or by their trade as garment workers. More than their older counterparts, their narratives tell of primary identities as wives and mothers. Factory work represented a means of subsistence, not the basis for self-esteem. Even before "working mothers" became an important policy issue, these women were negotiating the dual responsibilities of work and home. Only the oldest in this group (that is, Celeste, Francisca, and Elba) no longer had direct child care responsibilities. Perhaps this is what allowed Elba (about to turn sixty-five and negotiating the terms of retirement) to take a step back and look at changes in the economy and the meaning of work in more general, or impersonal, terms:

> Elba: It was easier [to get a job] before. Now it is more difficult. Because in the United States industry, the working American gets no respect. Because they [referring to the government] didn't, although the unions wanted to protect the worker; well, what they did was to live off the worker. But it didn't help the worker. Because, when they started exporting all jobs abroad, this city declined economically. They sent the industry to foreign countries, where they could pay the workers less. . . . So, what we are living is a depression, in part as a result of the lack of organization among United States workers.
>
> They started reducing the number of workers, then they cut working days, to distribute more evenly available hours and salary. And they also let go of many people. Many were left without work. It hasn't all been the workers' fault. It is that they [industry owners] prefer to hire an illegal alien than an American citizen, who was born here.

Displaced manufacturing workers were less likely to find similar employment. In fact, they frequently experienced significant earnings losses. Their chances of reemployment were significantly complicated by their age at the time of job loss. And women with marginal jobs were more likely to drop out of the labor force altogether. Celeste had experienced firsthand what Elba talked about in the abstract:

> Celeste: My husband got murdered in '83. After that, the factory where I worked for twenty-seven years moved to Florida. They wanted me to go along but I didn't want to. I couldn't leave my sons behind, because one's children come first. I decided to stay here, the union sent me to get unemployment, and I collected for six months. After six months, I had no choice but to go on welfare. . . . And I cannot live on [what I get]. I clean houses or do ironing, you know, I look around to make another dollar.
>
> We [she and her oldest son, who worked at the same factory for fifteen years] got laid off on March 30th of '89. It is now going to be four years. After that, he didn't . . . , because you know that foreigners will work at two dollars an hour and no Puerto Rican will do it. Not even I, old as I am, would do it. After I got laid off, I have looked for work, but they see your older face and behind you there's a twenty-year-old and that one gets the job someone who might not be as responsible and I, who am responsible, won't get it, because it is like that; I've looked for work.

Four of the women in this group of seven (younger) early migrants had never been on welfare. But Francisca, when she first arrived in Brooklyn; Gilda and Dora, after experiencing marital disruption; and Celeste, after job loss at the age of fifty-five, did not feel that they had any other option. They concurred with other women in their age group that jobs for women like themselves in New York City meant either a factory job or child-care work—neither of which would have enabled them to support their families on their own. The difference, again, appears to lie not in education or experience but in a combination of the availability of employment opportunities for the low-skilled and the presence (or absence) of social support networks.

Human capital differences appear insufficient to explain differences in the rate of employment. Rather, participation was higher for wives with husband present, regardless of educational attainment. A spouse, as a potential wage earner or surrogate caretaker, lent these households the flexibility to adjust to changing conditions in the labor market.

Single women among the early migrants followed somewhat different paths to employment. Women like Elba, Dora, Marta, Irene, and Damaris had migrated to the United States in their teens or early twenties, seeking independence or improvement in their marriage and job prospects. They often played a superfluous or nonessential role in their local economies, had the support and encouragement of a family member—usually the mother—and were willing (and able, since they had no dependents) to work for food and lodging in order to realize their self-improvement goal.

Elba ventured the five-day, 1,600-mile sea trip to New York and initially went to live with family:

Elba: I got here in 1947 on the last trip of that ship called, what was it called?, the *Merchant*, the. . . the *Marine Tiger*! . . . . I finished high school in Puerto Rico and I came to live here, with my sister Estela. And, then, on the second week here, I started working along with another sister who worked in the [garment] industry; we went to work at a factory in lower Manhattan. I started out from the bottom up, from the factory line to sample maker.[16]

Elba was keenly aware of changes in the economy and the workplace; she had lived through them. When asked why she thought Puerto Ricans kept coming to New York and to the United States, she replied:

Elba: I think that the Puerto Rican who is doing well in Puerto Rico has nothing to look for here. If someone has training and education, and a good job, why would they want to come here if they are better off in Puerto Rico? Those who come either don't have the resources or they have a problem. But to look for jobs? Not here!

The majority of Puerto Ricans migrating to New York before 1950 were from a skilled and semiskilled urban workforce (Maldonado 1979; Mills, Senior, and Goldsen 1950). Beginning in the late 1950s, allegedly relatively fewer migrants came from the largest cities and higher-skilled groups (Gray 1975). But whether the women's family origins were in agricultural or industrial labor, their successful integration into the labor force appears to have been mediated by a support network of family or kin who were also a source of job contacts.

Irene arrived in 1965. In her family, young males migrated first, recruited to work in agriculture; they left agricultural work at home for agricultural contract labor, and later on factory work, in the states.

Irene: I grew up in the countryside in Puerto Rico, and when I decided to come over to New York it was because of my brothers, who arrived first.

I had dropped out of school in Puerto Rico and helped out my mother at home. I was bored and restless, and not very hopeful about my future. My older siblings had left and they sent money home; they had factory jobs. I told my mom that I wanted to leave as well, to try my luck in New York. I was stubborn, I would tell her that everybody was going to New York and that it had to be something great—little did I know that the stories were not totally true.

My mother finally gave in. I got to New York. I had come to work but I was only sixteen and most jobs required that you be eighteen. I cleaned and cooked for my siblings, but I hoped and waited for a break to get a job. It finally happened. I got my first job, doing piecework, at the factory where my brothers worked.

Those who, because of their educational attainment, had aspirations beyond a factory job often faced a language barrier. Damaris arrived in New York City three years after her sister Irene:

Damaris: I came over in 1968, in August of '68, the 28th. Since I had those two years of college in Puerto Rico, I was thinking, I am not going into one of those crowded factories, because I went to school. In my mind, that's what I thought. I was up for a surprise. When I started looking for a job, my brother came along. The first place that I walked into, the man asked me if I spoke any English and I said that a little, thinking of the English that I'd learned while in Puerto Rico. Little did I know that that English wouldn't even help with basic communication. I could follow with some difficulty, but he said, "No, I don't have a job for you." So, we went to another place, but they only had factory jobs. My brother said, "Look, this is all there is." And we went, my sister Irene also came along, and we all got jobs, because there were jobs for everybody. Even my brother got a job, driving a truck. Our job was packing clothes.

But Damaris was determined to get an office job. She signed up for evening English classes at the Spanish Institute. She was growing confident and started looking for a new job. When a problem at work forced her to quit, she once again had to compromise:

Damaris: I looked and looked and I didn't find anything. After four or five months, I started getting nervous. My brother came along and took me to a place where one had to pay to get a job. It was for people without papers, you know. But we are American citizens, we shouldn't have to go through this—I thought. Well, he took me over there, somewhere on 14th Street, where one had to pay like fifty or sixty dollars, I don't remember.

The job was for three months only, after the three months, they kicked you out and they would take in a new person and start all over again. By Christmas I was, once again, without a job. I couldn't collect (unemployment); I didn't have enough time on the job.

Damaris had another factory job before she decided to enroll in school full-time. A chance occurrence landed her an office job in the factory where she worked, and she changed her admission status at Hunter College to part-time student, at night. That Damaris was single and that her working siblings could back her up financially if needed allowed her to persist with her occupational aspirations. Her employment history, like that of others in her age and migrant group (with the exception of Celeste), was characterized by frequent changes between firms and occupations.

Dora also came from a large family in Puerto Rico; she was one of thirteen siblings, twelve of whom are still living, four in the United States. She arrived in 1968. Dora had a high school degree and secretarial training but no job contacts on the Island. After her government youth employment program was over, she applied for jobs in Puerto Rico, including factory jobs, to no avail. A discouraged worker, she left for New York City:

> Dora: I came here when I was about twenty-two years old. Initially, to take care of my older brother's children. I took care of his kids for about a year and a half. I didn't even get paid for the job. I felt as if they had taken advantage of me. Because Mom had not sent me over to baby-sit anybody's kids, it was to look for a job, to move ahead, even if it meant a factory job. Finally, about nine months after I arrived, some cousins of mine, my brother's sisters-in-law, helped me out and found me a job at a factory. That was my first paid job here, packing clothes that would later go to department stores. . . . I worked for them first, for about six years, in New York and another six years in New Jersey, when they moved the factory.

This group of younger, unattached women had kin networks that facilitated their migration and socioeconomic incorporation. Their choice of New York as a location had to do with the concentration of family or friends and the prospect of higher wages and employment opportunities. They were also seeking an environment with more relaxed gender-role expectations, and a measure of independence, to prove their mettle.

Faded Visions of Opportunity: Negotiating Work and Welfare

The period from 1969 to 1977 brought about a massive employment decline in New York City, particularly in the production and transportation of goods. Manufacturing firm headquarters were also abandoning the city. But the shift from goods production to services was not a new development in the city's economic history. Blue-collar jobs, traditionally associated with manufacturing employment, declined by 32,000 in the 1950s, by 183,000 in the 1960s, and by another 225,000 in the 1970s (New York City Department of City Planning, 1993).

Meanwhile, Puerto Rico, despite the absolute wage gap relative to the United States, had been losing its competitive advantage to other low-wage countries. A reorientation of the Island's development strategy from a labor-intensive export sector to a capital-intensive sector (for example, petrochemicals and pharmaceutical firms) did not result in the expected total job and income generation (Ríos 1990). The unemployment rate increased steeply during this period. Overall, young people with less than a high school education and in blue-collar occupations were the most likely to be unemployed. Unemployed Puerto Ricans on the Island continued to perceive migration to the United States as an alternative to joblessness. But the 1970s was also a period of increased return migration to Puerto Rico, suggesting that emigration was losing its effectiveness as a "safety valve" (Dietz 1986).

By 1975, New York's garment manufacturing, the quintessential sex-typed immigrant job source, had shed a third of its 1969 recession-year labor force (Waldinger 1986). The industry was never to return to earlier employment levels, and Puerto Ricans were no longer a preferred source of labor. At a time when the majority of Puerto Ricans in New York were Island-born, when 43.8 percent of the Puerto Rican population in New York City was under the age of eighteen, and when an increasing number of other women were entering the labor force, Puerto Ricans were not in a position to profit from government-designed buffers, like large-scale public sector job creation.

Carmín and Mercedes left the Island to flee a life of poverty. Carmín was the seventh of twelve children. She went to school until the sixth grade and worked as a domestic in order to buy her own clothes and shoes. Her mother had abandoned the family when Carmín was a child and died when Carmín was barely an adolescent. When her mother left, Carmín went to live and work in the house of a man who claimed to be her father. At thirteen, she left to follow a man who was more than twice her age, who mistreated her. She left him and got work as a live-in domestic. She discovered that she was pregnant and ended up at a state group home for girls. The Department of Public Welfare in Puerto Rico took the child away from her; she ran away. She later met a man whom she married and who offered to help her regain custody of her child.

Since Carmín had transgressed the rigidly defined limits of sex-role behavior by having a child out of wedlock, a husband represented an opportunity to leave the group home and to regain custody of her child. Without any significant employment or occupational future in the local economy, she saw migration as a way to try her luck elsewhere:

Carmín: I came to the United States because I thought that the city of skyscrapers was something out of this world. That's what everybody said, all who had been here and went back. So I had this wish to come over. But what really happened was that the father of my children came first, he came ahead, to live with his brother, and he told me that he would send for me. He left me pregnant, he said that it wouldn't be long before I could join him. But once he got there all I got were letters. In the meantime, he fell in love with an American woman and had forgotten about me. You know, he didn't want me to come over, so he left me at my sister's; he didn't do as he promised. It was his older brother who sent me the plane ticket. So I came over to New York, to see snow. I was seventeen. And very naive.

As soon as the child was born, and as a condition for them to get back together, Carmín's reluctant husband had her apply for welfare:

Carmín: I was so embarrassed. I didn't want to. I cried. I just wanted to go back to Puerto Rico and to take my daughter with me. For thirty dollars every two weeks. . . . But it was the only way for us to get started. I started living off welfare and he worked.

Once her children were in school, Carmín first worked in a meatpacking freezer and then held a night-shift job as a machine operator in a New Jersey factory, sewing hospital curtains. The husband's presence allowed them to take on different shifts in order to accommodate child care. Eventually, Carmín got back custody of her older son. When her children were older, she signed up for a home attendant training program through the welfare office.

Since 1981, Carmín (a post-1970 immigrant) had been part of the new occupational ghetto for poor women. She was working as a home attendant, taking care of the elderly. This was part-time, low-wage, contractual work, with no employee benefits attached, and did not pay enough to live on.

Carmín worked from referrals, often off the books, so as not to risk losing her public assistance. She received housing assistance and food stamps and was eligible for Medicaid. Carmín was helping to raise her granddaughter so that her daughter could work and finish college. Because she worked for pay, she was able to enroll her children in parochial schools. Her older son, then thirty years old, was married and lived and worked in Maryland; her two daughters (ages twenty-six and twenty-seven) were married and worked as low-level managers in the hotel industry, and the older was finishing a college degree; her younger son had dropped out of school.

Mercedes, like Carmín, arrived in New York in the 1970s, when jobs were harder to come by. Their pathways to migration appear very similar:

Mercedes: I was raised by my grandmother, because my mother couldn't have me. She wasn't really my grandmother, but the one who raised my mother. The story repeats itself, you see? When she died, I went to live in a state home for girls, from age seven until I turned seventeen. The only way to get out of there was to get married. I got married, left the group home, got pregnant. We lived together for four months, we broke up, we got together again, for four months, always four months. He talked me into joining him in Connecticut. I was miserable. I couldn't stand it. I left him and came over to New York. I had never really lived before, I didn't really know the world. When I got to New York, I started going to dance places, to bars, I got a job doing piecework. I felt like a free woman.

Mercedes was fifty years old. She had just quit her home attendant job because of a disability, and she lived in public housing in the South Bronx with her partner of many years. She had four children: two daughters and two sons, ages twenty-two to thirty. She had raised three of them; the oldest one had been raised by a female friend. They were a bank clerk, a hospital technician, a phone company representative, and a recent college graduate (who was to start graduate school that year). Mercedes had been on and off welfare when her kids were growing up, yet she did what she had to do so that they could go to parochial schools. She held odd jobs most of the time (anything that would not require previous work experience or specialized training). She even started a small restaurant once, but for the past two years she had worked as a home attendant. Mercedes and Carmín both had a rocky work and personal history, but their children seemed to be navigating the labor market reasonably well.

Beatriz, the youngest in the recent migrant sample, was a single head of household with the equivalent of a ninth-grade education. She married at fifteen and divorced six years and three children later, at twenty-one. She had been on AFDC for three years, and one of her children was receiving Supplemental Security Insurance. Beatriz's mother had come over in 1983, seeking specialized health care for a child with a life-threatening heart condition. She brought her family of eleven along, since there was nobody left to take care of them. Beatriz's father had left home, and there was little that she could do in the depressed economy of her southern Island hometown (once a booming oil-refining center). They went to live with her sister's mother and their family of seven (five children and the parents):

> Beatriz: My aunt and uncle had told my mother that they had better health care and better hospitals here. That she could get welfare in the beginning and then get herself a job. We were still at school but we worked in the afternoons.
>
> My father had abandoned my mother. He left for the U.S., hooked up with another woman, and never sent for us. He didn't lift a finger to help us. It was my mother who had to sell the house, so that we could all come over. We came over to Brooklyn, and we haven't left Brooklyn.
>
> My aunt had been on welfare herself, and my uncle worked, and still they had a hard time making a living. My mom got a job as a cook and received some supplementary assistance. We got an apartment. In the meantime, my aunt moved away, they got a house, she quit welfare. She moved ahead. Now she has a job. My uncle has a job. And so far, so good.

Beatriz was confident that there was a way out of welfare; her aunt had found it. First, she said, she needed to get a new apartment, away from the disruptive influence and verbal abuse of her children's father. Her independence would come at a high cost; she would no longer live close enough to her former mother-in-law, who helped with child care, and she would have to forgo the little assistance that her former husband provided in terms of home repair and occasional child care. She would also have to wait until the child that she was expecting was at least two years old and could be in day care before she could think of going to school or getting a job:

Beatriz: My dream is to leave welfare, to make it on my own, to get to be someone. So that my children grow up, since their father is no good example, with my example, working to support them. So that when it's their turn to have a family, they know where their responsibilities lie. But first I need to leave this place. I need to leave this place.

But Beatriz was not kidding herself. She knew that, with four children, taking on a job would only leave her a marriage away from poverty and welfare receipt:

Beatriz: I am embarrassed. Right now, when I go to the hospital and I see all these women, talking about their husbands—who work, and help support the family, who take them out to a restaurant and everything. At times, I am at the verge of tears. . . . Here I have to do everything, if I don't take charge, nothing happens.

Still, asserted Beatriz, finding a job was easier in New York City than it was in Puerto Rico, where she knew the jobs were scarce, where one needed a car to move around, and where there were few or no jobs for the unskilled. It was a time of declining opportunities for the Island-born, single head of household with children and less than a high school education in New York City, but it was her best option. She was staying.

Social scientists and policy analysts (for example, Bean and Tienda 1987) have noted the changing relationship between nativity status and the occupational allocation of Puerto Rican women in the U.S. labor market. The decreasing number of factory jobs for women in New York City, and of Puerto Ricans in those jobs, suggest that Island-born Puerto Rican women have lost the comparative advantage that they had over the U.S. born or educated.

The experience of three recent (post-1970) migrants, Beatriz, Carmín, and Mercedes, tends to confirm this pattern. Their labor force participation seems to have been determined as much by their "personal" traits (for example, educational attainment, marital status, child-care responsibilities, and illness or disability) as by broader structural forces over which they had little or no control. The local economy and the structure of employment were significantly different at the time of their arrival than it had been, for instance, for Marina's or Elba's cohorts (that is, those arriving before 1970). Among other things, the conspicuous rise in overall labor force participation and the increase in women with small children entering the labor force that started in the 1960s significantly altered the nature of supply.

Not only did Beatriz, Carmín, and Mercedes enter the U.S. labor market between two major recessions, in 1975 and 1982, but long-term changes in the industrial composition of employment meant the steady erosion of relatively better-paid and unionized factory jobs for the low-skilled. The three women were not unlike Teresa, Nydia, and Solangel in terms of their personal characteristics, but they seemed to have had fewer and less stable options than their predecessors. Although they were not prepared to make the transition into a service sector of either part-time "female" jobs or higher-skill professional and managerial jobs, they expected that their children would.

Given that a decreasing number of Puerto Ricans in New York are Island-born, the poor socioeconomic standing of Puerto Ricans in the city cannot be attributed to a "declining quality" of immigrants.[17] In fact, Puerto Ricans migrating from Puerto Rico in the 1980s were younger and more educated than those from earlier cohorts, although they still lagged behind U.S.-born Puerto Ricans and the city's overall population in terms of educational attainment and income (New York City Department of City Planning 1993). Entry-level garment manufacturing or service jobs have not significantly upgraded the level of skill required, but they have become scarcer and less stable, and New York City employers have found a more pliable and abundant workforce in undocumented migrants (who are willing to work at menial jobs for lower wages, lack organizational experience, and assume a deferential attitude toward their employers). The policy concern becomes one of determining what combination of employment and income is needed for the less skilled to support themselves and their families and what would it take for them to attain both.

Turning Points: From Factory Jobs to Service Sector Jobs

Second-generation Puerto Ricans include those who migrated as children. Angela, Belén, Elisa, and Zulma fall into this category. They were the offspring of single and married mothers, they had arrived in the United States at anywhere from infancy to fourteen years of age, and they were in the United States for good. All had at least a high school education and, in this regard, had done better than their mothers had. How were their paths in and out of employment different from those of immigrants? What were their perceptions of work, welfare, and social opportunity?

Only one of my informants, Lida, was born in the United States. Zulma arrived when she was six months old, Elisa when she was four years old, and Belén and Angela at the age of fourteen. They were all a generation removed from the original migration—actually, a generation removed from that household or family member's decision to leave the Island for New York City—and they had attended school in the United States

Lida was the outgoing director of the Home Management Program (which teaches "survival skills," such as nutrition, child rearing, and consumer education to urban, low-income, mostly foreign-born women) in a settlement house in the Lower East Side. She was married and had three adult children:

Lida: I grew up in El Barrio on 115th Street, on 17th Street, on Lexington Avenue, Park Avenue, 5th Avenue; all over the place! My mother was from Puerto Rico and my father was originally from Spain. My mother used to run a boardinghouse, that's how they met. She didn't know how to write or anything, I used to read her the letters that she got from Puerto Rico. After she had me and my brother, she worked in hotels and watching babies at nights. My mother and father separated when I was six. We were very poor.

I went to a vocational training high school because my teacher, my counselor said that I didn't spell well enough to become a secretary and my mother didn't make enough money to send me to nursing school.

So, I took up fashion design and, when I graduated, I worked for a long, long time in a factory. I was what they called the draper, at this place where they made fine women's negligees. I would put on garments on the figurine, to see that everything was tip-top. I also learned how to do assortments, which is to prepare work for the operators. Then they closed.

After a few weeks, I was getting bored. So I went and worked in a neighborhood factory. They put me down as an operator; I hated it. She [the owner] went bankrupt and I went back to collect unemployment. Then, they called me from my old job and I stayed with them until I got married.

Lida worked for a total of sixteen years in the garment industry. She got married at age thirty-five to a Puerto Rican in the Merchant Marine. She got pregnant and quit her job to raise her children almost by herself, since her husband was at sea most of the time. She did volunteer work in the community and participated actively in the school decentralization and community control movement. Through her next-door neighbor, Lida found out about a new Manpower Development program that offered general equivalency diploma (GED) classes for people who had not completed high school. Though Lida had had both high school and a year of college, it had been a long time since she had been in a classroom, and she felt old and unprepared.

The GED led the way to an associate's degree in education at Brooklyn Community College and her present job. Lida talked about her job in terms of social-psychological rewards, as a source of pleasure and satisfaction and of social and political identity:

Lida: I love this job. I don't want to give it up, really. It is low pay—I was never paid a tremendous salary—but I enjoy what I am doing. And because I was married and thanks God I lived with my husband, I didn't see the need [to change jobs]. I was not looking for money. I was looking for satisfaction in what I did.

Growing up poor in New York City in the 1940s was a totally different experience than growing up poor there in the 1970s. Perhaps one of the most commonly recited explanations for the high rates of poverty among Puerto Ricans in the United States regards circular migration. The assumption is that Puerto Ricans move back and forth between New York City and the Island, which results in unstable market trajectories, which in turn lead to isolation from the political system and socioeconomic marginality, a higher probability of joblessness, or both; unemployment and underemployment; and, consequently, limited attachment to the U.S. labor market. As teachers in the public school system will attest, the reality is that Puerto Ricans move a lot but mostly within New York City neighborhoods. This pattern is not uncommon among poor families, who are more likely renters than homeowners (Cook and Rudd 1984). It is particularly common among urban, low-income, single mothers, who move often, for safety reasons or to seek better housing conditions (Oliker 1994). Zulma's story is a case in point:

> Zulma: When I came here to the United States, I was like six months old. So school for me was not difficult, because I was raised learning the English language. Although, I'd say, it [ethnic background] caused a lot of prejudice, especially when I started college.
>
> I was raised in a very low income home. So I got used to it. So I moved a lot. And, as an adult, I understand that I came from a dysfunctional family. Not that it wasn't hard as a child. It was hard. It was hard because I not only had the thing that I was Hispanic, but I also kept moving.
>
> I also knew that it was hard on my mother too, as a single woman, to be able to maintain a house. Because of the financial reason, my mother was always moving. After I was, like, sixteen years old my whole life got more stable. She stayed where she is at—she's been living there for the last fourteen years.
>
> I went to the worst high school in the Bronx, but I was an honor student, and that made my mom very proud of me. And then I went to college.

Zulma was twenty-four years old, the mother of three (the oldest was a child from her first marriage). She was a year shy of a bachelor's degree in accounting. Her husband had only an elementary school education. He had quit his unionized job as a printer to start a business of his own as a flea market vendor. Zulma had worked for two years as a vocational counselor, on commission, for two small private business schools. The job offered low pay and no fringe benefits. When one of her children was molested by a relative caretaker, she quit her job and began to help her husband as an unpaid family worker in his small business. Her personal aspirations were to finish school, stay off public assistance, get a job that provided medical benefits, and ensure that her children would do better than herself, because she had done better than her mother. It did not all look that clear when Zulma was eighteen:

> Zulma: He was Puerto Rican, I was eighteen years old, he was twenty, we were very young. And, of course, that was when I was going to college. So, I

wanted to do the right thing—not like people think all, or most, Puerto Ricans do. I got pregnant and I got married, and I still wanted to go to school, so I went to school.

Behind Zulma's fierce determination to prove people wrong was her mother, who had housed the young couple in her government-subsidized apartment and provided child care while receiving welfare assistance on the condition that Zulma not quit school. Zulma was highly critical of welfare recipients, even though she was "able to do better than her mother" because her mother went on welfare and even though she herself had applied for benefits when her husband quit his job and she had to quit hers.

Angela and Belén were the only children of Francisca, an early migrant, who had received public assistance when she first arrived in Brooklyn in 1963. The siblings had low-paying but relatively stable jobs with no benefits. Both had young children living at home and spouses with significantly lower educational attainment than themselves but with a stable history of employment (twenty-nine and thirty years, respectively) as cooks in two different city hospitals, jobs with good benefits packages. Belén had held a clerical job for the past fifteen years. Her sister, Angela, who became a licensed practical nurse when she graduated from high school, had just finished her pharmacy degree, at forty-four, and was doing her internship in a small neighborhood retail and drugstore close to her home. They were harsh in their assessment of those who receive public assistance and were particularly worried that some of the new arrivals might tarnish the image of hardworking people of the early immigrants and the U.S.-born.

Elisa was forty-four years old. She worked part-time as a bookkeeper in Manhattan and lived in Queens. She was divorced, but her children were grown and had left home; the oldest was in graduate school, and the youngest was working toward a bachelor's degree. Elisa was the youngest daughter of Teresa, who had worked as a garment presser and a domestic and had combined work and welfare so that her children did not have to. Yet Elisa, like Zulma, was highly critical of welfare participation. Her statements echoed the reemergent conservative view that poverty has a lot to do with character flaws and the inability to pull oneself up by the bootstraps:

Elisa: I mean, how much can you give them? How much do you have to do for these people? They have to do something for themselves. I mean, I sound very harsh, very cruel, but this is my opinion on this, you know, and that is it, and what can you do?

I mean, they [beggars and welfare recipients] make more money than I do and they don't have to pay [taxes]. They get food stamps, they get their welfare check, they get the Medicaid, they get all these for free and, if they have kids, they have that WIC [Women, Infants, and Children] program. I am talking about all of them, all these nationalities; Puerto Ricans also. It is not fair at all.

Here, the more kids that you have, the bigger your checks; and they just keep having them. So, I don't blame the government for everything at all. I blame it on the people. I mean, that is why, in some places they have people work for welfare. I agree a hundred percent.

Rather than seeing welfare as a source of income that enables people, primarily women with children, "to survive while avoiding unsafe and insecure jobs as well as unsafe and insecure marriages" (Abramowitz 1988, 10), Elisa and others interpret welfare as a sort of moral bankruptcy.[18] The idea that government benefits intrinsically induce dependency, undermine self-esteem, or break down family ties is challenged by the experience of not only the purposefully selected and nonrepresentative sample in this study but by the experiences of whole categories of people, such as political refugees and women and families in other industrialized countries with strong welfare states. The U.S.-born or -educated daughters of early migrants had an advantage over Carmín or Mercedes, but it was not automatic. Elsa's, Belén's, Angela's, and Zulma's mothers had worked at factory jobs or combined work and welfare so that their children did not have to.

It is difficult to speak of a second generation of Puerto Ricans as a group, since the open-ended character of migration from the Island to the United States often translates into a replenishment of first generationers whose children will come of age at different times. Thus Lida entered the labor market in the late 1940s; Angela, Belén, and Elisa in the mid-1960s; and Zulma in the 1980s. Their success in the labor market depended on local labor market conditions at least as much as on their native-born (or U.S.-educated) status.

DISCUSSION

Family disruption, welfare receipt, and limited educational attainment were not a barrier to employment in earlier periods of economic expansion. Thus Luisa, Celeste, and Solangel were just as likely to get employment in the goods manufacturing sector as their better educated counterparts, Marina, Marta, and Elba, were. But whether a woman with the above characteristics got and held on to a low-wage job depended not only on labor demand but also on household composition and resources. The expectation was that a woman would work as long as family (preferably herself or another female relative) could take care of the children, and kin support networks or government safety nets for the most part enabled participation.

In the 1970s, when the "underclass" and concentrated poor population in New York City grew dramatically, more Puerto Ricans left than came into the city. Though educational attainment influenced who among the stayers got the available jobs, the decline of blue-collar jobs in manufacturing meant that there was not much labor demand for those with lesser skills or experience. For first-time labor market entrants and immigrants (like Mercedes or Carmín), this change meant increased competition for fewer jobs. But for Puerto Ricans along every educational and occupational group, economic contraction meant fewer jobs and declining earning opportunities.

The recovery of the local economy in the 1980s rested on the rapidly growing service industries. But new jobs were created almost exclusively in Manhattan; the number of jobs in the Bronx and Brooklyn, where most New York Puerto Ricans (70 percent, as of the 1990 census) live, declined (Harris 1991; Gerard 1984). The transformation of New York City into a service and professional and managerial-oriented economy meant that the recovery bypassed those living in boroughs other than Manhattan and workers other than managers and professionals. The restructured economy, which was thought to benefit women through an expansion of "female" service sector jobs, also resulted in the erosion of wages for low-skilled workers and diminished flexibility for one-parent families. As a result of declining real wages for low-skilled workers, poverty among workers increased.

Women like Beatriz, recent immigrants with an interrupted education and limited skills, ended up with shorter work histories than their predecessors or with discontinued work histories. Below-average schooling and limited English language ability made them ill-equipped to effectively compete for the new jobs in the more stable and expanding industries. In theory, at least, Beatriz had an extended family support system, but it was also strained by labor market hardships. Within-group differences were becoming more important in 1993, and unskilled recent arrivals were perceived as a liability to their more established counterparts. Combined with conservative politics and eroding public safety nets, these factors amounted to hefty barriers for single, female family heads among the Island-born.

The good news for New York Puerto Rican women in the 1980s was that, as they effectively moved away from operative jobs, they were less affected by the continued decline or stagnation of blue-collar jobs in manufacturing. New York Puerto Rican women increased their labor force participation in the 1980s, as U.S.-born and married women experienced gains in employment and earnings and Island-born and single female family heads did worse overall.

It is tempting to conclude that assimilation is intergenerational—that the first generation of migrants realize only modest earnings growth after arrival in the United States but that their native offspring will prosper. For instance, the female children of first-generation Puerto Rican women (for example, Lida, Angela, Belén, Lisa, and Zulma) seemed to be doing better than their mothers had done in terms of education and occupational attainment. But that good news is tempered by evidence of discrimination, residential segregation, and persistently high rates of poverty and unemployment across education and family-type groups.

Yet, despite the complexity and diversity elaborated above, with persistent frequency the "problem" of Puerto Rican women's labor force participation has been framed in terms of culture versus economics. The conceptual framework that has dominated research on Puerto Rican families sees adherence to traditional gendered roles and family interdependence as obstacles to economic incorporation and social mobility. As a result, cultural values, as opposed to, for instance, changing labor markets, are assumed to determine Puerto Rican women's labor force participation.[19]

This view on families disregards change and variation among Island-born and U.S.-born Puerto Ricans. Further, it fails to acknowledge that cultural prescriptions are often modified by class or economic experiences. This is not to say that family and culture arguments are unimportant; rather, the extent of their influence becomes an empirical question, not a given (see, for example, Cooney and Ortíz 1983; Gerson 1985).

Qualitative analysis of these personal narratives corroborates a story of economic restructuring and population changes in the New York metropolitan area. The story also involves a seemingly increasing association between nativity and labor market outcomes and between marital status and labor market outcomes. Declining earnings and employment opportunities, in the face of changing family structure, mean poverty, particularly for the Island-born, who are losing the comparative advantage that they once had over the U.S.-born.

Different cohorts have access to different kinds of jobs, and labor force attachment depends on a combination of supply, demand, and institutional factors. My findings reaffirm the importance of adopting a historical-specific approach to understanding (the process of) labor market incorporation and invite further inquiry into the role that gender, ethnicity, and structural economic change play in the structuring of employment and earning opportunities for different groups in the United States. This approach can provide useful information that enlarges the context in which work, welfare, and antipoverty policies are designed.

The research reported here was supported by a dissertation fellowship from the Social Science Research Council Committee for Research on the Urban Underclass and by funds from the Ford Foundation to the Research and Training Program in Poverty, the Underclass, and Public Policy at the University of Michigan.

NOTES

1. The work of Waldinger (1986) on the transformation of the New York City garment industry suggests that the city's decline as a production center began in the 1930s, when manufacturers and contractors started abandoning it for lower-cost, labor surplus areas in the Northeast. Though World War II temporarily boosted demand, the erosion of garment industry jobs resumed in the postwar era.

    Waldinger describes the unmistakably downward trend: "Between 1947 and 1958 total apparel employment declined by 54,000 jobs; in the succeeding decade, yet another 72,000 jobs were lost. The pace of job slippage accelerated further in the late 1960s and early 1970s. The 1969 recession produced a loss of 20,000 jobs in one year alone"(p. 56).

2. Puerto Ricans are U.S. citizens and, technically, do not immigrate but rather migrate to the United States. But they exhibit distinct socioeconomic differences according to place of birth that resemble those of immigrants. To distinguish circulation behavior from the Island to the United States from internal migration (between states), I refer to Puerto Ricans of the first generation as immigrants.

3. There are two exceptions: the Puerto Rico Fertility and Family Planning Survey of 1982 and the New York Fertility, Employment and Migration survey of 1985. Both collected retrospective migration histories from respondents aged fifteen to forty-five at the time of the survey. The U.S. Census of Population allows only the identification of recent migrants by asking their place of residence five years before the survey.

4. Snowball sampling uses one sampling frame to produce another. In this case, earlier migrants (often former factory workers) introduced me to their neighbors, friends, and U.S.-born or -educated daughters. I used a number of different starting points to tap into different networks. Overall, when key informers were a result of a personal contact with kin, they generated further contacts. This was not the case with women accessed through an adult education program or through otherwise tenuous connections.

5. Since migration is a selective process, this is a nonrandom sample. Looking only at those who moved misses the story of those who considered moving but did not. Missing as well is the story of those who, finding themselves worse or better off after a move, went back to their communities of origin (that is, return migrants) or departed for other locations (that is, internal movers).

6. Notwithstanding observed patterns of return migration (to the Island) and increasing dispersion of the Puerto Rican population in the United States in recent decades, the New York metropolitan area remains a central part of the Puerto Rican migration experience. In 1985, approximately 60 percent of all Puerto Rican women in the United States (ages fifteen to forty-five) were residents of

New York City or one of its five adjacent counties (namely, Suffolk, Nassau, Essex, Passaic, and Hudson).

7. Not surprisingly in an older sample, most of the women were Island-born. According to a 1993 New York City Department of Planning report, only among those thirty-four years old and younger did the U.S.-born predominate. In all other age groups, over 50 percent were Island-born women.

8. Following Rogler and Cooney (1984), I assume that age on arrival in the United States denotes the cultural context of the women's early socialization. If a woman was born in the United States or arrived before the age of fifteen, the context is the United States (in this case, New York City); if she arrived at age fifteen or older, the context is Puerto Rico.

9. Home Relief is New York City's equivalent of General Assistance, an income support program for poor single adults without dependents. It typically involves low-level transfer payments and eligibility for food stamps, Medicaid, and housing assistance. Besides meeting income limit requirements, applicants must undergo a medical exam and, if able-bodied, show evidence of active job search.

10. California was the second largest state of settlement for Puerto Ricans from 1910 to 1950, largely as a result of the resettlement of contract canefield labor from Hawaii or the cotton fields of Arizona (Maldonado 1979). Farm workers seeking the better wages and work conditions of industrial employment and former military personnel formed the bases for the Puerto Rican community in California.

11. In the 1920s, the cigar-making industry on the Island was transformed from an organization of artisans into a competitive, labor-intensive, sex-segregated industry with a 53 percent female workforce. It was an industry with a well-defined work culture and an urban character, which stressed workers' rights and education, independence, and pride in their craft. After the Great Depression, the industry declined, and textile production picked up the displaced female workforce, first as a cottage industry and then in sex-segregated factories in the post–World War II years.

   For a history of women in the cigar-making and clothes-manufacturing industries in Puerto Rico, see Azize (1985).

12. In the 1950s, 20 percent of the Island population migrated to the United States—the largest migration of Puerto Rican men and women (Bose 1986).

13. Zavella (1991) summarizes women's contributions to family income in four hierarchical categories: from mainstay or principal provider to coprovider, secondary provider, and sole provider.

14. Namely, Marina, Teresa, Estela, Solangel, Marta, Luisa, and Nydia.

15. This is the group composed of Elba, Francisca, Celeste, Dora, Damaris, Gilda, and Irene.

16. The rather flat job ladder in a garment shop consists of floor workers, machine operators, and sample makers.

17. For two different positions on this debate, see Borjas (1991) and LaLonde and Topel (1990).

18. Others have discussed at length the transfer of public discourse (and social anxiety about the urban poor) into private discourse. See, for example, Fraser (1989) and Sapiro (1990). For an alternative interpretation of welfare in the lives of women and children, besides Abramowitz (1988), see Amott (1990); Gordon (1990); Pearce (1990); and Sidel (1986).

19. Culture is a questionable explanation in this case, argues the sociologist Christine Bose (1986), since other Hispanic women have a greater likelihood of labor force participation and all Hispanic groups (including Puerto Ricans) show higher rates of participation in the United States than in their countries of origin.

REFERENCES

Abramowitz, Mimi. 1988. *Regulating the Lives of Women: Social Welfare Policies from Colonial Times to the Present*. Boston: South End Press.

Amott, Teresa L. 1990. "Black Women and AFDC: Making Entitlement out of Necessity." In *Women, the State and Welfare*, edited by Linda Gordon. Madison: University of Wisconsin Press.

Azize, Yamila, ed. 1985. *La Mujer en la Lucha*. Río Piedras, P.R.: Editorial Cultural.

Bailey, Thomas, and Waldinger, Roger. 1991. "The Changing Ethnic/Racial Division of Labor." In *Dual City: Restructuring New York*, edited by John H. Mollenkopf and Manuel Castells. New York: Russell Sage Foundation.

Bean, Frank D., and Marta Tienda. 1987. *The Hispanic Population in the United States*. New York: Russell Sage Foundation.

Blau, Francine D, and Marianne A. Ferber. 1986. *The Economics of Women, Men and Work*. Englewood Cliffs, N.J.: Prentice Hall.

Blumberg, Rae Lesser. 1991. "The 'Triple Overlap' of Gender Stratification, Economy and the Family." In *Gender, Family and the Economy*, edited by R. L. Blumberg. Newbury Park, Calif.: Sage Publications.

Borjas, George J. 1991. "Immigrants in the U.S. Labor Market: 1940–80." *AEA Papers and Proceedings* 81(2): 287–91.

Bose, Christine E. 1986. "Puerto Rican Women in the United States: An Overview." In *The Puerto Rican Woman*, edited by Edna Acosta-Belén. New York: Praeger.

Cook, Christine C., and Nancy M. Rudd. 1984. "Factors Influencing the Residential Location of Female Households." *Urban Affairs Quarterly* 20(1): 78–96.

Cooney, Rosemary Santana, and Vilma Ortíz. 1983. "Nativity, National Origin and Hispanic Female Participation in the Labor Force." *Social Science Quarterly* 64(3): 510–23.

DeFreitas, Gregory. 1985. "Ethnic Differentials in Unemployment Among Hispanic Americans." In *Hispanics in the U.S. Economy*, edited by George J. Boras and Marta Tienda. Orlando, Fla.: Academic Press.

———. 1991. *Inequality at Work: Hispanics in the Labor Force*. New York: Oxford University Press.

Dietz, John L. 1986. *Economic History of Puerto Rico*. Princeton, N.J.: Princeton University Press.

Fraser, Nancy. 1989. *Unruly Practices: Power, Discourse and Gender in Contemporary Social Theory*. Minneapolis: University of Minnesota Press.

Gerard, Karen. 1984. "New York City's Economy: A Decade of Change." *New York Affairs* 8(2): 6–18.

Gerson, Kathleen. 1985. *Hard Choices: How Women Decide about Work, Career and Motherhood*. Berkeley: University of California Press.

Geschwender, James A. 1992. "Ethnogender, Women's Waged Labor, and Economic Mobility." *Social Problems* 39(1): 1–17.

Glazer, Nathan, and Daniel P. Moynihan. 1970. *Beyond the Melting Pot: Negroes and Puerto Ricans in a Changing Metropolis*. Cambridge, Mass.: Harvard University Press.

Gordon, Linda, ed. 1990. *Women, the State and Welfare*. Madison: University of Wisconsin Press.

Gray, Lois. S. 1975. "The Jobs Puerto Ricans Hold in New York City." *Monthly Labor Review* 98(10): 12–164.

Handlin, Oscar. 1962. *The Newcomers: Negroes and Puerto Ricans in a Changing Metropolis*. Garden City, N.Y.: Anchor Books.

Harris, Kathleen Mullan. 1991. "Teenage Mothers and Welfare Dependency: Working Off Welfare." Journal of Family Issues 12: 492–518.

Jensen, Joan M., and Sue Davidson, eds. 1984. *A Needle, a Bobbin, a Strike: Women Needle Workers in America*. Philadelphia: Temple University Press.

LaLonde, Robert J., and Robert H. Topel. 1990. "The Assimilation of Immigrants in the U.S. Labor Market. Paper presented to the Ford/National Bureau of Economic Research Immigration Conference on the Determinants and Effects of Immigration in the U.S. Cancún, Mexico (January 14–16, 1990).

Lewis, Oscar. 1966. *La Vida: A Puerto Rican Family in the Culture of Poverty*. New York: Random House.

Maldonado, Edwin. 1979. "Contract Labor and the Origins of Puerto Rican Communities in the United States." *International Migration Review* 13(March): 103–21.

Maldonado, Rita M. 1976. "Why Puerto Ricans Migrated to the United States in 1947–1973. "*Monthly Labor Review* 99(9): 7–18.

Mills, C. Wright, Clarence Senior, and Rose Kohn Goldsen. 1950. *The Puerto Rican Journey: New York's Newest Immigrants*. New York: Harper and Brothers.

Mollenkopf, John H., and Manuel Castells, eds. 1991. *Dual City: Restructuring of New York*. New York: Russell Sage Foundation.

Moore, Thomas S. 1990. "The Nature of Unequal Incidence of Job Displacement Costs." *Social Problems* 37(2): 230–42.

Morokvasic, Mirjana 1984. "Birds of Passage Are Also Women." *International Migration Review* 18(4): 886–907.

Muschkin, Clara G., and George C. Myers. 1989. "Migration and Household/Family Structure: Puerto Ricans in the United States." *International Migration* 23(4): 495–508.

New York City Department of City Planning. 1993. *Puerto Rican New Yorkers in 1990*. New York: New York City Department of Planning.

Oliker, Stacey J. 1994. Proximate contexts and workfare outcomes: A framework for studying poor women's economic choices. Paper presented at the annual meeting of the American Sociological Association. Los Angeles, Calif. (August 1994).

Pearce, Diana. 1990. "Welfare Is Not for Women: Why the War on Poverty Cannot Conquer the Feminization of Poverty. In *Women, the State and Welfare*, edited by Linda Gordon. Madison: University of Wisconsin Press.

Ríos, Palmira. 1990. "Export-Oriented Industrialization and the Demand for Female Labor: Puerto Rican Women in the Manufacturing Sector, 1952–1980." *Gender and Society* 4(3): 321–37.

Rogler, Lloyd H., and Rosemary Sastana Cooney, eds. 1984. *Puerto Rican Families in New York City: Intergenerational Processes*. Maplewood, N. J.: Waterfront Press.

Rosen, Ellen Israel. 1987. *Bitter Choices: Blue-Collar Women in and out of Work*. Chicago: University of Chicago Press.

Safa, Helen. I. 1978. "La participación diferencial de mujeres emigrantes de América Latina en la fuerza de trabajo de los Estados Unidos." ("Differences in participation of female migrants from Latin America in the United States labor force"). *Demografía y Economía* 12(l): 113–28.

Sapiro, Virginia. 1990. "The Gender Basis of American Social Policy." In *Women, the State and Welfare*, edited by Linda Gordon. Madison: University of Wisconsin Press.

Sassen-Koob, Saskia. 1985. "Changing Composition and Labor Market Location of Hispanic Immigrants in New York City, 1960–1981." In *Hispanics in the U.S. Economy*, edited by George J. Borjas and Marta Tienda. Orlando, Fla.: Academic Press.

Sidel, Ruth. 1986. *Women and Children Last: The Plight of Poor Women in Affluent America*. New York: Viking.

Smith, James P. 1988. "Poverty and the Family." In *Divided Opportunities: Minorities, Poverty and Social Policy*, edited by Gary D. Sandefur and Marta Tienda. New York: Plenum Press.

Tienda, Marta. 1989. "Puerto Ricans and the Underclass Debate." *Annals of the American Academy of Political and Social Sciences* 501(1): 105–19.

Tienda, Marta, Katherine Donato, and Héctor Cordero-Guzmán. 1990. "Queuing and Labor Force Activity of Minority Women." Paper presented at the Annual Meeting of the Population Association of America. Toronto (April 1990).

Waldinger, Roger D. 1986. *Through the Eye of the Needle: Immigrants and Enterprise in New York's Garment Trades*. New York: Plenum Press.

Zavella, Patricia. 1991. "Mujeres in Factories: Race and Class Perspectives on Women, Work and Family." In *Gender at the Crossroads of Knowledge: Feminist Anthropology in the Postmodern Era*, edited by Micaela di Leonardo. Berkeley: University of California Press.

Chapter 7

Mexican-Origin Women in Southwestern Labor Markets

Susan González Baker

Few groups display greater social and demographic diversity than Mexican-origin women in the southwestern United States. While the identifier "Mexican-origin" signifies a shared ancestry, it describes individuals with life experiences as varied as those of an undocumented Mexican-born immigrant working as a domestic laborer in a private household and a U.S.-born, Mexican-origin Ph.D. holder working in a university. "Mexican-origin" includes people whose connection to Mexico is profound and those who have never been there. It includes significant numbers who speak only Spanish and significant numbers who speak not a word of that language. Given this complexity, questions about Mexican-origin women in southwestern labor markets require an exploration of class, nativity, human capital, and the structures of industry and occupation in the Southwest (Baker 1996).

The period from 1970 to 1990 saw significant shifts in labor force participation for Mexican-origin women. For instance, in 1970 only 39.6 percent of Mexican-origin women were in the labor force, while black and non-Hispanic white women's participation hovered much closer to the 50 percent "labor force active" mark (Bean and Tienda 1988). By 1990, the scales had tipped, with 52 percent of the Mexican-origin female population aged sixteen and over joining the majority of African American and non-Hispanic white women in the labor force.

During the same period, significant shifts in industrial and occupational placement took place for Mexican-origin women. Owing largely to the Mexico-born component, Mexican-origin women showed job and industry placement patterns that differed from those of their black and non-Hispanic white counterparts. These differences emerged along two dimensions: (1) Mexican-origin women working disproportionately in blue-collar manufacturing and (2) Mexican-origin industry and occupation profiles shifting most dramatically toward service work over the 1970–90 period.

Set against this backdrop of demographic diversity and labor market change, this chapter examines the labor market experiences of Mexican-origin women in the southwestern United States. I begin with an overview of the labor market position of Mexican immigrant and U.S.-born (or "Mexican American") women in the Southwest. Drawing from the U.S. Census *Public Use Microdata Sample* (PUMS), I compare profiles for both groups in 1970, 1980, and 1990—the period covering the most dramatic shift in the Mexican-origin female population toward formal labor force participation. I also draw comparisons between Mexican-origin women and their black and non-Hispanic white counterparts at each point in time.

Next, I review the existing literature and present new analyses of the intergroup labor market dynamics characterizing Mexican-origin, African American, and non-Hispanic white women in the Southwest. Specifically, I assess whether the increasing presence of Mexican immigrant women has altered the labor market playing field in ways that either boost or depress the economic outcomes of U.S.-born women workers. Finally, I evaluate my findings in light of persistent scholarly and policy debates about the role of Mexican-origin women in the labor markets of the urban Southwest.

MEXICAN-ORIGIN WOMEN IN SOUTHWESTERN LABOR MARKETS

No treatment of Mexican-origin women in urban southwestern labor markets should overlook nativity profiles. While most labor-force-aged Mexican-origin women living in the urban Southwest are U.S.-born, the foreign-born still constitute a significant share. In 1990, 41.2 percent of Mexican-origin women aged sixteen to sixty-four living inside a metropolitan statistical area in the five southwestern states were Mexican born, a larger share than in 1980 (37.3 percent) and a much larger share than in 1970 (20.3 percent).

The importance of nativity differences becomes readily apparent in a review of the human capital repertoires characterizing the Mexican-origin population. Human capital comparisons of the civilian labor-force-aged female population in the urban Southwest in 1970, 1980, and 1990 reveal distinctions within the Mexican-origin group and across racial or ethnic identifiers (table 7.1). Life experiences vary considerably within the Mexican-origin female population. From 1970 to 1990, Mexican-born women lagged far behind their Mexican American counterparts in education, English proficiency, and employment experience. That said, the human capital repertoires of Mexican-born women still demonstrated aggregate improvement from 1970 to 1990, with a drop in both the percentage falling short of a high school education and the percentage with few or no English skills.

These human capital improvements seem to have done little to ameliorate Mexican immigrant women's comparative disadvantage, however. By

Table 7.1 / Human Capital Indicators for Women Aged Sixteen to Sixty-four Living in Southwestern Metropolitan Statistical Areas, 1970, 1980, 1990 (Percent)

| | Mexican-Origin | | | | | | Non-Hispanic Black | | | Non-Hispanic White | | |
| | Mexico-Born | | | U.S.-Born | | | | | | | | |
Indicator	1970	1980	1990	1970	1980	1990	1970	1980	1990	1970	1980	1990
Education												
Less than high school	81.1	77.4	70.9	57.3	55.2	40.2	45.2	36.1	27.1	26.5	30.0	14.7
High school	13.5	14.9	14.5	31.2	30.1	28.8	34.4	33.3	27.4	40.3	38.1	26.6
Post–high school	5.4	7.7	14.6	11.5	14.7	31.0	20.4	30.5	45.5	33.2	31.8	58.6
English												
Little or no English	—	56.9	51.1	—	7.0	5.1	—	0.6	0.3	—	5.1	0.3
Bilingual	—	41.2	44.4	—	71.3	65.9	—	3.9	2.8	—	22.5	3.5
Only English	—	1.9	4.4	—	21.6	29.1	—	95.5	96.9	—	72.4	96.2
Work experience												
Worked within past 2 years	49.4	55.4	59.7	57.9	63.6	71.5	68.9	67.2	76.0	63.8	70.5	80.8
Worked in the 3 to 9 years prior	7.8	9.8	9.1	8.5	8.6	8.3	6.1	9.8	9.2	10.4	10.1	8.9
Worked more than 10 years prior or never	41.5	32.7	31.2	32.2	23.6	20.2	22.2	19.6	14.7	24.1	17.0	10.2
Average age (years)	38.0	33.4	34.4	32.8	31.9	34.5	35.4	33.7	36.1	37.5	35.6	38.3

Source: U.S. Department of Commerce (1996).
Note: Includes metropolitan statistical areas (MSAs) in Arizona, California, Colorado, New Mexico, and Texas.

1990, the gap between Mexican immigrant women with less than a high school education and their U.S.-born counterparts was at its widest margin in two decades. Similarly, the percentage of Mexican immigrant women speaking little or no English grew from seven times to nine times that of Mexican Americans.

The only indicator on which Mexican immigrant women kept pace with their U.S.-born counterparts was the growth of their labor force participation. Though the absolute share of Mexican immigrant women reporting recent work experience fell short of the U.S.-born figures in each decade, the relative increases kept pace with U.S.-born groups, suggesting that all groups of women were churning through the labor market in greater numbers, offering the possibility of emergent intergroup effects.

Mexican American women showed much higher levels of schooling, English proficiency, and work experience than Mexican-born women did. Furthermore, these human capital levels increased over time, to the point, for example, that nearly a third of the 1990 sample of Mexican American women reported being monolingual English speakers (table 7.1). Yet Mexican American women's skill profiles do not yet approximate those of black and non-Hispanic white women in the urban Southwest.

The clearest indicator of persistent difference across racial or ethnic groups is in the data on high school completion. Not until 1990 did the census identify a majority of Mexican American women in the urban Southwest as high school graduates. Similarly, Mexican American work experience profiles in 1990 fell squarely between those of Mexican immigrants and non-Hispanic whites, not substantially closer to either end of the continuum.

In sum, the human capital profiles of women in the urban Southwest suggest three trends. First, over time, Mexican immigrant women in the urban Southwest have demonstrated higher levels of human capital, a profile consistent with immigrant Latinas' profiles in other regions, yet contrary to much of the literature on immigrant men (Repak 1994; Borjas 1990). Second, a distinct "pulling away" characterizes the immigrant–U.S.-born dynamic, with both the foreign- and U.S.-born improving their human capital positions but with the U.S.-born doing so at a greater rate. Third, Mexican American women defy easy comparison with their labor market counterparts. On several dimensions, they resemble the Mexican-born no more or less than they do the non-Hispanic, U.S.-born. What is clear is that Mexican American women have not pulled away from their immigrant counterparts as far or as fast as other U.S.-born groups in the race to acquire those assets that spell success in U.S. labor markets.

Although Mexican American women fall between immigrant and non-Hispanic, U.S.-born women on human capital characteristics, their family structure profiles place them squarely in the midst of their U.S. counterparts (table 7.2). On dimensions like marital status, household headship,

Table 7.2 / Marriage and Family Indicators for Women Aged Sixteen to Sixty-four Living in Southwestern MSAs, 1970, 1980, 1990 (Percent)

Indicator	Mexican-Born			U.S.-Born			Non-Hispanic Black			Non-Hispanic White		
	1970	1980	1990	1970	1980	1990	1970	1980	1990	1970	1980	1990
Marital status												
Married	66.4	66.5	63.7	63.5	54.8	51.8	52.8	39.1	35.8	69.3	61.9	61.5
Widowed	6.8	3.7	3.3	3.3	3.1	2.9	7.0	5.2	5.2	4.9	3.4	2.9
Divorced	4.2	4.1	4.7	5.6	7.3	10.4	10.3	12.9	15.3	6.9	9.7	12.7
Separated	3.6	3.6	4.4	3.4	3.5	3.6	9.3	7.9	8.1	1.8	2.8	2.3
Never Married	18.9	22.0	23.9	24.2	31.2	31.2	20.6	34.8	35.5	17.1	22.0	20.4
Heads of household	13.9	13.3	14.3	12.9	15.4	20.1	27.3	34.1	41.4	15.4	19.2	25.0
Children ever Born	3.2	2.7	2.5	2.5	2.1	1.9	2.2	1.9	1.9	1.8	1.7	1.6

Source: U.S. Department of Commerce (1996).
Note: Includes metropolitan statistical areas (MSAs) in Arizona, California, Colorado, New Mexico, and Texas.

and fertility, Mexican immigrant women are quite distinct from U.S.-born women. Furthermore, these distinctions seem to have grown over time. In 1990, Mexican immigrant women were far more likely to be married, were far less likely to be household heads, and demonstrated higher fertility than did U.S.-born women of any racial or ethnic group. Yet the time trends appear to be moving in a direction that mirrors the changes taking place in the U.S.-born groups—changes toward higher levels of marital instability and household headship, and lower levels of fertility.

Mexican American women, on the other hand, demonstrated marital and family structure changes from 1970 to 1990 that result in contemporary patterns much resembling those of African American and non-Hispanic white women. Notably, substantial increases in divorce left one in ten Mexican American women in the urban Southwest reporting divorced status by 1990, a near doubling of the rate from two decades earlier. Similarly, substantial drops in fertility left Mexican American women with profiles fully consistent with those of their non-Mexican counterparts by 1990. Thus Mexican American women and, to a lesser extent, Mexican immigrant women demonstrated a shift from 1970 to 1990 consistent with the marital and family conditions that are associated with an increasing likelihood of labor force participation, again setting the stage for potential intergroup influences on labor market outcomes.

From 1970 to 1990, changes took place not only in the labor-related characteristics of women workers but also in the occupational and industrial structures within which they found work (table 7.3). In 1970, Mexican-born women were concentrated in operative jobs and manufacturing industries. By 1990, that concentration had dissolved, replaced by a larger showing in service work. One category of service work—private household domestic work—demonstrated a slight decline in 1980 but increased as a share of total employment by 1990, at which point one in twenty Mexican-born women in the urban Southwest worked as a domestic in a private home.

Mexican American women showed a distinct upgrading of their job and industry placement, with a fourfold increase in management jobs and a doubling of professional and technical employment from 1970 to 1990. Nonetheless, the dominant job categories throughout the period continued to be clerical and service work. Mexican American women, like Mexican immigrants, exhibited a smaller presence in manufacturing work over time.

Disaggregating "service" jobs to isolate private domestic workers reveals an interesting racial and ethnic pattern among the U.S.-born groups. Specifically, African American women appear to have exited domestic labor at a staggering rate, moving from nearly 15 percent engaged in such work in 1970 to less than 2 percent two decades later. No obvious shift in another job category indicates where these domestic laborers might have gone.

Several possibilities exist. They may have aged out of the labor force

Table 7.3 / Occupational and Industrial Distributions of Women in the Labor Force, Southwestern MSAs, 1970, 1980, 1990 (Percent)

Occupation	Mexican-Born			Mexican American			Black			Other		
	1970	1980	1990	1970	1980	1990	1970	1980	1990	1970	1980	1990
Manager	0.8	1.9	4.2	2.2	4.2	8.9	1.7	5.9	9.3	4.6	6.9	14.8
Professional/technical	2.4	3.8	5.4	7.7	9.1	13.4	11.8	14.0	15.6	17.6	15.4	22.2
Sales	5.0	5.8	8.5	5.8	11.3	13.7	3.4	8.7	10.5	8.7	10.7	13.4
Clerical	14.2	13.3	12.4	31.8	29.5	29.9	24.2	30.8	28.9	42.5	31.9	29.0
Domestic	7.9	3.6	5.6	2.8	1.8	1.2	14.8	3.9	1.6	1.6	1.8	0.5
Service	17.0	17.7	23.6	20.4	20.3	18.5	25.8	23.6	22.0	13.5	16.8	12.5
Farmer	0.0	0.0	0.3	0.0	0.0	0.1	0.1	0.0	0.0	0.0	0.0	0.2
Farm labor	5.3	8.9	6.1	1.5	2.7	0.9	0.3	0.4	0.3	0.2	0.8	0.5
Craft	2.7	5.0	4.4	2.1	3.5	2.7	1.2	1.9	2.3	1.7	3.3	1.9
Operative	40.3	32.1	21.2	23.3	13.4	7.1	13.9	7.5	5.7	8.2	9.1	3.0
Laborer	1.9	7.5	4.0	1.0	3.9	1.8	1.1	2.3	1.5	0.7	2.3	1.1
Industry												
Agriculture	6.3	10.6	7.1	2.1	4.4	1.6	0.7	1.7	0.8	1.1	3.3	2.0
Construction	0.1	0.3	0.8	0.6	0.8	0.8	0.3	0.7	0.7	1.2	1.3	2.0
Manufacturing	33.1	40.4	24.4	23.4	19.2	11.6	11.8	11.7	9.7	14.1	16.9	9.4
Transport/Comm.	0.8	1.7	1.9	3.3	3.8	4.7	3.3	5.7	7.4	4.9	4.3	5.0
Trade	22.7	15.3	21.8	22.2	23.2	23.5	14.1	15.7	17.5	24.1	22.3	21.2
Finance, insurance real estate	3.6	5.4	2.6	9.2	9.2	7.5	6.3	13.2	7.9	12.5	12.5	10.4
Personal services	10.7	5.1	6.1	7.7	4.4	4.2	11.1	2.9	3.4	5.8	3.5	3.3
Professional Services	11.0	14.9	23.1	21.6	27.6	36.8	31.0	37.0	41.1	28.9	28.9	40.8
Public sector	1.1	2.2	2.0	5.5	5.9	6.2	6.8	6.3	7.1	4.8	5.6	4.1
Private household	7.7	3.9	5.8	2.6	1.8	1.4	12.4	4.6	2.0	1.6	2.0	0.7

Source: U.S. Department of Commerce (1996).
Note: Includes metropolitan statistical areas (MSAs) in Arizona, California, Colorado, New Mexico, and Texas.

altogether, and certainly this is part of the story. The median age of the African American domestic workers in the 1970 sample was forty-four years, well above the average for other job categories. Some workers may have changed jobs, crossing into another job category. Some may have exited the labor force while remaining in the civilian labor force age categories. What is interesting is how, if at all, the presence of a growing Mexican immigrant female labor force, particularly one with a persistent showing in this job category, might have influenced this change in African American occupational composition.

Finally, non-Hispanic white women demonstrate a very clear upgrading of their occupational position, albeit across broad occupational categories. Their managerial presence tripled from 1970 to 1990; clerical work dropped substantially. Again, as was the case for all other groups, operative and manufacturing work declined over time.

In summary, analyses of labor market experiences for working women in the urban Southwest take place against a backdrop of significant occupational and industrial change. Some of those changes—an exit from domestic work for African Americans, an upgrading of jobs for all U.S.-born labor groups—may bode well for those groups' aggregate outcomes. Yet the changes evinced by Mexican immigrant women are not so promising. What remains to be seen is how these changes may influence women workers across racial or ethnic and nativity categories.

INTERGROUP LABOR MARKET DYNAMICS

The question animating the research reported here is simple to ask and hard to answer: Does the presence of a particular group of women in a local labor market affect labor market outcomes for other working women? Specifically, in the urban Southwest, does the presence of Mexican immigrant women matter for the labor market outcomes of U.S.-born working women?

This question is particularly important to answer in the contemporary era for several reasons. First, social science research suggests that immigration has become a permanent, significant element in the American demographic equation—forays into restrictive immigration policymaking notwithstanding (Massey 1995). Thus, understanding U.S. labor markets, particularly in the high-growth sites of the urban Southwest, requires an understanding of immigration dynamics. Second, this persistent immigration flow has become increasingly feminized over time (U.S. Immigration and Naturalization Service 1996). Thus, more than ever before, questions about job displacement, wage suppression, and other potential negative effects upon U.S. workers require attention to gender in order to produce complete answers.

To date, surprisingly little direct empirical analysis has examined the way immigration might affect U.S.-born working women, at least in comparison with the extensive scholarship on men. Recent ethnographic work has explored how specific niches in the female labor market—domestic service work, for example—incorporate Central American or Mexican undocumented women (Hagan 1994; Hondagneu-Sotelo 1995). However, broader assessments of intergroup competition and complementarity between Mexican immigrants and U.S.-born workers have relied, for the most part, on male samples (Bean, Lowell, and Taylor 1988).

The sparseness of the information on Mexican women workers does not stem from their being demographically or socioeconomically insignificant to the southwestern region. On the contrary, nearly half of the Mexican undocumented population enumerated in the 1980 U.S. Census was female; and legal immigration to the United States has been net female for many years (Bean and Tienda 1988). Over 475,000 Mexican undocumented women legalized their status through the federal legalization or "amnesty" program in 1987–88 (U.S. Immigration and Naturalization Service 1993). Over two-thirds of that "amnestied" group reported having been active in the labor force during their undocumented residence in the United States, placing their labor force participation rates at levels comparable to those of Mexican American women.

Existing data and models allow for the systematic analysis of Mexican immigrant women's position in urban southwestern labor markets. I employ these data and models to examine the relationship between the presence of Mexican immigrant women in a local labor market and the earnings profiles of other groups of women workers.

My analyses begin with an overview of recent research on labor competition and complementarity between Mexican immigrants and U.S.-born workers. Since virtually all of this work has been conducted with male samples, I then outline some features of the female labor force experience that might imply different relationships among groups of women workers and present hypotheses derived from those observations.

With data describing both individual workers and the labor markets for the area in which they live, I estimate the net effect of the presence of Mexican immigrant women in a local labor force on the earnings and employment probabilities of Mexican American, African American, and non-Hispanic white women.

Immigrants in U.S. Labor Markets: Theories and Evidence

Two portraits of the U.S. labor market compete in most contemporary research on Mexican immigrant workers. First, a "unified labor market" perspective envisions immigrant workers as competitors pushing down the earnings and employment of U.S.-born workers (Briggs 1984; Marshall

1987). Relying with varying rigidity on the assumptions of (1) perfect substitutability between immigrant and native labor on productivity dimensions (that is, human capital equivalencies), (2) lower reservation wages for immigrants than for natives, and (3) little or no job growth emerging from the population growth to which immigration contributes, researchers adopting this perspective suggest zero-sum labor market operations in which immigrants can have no effect other than that the jobs they fill will leave native workers unemployed and the wages for which they will settle will depress wage rates overall.

In contrast, "segmented labor market" perspectives consider immigrants as benign influences on native-born employment, because immigrants restrict their labor force participation to the secondary sector, where low pay and meager benefits render jobs unattractive to natives (Piore 1979). Absent immigrants, the argument goes, the jobs themselves would not exist, falling victim to capital substitution or to exportation to low-wage, labor-intensive countries. By taking the worst jobs, immigrants leave higher-level jobs for natives in industries that depend on cheap labor for their survival.

The segmented labor market perspective also rests on rather rigid assumptions, the most prominent being that secondary-sector employment retains its unattractive features independently of labor supply. The purest specification of segmented labor market theory leaves little room for the possibility that wage offers might rise and working conditions improve in the secondary sector—thereby attracting native-born workers currently without jobs—should immigrant labor become scarce. The theory predicts only that the "immigrant" jobs will vanish, not that natives will take them. This assumption is important to question in an examination of immigrant women in the labor force, however, as the mechanisms of capital substitution and offshore job flight are less feasible when the jobs in question are the jobs immigrant women do—domestic household service, for example.

A third variant of labor market structure particularly relevant to analyses in places with high immigration rates is the "ethnic enclave" perspective—a type of labor market segmentation dependent upon the presence of an ethnic (often foreign-born) community that establishes a vertically integrated, ethnically homogenous economy-within-an-economy (Portes and Bach 1985). This perspective assumes that, other things being equal, employment in an enclave economy will produce distinct benefits for immigrant workers, an assumption that continues to be debated both theoretically and empirically.

What has the evidence demonstrated? Bean, Telles, and Lowell (1987) provide a useful typology of social science studies specifying the labor market effects of Mexican migration. First, local-area case studies delve deeply into a particular industry situated in a particular place, tracking the flow of Mexican workers, for example, through that industry and the attendant effects on other labor groups. Such projects are more likely than broad-scale efforts to include qualitative or ethnographic components. Second, "empirically based" studies quantify the effect of immigration on earnings or employment rates across a wider range of industries, occupations, geographical labor markets, or all three. Third, "model-based" studies specify estimable equations derived from aggregate production functions that treat labor groups as elements or inputs in the production process, yielding parameters that quantify the extent to which given labor groups substitute for or complement one another.

Across all three research strategies, evidence of native-born wage depression or job displacement at the hands of Mexican immigrants has been mixed. For instance, case studies in California found wage levels inversely associated with the presence of undocumented immigrants in the garment and restaurant industries, although no such effect was observed in those same industries in New York and New Jersey (Maram 1980; Vasquez 1981; Bailey 1987). Evidence of a rise in domestic agricultural employment following the halt of the Bracero Program in the 1960s is countered by more recent evidence demonstrating no undocumented labor effect on job displacement for native farm workers in California (Wise 1974; Mines and Anzaldua 1982).

Evidence of labor competition between U.S.-born women and Mexican undocumented women exists in some case studies, but not in others. Zavella (1987) notes that Chicana cannery workers in northern California complained regularly that their undocumented counterparts were both favored and exploited, with production supervisors assigning them to higher-paying jobs above their seniority levels in exchange for bribes, even as they threatened the workers with deportation. However, Hondagneu-Sotelo (1994) identifies a job hierarchy in household domestic work in which African American women and Chicanas position themselves as higher-paid "professional cleaners" while their undocumented counterparts engage in the "job work" and "live-in" work slots vacated by the native-born.

Empirically based studies tend to demonstrate modest negative effects of Mexican immigrant presence on wages and employment rates, particularly for native-born, low-skilled workers (Smith and Newman 1977; DeFreitas and Marshall 1984; McCarthy and Valdez 1986). Some studies, however, find no such effect, and others have revealed positive effects on black family income and employment (Simon and Moore 1984; Muller and Espenshade 1985). In those few cases where "undocumented immigrant" status is identified directly, some studies find labor competition with native men while others yield none (North and Houston 1976; Van Arsdol et al. 1979).

Few of these empirically based studies have included women in their analyses. One that did revealed greater similarities in occupational position and earnings profiles between unapprehended undocumented Mexican women and other Hispanic women than was true for men, implying a greater level of potential economic competition (Van Arsdol et al. 1979).

The evidence from model-based studies is more consistent. Most of these studies do not disaggregate immigrants by legal status, relying instead on model specifications that include total Hispanic immigrants and various native-born groups as labor inputs. The models also tend to control for differences in human capital across individuals and differences in economic conditions across area labor markets. Most find virtually no net effect of total Hispanic immigration on native-born economic outcomes (King, Lowell, and Bean 1986; Borjas 1987). A project attempting to distinguish Mexican legal from undocumented immigrants revealed a more complex relationship in the U.S. Southwest, with Mexican undocumented men operating as modest labor complements to black and non-Hispanic white men—boosting native earnings slightly—and Mexican legal immigrant men serving as slight labor substitutes with non-Hispanic white men (Bean, Lowell, and Taylor 1988).

Where women enter into model-based analyses, they have been included as a "total female" category alongside groups of men disaggregated by ethnicity and nativity, and have demonstrated both competition effects with Hispanic immigrant men and complementarity effects with Mexican undocumented immigrant men (Borjas 1986; Bean, Lowell, and Taylor 1988). Nothing can be said, however, in these analyses, about women's effects upon each other, as they are all collapsed into one labor input based on gender.

On balance, the only consistent finding across these research strategies is that the magnitude of Mexican immigration effects, positive or negative, is quite small. For instance, increasing the size of the Mexican undocumented male presence by 10 percent in the urban southwestern United States would yield no significant change in U.S.-born Mexican-origin men's earnings and would actually boost black and non-Hispanic white men's earnings, albeit by less than 1 percent (Bean, Lowell and Taylor 1988).

The assumption of neither unified nor strictly-segmented labor markets yields hypotheses that enjoy vigorous empirical support. The model yielding the most consistent findings tends to be one in which labor groups are assumed to possess the potential for acting either as substitutes or complements depending upon their relative concentration in the labor market, the human capital features characterizing each group, and the economic conditions in the labor market itself (Borjas 1984; Bean, Lowell, and Taylor 1988).

A striking commonality among many studies is their tendency either to omit women from the analyses altogether, or, in model-based studies, to treat them as a residual "female" category, setting aside any possibility for comparisons within the female population. Interestingly, this omission is either attributed to the fact that groups of women workers are too similar—that is, variation in the dependent variable (individual hourly wage or annual earnings, most often) is much smaller among women workers than among men or that they are too different—that is, differences in the fertility of immigrants and natives lead to different labor force activity patterns, making comparisons difficult (Bean, Lowell, and Taylor 1988; Borjas 1990). Still, several aspects of female labor market experience make it a particularly interesting arena for economic comparisons of immigrants and natives.

First, women are concentrated in fewer occupational categories than men are, owing to both supply-side and demand-side factors (England and Farkas 1986). If Mexican immigrant women enter into a system of work options constrained by pervasive gender segregation, they may be positioned to compete more directly with native-born women than men are. In other words, gender-based job crowding may exacerbate competition effects along nativity lines for women, even if it does not do so for men.

However, several factors may offset this competition effect. For instance, much female-typed work in the United States involves clerical skills or direct contact with the public, thus demanding English language fluency—a skill Mexican immigrant women are particularly unlikely to possess. Also, a significant share of immigrant women's employment, particularly in the urban Southwest, is in domestic service work that frees native-born women quite directly to engage in market work outside the home (Hagan 1994). These features of women's work experience imply possible complementarity between Mexican immigrant women and other female labor groups.

Thus the possibility exists that, positive or negative, the effects of Mexican immigration upon native-born economic position might well be more pronounced for women than for men and may depart from male patterns in sign, given the gender-based system (operating on both the supply and demand sides) that sorts people into the labor market in the United States.

Data and Methods

My analyses begin with data from the 1 percent PUMS of the 1980 and 1990 U.S. Census. For each decade, I limit my analyses to women in the civilian labor force aged sixteen to sixty-four who were living inside a standard metropolitan statistical area (SMSA) in one of the five southwestern states and who did not reside in group quarters. An additional filter excludes all women who reported zero dollars in earned income in the year preceding the census interview. Women are assigned to one of four groups: (1) Mexican-born; (2) U.S.-born, Mexican-origin; (3) non-Hispanic black; and (4) non-Hispanic white. Each data record includes information on the woman's sociodemographic characteristics, including human capital measurements, occupational position, and labor market outcomes. To each individual record I have appended an additional independent variable: the percentage of Mexican-born females in the total female civilian labor force in the SMSA of residence. This "percent Mexican immigrant" variable was derived from U.S. Census Bureau tabulations for the 1980 data set and was generated from the person-weights included in the 1990 PUMS.

For all its limitations, the PUMS provides the considerable advantage of including sufficient cases for separate analyses of each labor group. Thus I present results for each of the four labor groups in 1980 and 1990. I present two models estimating women's earned income. Model 1 includes only the basic set of human capital variables that are well recognized as contributing to earning power. Model 2 adds two additional types of information: the occupational position of the worker and the "percent Mexican immigrant female" in the female labor force present in the worker's SMSA.

Results

Table 7.4 presents summary statistics for the four labor groups in each decade. Restricting the analysis to the labor force active with earned income in the previous year did little to change the sociodemographic patterns identified earlier. Mexican-born women still demonstrated significantly lower levels of human capital. Mexican American women still fell rather squarely between their foreign-born and non-Hispanic, U.S.-born counterparts.

Table 7.5 presents the results of ordinary least squares regression equations estimating annual earnings for each of the four female labor groups in 1980 and 1990. Model 1 in table 7.5 presents a baseline human capital estimation of earnings for each female labor group. These coefficients behave as one might expect, with increased education producing higher annual incomes, some advantage accruing to older workers, and a distinct advantage accruing to those who were bilingual or monolingual-English speakers over those who spoke little or no English.

Model 2 builds upon the human capital equation by adding information about the respondent's occupation and a contextual variable estimating the effect of the percentage of Mexican-born females in the total female civilian labor force of the respondent's SMSA. Service employment is the omitted category in the occupational dummies.

The primary focus of the results presented in table 7.5 centers on the "percentage Mexican-born female" variable. In 1980, net of human capital and occupational position, Mexican-born women experienced a significant penalty associated with the presence of their own demographic group in the female labor force. Similarly, Mexican American women demonstrated lower annual earnings in labor markets with larger Mexican immigrant female shares. The story differs for African American and non-Hispanic white women. No significant effect of Mexican immigrant female concentration emerged for African American women's earnings; and the effect of

Table 7.4 / Means for Variables Employed in OLS Regression Estimating Annual Earnings for Four Female Labor Groups, Southwestern SMSAs, 1980, 1990

Variable	Mexican-Born	Mexican American	Non-Hispanic	Non-Hispanic White
1990				
Annual earnings (dollars)	10,154.13	13,541.55	16,956.87	18,581.87
Less than high school	65.08	27.75	15.13	11.05
High school graduate	16.59	31.93	27.01	24.44
Post–high school	18.32	40.31	57.86	64.49
Age (years)	33.44	33.59	36.24	37.09
No English	44.45	4.42	0.49	2.07
Bilingual	51.56	66.07	4.50	12.64
Only English	3.97	29.51	94.99	85.28
Manager	3.83	8.56	9.97	14.76
Professional/technical	5.31	13.28	16.88	22.32
Sales	8.01	13.60	10.23	12.77
Clerical	13.46	31.57	30.69	29.48
Domestic	4.98	1.25	1.63	0.87
Service	22.33	17.68	20.59	12.05
Farmer	0.29	0.00	0.00	0.00
Farm labor	6.98	1.06	0.24	0.42
Craft	5.07	2.79	2.41	2.16
Operative	24.20	7.99	5.79	3.85
Laborer	5.51	2.14	1.52	1.24
Percent Mexican-born female[a]	6.25	5.21	3.62	3.46
Percent Mexican-born total[b]	8.91	7.26	5.51	5.19
N	5,839	10,507	7,416	79,050
1980				
Annual earnings (dollars)	5,490.34	6,032.35	7,693.41	7,499.05
Less than high school	70.57	40.59	24.32	21.89
High school	18.83	37.70	35.71	40.76
Post–high school	10.58	21.69	39.97	37.33
Age (years)	32.65	31.59	34.05	33.92
No English	51.37	4.82	0.46	3.71
Bilingual	46.39	71.80	4.13	20.89
Only English	2.24	23.37	95.40	75.39
Manager	1.93	4.18	5.93	7.56
Professional/technical	3.80	9.13	13.99	14.59
Sales	5.79	11.26	8.73	12.33
Clerical	13.35	29.55	30.78	34.34
Domestic	3.64	1.80	3.86	1.72
Service	17.74	20.36	23.58	16.18
Farmer	—	—	—	—
Farm labor	8.93	2.75	0.40	0.73

(Table continues on p. 259.)

Table 7.4 / *Continued*

Variable	Mexican-Born	Mexican American	Non-Hispanic	Non-Hispanic White
1980				
Craft	5.01	3.53	1.86	2.70
Operative	32.06	13.44	7.46	6.76
Laborer	7.50	3.88	2.26	2.36
Percent Mexican-born female[a]	9.49	7.16	5.16	5.33
Percent Mexican-born total[b]	9.74	7.32	5.59	5.66
N	3,212	8,213	1,501	6,728

Source: U.S. Department of Commerce (1996).
Note: Includes metropolitan statistical areas (MSAs) in Arizona, California, Colorado, New Mexico, and Texas. Values in percent unless otherwise indicated.
[a]Percentage of Mexican-born females in the total female civilian labor force in the SMSA of residence.
[b]Percentage of Mexican-born workers in the total civilian work force in the SMSA of residence.

the presence of Mexican female immigrants on non-Hispanic white women's earnings was positive. In summary, disaggregating female labor groups by ethnicity reveals a differential impact of Mexican female immigration, such that the immigrant presence served as a depressor on all Mexican-origin women's earnings, a benign influence on African American women's earnings, and a boost to non-Hispanic white women's earnings.

Three adjustments to the 1980 equations reveal additional information. First, in an effort to incorporate the presence of both Mexican immigrant men and women into the model, I estimated the equations with a "percentage Mexican immigrant" variable for the total civilian labor force. The results were virtually unchanged. Second, I restricted the analyses to the sector of the population with more modest education—a high school diploma or less education. This adjustment changed the results in one case. For non-Hispanic white females with little education, the effect of Mexican immigrant women moved from significantly positive to not significant at $\alpha = .05$. Finally, I sought to adjust for potential geographical clustering of the four population groups by estimating a set of equations that controlled for MSA residence (table 7.5, last row). The negative effects for Mexican immigrant and Mexican American women preserved their sign but dropped to nonsignificance. The positive effect for non-Hispanic white women dropped to significance at $\alpha = .06$. Thus the most robust findings in the 1980 analyses suggest that Mexican immigrant women may have been modest competitors on their own terms and with Mexican American women, had little effect on African American women's earnings, and boosted the earnings of non-Hispanic white women.

The story changed, however, in 1990. Again, human capital predictors of

Table 7.5 / OLS Results: Estimation of Earned Income for Four Female Labor Groups, Southwestern MSAs, 1980, 1990

Predictor	Mexican-Born		Mexican American		Black		Other	
	(1)	(2)	(1)	(2)	(1)	(2)	(1)	(2)
1980								
Intercept	3,170.5	2,447.5	−842.6	−1,365.9	−1,173.3*	−1,987.6*	−181.0*	−1,305.5
High school	1,300.0	863.2	2,334.8	1,639.1	2,730.3	1,735.6	2,387.2	1,806.8
Post–high school	2,029.9	1,178.8	3,979.8	2,769.2	5,483.2	2,671.5	4,378.1	3,024.1
Age	45.8	52.7	117.3	115.4	133.8	136.4	116.3	101.2
Bilingual	732.1	507.2	1,375.6	923.2	311.6*	345.7*	994.9	795.7
Only English	1,153.0	1,138.3	1,872.4	1,334.4	1,183.6*	1,311.9*	1,219.5	972.9
Manager		4,368.7		4,921.4		6,060.2		6,243.1
Professional/technical		2,937.5		3,323.2		5,091.2		3,936.4
Sales		406.3*		632.6		−488.1*		946.1
Clerical		1,951.3		2,418.3		2,802.0		2,590.5
Domestic		−1,412.6		−1,883.4		−3,317.9		−1,017.9
Farm Labor		−729.5		−714.9		−1,707.3*		−1,118.3*
Craft		2,170.0		3,382.4		2,131.6		4,506.6
Operative		1,395.3		2,086.8		799.1*		2,119.9
Laborer		1,083.2		1,219.3		−529.9*		1,951.9
Percent Mexican-born female		−23.8		−18.2		46.2*		50.2
Percent Mexican-born female	−24.0*		−16.0*		73.9*		56.8*	
R² (adjusted)	0.06	0.12	0.15	0.22	0.16	0.27	0.12	0.20
N	3,212	3,212	8,213	8,213	1,501	1,501	6,728	6,728

(Table continues on p. 261.)

Table 7.5 / *Continued*

Predictor	Mexican-Born		Mexican American		Black		Other	
	(1)	(2)	(1)	(2)	(1)	(2)	(1)	(2)
1990								
Intercept	2,721.7	2,211.3	−1,074.4*	−1,897.0	−5,220.1	−7,517.5	−2,278.2	−5,388.2
High school	2,238.5	1,491.6	3,809.0	2,307.4	4,069.8	2,372.8	4,012.9	2,980.1
Post–high school	4,841.6	2,989.6	8,497.5	5,603.4	11,363.0	6,874.4	10,676.0	7,061.2
Age	137.3	138.2	265.2	243.6	318.1	300.4	274.9	240.0
Bilingual	2,906.8	2,098.4	383.6*	−432.2*	2,545.7*	1,643.1*	2,514.4	1,686.5
Only English	2,073.4	1,261.9	2,747.8	1,778.9	3,009.8*	2,691.2*	2,904.5	2,083.3
Manager		9,304.4		10,919.0		11,818.0		12,853.0
Professional/technical		5,873.5		7,680.8		9,144.5		10,124.0
Sales		1,242.7		2,066.6		1,632.2		5,072.8
Clerical		3,892.6		4,612.9		5,091.2		3,839.6
Domestic		−1,158.9		−3,563.2		−6,607.1		−2,395.5
Farmer		6,120.9		−128.1*		9,219.8*		−206.4*
Farm labor		−1,202.6		−1,916.8		1,269.9*		−450.6*
Craft		3,682.3		7,407.9		8,360.8		7,893.9
Operative		2,121.9		3,742.4		3,329.7		3,643.5
Laborer		1,431.4		1,963.9		536.1		1,684.4
Percent Mexican-born female		−88.4		−30.2*		438.3		428.7
Percent Mexican-born female (adjusted)		−118.6		−101.5*		520.9		309.6
R^2	0.09	0.14	0.15	0.22	0.18	0.28	0.11	0.18
N	5,839	5,839	10,507	10,507	7,415	7,415	79,050	79,050

Source: U.S. Department of Commerce (1996).
Note: Includes metropolitan statistical areas (MSAs) in Arizona, California, Colorado, New Mexico, and Texas.

annual earnings behaved much as one might expect, with a few exceptions. For all groups, educational attainment was associated with higher earnings, but the jump between a terminal high school degree and some postsecondary education was much broader for African American and non-Hispanic white women than for either Mexican-origin group. In addition, whereas being either bilingual or English-monolingual afforded an earnings advantage for Mexican American women in 1980 (over the omitted category of "speaking little or no English"), no such advantage accrued to bilingual Mexican American women in 1990. Bilingual Mexican American women appear no more likely than limited-English speakers, net of the other human capital factors specified here, to have commanded earned income.

Changes also took place in the influence of Mexican immigrant women's presence on the earnings of women workers. Again, large Mexican immigrant female populations were associated with lower annual earnings for Mexican-born women themselves. However, by 1990, any substitution effect with Mexican American women had disappeared. Furthermore, the effect of Mexican immigrant women on African American and non-Hispanic white women had become significant and substantial, such that each percentage point increase in the share "Mexican immigrant female" of the female labor force was associated with an increase of over $400 in annual income for African American and non-Hispanic white women.

Again, adjusting the model slightly provided additional insight. First, incorporating men into the "percentage Mexican immigrant" variable dropped the competition effect within the Mexican immigrant female sample to nonsignficance. All other patterns remained the same. Second, restricting attention to the low-credential end of the labor force yielded a significant depressor effect of Mexican female immigrants on the earnings of Mexican American women, with a significant coefficient of −54. Finally, the adjustment for geographic clustering did little to affect the substance of the results. In sum, it appears that the overall pattern of competition within the ranks of Mexican-origin women persisted, albeit only within the low end of the skill continuum for Mexican American women, while the relationship between Mexican immigrants and their non-Mexican female counterparts was consistent and positive.

To explore these dynamics further, I estimated the same set of equations for the natural log of hourly wages earned in the year previous to the census interview (table 7.6). Again, human capital and occupational variables behave as one would expect in 1980, with the one distinction being that high school completion accrued no advantage in hourly wage to Mexican-born women over their counterparts who had not finished high school.

The immigrant substitution effect seen for Mexican American women's annual incomes disappeared in the estimates of hourly wage. That is, while immigrant women may have reduced Mexican American women's annual

Table 7.6 / OLS Results: Estimation of ln (Hourly Wage), Four Female Labor Groups, Southwestern MSAs, 1980, 1990

Predictor	Mexican-Born (1)	Mexican-Born (2)	Mexican American (1)	Mexican American (2)	Black (1)	Black (2)	Other (1)	Other (2)
1980								
Intercept	1.10	1.03	0.78	0.73	0.98	0.83	0.73	0.65
High school	0.09	0.06*	0.18	0.14	0.23	0.11	0.18	0.13
Post–high school	0.20	0.13	0.38	0.28	0.48	0.18	0.39	0.26
Age	0.003	0.004	0.01	0.01	0.01	0.01	0.01	0.01
Bilingual	0.08	0.07	0.10	0.08	−0.21*	−0.19*	0.18	0.15
Only English	0.18	0.18	0.18	0.14	−0.17*	−0.16*	0.20	0.16
Manager		0.36		0.31		0.55		0.37
Professional/technical		0.34		0.36		0.55		0.40
Sales		0.17		0.05		0.11*		0.08
Clerical		0.19		0.16		0.35		0.20
Domestic		−0.32		−0.16		−0.40*		−0.24
Farm Labor		0.18		0.01		−0.24		0.03*
Craft		0.18		0.23		0.33		0.31
Operative		0.14		0.17		0.12*		0.17
Labor		0.24		0.14		−0.12*		0.18
Percent Mexican-born female		−0.008		−0.001*		0.007*		0.006
Percent Mexican-born female (adjusted)		−0.007*		−0.001*		0.011		0.010
R^2	0.02	0.06	0.07	0.10	0.08	0.16	0.10	0.14
N	3,195	3,195	8,186	8,186	1,492	1,492	6,697	6,697

(Table continues on p. 264.)

Table 7.6 / *Continued*

Predictor	Mexican-Born		Mexican American		Black		Other	
	(1)	(2)	(1)	(2)	(1)	(2)	(1)	(2)
1990								
Intercept	1.30	1.28	1.11	1.06	1.11	0.89	1.18	1.05
High school	0.16	0.12	0.23	0.15	0.21	0.12	0.22	0.16
Post–high school	0.29	0.18	0.47	0.31	0.58	0.35	0.54	0.36
Age	0.007	0.007	0.01	0.01	0.01	0.01	0.01	0.01
Bilingual	0.17	0.13	0.04*	0.001*	0.10*	0.07*	0.13	0.09
Only English	0.12	0.07*	0.18	0.13	0.06*	0.07*	0.13	0.09
Manager		0.48		0.47		0.53		0.48
Professional/technical		0.39		0.46		0.51		0.51
Sales		0.05*		0.11		0.16		0.16
Clerical		0.28		0.27		0.35		0.23
Domestic		−0.14		−0.15		−0.14		−0.17
Farmer		0.43		−0.09*		2.01		−0.27
Farm labor		0.13		0.04*		0.11*		−0.11
Craft		0.23		0.35		0.38		0.32
Operative		0.12		0.19		0.22		0.17
Labor		0.09		0.10		0.17		0.12
Percent Mexican-born female		−0.01		−0.002*		0.03		0.02
Percent Mexican-born female (adjusted)		−0.006*		−0.006*		0.03		0.02
R^2	0.06	0.10	0.13	0.18	0.15	0.23	0.13	0.20
N	5,839	5,839	10,507	10,507	7,416	7,416	79,050	79,050

Source: U.S. Department of Commerce (1996).
Note: Includes metropolitan statistical areas (MSAs) in Arizona, California, Colorado, New Mexico, and Texas.

earnings by a small fraction, they did not do so through a depressing effect on the Mexican American wage offer.

Many of the 1990 annual earnings patterns held up in the 1990 hourly wage analyses. Again in 1990, Mexican American women accrued no wage advantage from bilingualism; they seemed to serve, as a group, as a depressor on their own wages; and no significant effect on Mexican American hourly wage emerged as a function of Mexican immigrant women's presence. Any significant immigration effects that emerged were directed toward African American and non-Hispanic white women's wages and were positive in sign.

Adjustments to the models yielded the following insights. In 1980, restricting the analysis to workers with few credentials pushed the positive sign for Mexican immigrant presence on African American women's wages to significance but lowered the positive effect on white women's wages to nonsignificance. In 1990, neither of the adjustments—including immigrant men or restricting analyses to the low end of the skill continuum—affected the substance of the wage results. Controlling for geographic clustering dropped the 1990 intragroup substitution effect for Mexican immigrant women to nonsignificance.

Clearly, things changed from 1980 to 1990 in the urban Southwest. In 1980, Mexican-origin women, U.S.- and Mexican-born, appear to have been much more substitutable than they would be ten years later. In contrast, Mexican immigrant women appear to have been irrelevant to African American women's earning abilities at that point in time, although their influence ten years later would be substantial and positive. The only consistent patterns across time were those demonstrating a negative effect of immigrant presence on a Mexican immigrant woman's economic life-chances and a positive effect on non-Hispanic white women's outcomes.

Several themes can be derived from these findings. First, a decade of simultaneous Mexican female immigration and Mexican American women's entry into the labor force casts intergroup relationships into flux. These two groups are no longer empirically or theoretically reducible to one category. What may have once been a justifiable collapsing of working women into a "Mexican-origin" category without nativity distinctions is less justifiable today, given the substantial and widening differences between the groups on numerous social and economic dimensions.

Second, to the extent that the size of the Mexican-born population might be expected to increase the likelihood of an emergent enclave economy, thereby benefiting Mexican immigrant workers, there is not much evidence that this process improved the earnings of Mexican immigrant women. Mexican women seem to have hurt themselves more than they have hurt anyone else in the U.S. labor markets where they have settled, at least in terms of the earnings they have been able to command. At best, the geographically adjusted results suggest that large Mexican female populations

/ 265

have a benign influence on the earnings of constituent immigrants. Why Mexican immigrant women continue to settle and work in these communities leads outside the realm of individual earnings equations and requires the integration of these findings with the substantial literature on the migration process itself and its influences. Paramount among these influences, for women, are household and family structure—marital status, family formation, and the migration patterns and earnings profiles of men. Analyses of these influences on immigrant women's labor force participation and earnings will be necessary in order to understand the substitution effects that persist over time in these analyses.

Third, for all the hostility and rhetoric surrounding Mexican immigration, the net effect on the non-Hispanic white female labor force in the urban Southwest appears to have been largely positive. Where Mexican immigrant women go, higher wages and earnings for non-Hispanic white women have been evident. Similarly, the highly publicized discourse focusing on the "black versus brown" conflict emerging in urban America does not appear to have very deep roots in the economic dynamics between African American and Mexican immigrant women. To the contrary, the upgrading of African American women's job profiles in the Southwest may be partially attributable to the growth of Mexican immigrant women in service employment, as "racialized" employment decisions by employers, for example, may have evolved into decisions that take nativity into increasing account.

Fourth, disaggregating women to evaluate the immigration phenomenon did indeed yield patterns that could not have been anticipated solely on the basis of what has been determined for men. While men's dynamics have tended to reflect modest substitutability between Mexican immigrant and U.S.-born workers; women's dynamics demonstrate more consistent complementarity and of somewhat greater magnitude, at least in 1990. This divergence of experience has at least a few significant research and policy implications.

RESEARCH AND POLICY IMPLICATIONS

These analyses reveal labor market dynamics among women workers that could not have been predicted solely on the basis of results reported for men. Given the pervasiveness of female labor force participation in 1970–90 and the complexities of gendered labor market dynamics, researchers must take on the task of disaggregating groups of women workers as thoroughly as they have for men in order to understand how labor markets operate. Indeed, carrying out this task yielded, in this case, an alternative to the male pattern with respect to Mexican immigration, easily one of the most important demographic phenomena facing the urban Southwest.

Considerable research remains to be done on this topic. Even if the restrictive policies being considered at the close of the twentieth century lead to a reduction in Mexican immigration to the United States, the momentum for the continued influence of nativity differences upon labor market outcomes is substantial. Put bluntly, understanding both immigrant and U.S.-born women's work matters for understanding the labor markets of the Southwest, a vitally important region of the United States.

From a policy standpoint, two themes emerge from this work. First, it is important to consider the mechanisms producing the complementarity between immigrant and U.S.-born women workers. Mexican immigrant women may be inducing the complementarity effects seen for U.S.-born women by occupying niches in the labor market that are commensurate with what tend to be lower skills and thereby sustaining the ability of employers to keep their doors open and to employ higher-skilled U.S.-born women at higher rates of pay. This situation is not inconsistent with the interests of immigration and labor policy makers whose constituency is the U.S.-born workforce. On the other hand, if Mexican immigrant women are inducing the complementarity effect at their own expense, through "nativity"-driven job crowding and with the attendant risks of such demand-driven exploitation as wage, hour, and safety violations, it is purchased at a dear social cost.

Second, how, if at all, the immigration phenomenon is affecting the largest ethnic group of women workers in the Southwest—Mexican Americans—remains unclear. Mexican American women appear to have transcended the period when they were largely substitutable with their immigrant counterparts, but that separation is by no means complete. For all the differences characterizing Mexican American and immigrant women, risks of job competition continue to assert themselves, at least at the low end of the skill continuum. And what lies ahead? Long after their full-force entry into the labor market, their transition to family and household structure patterns that parallel their non-Mexican counterparts, and the entry and settlement of a Mexican-origin female workforce that might have been expected to take their place and boost them up in the U.S. job queue, Mexican American women continue to lag behind both African American and non-Hispanic white women on both human capital indicators and labor market outcomes. The fate of the Mexican American woman in the southwestern labor market appears to have less to do with the decisions of federal immigration policy makers than with the thousands of decisions made, for example, at the federal, state, and local levels that determine access to, retention in, and quality of public education. Educational experiences in the urban Southwest continue to differ in some important ways by race or ethnicity, and specifying those differences, coupled with maintaining the political will to eradicate them, will go further to improve Mexican American women's life-chances than will any revision of immigration policy.

REFERENCES

Bailey, Thomas R. 1987. *Immigrant and Native Workers: Contrasts and Competition.* Boulder, Colo.: Westview Press.

Baker, Susan González. 1996. "Demographic Trends in the Chicana/o Population: Policy Implications for the Twenty-First Century." In *Chicanas/Chicanos at the Crossroads: Social, Economic, and Political Change,* edited by David Macial and Isidro Ortiz. Tucson: University of Arizona Press.

———. 1997. "The Amnesty Aftermath: Current Policy Issues Stemming from the Legalization Programs of the 1986 Immigration Reform and Control Act." *International Migration Review* 31:(1): 5–28.

Bean, Frank D., B. Lindsay Lowell, and Lowell J. Taylor. 1988. "Undocumented Mexican Immigrants and the Earnings of Other Workers in the United States." *Demography* 25(1): 35–52.

Bean, Frank D., Edward E. Telles, and B. Lindsay Lowell. 1987. "Undocumented Migration to the United States: Perceptions and Evidence." *Population and Development Review* 13(4): 671–90.

Bean, Frank D., and Marta Tienda. 1988. *The Hispanic Population of the United States.* New York: Russell Sage Foundation.

Borjas, George. 1984. "The Impact of Immigrants on the Earnings of the Native Born." In *Immigration: Issues and Policies,* edited by Vernon Briggs and Marta Tienda. Salt Lake City, Utah: Olympus Publishing. pp. 83–126.

———. 1986. "The Sensitivity of Labor Demand Functions to the Choice of Dependent Variable." *Review of Economics and Statistics* 68(1): 56–66.

———. 1987. "Immigrants, Minorities, and Labor Market Competition." *Industrial and Labor Relations Review,* 40(3): 382–92.

———. 1990. *Friends or Strangers: The Impact of Immigrants on the U.S. Economy.* New York: Basic Books.

Briggs, Vernon. 1984. *Immigration Policy and the American Labor Force.* Baltimore: The Johns Hopkins University Press.

DeFreitas, Gregory, and Adriana Marshall. 1984. "Immigration and Wage Growth in U.S. Manufacturing in the 1970s." In *Proceedings of the Thirty-Sixth Annual Meeting, Dec. 28–30, 1983, San Francisco,* edited by Barbara D. Dennis. Madison, Wisc.: Industrial Relations Research Association.

England, Paula, and George Farkas. 1986. *Households, Employment, and Gender: A Social, Economic and Demographic View.* New York: Aldine de Gruyter.

Hagan, Jacqueline. 1994. *Deciding to be Legal.* Philadelphia: Temple University Press.

Hondagneu-Sotelo, Pierette. 1995. *Gendered Transitions: Mexican Experiences of Immigration.* Berkeley: University of California Press.

———. 1994. "Regulating the Unregulated?: Domestic Workers' Social Networks." *Social Problems* 41(1): 50–64.

King, Allan G., Lindsay Lowell, and Frank D. Bean. 1986. "The Effects of Hispanic Immigrants on the Earnings of Native Hispanic Americans." *Social Science Quarterly* 67(4): 673–89.

Maram, Sheldon L. 1980. "Hispanic Workers in the Garment and Restaurant Industries in Los Angeles County." Monograph. In U.S.-Mexican Studies 12. San Diego, Calif.: Center for U.S.-Mexican Studies, University of California, San Diego.

Marshall, Ray. 1987. "Controlling Illegal Immigration." in *Hearings before the Joint Economic Committee, Economic and Demographic Consequences of Immigration*. Washington: U.S. Government Printing Office.

Massey, Douglas. 1995. "The New Immigration and Ethnicity in the United States." *Population and Development Review* 21(3): 653–58.

McCarthy, Kevin F., and R. Burciaga Valdez. 1986. *Current and Future Effects of Mexican Immigration in California*. Santa Monica, Calif.: Rand.

Mines, Richard, and Ricardo Anzaldua. 1982. *New Migrants vs. Old Migrants: Alternative Labor Market Structures in the California Citrus Industry*. Monograph. In U.S.-Mexican Studies 9. San Diego, Calif.: Center for U.S.-Mexican Studies, University of California, San Diego.

Muller, Thomas, and Thomas Espenshade. 1985. *The Fourth Wave: California's Newest Immigrants*. Washington, D.C.: Urban Institute Press.

North, David, and Marion Houstoun. 1976. *The Characteristics and Role of Illegal Aliens in the U.S. Labor Market: An Exploratory Study*. Washington, D.C.: Linton.

Piore, Michael. 1979. *Birds of Passage: Migrant Labor and Industrial Societies*. Cambridge: Cambridge University Press.

Portes, Alejandro, and Robert Bach. 1985. *Latin Journey: Cuban and Mexican Immigrants in the United States*. Berkeley: University of California Press.

Repak, Terry. 1994. "Labor Market Incorporation of Central American Immigrants in Washington, D.C." *Social Problems* 41(1): 114–28.

Simon, Julian, and Stephen Moore. 1984. "The Effect of Immigration upon Unemployment: An Across-City Estimation." Unpublished paper.

Smith, Barton, and Robert Newman. 1977. "Depressed Wages along the U.S.-Mexico Border: An Empirical Analysis." *Economic Inquiry* 15(1): 51–56.

U.S. Department of Commerce, U.S. Bureau of the Census. 1996. *Public Use Micro Samples—1970, 1980, 1990*. Data files maintained at Population Research Center, University of Texas, Austin.

U.S. Immigration and Naturalization Service. 1993. *Statistical Yearbook of the Immigration and Naturalization Service, 1992*. Washington: U.S. Government Printing Office.

———. 1996. *Statistical Yearbook of the Immigration and Naturalization Service, 1994*. Washington: U.S. Government Printing Office.

Van Arsdol, Maurice, Joan Moore, David Heer, and Susan Paulvier Haynie. 1979. "Non-Apprehended and Apprehended Undocumented Residents in Los Angeles Labor Markets: An Exploratory Study." University of Southern California, Population Research Lab.

Vasquez, Mario. 1981. "Immigrant Workers in the Apparel Industry in Southern California." In *Mexican Immigrant Workers in the U.S.*, edited by Antonio Rios-Bustamante. Chicano Research Studies Center Anthology No. 2. Los Angeles: University of California.

Wise, Donald E. 1974. "The Effect of the Bracero on Agricultural Production in California." *Economic Inquiry* 12(4): 267–77.

Zavella, Patricia. 1987. *Women's Work and Chicano Families: Cannery Workers of the Santa Clara Valley*. Ithaca, N.Y.: Cornell University Press.

Chapter 8

Getting Off and Staying Off:
Racial Differences in the Work Route off Welfare

Kathryn Edin and Kathleen Mullan Harris

The welfare reform bill of 1996 was the culmination of several decades of growing social concern over non-work, low marriage rates, and welfare dependency among the poor. During the 1980s, the growing research and rhetoric about a phenomenon labeled the "underclass" heightened this concern. Journalists, politicians, and some scholars claimed that a new class of people was emerging in America's inner cities, a group entirely outside the economic class structure. Members of this new class were allegedly isolated from the world of work and trapped in a cycle of welfare dependency (Auletta 1982; Kaus 1986; Murray 1984; Wilson 1987). Some scholars argued that a broad range of social-structural factors that emerged in the 1970s underlay the creation of this underclass (Wilson 1987). Others claimed that welfare was the cause, because it supposedly discouraged work, encouraged nonmarital births and family breakup, and perpetuated an intergenerational welfare culture among poor inner-city residents (Gilder 1981; Mead 1992; Murray 1984).

Although most of the discourse about the underclass in the 1980s and early 1990s skirted issues of race, the statistical relationships between race and the attributes of the "underclass" made the racial connotation unmistakable. African American women have been overrepresented on the welfare rolls for several decades (approximately two-fifths of all welfare recipients are African American; U.S. House of Representatives 1995). African Americans have also had longer initial welfare spells, higher rates of welfare return once they have left the rolls, and longer cumulative receipt (Bane and Ellwood 1994; Ellwood 1986). Because marriage rates have always been lower and separation and divorce rates higher among African Americans than among whites, female-headed families and poverty have been much more prevalent among African Americans (Cherlin 1992; Garfinkel and McLanahan 1986). Furthermore, ongoing residential segregation by race has meant that poor African Americans have been much more likely to live in America's poor inner-city neighborhoods than poor whites have (Massey and Denton 1989). Thus it is not surprising that the media have used a welfare-reliant, unwed, African American mother as a standard icon of the underclass phenomenon.

The scientific evidence is mixed as to whether racial differences in patterns of welfare use persist once human capital and family and residential characteristics are taken into account (see Tienda 1990). A number of studies find that the duration of welfare receipt does not differ by race once these and other risk factors are controlled (Blank 1989; Fitzgerald 1991; Harris 1993, 1996; Harris and Edin 1998; Pavetti 1993; Rank and Hirschl 1988). Still others find small but significant effects of race on length of welfare receipt, though the effects are typically attributed to the lower marriage rates of African Americans (Bane and Ellwood 1983; 1994; Ellwood 1986; O'Neill, Bassi, and Wolf 1987).

Longitudinal studies have firmly established, however, that the vast majority of both black and white recipients have had substantial experience in the labor force (Harris 1993, 1996; Spalter-Roth and Hartman 1994b; Gritz and MacCurdy 1991; Pavetti 1993). These analyses show that work is the main route off welfare for mothers in both racial groups and that most mothers in each group exit welfare for work in less than two years (Harris 1993; Pavetti 1993). Furthermore, recent qualitative research has suggested that these surveys pick up only a portion of the work that African American and white recipients actually engage in while on the welfare rolls (Edin and Lein 1997; Edin and Jencks 1992).

Taken together, both survey and ethnographic data show that while welfare reform debates raged over issues of nonwork and ways to get welfare mothers into the workforce, both African American and white welfare-reliant mothers were already combining welfare with work or cycling between welfare and work (Edin and Jencks 1992; Edin and Lein 1997a, 1997b; Harris 1993, 1997; Spalter-Roth and Hartmann 1994a). Research shows, however, that work is not the panacea policy makers think it is. Some mothers do not make enough by working to leave welfare. Overall, two-thirds of single mothers who use welfare eventually leave welfare through a job (Harris 1993), but many of these mothers do not survive the labor market and must return to welfare again (Ellwood 1986; Harris 1996; Pavetti 1993).

In this chapter, we combine quantitative and qualitative data to examine the labor market attempts of African American and white mothers who left welfare for work between the mid-1980s and the early 1990s. Differences in the human capital and labor market opportunities of blacks and whites suggest that the process by which women work their way off welfare permanently should vary by race. Race should influence mothers' ability to leave welfare for work and to sustain a work exit from welfare in at least four interrelated ways.

First, African American mothers have less human capital than whites do on average. Though the black-white gap in education has been narrowing in recent decades, African American women's educational credentials are still not equal to white women's, and the wage premium employers place on education is increasing (Danziger and Gottschalk 1995, 85–87). In addition, in recent years African American women at the bottom of the income distribution have begun to work less than whites (reversing a long historical trend), leading to a widening race-based gap in work experience among women. Second, African American women's wages have fallen behind those of white women at all educational levels (see chapters 1 and 4). Third, the unemployment rate for African American women is more than twice that for whites (see chapter 1). Finally, the literature on racial inequality in the labor market indicates that African American women face a more restricted labor market than their white counterparts do, as a result of racial residential segregation, the industrial composition of local and regional labor markets, and employer discrimination (see chapters 4 and 5; Ellwood 1988; Massey and Denton 1993; Neckerman and Kirschenman 1991). All of these factors are likely to make the work route off welfare more precarious for African American women than for their white counterparts.

While research has shown that most welfare-reliant mothers in each racial group attempt to leave welfare for work, little in-depth analysis exists of racial differences in the process by which women work their way off welfare for good or fall back onto welfare when work fails to sustain them. Whether these mothers' wages or hours improve or decline over time is unknown, and not much is known about each group's work behavior or job security. Our main questions are what happens to women when they leave welfare for a job and how this experience varies by race. We focus on the experiences of mothers who have attempted the work route off welfare in recent years and explore whether African American and white single mothers can sustain their families at the jobs that facilitate their welfare exit. We also identify the factors that facilitate permanent work exits from welfare and the ways they differ for African American and white women.

We address these questions by integrating quantitative data that follows African American and white mothers who have left welfare for work with data from semistructured depth interviews focusing on the experiences of single African American and white mothers who have moved from welfare to a low-wage job. The quantitative data are drawn from the 1983 to 1988 panels of the Panel Study of Income Dynamics (PSID), a nationally representative longitudinal survey of families in the United States. The depth-interview data are drawn from the Edin-Lein Survival Strategies Study, in which data were collected from low-wage working single mothers (most of whom had recent welfare experience) in four U.S. cities between 1988 and 1992.

CONCEPTUAL MODEL

We use a conceptual framework that specifies a decision-making process in which poor women determine how to combine income from multiple sources by considering the trade-offs involved as they try to balance their provider and parenting roles. Poor women usually negotiate this balance by constructing "income packages" (Spalter-Roth and Hartmann 1994a). Low-income single mothers do not generally rely on a single income source over time (that is, either welfare or work) but combine income from various sources, including welfare, work, members of their personal networks, and nongovernmental charities, both simultaneously and over time (Duncan 1984; Edin and Jencks 1992; Edin and Lein 1997a; 1997b; Harris 1993; Spalter-Roth and Hartmann 1994a, 1994b). We extend this model to incorporate the dynamics of changing life circumstances, and we assume that trade-offs can vary over time (that is, family responsibilities can increase with another birth, income can increase with more education) and that women reevaluate their options as their situations change. Thus we expect that single mothers may make different decisions at different points in time.

We model the process by which women move from welfare to work and back to welfare as a function of the social structural, familial, and communal resources mothers may draw on as they develop and redevelop their income packages. We have included variables that measure three types of resources available to welfare-reliant mothers as they develop and maintain these income packages: individual-level resources (human capital), local welfare and labor market resources (structural variables), and family and community resources (social capital). Because the level and effectiveness of these resources vary by race, we expect that the processes of maintaining work exits from welfare are distinctive within racial groups. Blacks have fewer resources than whites do, and the resources they do have are often less effective. For instance, the social networks of African American women are often made up of others in similar structural positions. Therefore, we specify separate models for African American and white women to identify the key mechanisms that sustain welfare exits for each group. The model also includes measures of a mother's needs and constraints, including her age, the ages and number of her children, her prior welfare history, and the length of time she has managed to sustain her work exit from welfare.

We use two measures of mothers' human capital: years of formal education and work experience. We recognize that seniority and cognitive skills are also important measures of human capital (see chapter 4), but our data do not include these measures. We expect that mothers with more human capital will fare better in the labor market once they leave welfare and consequently will be less likely to return to welfare than will mothers with less education or work experience.

We also expect that our measures of human capital might have different effects for African Americans and whites as they attempt to sustain a work exit from welfare. Overall, white women are somewhat better educated and have a little more work experience than African Americans do (see chapters 1 and 4). However, African Americans might see lower returns to education than whites do because they may learn less on average in school (see chapter 4). Second, they may see less return to both education and work experience because of employer discrimination (Holzer 1996; Kirschenman and Neckerman 1990; Wilson 1997). Thus African Americans may earn less than whites even if they have similar or superior educational credentials and years of work experience. Finally, some have argued that African American women could see lower returns to education and work experience than whites do because they are more likely to work in peripheral industries or in jobs that require fewer cognitive skills, though the evidence for this hypothesis is mixed (see chapters 1, 4, and 12).

The second set of resources are structural and accrue from local welfare policies and labor market strength. Local welfare resources are measured by the maximum Aid to Families with Dependent Children (AFDC) guarantee specific to the family size, state of residence, and year. If generous benefits provide an incentive to rely on welfare, as many argue (Murray 1984), mothers who live in high-benefit states should be more likely to return to welfare. Racial differences in the incentive effects of welfare may exist both because African Americans are more likely to use welfare and because the states with the highest proportion of African American welfare recipients pay the least in cash benefits (U.S. House of Representatives 1995, table 10–25).

Labor market variables include county unemployment rates. We use county unemployment rates as a proxy for the potential employment opportunities, work hours, and income of ex–welfare recipients because tight labor markets generally improve workers' prospects in each of these areas (Levy and Murnane 1992; Lichter et al. 1992). Thus we expect that mothers living in areas with tight labor markets would be less likely to return to welfare (Edin and Lein 1997b). However, overall unemployment rates may have different effects on African Americans and whites because weak labor markets have a more harmful effect on the employment, wages, and working hours of African American women than on their white counterparts (see chapter 1).

The urban context might restrict the labor market opportunities of African American mothers as they attempt to work their way off welfare permanently. Much has been written about the deteriorating labor market conditions in the central cities of large urban areas as a result of the industrial transformation of the urban economy and the spatial mismatch of skill supply and demand (for example, Wilson 1987; Jencks and Peterson 1991; Kasarda 1989). America's decaying central cities provide few good job opportunities for those with little education and work experience because such jobs have moved to the suburbs, the Sunbelt, or overseas. Thus the unemployment rates of central-city residents are commonly much higher than for the urban area as a whole (county unemployment rates do not capture these differentials). Because African Americans are far more likely to live in central cities than whites are, we expect the urban context to present greater difficulties for African Americans than for whites.

Our third set of variables includes measures that represent a mother's social resources. The literature on social capital indicates that social ties have an important effect on both the cash and the noncash resources of families (Tienda and Angel 1982; Bordieu 1986; Coleman 1990; Edin and Lein 1997a; Hofferth 1984; Hogan, Hao, and Parish 1990; Martineau 1977; Marks and McLanahan 1993; Parish, Hao, and Hogan 1991; Stack 1974; Wellman and Wortley 1990). Important social ties include both a mother's own immediate and extended family (Stack 1974); her child's father and his kin; any boyfriend, neighbor, or associate within her exchange network; and her social contacts with community organizations, institutions, and workplaces. Because mothers' social ties vary, they have different kinds of social capital on which to draw as a result of these ties.

Once source of social capital stems from a mother's family of origin (Bordieu 1986; Coleman 1990). McLanahan and Sandefur (1994) suggest that children who live with only one parent during childhood may often lose access to the potential social capital available from their father or his kin. McLanahan and Sandefur argue that part of the disadvantage children of single parents experience as adolescents and adults (such as low levels of education and increased poverty rates) is a direct result of this loss of social capital. Because African Americans are more likely to have grown up in a one-parent family than whites (Garfinkel and McLanahan 1986), more African Americans may suffer this loss of social capital than whites and may be less likely to sustain a work exit from welfare.

Racial differences in the educational level of mothers' parents may compound the disadvantage African Americans face because it increases their chances of growing up poor and isolates them from social contact with those who might be able to link them to job opportunities as adults. In addition, maternal education is correlated with a mother's ability to negotiate the social world in a way that would benefit her daughter while growing up, especially in neighborhoods that are dangerous and bereft of other community resources (see Furstenberg 1993).

A second source of social capital is a mother's ties to others outside of her immediate family. These ties include her child's father and his kin, her current partner, her friends and neighbors, and her institutional ties. Because of the restrictions of our data, we are able to measure only whether a mother said she cohabited or married subsequent to her welfare spell and whether her partner worked. The presence of a working husband or partner should increase the economic security of the former recipient, reducing the mother's likelihood of welfare return. We expect the extent to which marriage or cohabitation provided economic security among poor women to vary significantly across racial groups, both because low-income African American women are less likely to marry and cohabit and because white mothers can expect their partners or husbands to earn more relative to what African American women can expect their partners to earn (Cherlin, 1992; Mare and Winship, 1991; Bumpass and Sweet 1989; Raley 1996; chapters 1 and 4; Wilson 1987; Spalter-Roth and Hartmann 1994b; Edin and Lein 1997b). Some evidence suggests that these effects might be partly mitigated by African American mothers' increased propensity to live with or near kin, who may lower mothers' living and child-care costs. However, most analyses find that African Americans' network ties are generally weaker and more restricted than whites' (Tienda and Angel 1982; Hofferth 1984; Hogan, Hao, and Parish 1990; Martineau 1977; 1978; Marks and McLanahan 1993; Parish, Hao, and Hogan 1991; Stack 1974; Wellman and Wortley 1990).[1]

A third source of disadvantage in family and community resources is the urban context. Not only does the urban context restrict labor market opportunities, as we described earlier, but it also restricts access to some types of social capital. Poor urban African Americans are much more likely to live among poor neighbors than are poor urban whites, who generally live in mixed-income neighborhoods (Mayer and Jencks 1989; Wilson 1987). Both Wilson as well as Massey and Denton (1993) have argued that residents of these racially and economically segregated neighborhoods are isolated from the social ties that might lead to work opportunities in the formal economy. Thus either growing up in or currently living in an urban context restricts the social resources of African American mothers more than it does for whites. As a result, we expect that African American mothers who experience the urban context as either a child or an adult would be less likely than white mothers to make a permanent transition from welfare to work.

In sum, we assume that mothers with few social resources—that is, mothers whose own mothers were poorly educated, mothers who grew up in a one-parent family, and mothers who grew up in or currently live in an urban area—will be less successful at working their way off welfare than mothers with more social resources. Social ties can therefore be construed as resources because they are the basis upon which social capital is built (Bourdieu 1986). These ties may facilitate a mother's attempt to make a permanent transition from welfare to work in a multitude of ways, including both in-kind and cash assistance that becomes part of a mother's income package. To the extent that African American mothers' social capital is restricted vis-à-vis white mothers', we expect that African American mothers will experience greater difficulty in permanently moving from welfare to work. Because African American women have both less and less effective social capital than white women do, they may have to rely more heavily on their own human capital and may be more sensitive to labor market resources in their attempts to make a permanent transition from welfare to work

Finally, we include a set of variables that measure mothers' constraints and needs that vary over time, such as her age, the number and ages of her children, her prior welfare history, the length of time she has been off welfare, and whether she had a child subsequent to her work exit. We assume that mothers who are very young, mothers who have young children, and mothers who have large families will have less success in sustaining a work exit off of welfare. As women age, they presumably gain skills in managing their finances, in balancing their caretaking and provider roles, and in being parents and potential employees. Age may also be a proxy for social resources, since a mother's social ties are likely to increase with age. The ages and number of a mother's children represent her income needs as well as her time and child-care constraints. Because African American women become mothers at an earlier age and have slightly more children than white women do, on average, their ability to make a permanent transition from welfare to work might be uniquely constrained.

The potential effects of a birth subsequent to a work exit from welfare are harder to predict. The birth may increase a woman's caretaking responsibilities, but it may also increase the responsibilities inherent in her provider role. The costs of child care could be high if the mother stays at her job, and the potential benefits from welfare increase. These factors may make it impracticable for a mother to keep working. We are not sure whether to expect racial differences in the likelihood that mothers will bear a child subsequent to leaving welfare for work or racial differences in the effect of a subsequent birth. It follows logically, however, that if white women are more likely to marry or cohabit, they might also be at greater risk of bearing an additional child. Also, the potential costs of working may be higher for whites, who tend to get less free child care from relatives than African Americans do (Marks and McLanahan 1993).

Our models include information about the length of a time a mother spent on welfare to examine whether the length of welfare receipt affects the permanency of work exits. We expect longer spells to inhibit the development of all forms of capital (human, social, and cultural) and thus make work exits less secure.

STUDY DESIGN AND DATA

In this study of the lives of mothers who attempt to leave welfare for work, we use the novel approach of employing both quantitative and qualitative data drawn from separate sources. We argue that neither quantitative nor qualitative data alone is sufficient to study the work route off of welfare. Only a combination of the two types of data can yield a full explanation of how women work their way off of welfare for good and how this process varies by race.

Quantitative Data

We examined work exits and returns to welfare quantitatively using monthly data from the PSID for 1983 to 1988. These data were drawn exclusively from respondents who participated in the AFDC program.[2] We analyzed patterns of welfare return among a subsample of women living with children less than eighteen years old who had at any time received welfare as single mothers and who had exited AFDC through work. We included only women who were single mothers at the time of work exit in the analysis to identify the group of women for whom work was the main source of welfare exit. Women remained in the sample as long as their children lived with them and were less than eighteen years of age and for as long as they were still present in the study during the observation period. The observation period spanned the seventy-two months from January 1983 to December 1988, and the sample included 265 women.

A fundamental concept used throughout the quantitative analysis is that of spells of welfare and nonwelfare. We define a spell of welfare as a period of one or more months of continuous welfare receipt, or sequential months in which AFDC was received; a spell of nonreceipt refers to a period of two or more sequential months in which welfare was not received following the end of a spell of welfare.[3]

Qualitative Data

The PSID data provide a representative picture of patterns of work and welfare and statistical tests of the causes of permanent welfare exit through word, but they tell only part of the story. We used qualitative data to lend insight into the findings of the quantitative study. The qualitative data come from a study of 165 low-wage working single mothers in four U.S. cities: Boston; Charleston, South Carolina; Chicago; and San Antonio. The study, conducted by Kathryn Edin and Laura Lein between 1988 to 1992, was designed to explore and document the economic survival strategies of low-income single mothers.

Edin and Lein conducted multiple, in-depth interviews with a broad range of low-wage working single mothers who had been introduced to them by a trusted third party. After establishing a high level of rapport and trust, Edin and Lein collected detailed work and welfare histories and open-ended data on mothers' assessments of the relative merits of welfare and work. They also collected detailed income and expenditure data to construct monthly budgets that included income from welfare and on-the-books work as well as off-the-books work; contributions from men, family, and friends; and assistance from community groups and nongovernmental agencies. In all sites, Edin and Lein interviewed roughly the same numbers of African American and white women.[4]

ANALYSIS PLAN AND METHODS

The analysis that follows has four parts. We begin by using quantitative data from the PSID to describe patterns of work and welfare return for African American and white women following work exits from welfare. Next, we look at the characteristics of both groups of women according to whether their work exit was followed by welfare reentry. Third, we look within racial groups and contrast the characteristics of those who left welfare permanently with those who cycled back onto welfare. We use life table techniques to examine the length of welfare receipt, subsequent non-receipt of welfare, and patterns of returns to welfare. We then apply event history methods to analyze the determinants of welfare return following work exits (Allison 1982; 1995; Kalbfleisch and Prentice 1980).[5] Explanatory variables include both fixed and time-varying variables.[6] Finally, we interpret our quantitative results by drawing on depth-interview data from the Edin-Lein Survival Strategies study.

Working off Welfare

More than a quarter of the mothers in the PSID sample who left welfare through marriage, work, or other reasons had returned within a year of leaving the rolls, and 41 percent had returned within two years (table 8.1). Of those who exited for work, 20 percent had returned within the first year after exit. By the end of the second year, one working mother in three had returned. Once the mothers in the sample had remained off welfare for two years or more, the rates of return dropped off substantially. Though women who left welfare for a job returned more slowly than the larger group of exiters did, their advantage evaporated over time. By the end of the six-year window observed, about 60 percent of both groups of women had returned to the AFDC program.

The rate of return to welfare following a work exit differed markedly by race. Nearly two-thirds of African Americans who left welfare for a job

Table 8.1 / Mothers Returning to Welfare, by Race and Time Since Exit, 1983 to 1988 (Percent)

	All Welfare Exits (n = 470)	Exits Ending in Work[a]		
Time Since Exit		All Mothers (n = 265)	African Americans (n = 208)	Whites (n = 57)
Three months	5	4	7	2
Six months	14	11	16	6
One year	47	20	29	12
Two years	41	34	40	28
Three years	48	39	43	36
Four years	52	45	43	44
More than four years	57	59	65	44

Source: Panel Study of Income Dynamics, 1983 to 1988 panels.
Notes: Estimates are computed using PSID inverse sampling probability weights.
[a]Race differences in the duration distribution of welfare return are significant at the .05 level.

eventually cycled back onto the welfare rolls. Almost half (45 percent) of these reentries occurred within the first year, and nearly two-thirds (62 percent) within the first two years. Though reentries dropped off dramatically for African Americans in the third and fourth year following exit, more than a quarter (26 percent) cycled back onto the rolls after the fourth year. This pattern indicates that African American women remained vulnerable to reentry even after they had remained off the rolls and on their jobs for many years.

For whites, the overall reentry rate following a work exit was much lower. Only 44 percent of whites cycled back onto welfare after leaving for a job, 27 percent within the first year and 64 percent within the first two years. Returns to welfare continued to accumulate during the third and fourth years off welfare, but no reentries occurred after the fourth year. Thus African Americans were 48 percent (0.65/0.44 = 1.48) more likely than whites to return to welfare after a work exit. African Americans also returned to welfare more rapidly and remained vulnerable to reentry for a much longer period than whites did.

To understand this racial discrepancy, we compared the level and effectiveness of African American and white mothers' human capital, structural conditions, and social and cultural capital as well as their changing life circumstances (table 8.2). The groups were similar in terms of the length of time spent on welfare, but more than two-thirds (68 percent) of the African American mothers lived in cities, compared with only about two of every five white mothers (42 percent).[7] As we argued earlier, this difference may

Table 8.2 / Characteristics of Mothers at Welfare Exit and Since Welfare Exit, by Race, 1983 to 1988

Characteristic	African Americans	P	Whites
At welfare exit			
Prior welfare spell > 24 months (%)	32		32
Urban residence (%)	68	**	42
Age (years)	32.0		30.0
3 or more children (%)	29		25
Preschool children (%)	50	*	64
Education (%)		**	
Less than high school	23		49
High school diploma only	32		13
More than high school	45		38
Work experience (years)	7.7		6.3
Hourly wage (1988 dollars)[a]	5.36		5.27
Hours worked[a]	31.1		32.6
Weekly earnings (1988 dollars)	166.70		171.8
Family income below poverty line (%)	80	**	53
Since welfare exit			
Continued working (%)	59	*	45
Until return	23	**	8
Until end of the survey, no return	36		37
Returned to welfare (%)	47	**	31
Not working at return	19	**	22
Working at return	28	**	8
Length of time worked as proportion of time off welfare	90		89
Subsequently married or cohabited (%)	9	**	56
Married	7	**	33
Cohabited	3	**	22
Had another child (%)	9		15
Obtained further education (%)	7		6

Source: Panel Study of Income Dynamics, 1983 to 1988 panels.
Notes: Estimates are computed using PSID inverse sampling probability weights. n = 265 work exits.
[a]Missing values on wages and hours reduce the n slightly for these indicators.
*Significant at .05 level. **Significant at .01 level.

indicate that the African American mothers faced more limited labor market opportunities or had less access to the social capital that their white counterparts enjoyed.

Given the differences between African American and white mothers in their rate of return to welfare (table 8.1), one might expect the African American group to have been younger, to have had larger families, or to have been more likely to have a preschool child than the white group. However, the only significant difference in life circumstances ran contrary to our expectations; African Americans were actually *less* likely than whites to have a preschool child (table 8.2, rows 3 to 5).

As for human capital differences between the two groups at the time of welfare exit, African American mothers' greater vulnerability to reentry leads one to expect their years of schooling, work experience, and overall earnings will be low relative to those of whites. Actually, the opposite was true: whites who left welfare for work were more than twice as likely to have dropped out of high school as African Americans. Furthermore, more African Americans had had post–high school training. African Americans also had had more years of work experience prior to their welfare spell and earned a little more per hour when they left welfare for work, though these differences were not significant. Finally, their overall weekly earnings were nearly identical to whites' at the time of welfare exit. One would expect African American mothers' earnings to have been higher than whites' because of the former's higher level of schooling, but their educational advantages did not translate into increased earnings, at least at the point of welfare exit.

Thus far, only two of the components identified help explain why the African Americans mothers who left welfare for work were more vulnerable to repeat welfare use than whites: the likelihood that a mother had been raised in an urban area as a child and the likelihood that she was currently living in an urban area. Furthermore, many of the other factors we thought might disadvantage African Americans (life circumstances and human capital variables) actually conferred a theoretical advantage.

Another difference between the African American and white mothers in our sample hints at a proximate answer to this puzzle, one that we revisit in a subsequent section. African American mothers' increased vulnerability to repeat reliance on welfare may be due to the fact that they were so much more likely to be poor at the time of welfare exit than whites were. Judging by the total household incomes of mothers who exited welfare for work, 80 percent of the African American households remained poor in the year that the mothers left welfare for a job, compared with only about half of the white households.

This large difference in family income could not have been due to African American mothers' wages relative to whites', since their weekly earnings were nearly identical at the point of welfare exit. Nor did large differences in earnings appear after the mothers had spent a number of years on the job. Since welfare rules did not allow mothers to have substantial assets or draw income from investments, the addition income must have come from elsewhere, although the source is hard to identify in the PSID.

As we have pointed out, welfare scholars know virtually nothing about the work behavior and job security of mothers who leave welfare for a job and the way these factors vary by race. Again, the higher rates of welfare return for the African Americans following a work exit would lead us to expect that they worked less steadily than their white counterparts. The PSID data do not allow us to distinguish whether respondents' work patterns were due to the behavioral characteristics of workers (whether they quit or were fired) or to the nature of the work they engaged in (whether their employers reduced their hours or laid them off altogether), but the data are interesting nonetheless. First, whites, not African Americans, were more likely to have stopped working at some time (table 8.2, panel 2). What is most striking is the proportion of African American mothers who returned to welfare even though they had worked continuously since their exit from welfare: fully 38 percent $(0.23/0.59 = 0.38)$. The figure for whites is only 18 percent $(0.08/0.45 = 0.18)$.

Focusing on those mothers who returned to welfare tells the same story: African Americans were more likely to work continuously and more likely to return to welfare while they were working. Among all African Americans who returned to welfare (47 percent) and for whom we have complete earnings data, 60 percent $(0.28/0.47 = 0.60)$ were working when they cycled back onto welfare (including both those who had worked continuously and those who had stopped working at some point). For whites, the rate was only 27 percent. These results clearly indicate that formal-sector work—especially if it is continuous and at nearly identical wages and hours—nearly guaranteed that white women (who were less educated on average) would not return to welfare, but continuous work did not provide the same assurance for African American women. Mothers in both groups spent about 90 percent of their time off welfare and in the labor force.

Finally, cohabiting men might have been an important source of additional household income for white women, though we could not test this directly. White women were much more likely to marry and to cohabit after leaving welfare for work. A third of white women who left welfare for work subsequently married, and more than one-fifth cohabited. Fewer than one in ten African American women either married or cohabited after exit.

Women Who Stayed off Welfare Versus Those Who Returned

We now examine differences between women who left welfare for work and did not return during the six-year period and those who left and cycled back on again. To determine whether an exit was "permanent," we imposed the rule that spells of nonreceipt had to consist of at least thirteen months without welfare reentry before the end of the observation period. Therefore, we omitted from the analysis spells that ended within twelve months of the end of the observation period or that were right-censored

Table 8.3 / Characteristics of Mothers Who Exited Welfare Permanently Through Work (Means), by Race, 1983 to 1988

Characteristics	African Americans	P	Whites
Family Background (%)			
Lived in a two-parent household	67		70
Mother had at least a high school education	41		37
Grew up in urban area	29		27
At welfare exit			
Prior welfare spell > 24 months (%)	25		21
Urban residence (%)	49	**	27
Age at welfare exit (years)	32.2		30.7
Family with 3 or more children (%)	29		39
Preschool children (%)	61		58
Education (%)		**	
Less than high school	24		37
High school graduate only	34		14
More than high school	41		48
Years of work experience	8.1		7.0
Hourly wage at exit (1988 dollars)	5.25		5.66
Hours worked at exit	35.0	*	31.9
Weekly wage (1988 dollars)	183.80		180.60
Family income below poverty (%)	84	**	31
At end of study			
Hourly wage (1988 dollars)	5.93		5.18
Hours worked	27.9		34.6
Weekly wage (1988 dollars)	165.50		179.20
Family income below poverty (%)	64	**	33

Source: Panel Study of Income Dynamics, 1983 to 1988 panels.
Notes: Percentages computed using PSID inverse sampling probability weights and based on 102 spells with permanent endings. Fifty-one spells were eliminated from the base because spells off welfare that could not be observed beyond twelve months since work exit were not considered permanent (that is, right censored < thirteen months since exit).
*Significant at the .05 level. **Significant at the .01 level.

within twelve months of exit from welfare.[8] Among mothers who got off and stayed off of welfare, African American and white women were similar in many ways (table 8.3). They came from similar family backgrounds, had the same past experience with welfare, and were at about the same point in the life course. They commanded similar hourly wages, worked about the same number of hours, and earned about the same weekly income overall, both at the time they exited welfare and over time.

However, African Americans who left for good were more likely to live in an urban area than were their white counterparts. They were also more

Table 8.4 / Characteristics of Mothers Who Returned to Welfare Following a Work Exit (Means), by Race, 1983 to 1988

Characteristic	African Americans	P	Whites
Family background (%)			
Lived in a two-parent household	40		59
Mother had at least a high school education	47		41
Grew up in urban area	82	**	49
At welfare exit			
Prior welfare spell > 24 months (%)	38		42
Urban residence (%)	84	*	68
Age (years)	31.4	*	25.3
3 or more children (%)	28		20
Preschool children (%)	42	**	87
Education (%)		**	
Less than high school	18		65
High school graduate only	29		12
More than high school	52		23
Years of work experience	7.2		4.2
Hourly wage (1988 dollars)	5.34		4.99
Hours worked	28.0		33.9
Weekly Wage (1988 dollars)	149.50		169.20
Family Income below poverty (%)	76		78
At return to welfare			
Hourly wage at welfare return or end of job (1988 dollars)	5.39		4.93
Hours worked at welfare return or end of job	29.3		29.3
Weekly wage (1988 dollars)	157.90		144.50

Source: Panel Study of Income Dynamics, 1983 to 1988 panels.
Notes: Percentages computed using PSID inverse sampling probability weights and based on 113 spells followed by welfare return.
*Significant at the .05 level. **Significant at the .01 level.

highly educated than the whites, and though this advantage increased their hourly wages over time, the low number of hours worked meant that they were earning a little less each week than the whites were at the end of the study. The most striking difference is that African Americans who stayed off welfare were much more likely to have exited into poverty and to have stayed impoverished. In this sense, the success of those in the African American group who stayed off the rolls is surprising.

African American and white mothers who cycled back onto welfare after leaving for work were different from one another in a number of ways (table 8.4). As was true of those who got off and stayed off welfare, among those who returned the African American mothers were more likely to have grown up in an urban area and to live in an urban area than the whites. They were older than the white mothers, and they were half as likely to have preschool children at home. In addition, the white mothers were much less educated than their African American counterparts. Two out of three whites who returned to welfare were high school dropouts, as opposed to less than one in five of the African Americans. Finally, the whites had less work experience, though the differences were not statistically significant.

The African American groups' life circumstances and educational advantages were evident in their slightly higher wage at exit from welfare (however, they worked fewer hours, so their weekly earnings were actually less than those for whites at exit). The earnings of African American returnees relative to whites did improve somewhat over time, but only because whites were working fewer hours at the point of return to welfare than they were at exit. Weekly earnings for African Americans who returned to welfare improved by about $8 over time, whereas earnings for whites who returned dropped by about $25 a week between exit and reentry. Most important, however, is the fact that more than three-quarters of mothers in both racial groups who eventually returned to welfare initially exited into poverty.

Event-History Models of the Process of Working One's Way Off Welfare

Event-history models provide a dynamic framework within which to explore the factors that determine which mothers sustained their work exit from welfare and which did not. We define the dependent variable as a return to welfare, and we assume that the factors that predict returns to welfare are the same as those that facilitate the opposite behavior, staying off welfare. The discrete-hazard model employs logistic regression to estimate the probability of returning to welfare using maximum likelihood methods. We argue that the process by which African American mothers work their way off welfare for good differs from the process among white women, and the results shown in tables 8.1 to 8.4 support this argument. Thus we conducted separate hazard analyses of the probability of African Americans' and whites' returning to welfare following a work exit (table 8.5).

We derived the hazard model from a model-fitting procedure in which we tested substantive sets of variables in a hierarchical fashion to arrive at a parsimonious set of explanatory variables (shown in table 8.5). Table 8A.1 shows a subset of the model-fitting procedure based on the entire sample of work exits, in which the final model shown (model 3) is used to generate the interactive models with race display in table 8.5). Because dividing the

Table 8.5 / Parameter Estimates of Repeat Welfare Dependency Following Work Exits, by Race, 1983 to 1988

Explanatory Variable	African Americans		Whites	
	b	SE	b	SE
Intercept	−4.90	0.88	−0.30	3.29
Time since work exit (months)				
1–3	1.46**	0.44	−1.48	1.29
4–6	1.34**	0.46	−0.78	1.07
7–12	1.80**	0.40	−0.45	0.91
13–18	1.00*	0.48	0.24	0.83
19–24	1.15*	0.49	−0.61	1.18
25+	—		—	
More than 2 welfare spells	0.42#	0.24	0.43	0.66
Prior welfare receipt > 24 months	0.13	0.25	0.39	0.76
Grew up in urban area	0.35	0.28	0.98	0.74
Age at welfare exit	−0.02	0.02	−0.26#	0.16
High school education or more	0.16	0.28	−1.31#	0.70
Years of work experience	−0.05#	0.03	0.24	0.17
3 or more children	0.35	0.25	0.99	0.73
Recent birth	0.52#	0.27	1.20#	0.68
Married or cohabiting	1.16	1.09	1.95	1.38
Married/cohabiting * partner's work status	−1.78	1.20	3.43*	1.56
Unemployment rate	−0.05	0.06	0.06	0.18
AFDC guarantee/100	−0.01	0.07	0.16	0.32
Summary statistics				
−2 log likelihood	816.6		142.9	
χ^2	58.9		32.6	
df	17		17	
Person-months	4,333		1,426	
Number of spells	208		57	

Source: Panel Study of Income Dynamics, 1983 to 1988 panels.
Significant at the .05 level. one-tailed test. *Significant at the .05 level, two-tailed test. **Significant at the .01 level, two-tailed test.

sample by race results in small subsamples, we present significance levels for both one-tailed and two-tailed tests.[9]

Focusing on the African American model, the duration effects indicate that the greatest risks of welfare return occurred soon after the African American women exited, with the highest rates occurring seven to twelve months following the exit to work. Among whites, the length of time since welfare exit was less important than other individual characteristics or changing life events. The welfare spell parameters were significant only in the African American model and suggest that, once African American women had cycled back onto welfare, they were less likely to sustain a subsequent exit to work. Note that none of the family background variables were significant (see table 8A.1).

The effects of work experience indicate that each year an African American mother worked after leaving welfare, the better her chances were of staying off for good. Taking the antilog of the work experience coefficient (-.05), we can interpret each additional year of work experience as reducing the odds of welfare return by 5 percent. Age and educational level did not seem to alter African American women's prospects for a successful work exit.

The factors that increased the likelihood that white women would get off and stay off were very different. For white women, age and education were important factors in facilitating a permanent transition from welfare to work. If a white woman had a high school education or more, her chances of returning to welfare were nearly 75 percent less than those of a white high school dropout.[10]

We have shown that the white women actually had lower levels of education at the time of welfare exit than African Americans did. Here the returns to education among women who completed high school or obtained education beyond high school were greater for white women than they were for black women. Evidently, a high school diploma or a year or two of post–high school training did not protect African American women from returning to welfare as well as it did whites.

Events that affected the balance between caretaking and breadwinning roles also affected mothers' ability to sustain work exits. The most important family event for both African American and white mothers was a recent birth. Child-care constraints and the higher costs and greater family responsibilities associated with a new baby surely affected the trade-offs involved when women worked, increasing the likelihood of welfare return by 68 percent for African Americans and by 231 percent for whites.

Finally, we assume that because whites had much higher probabilities of cohabitation and marriage than African American women did (Bumpass and Sweet 1989; Raley 1996), white women who left welfare for work were often able to subsequently combine their income with that of a male earner (who probably earned more than the woman did). Thus whites could trade reliance on the state for reliance on a man. This option was far less available to African American women, whose only viable alternative to reliance on the state was self-reliance through work. The kinds of jobs available to unskilled and semiskilled African American women who leave welfare seldom offered the possibility of true self-reliance. We return to this point in the next section.[11]

Surprisingly, labor market conditions (reflected by the county-level unemployment rate) had no impact on the longevity of work exits. Consistent with most previous evidence, the incentive effects of the size of the AFDC guarantee did not appear to be very strong either (see Moffitt 1992).

In sum, African American women enhanced their prospects of getting off and staying off with each additional year they remained in the labor market. They generally did not have the option of trading reliance on the state for reliance on a man when they left welfare for work. Nor could they depend on a high school diploma or a few years of post–high school training to sustain their work exits. White women were much more able to combine their earnings with other income—some of it presumably provided by a husband or cohabiting male—to help them stay off welfare. They could also rely more on a high school diploma or post–high school training to increase their earnings in the labor market substantially. Interestingly, the white mothers with the best educational credentials and highest earnings were also the most likely to marry or cohabit (see Lichter et al. 1992), thus leaving those white mothers with the least education and earnings very vulnerable to repeated spells on welfare.

The Edin-Lein Survival Strategies Study

Our analysis of the quantitative data derived from the PSID leaves a number of questions unanswered. First, we have established that the African American women had more difficulty in making a permanent transition from welfare to work than the white women did. Economists generally assume that individual-level human capital characteristics can explain discrepancies of this kind. In our analysis, this was not at all the case. The African American mothers were far less likely to have dropped out of high school and were more likely to have had post–high school training than whites were. They had had more years of work experience prior to their welfare spell, and they were more likely to have worked continuously while on the rolls than their white counterparts. These findings are unlikely to indicate that the African American mothers were simply less inclined to work, since so many of those African American mothers who returned to welfare had worked continuously since leaving welfare and were working at the time they returned. Beyond human capital, structural and life circumstance variables also failed to shed light on the puzzle of African American mothers' heightened vulnerability to welfare return. Even more puzzling, neither their hourly wages nor their earnings explained their higher rates of return. Something is missing that cannot be measured by using the PSID data.

Throughout the chapter, we have hinted that the solution to the puzzle may lie in the differential social capital of blacks and whites, yet we were able to employ few direct measures of social capital in our quantitative analysis. To supplement these data with more direct indicators of racial differences in mothers' social capital, we turn to qualitative data drawn from the Edin-Lein Survival Strategies Study. Between 1988 and 1992, Edin and Lein collected data from 165 low-wage working single mothers living in four U.S. metropolitan areas: Boston; Charleston, South Carolina; Chicago; and San Antonio. Edin and Lein contacted the mothers through referrals from a wide range of trusted grassroots community organizations. These organizations acted as intermediaries between the interviewer and the respondents and greatly enhanced the trust and rapport the interviewer established with each respondent. These respondents provided referrals to other mothers the respondents thought Edin and Lein would be less likely to contact through a community group. Through repeated open-ended interviews, Edin and Lein collected detailed budget data from each respondent, including income from formal, informal, and illegal work; cash contributions from family members, absent fathers, and boyfriends; and cash or voucher assistance from agencies, as well as a detailed account of the mothers' expenditures over a twelve-month period. Some of these budget data (income from illegal or informal work, for example) cannot be gleaned from nationally representative surveys. Furthermore, no national survey collects both detailed income and expenditure data.[12]

Like the women in the sample drawn from the PSID, the majority of Edin and Lein's respondents had worked their way off the welfare rolls at some point during the previous five years and reported earnings as well. They were broadly similar to the PSID group in terms of work experience, race, age, and number of children.[13] In sum, the working single mothers in Edin and Lein's study were similar enough to the PSID sample to lend insight to the quantitative findings.

The mothers Edin and Lein interviewed reported earning an average of $777 per month at their main jobs. However, no mother could live on her earnings from her main job; on average, the working mothers spent $1,243 per month.[14] Only 7 percent of this amount was spent on cable TV, videos, alcohol, cigarettes, the lottery, or other nonessentials, and no mother could have come close to living off her earnings had she not purchased these items. Twenty-seven percent of the mothers' total expenditures went for housing, 20 percent for food, and 46 percent for other items most Americans would consider necessities, such as child care, medical care, transportation, and clothing.[15] After paying for housing and food, the mothers living in private housing had $126 left per month to pay the rest of her bills. Mothers who lived with another family or received housing subsidies had very little ($257 and $223 respectively) left over each month after paying for housing and food.

To make ends meet, the working mothers Edin and Lein interviewed had to generate substantial income (roughly 35 percent of their total income on average) from other sources. Some relied on second jobs or overtime. Others relied on cash jobs. A few even engaged in vice to generate side income. But mothers who worked were pressed for time and could expect to generate only a small amount of money from side work. Therefore, mothers who wanted to stay off welfare generally had to convince a family member, their child's father, a boyfriend, or a community organization to provide the cash and in-kind support they needed to keep their job (see figure 8.1 for a breakdown of working mothers' supplemental strategies by race). While on welfare, most of these workers had paid little or nothing for child care and medical care and very little for transportation. Work required them to spend much more for these items and often required additional expenditures for clothing. Because work cost mothers more than welfare had, their ability to garner support from family members, boyfriends, and absent fathers was all the more important.

The PSID data suggest that it is precisely this kind of support that can explain much of the disadvantage African Americans face relative to whites in their attempt to make a permanent work exit from welfare. The data suggest that main difference between African Americans and whites is the quality of their private safety net. The existence of such a safety net is crucial, because most mothers who exit welfare for work will not be able to earn enough to meet their expenses. Without an adequate private safety net, mothers trying to make ends meet at a low wage job are more vulnerable to repeat dependency on the public safety net.

Edin and Lein's study found large racial differences in mothers' private safety nets, and the data provide a more detailed view of the forms these safety nets took. The African American workers Edin and Lein studied received significantly less cash help from kin, boyfriends, and their children's fathers than white workers did (see figure 8.1). They were therefore more reliant on their income from their main job and on whatever side work they could generate.

White mothers themselves pointed out the importance of a private safety net for sustaining a work exit from welfare. One white Charleston working mother said,

> If I didn't have my parents to fall back on, I would be out of a job. They pay all of the bills that I can't pay, which is a lot of them sometimes. They also make my car payment and keep up on my car insurance. Without the transportation, I couldn't afford to keep my job.

Figure 8.1 / Income Sources of 150 Low-Wage Working Mothers in Four U.S. Cities, by Race

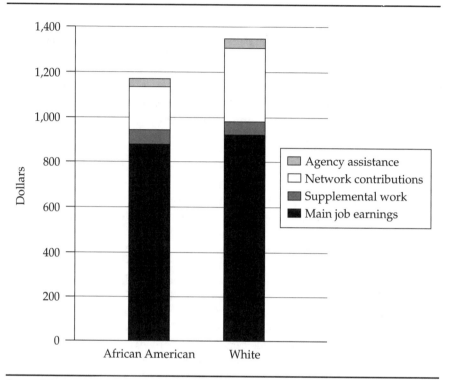

Source: Edin-Lein Survival Strategies study, see text.
Note: Excludes Latinas.

Another white Charleston worker commented,

My sister pays for the day care. That costs about $475 every month. That's how I can make it working now. Before, the day care just ate up everything I would have earned. That's when I was on welfare.

Edin and Lein did not interview any mothers who had married after leaving welfare for work, but the PSID data suggest that racial differences in mothers' private safety net were exacerbated by black women's lower propensity to marry. Theories that try to explain this phenomenon abound, and a thorough discussion of them is beyond our scope here. However, the qualitative data Edin and Lein collected did show some differences in attitudes toward marriage by race. In general, African American respondents tended to define men as an additional burden and believed that their economic futures depended mostly on what they themselves would be able to earn in the labor market. The PSID data bear this out. Edin and Lein found that whites were more likely to see reliance on a man as the long-term solution to their economic problems and were less likely to believe they would have to rely on their own earnings for long. Again, the PSID data suggest that their expectations fit reality.

When Edin asked one African American worker in Chicago if she had considered marriage, she replied, "I want somebody that I don't have to sit there and say, 'Is he going to work this week, is he going to work next week?'" Another African American worker told the interviewer, "A man simply don't earn enough money to support a family. I think this leads to couples finding it impossible to stay together." These comments are in stark contrast to the words of one white Charleston worker who had recently left welfare for work:

Tom is a wonderful man. He's got a steady job, he's had it for thirteen years. He works with DuPont. He has a house. We're moving in this weekend [and] we're planning to get married [within the year]. When I got rid of my [first] husband, I said "Things are going to get better now—that's all there is to it." And I found my boyfriend now through the ads in newspaper. That's where I got him. It's worked out and I love it.

Another white worker said of the mail carrier she had started dating,

I have just started dating a new man. I think that I could get married again. I guess that [we] will get married sometime in the [near] future, and I think that I would like just to stay home and raise my family. That would make me really happy.

Scholars have explained differentials in the marriage rates of blacks and whites in various ways. Along with the African American respondents quoted above, Wilson (1987) and others believe that the rapid decline in marriage rates for African Americans is rooted in the increasing economic marginality of African American men. Other scholars believe the difference is not primarily economic but cultural. Edin and Lein's African American respondents commonly expressed complex motivations for not marrying. Though they almost always cited economic factors, most of the African American respondents also said that their distrust of men made it difficult for them to consider marriage (see Edin 1998).[16] While a large minority of white women also expressed some reservations about the trustworthiness of men, most said they would consider marriage in the future if the right man came along.

The other major finding from the PSID data is the strong negative relationship between African American mothers' urban residence (both while growing up and at the time of the survey) and their ability to leave welfare for work permanently. Along with Wilson (1987) and Massey and Denton (1993), we believe that the physical, social, and economic isolation of African American urban residents limits their access to the level and quality of social capital they need to sustain.

CONCLUSION

Data drawn from the PSID and the Edin-Lein Survival Strategies Study have shown that understanding the full range of disadvantages African American women face in the low-wage labor market relative to whites requires looking beyond traditional explanations that focus on human capital and social structure. In our case, relying only on these explanations would have left us with a lot of unexplained findings. To tell the whole story of women who attempt the work route off welfare, we had to look at the level and effectiveness of a broader range of resources available to mothers from their families of origin, from the men in their lives, and from others in their communities. And to understand the full range of resources mothers had available to them, we had to rely on both quantitative and qualitative data.

We offer the following metaphor to summarize the role we believe the level and quality of these resources play in helping mothers exit welfare permanently for work. If welfare can be said to constitute even a minimal safety net for poor single mothers and their children, then the work route off welfare is a tightrope. Our data suggest that many will falter, but those with a strong private safety net can generally avoid falling back into the public safety net. Such mothers are disproportionately white. Those with a weak private safety net will likely fall back into the public safety net. Most of these mothers are nonwhite.

One of the most troublesome aspects of current state and federal welfare reform efforts is their potential to disproportionately disadvantage African American and Latino families headed by single mothers. If state and federal welfare reforms deliver on their promises, several million household heads will eventually be added to the pool of workers seeking jobs in the low-wage labor market. Even in the current labor market, women with few skills cannot expect to earn much. By adding several million more women with similar characteristics to the labor force, low-wage employers may be able to offer less in pay and benefits. In addition, increasing the supply of white unskilled women workers might allow employers to more easily avoid hiring or promoting nonwhite women.

We cannot be sure exactly what will happen to these workers and their families as they try to sustain themselves on their earnings from low-wage jobs. We believe, however, that the absence of a private safety net will mean that African American welfare recipients will face more difficulty on average than whites will. Therefore, we advocate federal and state policies that would simulate this private safety net for those without one. Simply put, the challenge for states under the new welfare law is to transform a system that supports not working (the old welfare system) with a system that supports work.

State efforts to create a work-based safety net could (and do) take a variety of forms. All states must offer some form of transitional child care and health care to welfare mothers who leave for work, but the duration of these benefits is short, and most exiters' wages will not increase quickly enough (if at all) to pick up the costs of child care and health care once their transitional benefits lapse. States vary widely in their provision of subsidized day care for workers once they exhaust these benefits. New legislation means that most of the children of these workers will have health insurance, but the workers themselves will not (unless their employers insure them).

The reason states must work to create a work-based safety net is that generating employment that pays enough to live on will probably be very difficult for all but the most highly skilled former welfare recipients. Since the 1996 federal welfare legislation does not allow states to offer any long-term training to welfare recipients, the skills of mothers who exit the rolls in one, two, three, or five years will be quite limited on average. Therefore, few will be able to command a living wage on the basis of their human capital.

As more and more welfare-reliant mothers reach the end of their time limit, legislators and taxpayers may prove willing to assist needy working mothers by helping them either to reduce their expenses or to improve their wages (through subsidies or training that can be combined with work). At this point, it is reasonable to predict that states will vary dramatically in their ability and willingness to provide a work-based safety net. Providing such a safety net is, after all, far more appealing than paying mothers to stay at home. Thus the effects on poor families, particularly those without a safety net of their own, will probably vary quite dramatically as well.

APPENDIX

Table 8A.1 / Parameter Estimates of Repeat Welfare Dependency Following Work Exit, 1983 to 1988

Explanatory Variable	Model 1		Model 2		Model 3	
	b	SE	b	SE	b	SE
Intercept	−5.525	0.54	−4.364	0.66	−3.970	0.77
2 or more welfare spells	0.248	0.22	0.370	0.21	0.348	0.21

(Table continues on p. 296.)

Table 8A.1 / *Continued*

Explanatory Variable	Model 1 b	Model 1 SE	Model 2 b	Model 2 SE	Model 3 b	Model 3 SE
Time since work exit (months)						
1–3	1.235**	0.38	1.292**	0.38	1.145**	0.39
4–6	1.237**	0.39	1.219**	0.39	1.059**	0.40
7–12	1.557**	0.34	1.564**	0.33	1.473**	0.34
13–18	0.931*	0.40	0.975**	0.40	0.895*	0.40
19–24	0.834	0.44	0.914*	0.43	0.812	0.44
25 +	—		—		—	
Prior welfare receipt >24 months	0.147	0.21	0.228	0.21	0.279	0.22
White	−0.285	0.30	−0.454	0.32	−0.470	0.30
Mother had a high school education or more	−0.092	0.21				
Grew up with two parents	−0.029	0.21				
Grew up in urban area	0.524*	0.24	0.289	0.25	0.395	0.25
Age at welfare exit	—		−0.046**	0.02	−0.053**	0.02
Lives in South	—		−0.007	0.21		
Urban residence	—		0.024	0.25		
High school education or more	—		—		−0.206	0.23
3 or more children	—		—		0.341	0.22
Recent birth	—		—		0.604**	0.23
Married or cohabiting	—		—		1.419	0.78
Married and cohabiting * partner's work status	—		—		−1.905*	0.87
Unemployment rate	—		—		−0.034	0.05
AFDC guarantee/100	—		—		0.004	0.07
Summary statistics						
−2 log likelihood	968.47		10,16.98		984.05	
χ^2	42.43		56.90		72.95	
df	11		12		17	
Person-months	4,989		5,786		5,759	
Number of spells	246		260		259	

Source: Panel Study of Income Dynamics, 1983 to 1988 panels.
*Significant at the .05 level. **Significant at the .01 level.

This research was supported by grants to both authors from the William T. Grant Foundation through the Faculty Scholars Program, and by support to Kathryn Edin through a grant from the Russell Sage Foundation.

NOTES

1. African American mothers get less cash help from kin than do whites on average.

2. We include receipt of "other welfare" with reports of AFDC receipt because evidence suggests that "other welfare" receipt picks up misreporting of AFDC (Ellwood 1986).

3. Most women had only one spell of nonreceipt, but some had several. Women who experienced multiple spells of nonreceipt had already returned to welfare and exited again at least once. Therefore, first spells of nonreceipt all followed the first welfare spell, and return spells of nonreceipt all followed a second or higher-order exit from welfare.

4. We also interviewed a small group of Latinas in San Antonio.

5. We used a discrete-time model since the monthly determination of eligibility makes the process inherently discrete, where the dependent variable is a return transition to welfare indicated by a change in welfare status from nonreceipt in one month to receipt in the following month.

6. Time-invariant factors include family background variables and individual characteristics that do not change over time in a spell of nonwelfare. Time-varying covariates change either monthly or annually. On a monthly basis, changes in welfare and work status are known. The occurrence of marriages and births are updated each year. On a yearly basis, changes in education, cohabitation status, residence, unemployment rates, and AFDC benefits are recorded. Other time-varying covariates represent the cumulative effects of such factors as age, family size, and work experience.

   In a discrete-time model, the dependent variable is the probability that a return to welfare will occur at a particular duration for those who have exited welfare through work. To explain the process of returning to welfare, the return probability, denoted as P_t, is estimated as a function of the explanatory variables using a logit transformation. Using maximum likelihood methods, the basic model estimated is $\log P_i t /(1 - P_i t) = \alpha + \beta X_i + \phi Z_i t$, where $P_i t$ is the probability of a return to welfare for individual i at time t; X is a vector of time-invariant independent variables; and Z_t is a vector of time-varying independent variables at each time t.

   As P_t varies between 0 and 1, the left-hand side of the equation, the logit, varies between minus and plus infinity for $t = 1, \ldots .72$. The X variables vary across individuals but are constant over time and thus measure between-subject variation (for example, race, mother's education). The Z variables measure between- and within-subject variation, as values on each specific variable can vary over time for an individual (for example, family size, education). The coefficients β and ϕ estimate the effects of differences across individuals and across time. Duration is specified in the model by allowing a different base (or intercept) return probability during three- and six-month intervals throughout the first two years following welfare exit, and for durations off welfare beyond twenty-four months. This specifies that the rate of welfare return differs in each interval within two years of welfare exit but that, beyond twenty-four months of nonreceipt, the rate of return does not vary with time. Note that in the descriptive analyses we use the weighted data, while the multivariate analyses employ the unweighted observations.

7. Nor were there significant racial differences in the average length of the previous welfare spell.

8. This eliminates fifty spells from the analysis since we could observe the time off welfare long enough to assess whether the exit was permanent.

9. Because individual women contribute multiple observations to the person-month analysis file, the person-month observations are not independent, which may bias the standard errors downward. If the model specification of duration is correct, this bias is minimized. Nevertheless, we interpret the significance of the parameter estimates cautiously.

10. This is the antilog of the coefficient, -1.31.

11. Note, however, that the marriage or cohabitation fostered permanent welfare exits for whites only if the woman's partner worked, as revealed by the interaction term between married and cohabiting status and partner's work status. White married and cohabiting women whose partners did not work were just as likely (and perhaps more likely) as unmarried or noncohabiting mothers to return to welfare, indicated by the coefficient on "married or cohabiting." However, marriage or cohabitation reduced the risks of returning to welfare by 97 percent for whites when the woman's partner worked (as was generally the case).

12. To our knowledge, only the Consumer Expenditure Survey collects detailed expenditure data, and this survey contains only very simple estimates of income.

13. One difference between the two groups is that the Edin-Lein data were gathered between 1988 and 1992, whereas the PSID data were collected during the mid-1980s. This problem is not a serious one for our purposes, since wages (for this population) were stagnant and inflation was low during the mid-1980s and early 1990s. A second difference is that the Edin-Lein respondents were all urban residents, which likely means that they had to spend more for some items (housing) and less for others (transportation) than the PSID group did. A third difference is that Edin and Lein oversampled workers who lived in subsidized housing. Thus, the expenditure data Edin and Lein report are lower bound. Finally, Edin and Lein interviewed only mothers who made $8 or less per hour. The PSID sample includes all mothers who worked their way off welfare during the six-year window studied, regardless of their hourly wage. A more serious difference is that the Edin-Lein group did not include any mothers who had married subsequent to leaving welfare for work. Since subsequent marriage was common among the whites we studied in the PSID, and the whites who married had the most human capital, we suspect that the Edin-Lein sample captured a less skilled group of white mothers than would be found in the general population of women leaving welfare for work.

14. Though the PSID contains income data, it does not contain information on expenditures.

15. Other necessary items include phone charges, laundry supplies, toiletries, cleaning supplies, diapers and formula, school supplies, furniture and appliances, life or burial insurance, and haircuts.

16. This distrust was manifest in several common complaints, including male infidelity, traditional sex role expectations, domestic violence, sexual abuse of children, criminal behavior, and substance abuse.

REFERENCES

Allison, Paul D. 1982. "Discrete-time Methods for the Analysis of Event Histories." In *Sociological Methodology*, edited by Samuel Leinhardt. San Francisco: Jossey-Bass.

———. 1995. *Survival Analysis Using the SAS System: A Practical Guide.* Cary, N.C.: SAS Institute.

Angel, Ronald, and Marta Tienda. 1982. "Determinants of Extended Household Structure: Cultural Pattern or Economic Need?" *American Journal of Sociology* 87(6): 1360–83.

Auletta, Ken. 1982. *The Underclass.* New York: Random House.

Bane, Mary Jo, and David T. Ellwood. 1983. *The Dynamics of Dependence: The Routes to Self-Sufficiency.* Report prepared for the assistant secretary for planning and evaluation, Office of Evaluation and Technical Analysis, Office of Income Security Policy, U.S. Department of Health and Human Services.

———. 1994. *Welfare Realities: From Rhetoric to Reform.* Cambridge, Mass.: Harvard University Press.

Blank, Rebecca M. 1989. "Analyzing the Length of Welfare Spells." *Journal of Public Economics* 39(3): 245–73.

Bourdieu, Pierre. 1986. "The Forms of Capital." In *Handbook of Theory and Research for the Sociology of Education*, edited by John G. Richardson. New York: Greenwood Press.

Bumpass, Larry L., and James A. Sweet. 1989. "National Estimates of Cohabitation." *Demography* 26(4): 615–25.

Cherlin, Andrew J. 1992. *Marriage, Divorce, Remarriage.* Cambridge, Mass.: Harvard University Press.

Coleman, James. 1990. *Foundations of Social Theory.* Cambridge, Mass.: Harvard University Press.

Danziger, Sheldon, and Peter Gottschalk. 1995. *Uneven Tides.* New York: Russell Sage Foundation.

Duncan, Greg J. 1984. *Years of Poverty, Years of Plenty.* Ann Arbor: University of Michigan, Institute for Social Research.

Edin, Kathryn. 1998. "Why Don't Single Mothers Get Married (Or Remarried)." Paper presented at the Russell Sage Foundation Visiting Scholar Seminar Series. New York (June 1998).

Edin, Kathryn, and Laura Lein.1997a. "Work, Welfare, and Single Mothers' Economic Survival Strategies." *American Sociological Review* 62(2): 253–66.

———. 1997b. *Making Ends Meet: How Single Mothers Survive Welfare and Low-Wage Work.* New York: Russell Sage Foundation.Edin, Kathryn, and Christopher Jencks. 1992. "Welfare." In *Rethinking Social Policy: Race, Poverty, and the Underclass*, edited by Christopher Jencks. Cambridge, Mass.: Harvard University Press.

Ellwood, David T. 1986. "Targeting Would-Be Long Term Recipients of AFDC." *Mathematica Policy Research.*

———. 1988. *Poor Support: Poverty in the American Family.* New York: Basic Books.

Fitzgerald, John. 1991. "Welfare Durations and the Marriage Market: Evidence from the Survey of Income and Program Participation." *Journal of Human Resources* 26(3): 545–61.

Furstenberg, Frank. 1993. "How Families Manage Risk and Opportunity in Dangerous Neighborhoods." In *Sociology and the Public Agenda*, edited by William Julius Wilson. Newbury Park, Calif.: Sage Publications.

Garfinkel, Irwin, and Sara S. McLanahan. 1986. *Single Mothers and Their Children.* The Changing Domestic Priorities Series. Washington, D.C.: The Urban Institute Press.

Gilder, George F. 1981. *Wealth and Poverty.* New York: Basic Books.

Gritz, R. Mark, and Thomas MacCurdy. 1991. "Welfare Entrances, Durations, and Exits: A Comparison of NLSY and PSID." Paper presented at the Panel Study on Income Dynamics Event History Conference. Stanford, Calif., June 30–July 2.

Harris, Kathleen Mullan. 1993. "Work and Welfare among Single Mothers in Poverty." *American Journal of Sociology* 99(2): 317–52.

———. 1996. "Life after Welfare: Women, Work, and Repeat Dependency." *American Sociological Review* 61(3): 407–26.

———. 1997. *Teen Mothers and the Revolving Welfare Door.* Philadelphia: Temple University Press.

Harris, Kathleen Mullan, and Kathryn Edin. 1998. "From Welfare to Work and Back Again: A Quantitative and Qualitative Perspective." Paper presented at the Joint Center for Poverty Research Seminar Series, University of Chicago, Ill. (February 26, 1998).

Hofferth, Sandra L. 1984. "Kin Networks, Race, and Family Structure." *Journal of Marriage and the Family* 46(4): 791–806.

Hogan, Dennis P., Lingxin Hao, and William L. Parish. 1990. "Race, Kin Networks, and Assistance to Mother-Headed Families." *Social Forces* 68(3): 797–812.

Holzer, Harry. 1996. *What Employers Want: Job Prospects for Less Educated Workers.* New York: Russell Sage Foundation.

Jayakodi, Rukmalie, Linda M. Chatters, Robert J. Taylor. 1993. "Family Support to Single and Married African-American Mothers: The Provision of Financial, Emotional, and Child Care Assistance." *Journal of Marriage and the Family* 55(2): 261–76.

Jencks, Christopher, and Paul E. Peterson. 1991. *The Urban Underclass.* Washington, D.C.: Brookings Institution.

Kalbfleisch, J.D., and Prentice, R.L. 1980. *The Statistical Analysis of Failure Time Data.* New York: John Wiley and Sons.

Kasarda, John. 1989. "Urban Industrial Transition and the Underclass." *The Annals of the American Academy of Political and Social Science* 501(Jan.): 26–47.

Kaus, Mickey. 1986. "The Work Ethic State: The Only Way to Break the Culture of Poverty." *The New Republic,* 7 July, 22–32.

Kirschenman, Joleen, and Kathryn Neckerman. 1990. "We'd Love To Hire Them But . . ." In *The Urban Underclass,* edited by Christopher Jencks and Paul E. Peterson. Washington, D.C.: The Brookings Institution.

Levy, Frank, and Richard Murnane. 1992. "U.S. Earnings Levels and Earnings Inequality: A Review of Recent Trends and Proposed Explanations." *Journal of Economic Literature* 30(3): 1333–81.

Lichter, Daniel T., Diane K. McLaughlin, George Kephard, and David J. Landry. 1992. "Race and the Retreat from Marriage: A Shortage of Marriageable Men?" *American Sociological Review* 57(6): 781–99.

Mare, Robert D., and Christopher Winship. 1991. "Socioeconomic Change and the Decline of Marriage for Blacks and Whites." In *The Urban Underclass,* edited by Christopher Jencks and Paul E. Peterson. Washington, D.C.: The Brookings Institution.

Marks, Nadine S., and Sara S. McLanahan. 1993. "Gender, Family Structure, and Social Support Among the Poor." *Journal of Marriage and the Family* 55 (2): 481–93.

Martineau, William H. 1977. "Informal Social Ties among Urban Black Americans: Some New Data and a Review of the Problem." *Journal of Black Studies* 8(1): 83–104.

Massey, Douglas S., and Nancy A. Denton. 1993. *American Apartheid: Segregation and the Making of the Underclass*. Cambridge, Mass.: Harvard University Press.

Mayer, Susan, and Christopher Jencks. 1989. "Poverty and the Distribution of Material Hardship." *Journal of Human Resources* 24(1): 88–113.

McLanahan, Sara, and Gary Sandefur. 1994. *Growing Up with a Single Parent: What Hurts, What Helps*. Cambridge, Mass.: Harvard University Press.

Mead, Lawrence. 1992. *The New Politics of Poverty*. New York: Basic Books.

Moffitt, R. 1992. "Incentive Effects of the U.S. Welfare System: A Review." *Journal of Economic Literature* 30(1): 1–61.

Murray, Charles. 1984. *Losing Ground: American Social Policy, 1950–1980*. New York: Basic Books.

Neckerman, Kathryn M., and Joleen Kirschenman. 1991. "Hiring Strategies, Racial Bias, and Inner-City Workers." *Social Problems* 38(4): 433–47.

O'Neill, June A., Laurie J. Bassi, and Douglas A. Wolf. 1987. "The Duration of Welfare Spells." *Review of Economics and Statistics* 69(2): 241–49.

Parish, William L., Lingxin Hao, and Dennis P. Hogan. 1991. "Family Support Networks, Welfare, and Work among Young Mothers." *Journal of Marriage and the Family* 53(1): 203–15.

Pavetti, LaDonna A. 1993. "The Dynamics of Welfare and Work: Exploring the Process by Which Young Women Work Their Way off Welfare." Ph.D. diss., Harvard University, John F. Kennedy School of Government.

Raley, R. Kelly. 1996. "A Shortage of Marriageable Men? A Note on the Role of Cohabitation in Black-White Differences in Marriage." *American Sociological Review* 61: 973–83.

Rank, Mark R., and Thomas A. Hirschl. 1988. "A Rural-Urban Comparison of Welfare Exits: The Importance of Population Density." *Rural Sociology* 53(2): 190–206.

Spalter-Roth, Roberta M., and Heidi I. Hartmann. 1994a. "AFDC Recipients as Care-Givers and Workers: A Feminist Approach to Income Security Policy for American Women." *Social Politics: International Studies in Gender, State, and Society* 1: 190–210.

———. 1994b. "Dependence on Men, the Market, or the State: The Rhetoric and Reality of Welfare Reform." *Journal of Applied Social Sciences* 18: 55–70.

Stack, C. 1974. *All Our Kin: Strategies for Survival in a Black Community*. New York: Harper and Row.

Tienda, Marta. 1990. "Welfare and Work in Chicago's Inner City." *American Economic Review* 80(2): 372–376.

Tienda, Marta, and Ronald Angel. 1982. "Headship and Household Composition among Blacks, Hispanics, and Other Whites." *Social Forces* 61(2): 508–31.

U.S. House of Representatives. Committee on Ways and Means. 1995. *1995 Green Book: Overview of Entitlement Programs*. Washington, D.C.: U.S. Government Printing Office.

Wellman, Barry, and Scot Wortley. 1990. "Different Strokes from Different Folks: Community Ties and Social Support." *American Journal of Sociology* 96(3): 558–88.

Wilson, William Julius. 1987. *The Truly Disadvantaged: The Inner City, the Underclass, and Public Policy*. Chicago: University of Chicago Press.

Chapter 9

Stereotypes and Realities: Images of Black Women in the Labor Market

Irene Browne and Ivy Kennelly

As the chapters in this volume illustrate, opportunities for success in the U.S. labor market remain linked to gender and race, and African American women continue to be among the most severely disadvantaged. Black women still earn lower wages than black men, white women, and white men (see chapter 4). Black women also face restricted opportunities for upward mobility; when they secure positions of authority in the workplace, they most often hold positions in which they supervise only other black women (Browne, Tigges, and Press forthcoming).

Why do black women continue to remain at the bottom of the wage and authority hierarchy? Stratification in the labor market emerges through the interplay of labor supply, labor demand, and social processes that match workers to positions. The dynamics of this interplay are the source of heated debate among economists and sociologists (Bills 1992; Granovetter 1995). Theories of discrimination in particular stress that workers' gender and race influence employers' attitudes and practices, producing inequality through the matching process (Granovetter 1995; Rosenbaum and Binder 1997). Yet very little is known about how employers actually perceive different groups in the labor force (Holzer 1996).

Black women in particular are absent from research on employer perceptions. Inquiries into how employers view black workers focus on black men, while studies of employers' attitudes toward women in the workforce focus on white women (Struyk, Turner, and Fix 1991; Kirschenman and Neckerman 1991; Neckerman and Kirschenman 1991; Moss and Tilly 1995a, 1995b).[1] In addition, almost no research compares employers' perceptions with the actual pool of workers in local labor markets. Information on labor demand is uncoupled from labor supply, although theories of labor markets stress that demand and supply move together.

In this chapter, we address these gaps in the literature and concentrate on how employers view black women workers. We address two questions:

- How do white employers perceive black women in the workforce?
- How do these perceptions compare with profiles of the actual labor pool of black women in their local labor market?

We examine these questions by using a special data set that allows us to contrast employers' perceptions with the experiences of a matched sample of women and men in the labor force. Members of 1,600 households in the Atlanta metropolitan area were surveyed, providing information on labor supply. We then collected the names of the employers of a subsample of the men and women in those households. The employers were contacted and interviewed face to face. We are thus able to assess how well employers' views of black women workers correspond to the reports of those workers.

We cover theories in two separate fields—labor markets and cognitive psychology—that motivate our investigation. In the labor market literature, theories pertaining to statistical discrimination, status closure, and black feminism argue that employers will base perceptions on group status such as race and gender, shaping decisions about hiring and placing workers. The literature in cognitive psychology suggests that individuals regularly use popular stereotypes to form perceptions and filter information about individuals. We do not test these theories but describe them to place our research in the context of the debates about black women in the labor market.

We then discuss how we use the in-depth interviews with employers to investigate their views of black women in the labor force, and we compare the interviews with reports from the household surveys. Finally, we return to the theories to guide our interpretation of the results and discuss the relevance of our study to debates in scholarship on labor markets, particularly theories of discrimination.

EMPLOYERS' PERCEPTIONS

Theories of the Labor Market

Early neoclassical economic theory assumed that employers base decisions about hiring, placement, and wages on individual workers' productivity in the context of overall labor supply and demand. Presumably, if gender and race are unrelated to productivity, these characteristics should not influence an employer's evaluation of the suitability of an individual for a particular position.

The New Information Economics recognized that there are costs to obtaining information about worker productivity and incorporated this insight into economic theory. Economists propose the theory of "statistical discrimination" to explain why employers use gender and race in making decisions about workers in a competitive labor market. Given that it is costly and time-consuming to assess the merits of every employee or potential employee individually, employers may decide who their most desirable workers are by substituting the characteristics they associate with groups for information about individuals (Aigner and Cain 1977; Arrow 1973; Bielby and Baron 1986; Kirschenman and Neckerman 1991; Moss and Tilly 1991). If employers could obtain complete information on the skills and productivity of each job applicant, race and gender would presumably cease to be relevant in hiring and placement decisions.

Generally, the theory of statistical discrimination assumes that employers' perceptions of the workforce are fairly accurate assessments of group differences—in terms of either means or variances (Aigner and Cain 1977; Bielby and Baron 1986; England 1992). Since mistaken assessments of worker capabilities can lead to a poor fit between the worker and the job, and thus low productivity, employers have an incentive to avoid basing decisions on inaccurate perceptions or stereotypes (a "conventional and usually oversimplified conception or belief"; *American Heritage Dictionary*, 1987).[2] However, there is some debate over the extent to which systematic erroneous perception can be considered "statistical discrimination." We include both the "strong" and the "weak" versions of the theory of statistical discrimination in our definition (Tomaskovic-Devey 1993).

Sociological theories of social closure argue that the stereotyping of workers on the basis of gender and race by white male employers is not simply a problem of incomplete information but is an endemic feature of social institutions in which one group attempts to maintain control over valued social resources (Ridgeway 1997; Squires 1977; Tomaskovic-Devey 1993). White men in powerful positions benefit from the social status hierarchy grounded in gender and race and therefore attempt to reproduce that hierarchy (Blumer 1965; Jackman 1993; Lieberson 1980; Reskin and Roos 1990; Ridgeway 1997; Squires 1977; Tomaskovic-Devey 1993). These labor market benefits for white men include relatively higher wages, better chances for promotion, and greater job authority (Federal Glass Ceiling Commission 1995).

A number of theories of social closure can explain the position of African American women in the labor market (see Tomaskovic-Devey 1993 for a review of theories of social closure based on gender and race). Blumer's theory of race relations is one of the most well developed, and it finds substantial empirical support (Bobo 1983, 1988; Bobo and Hutchings 1996; Bobo and Kluegel 1993). According to Blumer (1958, 1965), individuals form identities, allegiances, and normative ideas based on the economic and social position of their group. This resulting sense of "group position," grounded in existing economic and social conditions, generates perceptions of superiority and entitlement to coveted social and economic resources. Individuals who belong to a group that already receives societal benefits (that is, whites) and who perceive an economic threat, such as competition for jobs from members of another group (that is, blacks), will develop negative attitudes toward that group. These negative attitudes often crystallize into stereotypes and then work to rationalize further the dominant groups' sense of superiority and entitlement.

Jackman (1993) argues that, while they legitimate the existing stratification in social institutions, stereotypes need not be negative to undergird status hierarchies. For instance, common stereotypes of women as nurturing and considerate are generally esteemed as feminine traits but are still used to justify the concentration of women into lower-paying occupations in which they may not have to be as tough or detached. Thus employers do not invoke stereotypes simply to exclude individuals from the labor market. Rather, employers rely upon gender and racial stereotypes to sort individuals into different positions. White men are disproportionately allocated into jobs with the greatest rewards, while black women are restricted to positions with low earnings and little authority.

Black feminist theorists critique theories of gender inequality as well as theories of racial stratification such as Blumer's for failing to consider how the dynamics of race and gender inequality operate simultaneously and interact (King 1988). Racial stereotypes are "gendered" in important ways, and stereotypic portrayals of women vary by race (Collins 1990; Essed 1991; Guy-Sheftall 1990; Landrine 1985; St. Jean and Feagin 1997). This combination of gender and racial stereotypes puts black women at a unique disadvantage in the labor market. Congruent with the position of social closure theorists, Collins (1990) argues that unequal power in the workplace enables employers to define black women in terms of pervasive stereotypes and use these "controlling images" to reinforce and legitimate the status quo.

Black feminist theory, theories of statistical discrimination, and social closure all suggest that employers have economic incentives to hold attitudes that are shaped by workers' group affiliations, particularly their gender and their race. These theories counter the assumptions inherent in older versions of orthodox economic theory that individual productivity will determine a worker's job and wages (England 1992). However, the theories differ in what they see as the main impetus for the influence of gender and race on employers' perceptions of individual workers. Specifically, social closure and black feminist theories assume that the evaluations of black women workers made by white employers are filtered through biased perceptual lenses. This assumption raises the question of how employers' descriptions of black women workers compare with characteristics of the actual labor pool.

Theories of Stereotyping

Research in cognitive psychology suggests that the economic incentives for employers to stereotype described by theories of statistical discrimination, social closure, and black feminism may actually reinforce or exacerbate, rather than create, common perceptual processes. Individuals' perceptions are routinely selective and biased (Fiske and Taylor 1991; Hoffman and Hurst 1990). Because capacity for information processing is limited, individuals focus upon selected aspects of their environment to organize the massive volumes of information they encounter daily. Social groups provide a readily accessible selection criterion that allows individuals to situate others cognitively in relation to "self" (Fiske and Taylor 1991). To simplify further the amount of information processed, individuals tend to generalize from their assumptions about social categories to specific individuals within those categories, leading to potential bias (Read 1983). Bias also arises from the tendency to make positive attributions about individuals perceived as "like oneself" and to attribute relatively more negative qualities to individuals perceived as "unlike oneself" (Pettigrew 1979).[3] Once the generalizations and their concomitant evaluative labels are activated, individuals who fit those preconceived notions become more visible, and those who deviate from preconceived notions are considered "exceptions" (Heilman 1995). Through the cognitive processes that maintain people's everyday perceptions of the social world, group differences are exaggerated while diversity among individuals within groups is minimized (Fiske and Taylor 1991).

Stereotyping is thus a common facet of social interaction, as individuals tend to differentiate others in terms of social categories and filter their perceptions and subsequent interactions on the basis of those categories (Jones 1981; Ridgeway 1997; Tajfel and Turner 1986). Gender is one of the primary social categories that individuals use to classify themselves and others for any interaction (Ridgeway 1997). Yet even though categorizing by gender is common, it can disadvantage women in the workplace when it dictates what employers should expect of them. "If the cultural construction of sex as a simplified, prior categorization system is related to its uses in interaction, then the cultural development of *gender stereotypes* is likely; these describe what behaviors can be expected from a person of a given category" (Ridgeway 1997, 220–21; italics in original). Stereotypes facilitate interaction by giving actors a cultural script based on an oversimplified, widely shared schema.[4]

Members of all groups are potentially subject not only to gender stereotyping but also to racial stereotyping and to stereotypes based on their combination of race and gender. Yet because most employers are white men, theories of stereotyping would suggest that employers perceive workers who are not white men as being unlike themselves, making negative stereotypes of these workers prominent. Since black women are "others" to white men both in gender and race, negative stereotypes about black women may seem particularly salient to employers. This situation also raises the question of how employers' perceptions compare with the profiles of the local labor force.

Because research on racial stereotypes in the workplace has almost always focused on men, and because research on gender stereotypes has largely ignored racial variations, the perceptions and stereotypes specifically about black women in the workplace have not been adequately documented. No study systematically investigates the extent to which employer perceptions reflect the characteristics of labor supply. Yet theories of labor market disadvantage and theories of stereotyping such as Ridgeway's (1997) assume that employers do not objectively report patterns in the workforce and the actual problems that they encounter with their employees. Instead, employers view groups of workers through perceptual lenses that contain biases. To illuminate the race- and gender-specific biases that white employers have toward black women workers, we compare those biases with the patterns that actually exist in the labor market. Our study is a first step in uncovering the relationship between employers' perceptions and the difficulty that black women face in the workplace.

Methods

Studying employers' perceptions of black women presents a dilemma. Researchers know that white men are hired at greater rates and are paid higher wages than are black women, white women, and black men of comparable education and training (see chapter 4; Smith 1997; Farkas et al. 1997). That is, race and gender—or characteristics associated with race and gender—clearly influence the process through which employers sort workers into jobs. Yet discovering the ways in which employers use gender and race as criteria in evaluating workers is a difficult feat. Even employers with strong prejudices that lead them to systematically deny jobs to certain groups may be reluctant to state openly views that could be interpreted as "discriminatory" (Moss and Tilly 1995b). Such survey questions as "Do you think black workers are less skilled than white workers?" or "Do you prefer to hire white men for the higher-paying jobs?" might therefore yield little variation. Employers will say "no" or refuse to answer these potentially incriminating queries.

Employers are more likely to speak of race in circumspect or general ways that cannot be construed as racist and do not directly implicate them in unfair hiring practices. For instance, in conducting in-depth interviews with employers about a range of employment issues, Kirschenman and Neckerman (1991) found that employers did not often refer to race directly but instead "coded" race in terms of space, using terms such as "the people from the inner city" to refer to low-skilled black men.

In our study, we followed Kirschenman and Neckerman's (1991) strategy, using data from in-depth, open-ended, face-to-face interviews with employers. A series of questions were asked about their personnel needs and their ability to find suitable workers to meet those needs. The survey included questions that encouraged employers to speak about race and gender using their own frameworks, which gave them ample latitude to discuss their views of black women. While employers were asked about "blacks" in the labor force and "women" in the labor force, no questions specifically referred to "black women." Thus, when they spontaneously mentioned black women as a distinct group, employers were imposing their own race-gender schemas onto their descriptions of the labor force.

Employers discussed black women workers in response to such questions as:

- What skills and qualities do you look for in a worker for [sample job]?
- What are the main problems you face with your workforce, thinking specifically about [sample job]?
- We've talked to quite a few other managers who say there are significant differences between black and white workers, and I'm wondering what you think. Have you seen these differences? (Probe: We do know from other research that blacks and other minorities are doing badly in the labor market. Why do you think that is?) Do you see any differences between men and women? city and suburban workers?

When analyzing the responses to these and other questions in the interview transcripts to identify employers' perceptions of black women, we watched for themes to emerge—opening our vision to those themes that resonated with the literature as well as those that were unexpected or new. We found that many white employers easily characterized workers in terms of race and gender and that these characterizations were consistent with theories of discrimination and stereotyping.

To analyze the interview transcripts, we adopted a coding scheme approximating the open, axial, and selective coding strategies as laid out by Strauss and Corbin (1990). In the initial coding phases we noted and recorded repetitive themes in employers' descriptions of workers, guided by research literature and themes introduced by the employers themselves. We found at this stage that the concepts of "family" and "motherhood" came up often in white employers' discussions of women employees and applicants but not as often and in different ways in their discussions of men. In further coding phases in which we examined these concepts in different contexts than those we had originally seen, we realized that employers were not simply talking about their *men and women* employees differently but that they also differentiated between *black and white women* employees and applicants. In descriptions of white women, many employers referred to "motherhood," but when speaking about black women, employers invoked the image of "single motherhood." We then reexamined the data to explore the prevalence of this image and search out deviant cases. Selective coding strategies allowed us to focus more specifically on the category of single motherhood and identify the contexts and ways in which it was used.

After the theme of single motherhood emerged, we found questions in the matched household survey of Atlanta residents with which we could compare the employers' depictions of black women in the local labor market. The picture that employers painted of the labor market highlighted some dimensions of the local labor force but ignored other dimensions.

Data

Our study site is the Atlanta metropolitan area, which encompasses the nine counties defined by the Atlanta Planning Department.[5] Atlanta enjoys the reputation of being the "city that's too busy to hate," where racial tolerance abounds and African Americans are welcomed into a flourishing economy. Many black Americans refer to the city as "the black Mecca," and approximately 24 percent of employed Atlantans are black (Jacobs 1996). Indeed, African Americans encounter an array of opportunities in Atlanta that are unavailable in many other major cities in the United States. Atlanta has a large black middle class, and many blacks hold positions of political power. While it could be argued that whites in Atlanta, a southern city, hold more negative racial attitudes than whites in the North do, the evidence on southerners being more prejudiced than northerners is quite mixed (see Kuklinski, Cobb, and Gilens 1996 for a review). In fact, Atlanta's white residents appear to express slightly more tolerance towards blacks than whites in Detroit or Boston do (Bobo and Massagli forthcoming).

The data we used were collected as part of the Multi-City Study of Urban Inequality (MCSUI), which focuses on labor market inequality, residential segregation, and racial and ethnic attitudes (Johnson, Oliver, and Bobo 1994).[6] The study involved three components: interviews of household respondents, a telephone survey of employers, and face-to-face interviews with employers. We used data from the household survey and the in-depth interviews with employers in the Atlanta metropolitan area.

For the household survey, we drew a representative sample of Atlanta households and interviewed one adult member from each sample household face-to-face (Hall 1994).[7] The total sample size for the household survey was 1,528, which included 651 white respondents, 829 African Americans, and 49 respondents of other races.

Our sample of household respondents included individuals between the ages of twenty-one and sixty-four who were in the labor force in 1992 or 1993, which is the labor pool that the employers encountered during the interview period. Since the employer interviews focused on jobs that required no more than a high school degree, we also provide information on men and women with a high school diploma or less education for comparison. The advantage of the full sample is that the numbers are relatively large and that they address the fact that, in some cases, the employer interviews referred to black workers in general rather than those in the sample job. In almost all cases, the patterns for the full sample and the low-skilled sample were the same.

The names of the employers for the face-to-face interviews were drawn randomly from a list of employers whom respondents had identified in the household survey. We thus obtained a matched sample of employers and paid workers with which to make our comparisons.

Two interviewers, a white woman and a white man, conducted structured, in-depth interviews with Atlanta employers in forty-five firms from July 1994 to March 1995, obtaining a 75 percent completion rate in their final sample. The three persons targeted for interviews in each firm included the president or chief executive officer (CEO) of each firm, a human resource representative, and the direct supervisor of the job as named by the household respondent. Because some firms did not have each of the three targeted positions and some potential respondents in each position refused to be interviewed, the average number of interviews per firm was 2.16. Of the ninety-seven interview respondents, 57 percent were white men, 24 percent were white women, 12 percent were black men, 6 percent were black women and 1 percent were Asian women.

Here we analyze only the responses of the seventy-eight white employers, since the relevant theories—social closure, black feminist, and stereotyping—assume that perceptions differ systematically by the race of the perceiver. In addition, strong evidence in the stereotyping literature shows that whites hold different perceptions of blacks than blacks hold of their own racial group.[8] In our sample of employers, twenty-seven white respondents (34.6 percent) were presidents or CEOs or held related positions, twenty-two (28.2 percent) were human resource representatives, and twenty-nine (37.2 percent) were supervisors of the sample job. Twenty-three white respondents (29.5 percent) were women; fifty-five (70.5 percent) were men.

Originally, the employer study was designed to test theories of industrial restructuring and the changing skill needs of employers for low-skilled workers. Therefore, all of the sample jobs in the employer survey were positions considered "low skill," that is, requiring a high school diploma or less education (see table 9A.1 for a summary of the characteristics of the firms and jobs). Common sample jobs included clerical worker, cashier, and sales representative. The average hourly wage for all jobs combined was $7.93, ranging from $4.25 (forklift operator) to $23.08 (salesperson).

Women as Mothers, Black Women as Single Mothers

Employers' Perceptions   When employers talk about women workers, they often talk about mothers. Family responsibilities are one of the primary concerns employers have about women workers. Forty-two percent of the white employers mentioned parenthood, family, or both when they discussed women, while only seven employers mentioned this topic when they talked about men. To these white employers, family in relation to men meant wages, since they assumed that men had the monetary responsibility of supporting their families. Only one employer indicated that responsibilities for their children could be problematic for men at work.

While white employers often brought up motherhood when they discussed their women employees and applicants, these employers were more specific when they referred to black women. Not only did they invoke the image of motherhood when talking about black women as mothers, but they also spoke about black women in terms of single motherhood. Over one-third of the white respondents referred to black women by using the image of the single mother at some point in their interviews, even though the interview instrument included no questions specifically mentioning motherhood or single motherhood. White employers spoke about "black women" differently from the way they spoke about "women," which signifies that the category of "women" probably often meant "white women." This usage indicates that not only black women's gender but also their race was salient to the white employers. The *combination* of gender and race creates perceptions of black women that are unique (Essed 1991; King 1988).

White employers did not associate single motherhood with any other gender and racial groups with nearly this frequency. Twelve percent of employers referred to either "white women" or "women" with no clear racial characterization as single mothers. No employers brought up the idea that black men or white men were single parents whose family responsibilities made their work in the paid labor force difficult.

Survey Data   How do these depictions of employed women as "mothers" and employed black women as "single mothers" compare with the actual characteristics of the local labor force? After all, motherhood remains one of the primary social roles for women, and the relatively high rates of single parenthood among black families is an abiding concern among scholars and policy makers.

Responses to the household survey revealed a disjuncture between employers' depictions of most female workers——black or white—as mothers

Table 9.1 / Parenthood Status, Employed Respondents, by Gender and Race (Percent)[a]

Group	Women		Men	
	Black	White	Black	White
Total sample				
Parent[b]	39.3	39.6	34.7	28.8*
Single parent[c]	19.6	5.4**	5.6**	1.0**
N	317	202	195	205
Low-skilled sample				
Parent[b]	41.6	32.1	27.2*	32.1
Single Parent[c]	22.1	6.2**	1.9**	2.6**
N	149	81	103	78

[a]Significance tests are comparisons with estimates for African American women.
[b]Respondents with a child under age eighteen in the household.
[c]Respondents who were not living with a spouse or partner and who had a child under age eighteen in the household.
*$p < .05$. **$p < .01$.

and the women in Atlanta's workforce. In fact, most women workers in our representative sample of households were not living in families with children under the age of eighteen. An equal percentage (39 percent) of black and white women in the labor force had a child in their household at the time of the interview (table 9.1). Among the low-skilled, a slightly higher percentage of black women (41.2 percent) than white women (32.1 percent) were parents, but this difference is not statistically significant. Although these percentages are not small, they make it clear that not all or even most women in the labor force are mothers, despite employers' stereotypes.

The employed individuals who had children under eighteen years old maintained a pattern that is consistent with the remarks of employers; black women in our household survey were indeed more likely than white women to be single mothers (20 percent versus 5 percent, respectively). The patterns are similar among the low-skilled respondents. Yet, while single motherhood was more common among the African Americans than among the whites in our sample, the majority of black women in the labor force are *not* single mothers. Theories of statistical discrimination and research on stereotyping would explain these contrasts by arguing that employers attend to the information on black-white differences in family structure rather than the actual levels of single motherhood for each group.

Motherhood and Job Performance

Employers' Perceptions   Employers' perceptions regarding women as mothers is important for understanding labor market stratification by gender, as employers often associated the role of mother with tardiness and absenteeism. One employer at an insurance company that employs a roughly equal number of men and women stated,

> If I look at our attendance record I would in fact not doubt that the people who have been documented and who have been terminated for attendance reasons were women, and those people are primarily out not because they're ill, but because kids are ill, or the husband is ill, or the parent. (Man; human resources manager; insurance company)

Another employer, a regional manager of sales representatives, posed a question he would like to ask applicants:

> Now, Ms. Jones, you're going to have somebody who can, y'know, if your children get sick I still need you to come to work here. So do you have somebody who can take care of those people? (Man; regional manager; pest control company)
>
> He laments over how he "used to be able to ask that question as an employer. I can't ask that question anymore. It's against the law." Eighty-nine percent of workers in his firm are men; 100 percent of his sales representatives are men.

For many of the employers, the problems with job performance wrought by the pressures of motherhood were especially keen among *single* mothers. A dominant theme for employers who depicted black women as single mothers was that black women heading families alone were poor workers. However, some employers actually cast black single mothers as reliable workers. Although these images may seem contradictory, employers brought them up in ways that were not mutually exclusive.

According to some white employers, single black mothers had conflicting loyalties, which made them poor workers. Since single mothers presumably had the greatest family responsibilities of all groups, employers assumed that they would be late to work, distracted, and absent more often than others. One supervisor of clerical workers explained how single motherhood could be a difficult issue for her to manage:

> Many of the young ladies that report to me are single mothers. And, it's, . . . when a child is sick and they get a call from day care (and probably rightfully so), you find them extremely distracted. And sometimes even just unable to focus at all on the task at hand. It's very hard—how strict will you be with

something like that? . . . . The single-mother thing, I think, is huge. (Woman; supervisor; delivery company)

That "the single-mother thing is huge" was a view shared by a good number of employers. In the context of talking about the problems of the inner city, the interviewer asked a plant manager what the single biggest problem with his workers was. He replied, "I'd say single-parent moms." When the interviewer asked why, he said simply, "Missing work. . . . When somebody's sick, they've got to go." (Man; plant manager; manufacturing plant)

Another employer made the connection between single motherhood and black women more explicit. This manager of laundry workers, all of whom were black and three-fourths of whom were women, brought up the term "family structure." When asked about his satisfaction with the available labor pool, he said he was dissatisfied with applicants because they carried the markings of the inner-city "family structure"—meaning single black women with children. This employer then tied this assumed family structure to black women's job performance. The interviewer asked him, "Does that have an impact, does family structure have an impact on, on their job performance?" He replied, "I think it's everything. I think it's the major thing that we have here that's a problem." Then he generalized a bit further and explained why single motherhood was so problematic in the paid labor force:

Well, right off the bat you've got a, a child-care problem. With a single mother, there's a, a child-care problem. Of course obviously there's a big financial problem. . . .You're gonna have a, experience a higher absenteeism rate and tardiness rate because of the fact that the children obviously are very important and come first, and there's a whole set of things that happen where the mother has to be, ah, y'know, off her job for one reason or another. So you have a workforce where it's, it's a high rate of absenteeism. (Man; laundry-valet manager; hotel)

This employer, whose workforce was largely made up of black women, perceived the poor job performance of single mothers as his biggest problem because of the absenteeism it created. When the interviewer asked him if he had the same problems, like absenteeism, from men, he replied,

Well, I have. The, . . . I realize that for the most part the men are not tied down with, with the kids. I know that. But yes, we have, have the same type of problems as far as basic work habits and coming to work with the men as we do with the ladies, but it's for a different set of reasons I believe. [Interviewer: Do you have any idea what their reasoning is?] Well, I think black men has a very low self-esteem level. (Man; laundry-valet manager; hotel)

This employer made it very clear that both men and women had absenteeism problems. Yet the problem he perceived to be the greatest was women's absenteeism, because of its association with single motherhood.

Seemingly in disagreement with the employers mentioned above, some white employers indicated that black single mothers were hard workers. This work ethic was not seen as a completely positive characteristic, however. Instead, half of the white employers who assumed that single mothers were desperate for their paychecks remarked that it was this desperation rather than a more noble force that made black single mothers work hard. For example, one employer compared his black employees with his white employees in this statement:

> The number of single parents in the inner city obviously is a much higher percentage. Those people absolutely have got to have income. They are supporting a family with one person running the household. From an ethic standpoint though, I would tell you it is more of a need to work than it is a real true work ethic. (Man; vice president for merchandising; grocery store)

This employer gave inner-city (read: black) single mothers credit for working hard but simultaneously devalued this attribute because of its assumed source.

The same supervisor of laundry workers who was quoted as saying that black women were the weakest link in his workforce because of their absenteeism gave this somewhat disjointed answer when asked if he noticed any differences between his men and his women workers:

> I think the ladies are much more responsible than the men for the most part, because I think they have more responsibilities. They have the burden of raising the family for the most part, and the men don't. . . . I think that, um, off the record, that our welfare system promotes a single family, a single-parent family. I think, I think that's wrong. (Man; laundry-valet manager; hotel)

Although this employer was talking about the women who worked at his organization, he brought up their perceived single motherhood in the context of welfare, which would seem to refer to women outside the labor force. Stereotypes like this one surrounding single motherhood are often negative and can be used by white employers even when they do not directly apply to black women employees' situations. Thus, while employers gave black women credit for being responsible because of their assumed heavy family load, they were associated with the negativity tied in with the single-mother stereotype.

While the stereotype of the hardworking black single mother may arguably prompt employers to hire black women over members of other groups (Kirschenman 1991), the imagery employers used makes it more likely that they held a negative view even of the potential advantages in the matriarch stereotype. Employers may even have felt that they could exploit black women, since the employers assumed that single mothers are so desperate for their income.

These two images—the black woman as poor worker and the black woman as reliable worker—indicate that white employers did stereotype black women in a racialized and gendered way and that the stereotype of black women was unique. The black woman was not seen as "lazy" or "scary," as the black man was (Kirschenman and Neckerman 1991), nor was she seen as the secondary earner in a nuclear family, as the white woman was. The black woman, according to the white Atlanta employers interviewed, was a single mother who was either reliable in a suspicious sort of way or the most likely person to be late, distracted, and absent because of her child-care concerns.

While employers brought up single motherhood most often in a negative context, a handful of employers did not use this as a pejorative label but remarked upon some of the ways they felt the workplace could change to accommodate the needs of single parents. An additional 6 percent of all white employers specifically noted that their places of employment practiced some racist and sexist actions that they felt should not be tolerated.

Motherhood and Job Performance

Survey Data   Employers stated that their women employees often faced conflicts between child-care and job responsibilities. Is this view reflected in the experiences of Atlanta's workforce? Individuals in the household survey sample who had children under the age of eighteen in the household during the interview period were asked the following questions regarding potential child-care conflicts: "In the past twelve months, have concerns about child care ever led you to: be late from work; be absent from work; change your hours?" Respondents could answer "yes" to any or all of these questions. We created an additional variable indicating whether a respondent answered "yes" to at least one of these questions.

Because most of the women in Atlanta's labor force were not raising children at the time of the survey, the majority did not face conflicts due to child-care responsibilities (table 9.2). Only 17 percent of black women and 21 percent of white women reported that concerns over child care led them to be late, to be absent, or to change their hours of work at least once over the past year. Among the low skilled, black women were slightly more likely than white women to face conflicts between job demands and child-care needs, but this difference is not statistically significant. Black women did face child-care conflicts significantly more often than black men did, however. Thus, although black women were over three times more likely than white women to be single mothers, being a black female head of a

Table 9.2 / Conflicts between Job and Child Care among Employed Respondents, by Gender and Race (Pecent)[a]

	Women		Men	
Group and Conflict	Black	White	Black	White
In the past twelve months, have concerns about childcare ever caused you to . . .				
Total sample				
Be late for work	9.1	9.9	7.1	6.8
Be absent from work	13.2	15.3	7.7	8.3
Change hours	7.2	10.4	7.7	5.9
Any of the above	17.0	21.3	10.7	11.7
N	317	202	195	205
Low-skilled sample:				
Be late for work	10.0	4.9	2.9*	5.1
Be absent from work	15.3	12.5	4.9*	6.4
Change hours	4.0	6.2	5.8	3.8
Any of the above	18.7	14.8	8.7*	9.0
N	149	81	103	78

[a]Significance tests are comparisons with estimates for African American women.
*$p < .05$. **p .01.

household did not necessarily lead to higher levels of work conflicts for black women as measured by our survey questions.

Employers' perceptions of black women as "single mothers" and therefore "poor workers" clearly carry negative connotations. Yet employers' perception that single mothers were the group most likely to be late, distracted, or absent from their jobs may have been an accurate assessment. The paid labor market is not structured around a single parent's needs or even a married parent's needs. The survey data enable us to address this question.

Even among women with children, black women were not more likely than white women to have conflicts between work and child-care responsibilities. Employers were correct in assuming that women who had children in their household often faced difficulties that could affect job performance (table 9.3). Among the women in our sample with children below age eighteen, a relatively high percentage of both black and white women reported problems with child care that led to tardiness, absences, or changes in work hours. Yet it is striking that black women were no more likely than white women to report work conflicts arising from child-care concerns. Forty-three percent of black mothers and about 54 percent of white mothers reported that they were late, were absent from their job, or

Table 9.3 / Job and Child Care Conflicts Among Employed Respondents with Children Under eighteen, by Gender and Race of Respondent (Percent)[a]

Conflict and Group	Women		Men	
	Black	White	Black	White
In the past twelve months, have concerns about childcare ever caused you to . . .				
Total sample				
Be late for work	23.6	25.0	20.6	24.1
Be absent from work	34.1	38.8	22.4	29.3
Change hours	18.9	26.3	22.4	20.7
Any of the above	43.2	53.8	30.9	40.7
N	125	80	68	59
Low-skilled sample:				
Be late for work	24.6	15.4	10.7	16.0
Be absent from work	37.7	38.5	17.9	20.0
Change hours	9.8	19.2	21.4	11.5
Any of the above	45.2	46.2	32.1	28.0
N	61	26	28	25

[a]Significance tests are comparisons with estimates for African American women.
*$p < .05$. **$p < .01$.

changed hours as a result of child-care concerns (a difference that is not statistically significant).

In addition, white men with children were equally as likely as black women with children to face conflicts between child-care responsibilities and work demands. Our data reveal that child care presented difficulties for a sizable minority of fathers. About 41 percent of white fathers and 31 percent of black fathers reported that concerns with child care led them to be late, to be absent, or to change their hours of work. Yet employers' perceptions of male workers excluded the demands of fatherhood completely. Although a higher proportion of black women than white women in the low-skilled sample stated that child-care concerns made them late for work, this difference is not statistically significant. Given the lack of overall significance for any of the estimates, the patterns for the total sample and the low-skilled sample are the same (table 9.3).

Our data suggest that employers' perceptions of black women do not reflect the characteristics of Atlanta's labor force in a simple way. Employers invoked images of black women as single mothers who faced constant conflicts between their responsibilities at home and at work. While black women are more likely than white women to be the sole family head, the majority of black women in the labor force are not single mothers, even among the low-skilled. Further, the data indicate that employers may have been incorrect in assuming that because black women more often serve as the single head of a family, they have more protracted difficulties in balancing home and family.

This second finding is puzzling. After all, it seems reasonable to assume that the absence of a second adult in the household would place additional child-care burdens on single mothers. We suspect that the ability to balance work and child care is so difficult and precarious for single mothers that only those who successfully make adequate arrangements are in the labor force (see chapter 8). Another explanation could rest in the kinship relationships that black women may form with family members and neighbors. Researchers have documented that black women may develop a community of "othermothers" and "fictive kin" to help each other with the burdens associated with balancing work for pay outside the home and work without pay inside the home (Collins 1991; Stack 1974; Troester 1984; hooks 1984). The prevalence of this type of support network may make the presence or absence of a biological father less important in determining the ability of black women to resolve conflicts between child-care needs and the demands of their job.

Finally, black women may face constraints from child-care responsibilities more times over the course of a year than white women do. Our survey questions asked only whether the respondent had been late, had been absent from work, or had changed hours "at least once" during the previous twelve months. Thus, among those who answered "yes" to these questions, we do not know how often these difficulties occurred.

DISCUSSION

When asked to discuss their employment needs and the problems that they encounter in meeting their needs, many white employers invoked specific imagery in relation to black women. These white employers described black women in the workforce as "single mothers," whose difficulties led them to be either poor workers or desperate yet reliable workers.

Our data from the matched sample of employed Atlanta employers and workers highlight the ways in which employers' perceptions are, at best, selective and, at worst, inaccurate. Theories of status closure and stereotyping, and black feminist theories provide insight for interpreting our results. As employers used stereotypes to formulate impressions of their labor pool based on gender and race, they appeared to accentuate some patterns while ignoring others. Employers discussed black women workers as "single mothers" who brought the problems related to child-care responsibilities to work, although the majority of black women in the labor force were not single parents. Black women's assumed single motherhood was salient to employers, while employers did not seem to notice men's child-care responsibilities or the potential conflicts with paid work that these responsibilities can create for members of any gender or racial group. Group differences among paid workers were highlighted and exaggerated in employers' descriptions.

These perceptions reflect attitudes that are prevalent in the dominant U.S. culture. The stereotype of black women as single mothers carries negative connotations for employers. Status closure theory and black feminist theory would argue that employers use the unfavorable image of black single motherhood as a trope to keep black women in the lowest-paid positions. Indeed, the "black matriarch" has been a central theme within mainstream white culture since slavery. White clergy and intellectuals writing at the turn of the century characterized black mothers as "immoral" women who caused problems within the black family and were responsible for the "deterioration of the black community" (Guy-Sheftall 1990). In the 1960s, Moynihan (1965) specifically cited the "matriarchal" family as the predominant black family structure and argued that its pathological and emasculating consequences were the source of black men's economic distress. Other recent depictions of the black matriarch include the impoverished single woman whose work ethic is not an adequate model for her children (Collins 1990).

Theories of statistical discrimination would disagree that employers' perceptions are motivated by attempts to maintain status hierarchies and regulate access to social and economic rewards on the basis of gender and race. Rather, those theories hold, white employers are just being rational. Given a woman applicant and a man applicant, the odds are higher that the woman rather than the man is shouldering child-care obligations that could interfere with job performance. Given a white woman applicant and a black woman applicant, the odds are higher that the black woman rather than the white woman is a single mother. Note that these "rational" decisions still lead to systematic disadvantage for black women in the labor market, as these women are evaluated in terms of "average" differences between groups rather than individual merit.

Our data do not allow us to differentiate between the motivations behind employers' perceptions. What our study does provide is a test of the basic assumptions common to theories of statistical discrimination, social closure, black feminism, and stereotyping: that is, that employers evaluate workers on the basis of gender and race and that these evaluations evidence discernible patterns. Further, we show that these patterns in employers' perceptions do not follow the contours of the labor force in a simple or straightforward manner.

In suggesting that employers may be filtering their perceptions of black women through preexisting stereotypes, we do not mean to downplay the difficulties that black women who *are* single mothers encounter as the sole providers for their families. Rather, our data suggest that employers are apt to focus upon this status as the defining characteristic of black women, regardless of its accuracy. Small differences in the population can become exaggerated when filtered through employers' gendered and racialized perceptions. Employed black women who are not mothers of young children or who have actually resolved conflicts between child care and paid work are less visible to employers than are black women who fit the common cultural stereotype of the matriarch. The literature on stereotyping suggests that regardless of her family status, any black woman is susceptible to an employer's negative image of the black woman as single mother.

Regardless of which of the theories best describes the underlying mechanism shaping employers' perceptions, all of the theories imply processes of systematic discrimination against black women in the labor market. Our findings are therefore especially pertinent amid the current judicial and legislative trend to do away with policies of affirmative action that attempt to counteract the prejudicial attitudes that factor into hiring, firing, promotion, and wage rate decisions. The MCSUI data indicate that equal employment opportunity is not enough to guard against employers' negative prejudicial images of specific groups of workers and that affirmative action policies continue to be necessary, especially for black women. Further, the study suggests that despite employers' formal proclamations of nondiscrimination, the potential for discrimination lurks within the everyday practices of organizational life. Clearly, the next step in the research agenda is to demonstrate the extent to which employers' perceptions work to keep black women at the bottom of the labor market reward structure.

APPENDIX

Table 9A.1 / Characteristics of Firms and Sample Jobs in Employer Survey

Characteristic	Number	Percent
Firms		
Industry		
Manufacturing	11	24
Transportation, communication, and other public utilities	2	4
Retail trade	10	22
Finance, insurance, and real estate	3	7
Business and repair services	2	4
Personal services	4	9
Professional and related services	9	20
Public administration	4	9
Total	45	100

(Table continues on p. 322.)

Table 9A.1 / *Continued*

Characteristic	Number	Percent
Size (employees)		
1–10	1	2
11–50	13	29
51–500	16	36
500+	8	18
Missing	7	16
Total	45	100
Sample jobs		
Occupation		
Managerial and professional specialty		13
Technical, sales, and administrative support		55
Service		13
Precision production, craft, and repair		9
Operators, fabricators, and laborers		9
Black women in Sample Job (%)[a]		
None		33
1–25		16
26–50		16
51–75		20
76–100		2
Missing		13

[a] These figures can be interpreted as follows: There were no black women in 33 percent of the sample jobs. In .02 percent of the sample jobs, black women constituted over 75 percent of the employees.

This research was supported by grants from the Russell Sage Foundation, the Ford Foundation, and the Rockefeller Foundation. We would like to thank Paula England, Joya Misra, Linda Grant, Cathryn Johnson, and Rick Rubinson for their insightful comments and suggestions.

NOTES

1. As noted by Berry in the foreword to *All the Women Are White, All the Blacks Are Men, Some of Us Are Brave* (Hull, Scott, and Smith 1982), the "invisibility" of black women is common throughout social science research, although the pattern is slowly changing.

2. The literature on stereotyping includes a wide range of definitions and debates. We use a definition that does not privilege a particular theory or assume that stereotypes are necessarily negative, consensual, or false (see Miller 1982 for a

review of these definitional debates). Instead, we see stereotypes as oversimplified generalizations about a group.

3. The "similarity-attraction" hypothesis provides a formalized explanation of these processes and receives much empirical support (see Tsui and O'Reilly 1989).

4. The degree to which gender stereotypes are activated depends on the organizational features of the firm, the context of the interaction, and the other salient identities, such as race (Kanter 1977; Ridgeway 1997). In her landmark study, Kanter (1977) argued that stereotyping on the basis of gender (and, by extension, race) varies with the requirements of the job, access to power and mobility, and the relative size of gender and race groups. Individuals who are "tokens" within an organization are more likely to be stereotyped by coworkers.

5. These counties are Clayton, Cobb, DeKalb, Douglas, Fayette, Fulton, Gwinett, Henry, and Rockdale.

6. This study was also carried out in Boston, Los Angeles, and Detroit.

7. Specifically, the household sample is a multistage, stratified area-probability design of the nine-county Atlanta metropolitan area. Areas (census tracts) with a high proportion of low-income persons and African American residents were oversampled. The total completion rate was 75 percent. See Johnson, Oliver, and Bobo (1994) for a complete description of the study design.

8. In subsequent research, we plan to investigate a related question about differences in white and black employers' perceptions of black employees. Here we are concerned with establishing how white employers perceive black women and with comparing these perceptions to the responses to our household survey.

REFERENCES

Aigner, Dennis J., and Glen C. Cain. 1977. "Statistical Theories of Discrimination in Labor Markets." *Industrial Labor and Relations Review* 30(2): 175–87.

Arrow, Kenneth. 1973. "The Theory of Discrimination." In *Discrimination in Labor Markets,* edited by Orley Ashenfelter and Albert Rees. Princeton, N.J.: Princeton University Press.

Bielby, William T., and James N. Baron. 1986. "Men and Women at Work: Sex Segregation and Statistical Discrimination." *American Journal of Sociology* 91(4): 800–37.

Bills, David B. 1992. "A Survey of Employer Surveys: What We Know about Labor Markets from Talking with Bosses." *Research in Social Stratification and Mobility* 11: 3–31.

Blumer, Herbert. 1958. "Race Prejudice as a Sense of Group Position." *Pacific Sociological Review* 1(1): 3–7.

———. 1965. "Industrialization and Race Relations." In *Industrialization and Race Relations: A Symposium,* edited by Guy Hunter. New York: Oxford University Press.

Bobo, Lawrence. 1983. "Whites' Opposition to Busing: Symbolic Racism or Realistic Group Conflict?" *Journal of Personality and Social Psychology* 45(6): 1196–1210.

———. 1988. "Group Conflict, Prejudice, and the Paradox of Contemporary Racial

Attitudes." In *Eliminating Racism: Profiles in Controversy*, edited by Phyllis A. Katz and Dalmas A. Taylor. New York: Plenum Press.

Bobo, Lawrence, and Vincent L. Hutchings. 1996. "Perceptions of Racial Group Competition: Extending Blumer's Theory of Groups Position to a Multiracial Social Context." *American Sociological Review* 61(6): 951–72.

Bobo, Lawrence, and James R. Kleugel. 1993. "Opposition to Race-Targeting: Self-Interest, Stratification Ideology, or Racial Attitudes?" *American Sociological Review* 58(4): 443–64.

Bobo, Lawrence, and Michael Massagli. Forthcoming. "Racial Identity, Stereotypes and Perceived Group Competition." In *The Multi-City Study of Urban Inequality*, edited by Alice O'Connor, Chris Tilly, and Lawrence Bobo. New York: The Russell Sage Foundation.

Browne, Irene, Leann Tigges, and Julie Press. Forthcoming. "Inequality through Labor Markets, Firms, and Families: Race, Ethnicity, and Wages among Women in Three Cities." In *The Multi-City Study of Urban Inequality*, edited by Alice O'Connor, Chris Tilly, and Lawrence Bobo. New York: Russell Sage Foundation.

Collins, Patricia Hill. 1990. *Black Feminist Thought: Knowledge, Consciousness, and the Politics of Empowerment*. London: Unwin Hyman.

England, Paula. 1992. *Comparable Worth: Theories and Evidence*. New York: Aldine de Gruyter.

Essed, Philomena. 1991. *Understanding Everyday Racism: An Interdisciplinary Theory*. Newbury Park, Calif.: Sage Publications.

Farkas, George, Paula England, Kevin Vicknair, and Barbara Stanek Kilbourne. 1997. "Cognitive Skill, Skill Demands of Jobs, and Earnings among Young European American, African American, and Mexican American Workers." *Social Forces* 75(3): 913–40.

Federal Glass Ceiling Commission. 1995. *Good for Business: Making Full Use of the Nation's Human Capital*. Washington: U.S. Government Printing Office.

Fiske, S.T., and S.E. Taylor. 1991. *Social Cognition*. New York: McGraw-Hill.

Granovetter, Mark. 1995. *Getting a Job, 2nd Edition*. Chicago: University of Chicago Press.

Guy-Sheftall, Beverly. 1990. *Daughters of Sorrow: Attitudes toward Black Women, 1880–1920*. Brooklyn, N.Y.: Carlson Publishers.

Hall, John. 1994. "Sample Design and Weighting Procedures for the Atlanta Survey for the Urban Inequality Study." MPR Report 8111. Princeton, N.J.: Mathematica Policy Research, Inc.

Heilman, Madeline. 1995. "Sex Stereotypes and Their Effects in the Workplace: What We Know and What We Don't Know." *Journal of Social Behavior and Personality* 10(6): 3–260.

Hoffman, Curt, and Nancy Hurst. 1990. "Gender Stereotypes: Perception or Rationalization?" *Journal of Personality and Social Psychology* 58(2): 197–208.

Holzer, Harry J. 1996. *What Employers Want*. New York: Russell Sage Foundation.

hooks, bell. 1984. *Feminist Theory: From Margin to Center*. Boston: South End Press.

Hull, Gloria T., Patricia Bell Scott, and Barbara Smith, eds. 1982. *All the Women Are White, All the Blacks Are Men, But Some of Us Are Brave: Black Women's Studies*. Old Westbury, N.Y.: Feminist Press.

Jackman, Mary. 1993. *The Velvet Glove*. Berkeley, Calif.: University of California Press.

Jacobs, Jerry A.. 1996. "Gender, Race, Local Labor Markets, and Occupational De-valuation." *Sociological Focus* 29(3): 209–30.

Johnson, James H., Jr., Melvin L. Oliver, and Lawrence D. Bobo. 1994. "Understand-ing the Contours of Deepening Urban Inequality: Theoretical Design of a Multi-City Study." *Urban Geography* 15(1): 77–89.

Jones, Russell. 1981. "Perceiving Other People: Stereotyping as a Process of Social Cognition." In *In the Eye of the Beholder: Contemporary Issues in Stereotyping*, edited by Arthur G. Miller. New York: Praeger.

Kanter, Rosabeth Moss. 1993. *Men and Women of the Corporation*. New York: Basic Books.

King, Deborah. 1988. "Multiple Jeopardy: The Context of a Black Feminist Ideol-ogy." *Signs* 14(1): 42–72.

Kirschenman, Joleen. 1991. "Gender Within Race in the Labor Market." Paper pre-sented at the Urban Poverty and Family Life Conference, Chicago, Ill. (Oct. 10–12, 1991).

Kirschenman, Joleen, and Kathryn M. Neckerman. 1991. "'We'd Love to Hire Them, But . . .': The Meaning of Race for Employers." In *The Urban Underclass*, edited by Christopher Jencks and Paul E. Peterson. Washington, D.C.: Brookings Institution.

Kuklinski, James H., Michael D. Cobb, and Martin Gilens. 1996. "Racial Attitudes and the 'New South.'" Working Paper 49. Urbana–Chamaign, Ill.: University of Illinois, Institute of Government and Public Affairs.

Landrine, Hope. 1985. "Race * Class Stereotypes of Women." *Sex Roles* 13(1–2): 65–75.

Lieberson, Stanley. 1980. *A Piece of the Pie: Blacks and White Immigrants since 1880.* Berkeley: University of California Press.

Miller, Arthur G. 1982. "Historical and Contemporary Perspectives on Stereotyp-ing." In *In the Eye of the Beholder: Contemporary Issues in Stereotyping*, edited by Arthur G. Miller. New York: Praeger.

Moss, Philip, and Chris Tilly. 1991. *Why Black Men Are Doing Worse in the Labor Market: A Review of Supply-Side and Demand-Side Explanations*. Monograph. New York: Social Science Research Council.

———. 1995a. "'Soft' Skills and Race: An Investigation of Black Men's Employment Problems." Working Paper 80. New York: Russell Sage Foundation.

———. 1995b. "Raised Hurdles for Black Men: Evidence from Interviews with Em-ployers." Working Paper 81. New York: Russell Sage Foundation.

Moynihan, Daniel Patrick. 1965. *The Negro Family: The Case for National Action*. Washington, D.C.: U.S. Government Printing Office for U.S. Department of Labor, Office of Policy Planning and Research.

Neckerman, Kathryn M., and Joleen Kirschenman. 1991. "Hiring Strategies, Racial Bias, and Inner-City Workers." *Social Problems* 38(4): 433–47.

Pettigrew, Thomas F. 1979. "The Ultimate Attribution Error: Extending Allport's Cognitive Analysis of Prejudice." *Personality and Social Psychology Bulletin* 5(4): 461–76.

Read, Stephen J. 1983. "Once Is Enough: Causal Reasoning from a Single Instance." *Journal of Personality and Social Psychology* 45(2): 323–34.

Reskin, Barbara, and Patricia A. Roos. 1990. *Job Queues, Gender Queues: Explaining Women's Inroads into Male Occupations*. Philadelphia: Temple University Press.

Ridgeway, Cecilia. 1997. "Interaction and the Conservation of Gender Inequality: Considering Employment." *American Sociological Review* 62(2): 218–35.

Rosenbaum, James E., and Amy Binder. 1997. "Do Employers Really Need More Educated Youth?" *Sociology of Education* 70(1): 68–85.

Smith, Ryan A. 1997. "Race, Income, and Authority at Work: A Cross-Temporal Analysis of Black and White Men (1972–1994)." *Social Problems* 44(1): 19–37.

Squires, Gregory. 1977. "Education, Jobs, and Inequality: Functional and Conflict Models of Social Stratification in the United States." *Social Problems* 24(4): 436–50.

Stack, Carol D. 1974. *All Our Kin: Strategies for Survival in a Black Community*. New York: Harper and Row.

St. Jean, Yanick, and Joe Feagin. 1997. "Black Women, Sexism, and Racism: Experiencing Double Jeopardy." In *Everyday Sexism in the Third Millenium*, edited by Carol Rambo Ronai, Barbara Zsembik, and Joe R. Feagin. New York: Routledge.

Strauss, Anselm, and Juliet Corbin. 1990. *Basics of Qualitative Research: Grounded Theory Procedures and Techniques*. Newbury Park, Calif.: Sage Publications.

Struyk, Raymond J., Michael A. Turner, and Michael Fix. 1991. *Opportunities Diminished: Discrimination in Hiring*. Washington, D.C.: Urban Institute Press.

Tajfel, Henri, and Jonathan Turner. 1986. "The Social Identity Theory of Intergroup Behavior." In *Psychology of Intergroup Relations*, edited by Stephen Worchel and William Austen. Chicago: Nelson Hall.

Tomaskovic-Devey, Donald. 1993. *Gender and Racial Inequality at Work: The Sources and Consequences of Job Segregation*. Ithaca, N.Y.: ILR Press.

Troester, Rosalie Riegle. 1984. "Turbulence and Tenderness: Mothers, Daughters, and 'Othermothers' in Paule Marshall's *Brown Girl, Brownstones*." *Sage: A Scholarly Journal on Black Women* 1(2): 13–16.

Tsui, Anne S., and Charles A. O'Reilly. 1989. "Beyond Simple Demographic Effects: The Importance of Relational Demography in Superior-Subordinate Dyads." *Academy of Management Journal* 32(2): 402–23.

Chapter 10

Perceptions of Workplace Discrimination Among Black and White Professional-Managerial Women

Elizabeth Higginbotham and Lynn Weber

D espite recent gains, both African American and white women professionals and managers still earn far less than white men do and remain segregated in segments of the workforce with limited advancement opportunities and "glass ceilings" (see Federal Glass Ceiling Commission 1995; McGuire and Reskin 1993). And black women professionals and managers earn less than white women (Higginbotham 1987, 1994; Reskin and Roos 1990; Sokoloff 1992; Woody 1992). Yet knowledge of how black and white women experience and understand systems of racial and gender-based inequality is quite unsystematic and is based largely on anecdotal evidence and qualitative studies of small, racially homogeneous groups of women. Understanding the ways women perceive race- and gender-based inequity in the workplace is important for many reasons, one of the most important being the quest for common ground on which to forge collective action to redress inequities. Efforts to forge multiracial coalitions among women have often failed when women of color have been expected to accept a women's political agenda that does not reflect their sense of the problems (Baca Zinn et al. 1986; Spelman 1988). Thus understanding the nuances in the ways that black and white women—especially in the same structural locations and workplaces—perceive and respond to racial and gender inequality is a critical project in achieving social change.

The research described here seeks to contribute to that project by directly assessing three basic questions about the nature of black and white professional and managerial women's experiences with discrimination in the workplace. First, we assess the extent to which black and white women professionals and managers perceive discriminatory treatment in key dimensions of their work, including the reward structures of rank, pay, and promotions as well as everyday interactions in which they confront controlling images of women. Second, we identify similarities and differences in the ways that black and white women professionals and managers perceive both racial and gender discrimination. Third, we examine the ways in which different racial experiences with gender inequality shape career plans.

RESEARCH ON RACIAL AND GENDER DISCRIMINATION

We review two types of studies that address racial and gender discrimination. First, studies of structural inequality, typically based on quantitative analyses of census data or large-scale surveys, control factors such as experience and credentials and we document racial and gender differences in rewards such as pay, rank, and promotions. Second, experiential studies explore women's perceptions of equity, discrimination, rewards, and opportunities. These studies are typically based on in-depth interviews with small, racially homogeneous samples. Unlike the quantitative studies, they do not typically control or analyze other factors, such as class or credentials, that influence workplace perceptions.

Structural Discrimination in Rank, Pay, and Promotion

Survey- and census-based research consistently documents that professional-managerial women's authority and wages are lower than white men's (see Federal Glass Ceiling Commission 1995; McGuire and Reskin 1993; Sokoloff 1992; Woody 1992). Two processes are implicated. First, women have lower credentials (that is, education and experience) than white men. Second, women receive lower wages and have less authority (rank) even when they have the same education and experience and work in the same industries (see McGuire and Reskin 1993; Sokoloff 1992; Woody 1992). These patterns occur largely because women are channeled and clustered into sectors of the labor force that pay the least and that restrict advancement opportunities (Higginbotham 1987, 1994; Reskin and Roos 1990; Sokoloff 1992; Woody 1992). Reskin and Roos highlight one aspect of this process by documenting wage declines that occurred as white men left and women and people of color entered certain occupations, including book editing, pharmacy, and bank management. They also demonstrate that women are channeled into sectors, such as customer service banking, that generate no profit and restrict opportunities to move into top management. Across the labor force, Morrison and Von Glinow (1990) report, the majority of women in management hold staff positions rather than the line positions from which promotions take place.

Although recognizing that black women experience even greater disadvantage than white women on both credentials and returns to them, feminist scholars are often reluctant to compare the status of black or other women of color directly with that of white women (McGuire and Reskin 1993). As McGuire and Reskin caution, comparisons between black and white women are diversionary and divisive since the gap between either group and white men is far larger and more significant.

Perceptions of Racial and Gender Discrimination

Qualitative, in-depth studies reveal people's interpretations of the circumstances of their jobs and insights into the actions they are likely to take to remedy whatever job dissatisfaction they experience. In these studies lies the potential for understanding whether wage gaps are produced, experienced, and interpreted in the same way among white women and women of color. Yet studies of professional-managerial women's perceptions of oppression have avoided direct comparisons of white women with women of color.

Both popular personal narratives (Nelson 1993; Williams 1991) and qualitative research studies describe black middle-class women's everyday encounters with racial discrimination in the workplace. They vividly detail African American professionals' and managers' experiences of repeatedly having to "prove" their competence, failing to move up as a result of discrimination in evaluation and promotion processes, being excluded from critical networks, lacking mentoring, feeling marginalized and isolated, and coping in an unpleasant environment created by racist and sexist remarks (Bell 1990; Davis and Watson 1982; Denton 1990; Feagin and Sikes 1994; Fulbright 1986; Nkomo 1988).

Most black professional-managerial women see sexism as well as racism implicated in the discriminatory treatment that they face (Hochschild 1993; Williams 1991). But how do their perceptions compare with those of white women? Are black women as likely as white women to perceive sexism in professional-managerial work? Do black and white women define the obstacles they encounter in the same ways? Certainly, white women professionals and managers have identified lack of mentoring, feelings of marginality, and glass ceilings as obstacles (Federal Glass Ceiling Commission 1995; Morrison and Von Glinow 1990; Northcraft and Gutek 1993), but do white women in the same structural locations in the workforce perceive their constraints similarly as black women? While black women see sexism as restricting their opportunities, do white women see the ways that racism oppresses their African American counterparts, or do they hold negative images of black women? How pervasive are these varied views?

Recent scholarship on race indicates that the dominant racial ideology in the United States today is a "colorblind" ideology in which white people not only fail to perceive racism but believe that to acknowledge racial difference is to be racist (Frankenberg 1993; Omi and Winant 1994). White women with a "colorblind" ideology who perceive gender discrimination may thus be unlikely to perceive racial discrimination in their same work environment. Despite the prevalence of the "colorblind" ideology, some white people are "color conscious" and recognize racial discrimination, while others are "color conscious" and hold racist views. When they recognize racial discrimination, white people can form the basis of coalitions with people of color that can redress injustices (Collins 1990; Frankenberg 1993). Some who hold "color-conscious" racist ideologies actually see white people as racial victims in a process labeled "reverse discrimination." Little is known about the extent or character of such "colorblind" or "color-conscious" views in professional-managerial workplaces where antidiscrimination has broader support but affirmative action much less (see, for example, Tickamyer et al. 1989), and men's experiences have formed the basis for the images that are available (for example, the *Bakke* court case).

Since most of the studies of workplace discrimination have involved racially homogeneous groups, it is not known whether racial differences that appear across studies are based on the different social locations of white and African American women, different treatment in the same locations, different perceptions of the same treatment, or some combination of these factors (Cannon, Higginbotham, and Leung 1988). Similarly, the existing literature does not reveal whether issues such as mentoring and promotion obstacles, which appear in the discussions of both black and white women, are as frequent in each group, are interpreted similarly in each group, and have the same or different effects on career plans.

THE STUDY

The research described here combines features of both structural and experiential research by looking at the interpretations and meanings attached to workplace structures by African American and white women in a study that controlled for other key structural factors affecting workplace rewards, treatment, and perceptions. We compare the perceptions of global racial and gender discrimination, equity in specific reward structures, and career plans of same-aged African American and white women who were situated in the labor force in the same occupations and industries and who shared educational credentials, experience, economic standing, and social class histories.

The goal of these comparisons is twofold. First, we seek to provide personal interpretations that may help explain the dynamics behind the findings of large-scale demographic studies of job rewards, which indicate that African American women receive similar although slightly lower levels of job rewards than white women. Second, we seek to provide this interpretive picture in a qualitative study that, through a combination of controlling variables and matching subjects, eliminates a series of structural factors beyond race that typically confound qualitative studies based on small samples, including age, education, direct route to college, employment status, occupation, industrial sector, and social class background. We employ a sample of two hundred, far exceeding the twenty to fifty subjects typical in qualitative studies.

METHOD

Research Design

The data for this study were taken from a larger exploratory project that examined the relationships among race, class background, and the gender composition of occupations on a wide range of family, work, and health issues in a sample of two hundred full-time employed women professionals, managers, and administrators in the Memphis metropolitan area. The research instrument contained closed- and open-ended questions that elicited a general life history of the women, focusing on family history, school experiences from elementary school through higher education, current employment, family and personal life, and general well-being and health. Data were collected from 1985 to 1987 in face-to-face interviews lasting two and one-half to three hours each.

Sample

We selected a sample of black and white women who were matched on other important characteristics affecting workers' experiences and perceptions. The sample was restricted to women of the baby-boom cohort (that is, women who were twenty-five to forty years of age at the time of the study); college graduates who went directly from high school to college or did so within two years of graduation; women who were currently working full-time as professionals, managers, or administrators (that is, in "middle-class" occupations; Vanneman and Cannon 1987). (For a discussion of the rationale for selecting these groups and selection procedures, see Cannon, Higginbotham, and Leung 1988.) All subjects were defined as currently middle class by virtue of their employment in either a professional, a managerial, or an administrative occupation as specified in Braverman (1974), Ehrenreich and Ehrenreich (1979), and Vanneman and Cannon (1987) (see Vanneman and Cannon 1987 for exceptions). We classified subjects as either professional or managerial-administrative on the basis of the designation of occupations in the 1980 U.S. Bureau of the Census (U.S. Department of Commerce 1983). Managerial occupations were defined as those in the census categories of managers and administrators, and professional occupations were defined as those in the professional category, excluding technicians (Braverman 1974).[1] At the time of the study, the majority of the black and white women had advanced degrees (master's degrees: fifty-seven black women, fifty-five white women; law degrees: seven black women, eight white women; doctorates: three black women, eight white women).

We employed a quota sample stratified by three dimensions of inequality: race, the social class background of the respondent, and the gender composition of her occupation. Each dimension was operationalized into two categories: black and white; raised working class—upwardly mobile and raised middle-class—middle-class stable; and female dominated and male dominated. Twenty-five cases were selected for each of the eight cells of this two-by-two-by-two design.[2]

To avoid confounding race, class background, and occupation, we selected subjects so that the different race and class-background categories contained women from the same or closely related occupations. To prevent overrepresentation of any age group in a race, class background, or specific occupational category, subjects were also sorted into three age groupings defined by birth cohort (1945 to 1950, 1951 to 1955, and 1956 to 1960).

Procedures

Every few weeks, volunteers who met all study parameters (twenty-five to forty years of age; full-time employed professionals, managers, or administrators; and college graduates who went directly to college) were sorted according to all of the stratifying variables (race, class, sex composition of occupation, professionals versus managers and administrators; specific occupation; and age category). We then randomly selected subjects to be interviewed from each pool. From the responses, we assessed subjects' perceptions of global racial and gender discrimination, reward structures, and career plans in a series of open-ended questions and developed categories for the responses.

GLOBAL PERCEPTIONS OF SEXISM AND RACISM

In the findings as presented here, all analyses are presented by race only. Separate analyses including class background and gender composition of occupation did not explain any of the racial differences reported here and are not presented.

Sexism

We asked, "Do you feel women are treated differently in any ways than the men in your workplace?" If the answer was "yes," we asked, "In what ways?" While a majority of respondents indicated that women were treated differently, black women were far more likely to do so. Roughly three-fourths of the black women (73.7 percent) and slightly over one-half of the white women (56.1 percent) stated that they perceived different treatment of women (see table 10.1). Among those who perceived different treatment, however, black and white women were equally likely to mention the same four major areas of concern: treatment as inferior or subordinate, soft, emotional, or helpless based on sexist stereotypes ($N = 30$); hiring and promotion discrimination ($N = 26$); necessity of "proving" themselves, working harder, and attaining more qualifications ($N = 16$); and lower salaries and other compensation ($N = 12$). Other areas mentioned by a few respondents included exclusion from the "good-ole-boy" network, sexual harassment, and preferential treatment of males. Finally, four women indicated that women were treated in stereotypic ways, such as having the door opened for them, but they interpreted this behavior as preferential, not inferior, treatment.

The comments of Lynn Johnson, an African American health care administrator in a major hospital, typify the way many black and white women described their daily struggles against traditional stereotypes of women:

> You can't be just a normal woman in that environment. They take you too much for granted, and they want to treat you like you're helpless. You've got to be very aggressive, which they consider abrasive. . . . They still promote men because men "need" it and women don't "need" it. You're still fighting the same old "isms."[3]

Although wage equity has been a cornerstone of the struggle for women's rights, wages per se were not the first thing these women mentioned. In addition to struggling against limiting stereotypes, black and white women most often saw barriers to hiring and promotions as the crux of the inequities they faced. These barriers were and continue to be especially troublesome in professional-managerial work, in which expectations are that careers will be characterized by steady progress up the ladder of success (Vanneman and Cannon 1987). These women's perceptions validate recent work that finds that women's wages are depressed most often through ghettoization in lower-paying job titles and sectors of the workplace and less often through unequal pay in the same jobs, a practice explicitly prohibited by Civil Rights legislation (McGuire and Reskin 1993; Reskin and Roos 1990). Furthermore, in many public sector work settings, salaries are set for entire categories of workers, such as teachers or attorneys, and the main way to achieve a significant salary increase is through a promotion. Finally, one of the features of professional-managerial work is relatively high wages, and research has demonstrated that, among professional-managerial women and men, subjective job rewards affect job satisfaction more than salary-related factors do (Phelan 1994). The women, especially African American women, expressed considerable dissatisfaction about salaries,

Table 10.1 / Perceptions of Work-Related Treatment, Opportunities, Rewards, and Career Goals, by Race (Percent)

Question and Answer	Race (%)		χ^2	p	N
	Black	White			
Are women treated differently? (yes)	73.7	56.1	5.77	.02	193
	(70)	(55)			
Are blacks treated differently? (yes)	68.1	44.3	8.85	.00	170
	(62)	(35)			
Have you been treated unfairly because of (race) sex? (yes)	42.0	25.0	5.75	.02	200
	(42)	(25)			
Do you occupy the position you deserve based on your training and experience?	(99)	(96)	9.15	.01	195
Yes	74.7	80.2			
	(74)	(77)			
No, overqualified	24.2	12.5			
	(24)	(12)			
No, underqualified	1.0	7.3			
	(1)	(7)			
Are you adequately paid relative to co-workers?	(98)	(91)	10.88	.03	189
Yes	51.0	71.4			
	(50)	(65)			
Adequate compensation	34.7	57.1			
	(34)	(52)			
Same compensation for all coworkers	16.3	14.3			
	(16)	(13)			
No	48.9	28.6			
	(46)	(26)			
Inadequate compensation for all co-workers	17.3	10.2			
	(17)	(9)			
Unfair evaluation	26.5	14.3			
	(26)	(13)			
Race or sex discrimination	5.1	4.4			
	(5)	(4)			
Do your chances for promotion reflect your talent and ability?	(98)	(95)	14.96	.06	193
Yes	44.9	47.4			
	(44)	(45)			
Fair policies	17.3	20.0			
	(17)	(19)			

Table 10.1 / *Continued*

Question and Answer	Race (%)		χ^2	p	N
	Black	White			
Self-confidence	17.3	13.7			
	(17)	(13)			
Supervisor's validation	6.1	5.3			
	(6)	(5)			
Personal experience	4.1	8.4			
	(4)	(8)			
No	55.1	52.6			
	(54)	(50)			
Ability not deciding factor					
Unfair system (politics)	20.4	17.9			
	(20)	(17)			
Racism	8.2	0.0			
	(8)	(0)			
Sexism	1.0	3.2			
	(1)	(3)			
Structural obstacles	21.4	27.4			
	(21)	(26)			
No interest in promotion, burnout	4.1	4.2			
	(4)	(4)			
What are your current career goals?	(100)	(97)	17.84	.00	197
New job through					
Promotion	24.0	24.7			
	(24)	(24)			
New employer	18.0	15.5			
	(18)	(15)			
Self-employment	15.0	11.3			
	(15)	(11)			
Continued education or training	20.0	8.2			
	(20)	(8)			
Current job	12.0	34.0			
	(12)	(33)			
None, unsure	11.0	6.2			
	(11)	(6)			

Note: Figures in parentheses are Ns.

but pay was not the first thing they mentioned when asked about inequities.

Awareness of structural barriers to advancement was common among the women in both male- and female-dominated occupations. The comments of Wendy Robinson, a white lawyer and bank trust officer, are typical:

It's obvious that the top echelon at the bank is all male. There are a lot of vice presidents and a lot of them are female, but nonetheless there are so many it's almost a meaningless title. All the people who have the lowest jobs are female. And all the people who have the highest jobs are male. It's just obvious.

Black women also identified a subtle process of limiting women's advancement. Eleven black and only two white women identified differences in work assignments and responsibilities as a part of the process that ultimately prohibited promotions. Specifically, they mentioned that women were given token, less challenging, and more "secretarial" types of jobs; were kept off committees and boards; and were excluded from tough work that often serves as the proving ground for further advancement. Patricia Moore, an African American journalist, talked about such barriers:

A lot of women aren't given some of the "primo" assignments like City Hall. They think that somehow we're not as astute politically as men since it's mostly men in the city and county administration. They figure that men would understand them better, I suppose.

The data show that black women were significantly more likely to perceive gender inequities in the workplace and to express a more nuanced understanding of the dynamics of gender inequities. Yet among those who perceived inequity, both black and white women focused on the same arenas: the limitations imposed by stereotypical images of women and discrimination in hiring and promotions. Salaries per se were much less frequently mentioned.

Racism

Thirty women (9 black and 21 white) worked in racially homogeneous workplaces. We asked the remaining 170 respondents, "Do you feel blacks are treated differently in any ways than whites in your workplace?" Just over 68 percent of the blacks and 44.3 percent of the white women indicated that black people were treated differently, but one-third (34.3 percent, $N = 12$) of those white women stated that black people received *preferential* treatment, and some contended that white people faced "reverse discrimination." Among the white women, 44 (55.7 percent) perceived no differences in treatment, 12 (15.1 percent) perceived preferential treatment for black people, and 23 (29.1 percent) perceived discriminatory treatment. Taken together, close to three-fourths (70.9 percent) of the white women perceived no negative treatment of black people while 68.1 percent of black women perceived negative treatment—a striking contrast.

Interestingly, both the black women and the white women who perceived discriminatory treatment described the discrimination as occurring in the same two areas most commonly mentioned in response to the question about differential treatment of women: hiring and promotions ($N =$ 31) and disrespectful treatment by coworkers and clients based on stereotypes of black people as inferior, incompetent, or less able ($N = 27$). A few women also mentioned salary, exclusion from social networks, and tokenism—being put in positions that lack power.

Black Women Racial discrimination in hiring and promotions was commonly cited by black women. Cheryl Waddell, a black medical social worker at a private hospital, said,

> I think the blacks are confined to the lower positions—lower-status positions—promotional opportunities are not as available to them as the whites. It's not easy . . . it's definitely there.

Talking about another work sphere, Janice Freeman, a thirty-six-year-old black associate professor in a community college, described black women's confrontations with negative stereotypes:

> Yes, I do and I hope that I'm being objective, but I think that they're treated differently because of their color and because of that other person's personal expectation of what this person can do that's ingrained in them culturally over the years or over the decades so that we have to prove more, be twice as good, and be damned near flawless to meet even their mediocre standards. And that to me is not right!

White Women and the Colorblind Perspective In contrast with these black women's views, the majority of the white women (55.7 percent), even though they worked in integrated environments, simply did not perceive that black people were treated any differently in the workplace. If most of the white professional-managerial women in this sample who worked in all-white environments (21 percent) were even less likely to perceive racial discrimination, the profound extent of middle-class white women's unawareness of racism is evident. The position of these women represents the "colorblind" racial ideology that defines the dominant culture discourse on race in the United States (see Omi and Winant 1994; Frankenberg 1993). This stance has proven to be a powerful force for the preservation of the racial status quo and a persistent barrier to a unified women's movement.

The vast majority of these white women simply responded "no" when asked if blacks were treated differently in their workplaces. No further comment or elaboration appeared necessary when they saw no differences. Among those who elaborated on their response, several explicitly presented a "colorblind" perspective, claiming not to notice race. Some women went so far as to acknowledge the difference between their perceptions and those of black people in their workplaces. Sharon Anderson, an occupational therapist, said, "No, but I know some blacks who do." And a few women overtly evoked the language of "colorblindness," saying, "We try to be colorblind" or "I forget that Ethel is black."

An interesting variant on the "colorblind" perspective is reflected in a group of women who claimed that people in their workplace held prejudicial attitudes but did not discriminate on the basis of race. These women tended also to implicate black and white people equally in holding prejudicial attitudes. By highlighting what they saw as a balance of views, they minimized the significance of stereotypic attitudes and power differences across races. Donna Latimer, a manager at a utility, said,

> A good part of the company has an attitude that the majority of blacks are inferior to whites, and some of the blacks feel that the whites are inferior [yet] policywise, there can be no discrimination.

Equating black and white workers sends the message, in the words of Alice Norwood, one of the respondents:

> In the final analysis, I believe it is very equal and it all comes out the same in the wash, but in the process of hiring and firing, that's [race] always a big topic of conversation.

White Women and Color Consciousness   When they are conscious of the existence of racial discrimination, as over one-fourth were, the white women in this sample were often in a singular position to observe the everyday practice of racism. Barbara Worthington, a forty-year-old white college professor, clearly saw racism in her work environment. She discussed the way racially exclusionary practices were carried out in the science department at her university:

> First, we have no blacks in this department. The few that have applied while I've been here have been automatically eliminated from consideration. Part of the reason was that they told in their original application that they were black. There is a standard equal opportunity form . . . and some people make a big point of saying, "I'm a black applicant." And this does not confer a special advantage. Especially to many of my colleagues it's a disadvantage, because they feel that if this person were adequately trained, competitive, etc., with similar qualifications, they would not need to declare themselves a black candidate up front. So they feel that by doing that, they are asking for special consideration. That's a kind of backlash and that's not something you can take to court.

Mary Ellen Madsen, a white public school teacher, discussed the open challenging of black people's competence. She said,

> The one black assistant principal we have is on a regular basis called incompetent in front of others. I think it's really because he's black. I don't think

he's incompetent at all. I think he has not been given the opportunity to prove extreme competence. When you're only in charge of the buses. . . . On occasion, I've heard remarks made [about a teacher] like, "Well, she's black, what do you expect?" No, I don't think they're treated fairly. There are some excellent black teachers in my school, and no one will ever know it purely because they're black.

And finally Toni McKenna, a white librarian, mentioned more structural concerns:

So many blacks in the organization are in the lower levels of the spectrum. So many more clerks are black than are white. They have lower salaries, they have lower positions and rank, and all that other stuff.

The comments of the twelve white women who thought black people received preferential treatment are also revealing. Two of the women indicated that their workplace gave advantages to black workers, but they saw the need for the perceived advantage. For example, Nicole Osborne, a legal aid attorney, said,

Legal aid is a different type of practice of law. . . . In legal aid we go overboard in trying to provide opportunities because our clients are black and I think that is important. I think we are sensitive to the need for minorities to have opportunities in the professions, and it has been a good opportunity for many minorities to get a job and get good experience practicing law. But I think there has been some concern that it has worked against whites who also were sensitive to the needs of legal representation for poor people and want that opportunity too. . . . Sometimes color is a factor.

The remaining ten white women expressed varying degrees of dissatisfaction with the preferences they observed. Perhaps the most vociferous in her response was Jeannette Wilson, a thirty-six-year-old senior marketing consultant at a radio station:

They [blacks] are given opportunities that most of them are not . . . maybe I better rephrase that. They are given opportunities . . . people that apply that are white would be better qualified, but because of the fact that there is a black quota that has to be met, they have to take the inferior persons and that really chaps me!

Katherine Davis, an administrator with a youth agency for girls, was more cautious in her comments:

There has been some reverse discrimination. There were some opportunities given to black staff members that were not given to white staff members.

These comments reflect not the rantings of crazed white supremacists but rather the views of middle-class white women, who were conscious of race and saw black people as advantaged. They represented about 15 percent of our sample, a large enough group to constitute a force to be reckoned with in the workplace. The group was only one-half the size of the group of white women who clearly perceived racial discrimination. If these two groups captured the bulk of the perceptions of white professional managerial women, antiracist movements would have achieved far more than they have. Rather, the larger obstacle to achieving white women's support for black people's struggles against racism is the pervasive belief in a "colorblind" ideology and practice. This ideology is a set of beliefs that minimizes the importance of race either by not noticing it or by recognizing race while denying power differences among races, thereby interpreting any observed differences in negative treatment as unimportant.

PERSONAL EXPERIENCES WITH SEXISM AND RACISM

General Assessment of Discriminatory Treatment

We next asked the women about any personal experiences of unfairness: "Do you feel you have received any unfair treatment at work because you are a (black) woman?"[4] Forty-two percent of the black women but only 25 percent of the white women felt that they had been treated unfairly because of their gender or because of their race and gender. Furthermore, eight of the white women but only two of the black women indicated that the unfairness had happened to them on a previous job—not in their current workplace.

When discussing their personal experiences with inequities, both black and white women most often discussed the subtle, indirect, and informal ways they were treated—racist and sexist jokes, exclusion from networks, subtle putdowns, and sexual innuendoes. Twelve black women and only one white woman specifically referred to overt sexual harassment or used the term sex or race discrimination. Hiring and promotions were also frequently mentioned, although less often than the informal mechanisms listed. These subtle and informal mechanisms of control were captured by Sandra Maxwell, a twenty-eight-year-old African American corporate attorney:

> Basically I feel like there are periods where colleagues feel very threatened by you. They feel that you move faster, that your work is better and is noted more by some of the senior people. So things are done to bring you down. They are done to "put you back in your place" so they say. And I have run into that more than a number of times. And you feel—maybe I should wait until my time—or you come to the feeling that I want to fight it all the way.

Joan Harden, a black associate news producer at a television station, said,

They tell a lot of racial jokes. They're always categorizing people differently, especially blacks. They seem to be quite prejudiced.

Margaret Ford, a private attorney, described pay and the job ceiling:

Well, the initial compensation that I received [was low], and the fact that there's no partnership track or any real interest in making me a partner.

Comments on discrimination were not only less frequent among the white women than among the black women, but they were even more likely to focus on the subtle and indirect nature of the inequality. Julie Townsend, an elementary school principal, said,

I think I receive subtle sexual harassment. For example, yesterday I was meeting with a male professor, who used to meet with the assistant director and me, and she couldn't be there, so he said, "Well, at least I get to meet with one good-looking dame." The stuff that is totally inappropriate because it has nothing to do with what you are doing.

Barbara Worthington, the college science professor, was atypical of the white women in that she described in great detail the overt sex discrimination that was pervasive in her department. Recall that she was also quite aware of the way racism operated to exclude African American candidates from her department. As her comments indicate, a lawsuit surely heightened her awareness:

I don't think that I have received the same amount of opportunities as men—the same amount of research support, which is monetary support, travel money to attend professional meetings, for professional advancement . . . . I was hired here primarily because they saw this [position] as a woman's job. They had a sex discrimination suit in this department which the department lost, and when the lawyer called on me to testify, I asked not to because I needed the job and I was not willing to perjure myself to keep the job, and he said he understood. . . . I hope the experience will make me a little more sensitive to people's feelings about professional status, promotion, pay, etc.

Far fewer women, both black and white, said they had personally experienced unfair treatment than identified global racism, sexism, or both in their workplaces. Crosby (1984) reports that denial of personal disadvantage, even when people recognize broad patterns of discrimination, is quite common. These people felt they were generally treated fairly in a system that they recognized as unfair. The comments of Darlene Hooks, a black woman librarian, are instructive. Darlene recognized that the sexism in the system constituted a "glass ceiling" for all women:

> Women are not given the same employment opportunities. The men hold the top management levels in my business, and the women are all the subordinates. So there is no way women have the same opportunities, because men hold all the top levels, and the women will hold the second-level positions.

When asked about personally being treated unfairly, Darlene said she was not, because "there are not many black librarians in the field, so people seek me out." Yet in reality there was still a glass ceiling that Darlene knew she would not penetrate. The issue of age and job tenure can be a factor in shaping women's likelihood of experiencing treatment that they consider discriminatory. Women at early career stages may not yet have felt the denial of promotions and the significance of informal differential treatment.

Assessment of Discriminatory Treatment in Rank, Pay, and Promotion Opportunities

All the women in our study were college graduates, many with advanced degrees. As McGuire and Reskin (1993) note, however, women do not receive the same pay, authority, or other returns to education as their male counterparts do. Research on job satisfaction has long documented a positive bias in response to global questions about job satisfaction (or dissatisfaction) that is less common when respondents are asked about specific aspects of the job, for example, pay, promotions, and benefits. Therefore, we asked specific questions about the women's perceptions of equity in their rank, pay, and promotion opportunities.

Rank We asked, "Is the position you currently occupy what you feel you deserve based on your training and experience?" and "Why do you say that?" The majority of women, 74.7 percent of the black women and 80.2 percent of the white women, thought they deserved the position they currently held (see table 10.1). Toni McKenna, a white woman heading a branch of the public library, is typical of the black and white women in both traditionally male and female occupations who felt as if their careers were on track:

> I spent my early years in librarianship in reference and public service. My most recent job to this one [branch head] was being a first assistant to someone in a branch, and it was there that I learned more about the nitty-gritty details of how to run a branch: the paperwork that is required, the maintenance kinds of things, security issues and the like. And I think the combination of the two has served me well.

Most of the black and white women who answered that their current positions did not match their training and experience (24 percent and 12 percent respectively) felt they were *overqualified* for the positions they currently held. The perceptions of the women in this study run counter to myths that depict black people, especially black women, as working in jobs for which they are not adequately prepared. For example, Carolyn Blackman, an account executive for a private corporation, responded,

> At this point, no. It's time to go higher. Because with this company and with certain companies, you have so many years that you do this, then you move on and you try not to become stuck in one [position] over a period of years. So really, three or four years or three to five years is the most in this job title. It's time for another job title. It's time to move.

Some white women also voiced these complaints, but black women were twice as likely to do so. While these women may have been hired and even welcomed into their workplaces, many had not been able to advance in their careers as they had planned.

Finally, seven of the white women and only one black woman thought they were *underqualified* for their positions based on their training and experience. For example, Wendy Johnson was in the trust department of a bank. She noted,

> I'm not particularly well trained for this job. And I feel I could do more of what I was trained to do in another part of the bank.

Sally Faulkner, a white woman manager, knew that she did not get her position because of training or experience. She explained,

> The president of the company, whose primary background is as a salesman, is very intelligent but lacks managerial skills, as do I. I think one of the main reasons that I got this job wasn't because of my management skills, because I had none, but it was more my dedication. He [the president] made this comment to many people many times: "I can always count on Sally to get things done no matter what."

In sum, although the majority of women thought they were in jobs appropriate for their educational attainment and training, some felt overqualified and a few felt underqualified. Contrary to popular myths, the black women were twice as likely to feel overqualified, and the white women were more likely to feel underqualified for their jobs.

Pay When asked, "Relative to your coworkers, do you think you are adequately paid for the work you do?" and "Why do you say that?" the respondents again revealed substantial racial differences. Fully 71.4 percent of the white women but only 51.0 percent of the black women thought their pay was adequate. Jamie Larson, a white branch head in the public library system, expressed a common sentiment when she said,

> I am making three times as much as I started out at nine years ago, and I think that is pretty good. I hear a lot about people not getting enough money for what they do, but I am very satisfied.

In contrast, 48.9 percent of the black women and 28.6 percent of the white women indicated that they were not adequately compensated in relation to their coworkers. Even though the question asked them only to compare their situations with that of their coworkers, seventeen black women and nine white women added that they and their coworkers were all underpaid.[5]

Twenty-six black women and twelve white women spoke of a variety of unfair compensation practices, such as inconsistent pay practices and failure to be compensated for additional schooling, extra effort, more work, longevity, experience, or competency. Wilma Davidson, an African American information analyst working in city government, was not rewarded for her additional schooling. She remarked,

> I think if you make an extra effort to go to graduate school that you should be compensated. Not everyone here has a master's degree.

Finally, five black women and four white women specifically mentioned race or sex discrimination as an issue in compensation. Karen Williamson, a black bank branch manager, commented, "I really believe that men make more. I think overall that whites make more." Michele Addison, a white woman attorney in the public defender's office, was concerned about her own salary and the treatment of women and black people in her office:

> I am the highest-paid person who is not a white male in the office, and I make $10,000 less than a [white] man who started two years after me. There is a large discrepancy due in part to past discrimination that has not been rectified. There was a change in the salary schedule right about the time when more blacks and women were being hired. And that is partly responsible for the disparity. And blacks and women do not stay long. There is a large turnover as a result of pay differences.

Some women, like Eleanor Hillerman, a white social worker, discussed structural problems with pay. Eleanor noted,

> There are a couple of people who have been there a year who are making the same salary [as me], and I've been here five years. We've got compression real bad.

A substantial minority, 40 percent of the sample, indicated that they were not adequately compensated in relation to their coworkers. This number suggests a rather pervasive feeling of inadequate compensation among professional-managerial women in the workforce. Clearly, though, the black women were significantly more likely to experience dissatisfaction with their pay than were their white counterparts. The black and white women in this study were the same age, worked in the same occupations and in the same industrial sectors, earned the same average wages, had the same levels of education, and came from the same class backgrounds. Yet the black women were more likely to feel overqualified and undercompensated—a perception that can reflect both greater sensitivity to inequality among black women and a greater likelihood that they were located in less remunerative sections of the same workplaces.

Promotion Opportunities   As noted in the discussions of the respondents' comments on racism and sexism in the workplace, the most common concern expressed was not about salary. Women most often spoke about restrictions on promotions and career advancement possibilities. We asked directly about this area: "Do you think your chances for promotion or advancement in your workplace truly reflect your talents or abilities?" And then we asked, "Why do you say that?"

Unlike the tendency in the other areas, white women were equally likely to express discontent with advancement opportunities as black women were. About promotions, white women expressed their highest levels of discontent. About one-half of both white women (52.6 percent) and black women (55.1 percent) felt their chances were not based on ability or talent. Both black and white women expressed similar reasons for their beliefs in the fairness or unfairness of the promotion possibilities in their workplaces—with the single exception of black women who identified racism as affecting their chances. In this light, it is interesting that none of the white women mentioned reverse race discrimination as *limiting their promotion opportunities*—even those who previously mentioned reverse racism in their workplaces.

Forty-seven percent of the white women and 44.9 percent of the black women felt their chances for promotion were fair. When asked to elaborate, the women referred to the fairness of policies, to their belief in their own abilities and talents, to statements that they had the support of their supervisors (often in the form of positive evaluations), and to the fact that they had already been promoted or advanced.

On the other hand, fifty-four black women and fifty white women did not think that their chances for promotion or advancement reflected their talents or abilities. Upon elaboration, twenty black women and seventeen white women indicated that ability was not the deciding factor; instead, whom you knew and the internal politics of the firm or agency were primary. For example, Josephine Franklin, a black public school teacher, talked about what she saw as key for advancement in her system:

> You can be the best and never get to do a supervisor's job because you're not married to the right person or you're not anybody's wife. First of all, you're not anybody's wife. They prefer settled people over single people.

Black and white women also acknowledged the need to be "in" with a small circle to gain promotions. Cassandra Adams, a black psychiatric social worker working in a private hospital, acknowledged that there were few opportunities for advancement "unless you were very familiar with the people who run the organization. You have to have a personal relationship with them. They do not tell you that, but that's the way it is."

Eight black women indicated that racism was a primary barrier to their advancement. For example, while she was clearly on a social-work career ladder and was currently the director of a unit in a hospital, Cheryl Waddell did not think she could move very far. She noted,

> I think certain individuals get typecast, and it would be very difficult for a black to move into a vice presidency [in the hospital] in my lifetime.

Her comments echo a common theme in research on women and minorities in management, which suggests that membership in a historically disadvantaged group works against individuals when supervisors, coworkers, and subordinates view such membership as incongruent with holding key management positions (Bell, Denton, and Nkomo 1993; Morrison and Von Glinow 1990).

Karen Williamson talked about the slow progress of black people involved in banking. Currently a branch manager, she spent six years as an assistant manager. She remarked,

> We [African Americans] have to be "superpeople" to get the recognition that other people get just by association. I think I had to do some super things to get this position as branch manager, and I've only been here four months. I was under the impression that I would not get promoted until I got my degree [master of business administration]. Whereas there are [white] people here in management positions and who are branch managers that do not have their degrees. They may have experience, but they do not have the degree.

Sexist practices were also explicitly referenced by one black woman and three white women. Myra Jackson, a white woman currently in management, noted the sexism in the banking industry:

> I think the banking industry has a very tight "good-ole-boy" club atmosphere that's very difficult to break into. I don't think I'd get promoted any higher

than I am at State Bank. I think I'd have to go outside the bank [for advancement].

Women and minorities often cite rigid corporate structures as reasons for relocating to other firms or starting their own businesses (Morrison and Von Glinow 1990).

Twenty-one black women and twenty-six white women in both male- and female-dominated occupations indicated that their mobility was blocked by systemic or structural obstacles. Some noted, for example, that their location in a branch office of a national firm worked to their disadvantage, since few people from the Memphis office were promoted. Others said management employed inflexible criteria, such as hours of additional education or scores on tests that determined promotions, regardless of an individual's ability to do the job.

Structural arguments also included the inability of a company to develop career tracks for employees. For example, Phyllis Tyler, a white respondent employed as a computer systems analyst, was having trouble moving up within her firm. She indicated that at her company upper-level managers failed to assess skills and consider internal advancement. Phyllis had even talked with the personnel manager about the issue. She said,

> Unfortunately, the company I work for tends to put you in a nice slot and leaves you there. They don't necessarily have a fast track or a program to keep track of the skills and abilities of the people that work for them.

Phyllis's management skills were not seen as transferable to another division of the company, so she was expected to remain in her slot.

Where structural reasons end and individual discrimination begins is sometimes hard to identify. Etta Washington, a black woman professor in a community college, said, "Promotions are given here based on longevity or number of years you have been on the job as opposed to your credentials or your performance as such." She thought the decisions had "racial overtones" because white men and women had been in the occupations longer and were therefore more likely to get promoted.

CAREER GOALS AND PLANS

Having explored their perceptions of obstacles and opportunities in the workplace, we sought to understand what the women planned to do in the future. As we have shown, the opportunity to advance is central to the thinking of professional-managerial women, and planning for one's career is expected. Assessing career plans can also reveal a sense of the behavioral consequences of the differing experiences of black and white women in the workplace as well as the way they might choose to deal differently with the same experiences. What women do when they see opportunities for advancement is quite different from what they do otherwise.

We asked, "What career goals do you currently have for yourself?" The responses confirm that this group of women had a long-term commitment to employment, and many women had advancement on their agendas (see table 10.1). Roughly equal percentages of black and white women (57 percent and 51.5 percent, respectively) were currently seeking a new job. About one-fourth of each racial group voiced an interest in securing a promotion or advancement in the same agency, firm, or company as their current career goal. Nancy Fitzgerald, a white woman who was a training specialist, gave a typical response:

> I want to be training director at forty, then at forty-five to forty-eight, I'd like to be vice president of the human resource area. At fifty-five, I want to retire and go into business for myself or go into education and do something part-time.

Some black women also voiced such sentiments. Cheryl Waddell, who was directing a social work division in a hospital, anticipated moving up in hospital or public administration. These women were more likely to see the opportunity structure as open or had already seen evidence that they were on an appropriate career track.

Eighteen percent of the black and 15.5 percent of the white women planned to change employers. A few mentioned relocating to a new city or finding a position that had greater flexibility or was more challenging. An additional 15 percent of the black women and 11.3 percent of the white women wanted to be self-employed. This response is common for women and racial minorities in management, where many desire self-employment as a reaction to negative experiences in their work settings (Morrison and Von Glinow 1990).

Some of the women were considering alternative careers, especially in the service area. Kimberly Joyner, a black woman employed as program director of a social service agency, wanted to get a master's and a doctorate and then become self-employed to consult and develop curricula in the same field.

The number of women who were interested in continuing their education or training to improve their employment prospects differed strongly by race. Even though the same number of black and white women had advanced degrees, black women were two and one-half times as likely to plan to continue their education as were white women. Such plans were common for women not only in education, teachers and counselors, but also in social services and in business.

Donna Oliver, a black woman employed as a day-care center director, was typical of many of the black women:

> Right now, I am attending Regional University, and I'm trying to get a degree in management. I'm planning on switching over to some type of business profession.

Women like Donna did not think that they could make the move to the careers they had in mind without additional educational credentials.

Three times as many white women (34 percent) as black women (12 percent) were content with their current positions. Connie Baxter, a white woman, said,

> I want to teach for twenty to twenty-five years and then retire.

Debbie Armstrong, another white respondent, was also content with her position as an administrator in a public school system:

> I'm pretty satisfied right now to stay where I am. I might have some aspirations in five years, but no immediate ones.

All these women had strong mobility aspirations and expectations. They had well-defined plans for advancement even in the face of structural obstacles. For black women, those plans more often included further education; for white women, they more often involved staying in the current job. For both, their current contexts clearly shaped their plans.

CONCLUSIONS

The women in this study had much in common. They were full-time professionals and managers who displayed a strong commitment to their careers. They shared workplaces, occupations, credentials, experience, age, industrial locations, and even class backgrounds. These many similarities form the backdrop against which to assess more clearly the ways that race shapes professional-managerial women's work experiences.

The majority of white women (56 percent) and a much greater proportion of black women (74 percent) believed that women were treated differently in their workplaces. When asked about the treatment of black people, a large majority of black women (68 percent) perceived different treatment, while about 30 percent of white women saw black people as disadvantaged in their workplaces. The vast majority of white women perceived no discrimination, in a stance that affirms the pervasive extent of a colorblind ideology, and a significant minority (about 15 percent) felt that black people were advantaged and whites disadvantaged in their workplaces. The range of perceptions of racism among white women indicates both potential obstacles for their black coworkers and the potential for white women to work in coalitions with black colleagues against racial injustice in the workplace. Only through comparative studies that document the meaning of race to white and black women can the foundation for such coalitions be assessed.

Both black and white women were far more likely to identify group rather than personal disadvantage, affirming Crosby's (1984) contention that people deny personal disadvantage even when they know it affects their group. Still, 42 percent of the black and 25 percent of the white women identified personal experiences of discriminatory treatment. When speaking of the types of discrimination they faced, whether group or individual, the women repeated common themes. Lack of opportunities for promotion, treatment based on stereotypes, and having to work harder and to "prove" themselves were most often cited, while salary differentials were less often mentioned.

Lack of opportunities for promotion and lack of fairness in the promotion process were what united the black and white women and were the areas about which they expressed their greatest discontent. Over one-half of both groups felt their promotion chances were not related to their talents or abilities. This finding is particularly significant for these women, who were in relatively early career stages (ages twenty-five to forty) and, like most professional people, had entered careers in which upward mobility is expected. Blocked mobility could become increasingly problematic as these women enter midcareer stages.

Different experiences of unfair treatment related to different career plans for black and white women. Although significant numbers of black and white women planned to leave their current jobs, black women were much more likely to be planning additional education, a process that may only partly resolve their dilemma, since the returns they receive on education are less than those for white men or women.

This study reveals that black women experience more and different forms of discriminatory treatment in the workplace than do white women as well as experiencing some of the same forms that white women face. Blocked mobility, the sense that merit does not matter, and continuous struggles against controlling images of black and white women are critical elements in the personal experience of discrimination and in shaping women's immediate career plans. Leaving their current employer and pursuing further education are individual career strategies that may obviate individuals' immediate needs but cannot alter the structure of the race-gender system that is producing the blocked opportunities for them. Collective action is critical to systemic change, and the colorblind perspective of most white women may represent the most significant deterrent to this action. Simply noting the structural similarities in black and white women's positions in relation to white men's will not itself overcome the different ways black and white women experience and interpret these barriers. Our data suggest that effective coalition building may also require increased awareness of racial discrimination among white women.

This research was supported by National Institute of Mental Health grant MH38769. We acknowledge Jean Bohner, Andreana Clay, Melissa Fry, Stephanie Messer, Claire Porter, Lauren Rauscher, Christine Robinson, Tonye Smith, and Yang Su for their assistance. We also appreciate the comments of the editor, the conference participants, and the reviewers.

NOTES

1. Subjects were defined as upwardly mobile (from a working-class background) if neither of their parents had worked in a professional or managerial occupation before the subject was thirteen years old. Subjects were defined as stable middle class if either of their parents had worked in a professional or managerial occupation before the subject was thirteen years old.

2. Within each of these cells, we selected subjects to reflect the proportions of professionals, managers, and administrators in the Memphis standard metropolitan statistical area (SMSA) (60 percent professionals and 40 percent managers and administrators in the male-dominated occupations, and 76 percent professionals and 24 percent managers and administrators in the female-dominated occupations). Within each gender composition category, we selected particular occupations for inclusion in the sample based on their proportions among professionals, managers, and administrators in the SMSA.

3. All names are pseudonyms.

4. We asked black women, ". . . because you are a black woman?" To white women we said, ". . . because you are a woman?" We used different wording to approximate more closely the ways that black and white women think about their race and gender status. As noted in our study and in the recent literature on whites and race, the most common view of race among white people is a "colorblind" view, in which the race of black people is not acknowledged as significant in everyday life and white people are viewed as not having a race. In that context, had we used the phrase "white woman," we think that many women would have thought we were asking about their experiences of "reverse discrimination," which was not our intent. Frankenberg (1993) describes a similar negative reaction when she sought subjects for her study of white women and race. Many women thought she was looking for *white racists*—since to acknowledge race from the dominant "colorblind" perspective is *to be racist*. In contrast, black women most commonly experience both their race and gender simultaneously as real and significant (see Collins 1990). So we sought not to ask black women to dissociate their race from their gender in thinking of their experiences of unfair treatment. In a few cases, black respondents did discuss incidents of discrimination and talked about whether they thought of them as based more on gender or on race, but most made no attempt to separate the two.

5. In the population at large as well as in our sample, women in male-dominated occupations (X = \$32,015) earned more than women in female-dominated occupations (X = \$23,420). However, these groups did not differ in their responses to this question, probably because the question asked respondents to compare their salaries with those of their coworkers.

REFERENCES

Baca Zinn, Maxine, Lynn Weber Cannon, Elizabeth Higginbotham, and Bonnie Thornton Dill, eds. 1986. "The Costs of Exclusionary Practices in Women's Studies." *Signs: Journal of Women in Culture in Society* 11(2): 290–303.

Bell, Ella Louise. 1990. "The Bicultural Life Experiences of Career-Oriented Black Women." *Journal of Organizational Behavior* 11(B): 459–77.

Bell, Ella Louise, Toni C. Denton, and Stella Nkomo. 1993. "Women of Color in Management: Toward an Inclusive Analysis." In *Women in Management: Trends, Issues and Challenges in Managerial Diversity*, edited by Ellen Fagenson. Newbury Park, Calif.: Sage Publications.

Braverman, Harry. 1974. *Labor and Monopoly Capital.* New York: Monthly Review Press.

Cannon, Lynn Weber, Elizabeth Higginbotham, and Marianne Leung. 1988. "Race and Class Bias in Qualitative Research on Women." *Gender & Society* 2(4): 449–62.

Collins, Patricia Hill. 1990. *Black Feminist Thought: Knowledge, Consciousness and the Politics of Empowerment.* New York: Routledge.

Crosby, Faye J. 1984. "The Denial of Personal Discrimination." *American Behavioral Scientist* 27(3): 371–86.

———. 1993. "Affirmative Action Is Worth It." *Chronicle of Higher Education*, 15 December, B1–B2.

Davis, George, and Glegg Watson. 1982. *Black Life in Corporate America.* Garden City, N.Y.: Anchor Press/Doubleday.

Denton, Toni C. 1990. "Bonding and Supportive Relationships among Black Professional Women: Rituals of Restoration." *Journal of Organizational Behavior* 11(B): 447–57.

Ehrenreich, Barbara, and John Ehrenreich. 1979. "The Professional-Managerial Class." In *Between Labor and Capital*, edited by Pat Walker. Boston: South End Press.

Feagin, Joe R., and Melvin P. Sikes. 1994. *Living with Racism: The Black Middle-Class Experience.* Boston: Beacon Press.

Federal Glass Ceiling Commission. 1995. *Good for Business: Making Full Use of the Nation's Human Capital.* Washington: U.S. Government Printing Office.

Frankenberg, Ruth. 1993. *White Women, Race Matters: The Social Construction of Whiteness.* Minneapolis: University of Minnesota Press.

Fulbright, Karen. 1986. "The Myth of the Double-Advantage: Black Female Managers." In *Slipping through the Cracks: The Status of Black Women*, edited by Margaret C. Simms and Julianne Malveaux. New Brunswick, N.J.: Transaction Press.

Higginbotham, Elizabeth. 1987. "Employment for Professional Black Women in the Twentieth Century." In *Ingredients for Women's Employment Policy*, edited by Christine E. Bose and Glenna Spitze. Albany: State University of New York Press.

———. 1994. "Black Professional Women: Job Ceilings and Employment Sectors." In *Women of Color in U.S. Society*, edited by Maxine Baca Zinn and Bonnie Thornton Dill. Philadelphia: Temple University Press.

Hochschild, Jennifer L. 1993. "Middle-Class Blacks and the Ambiguities of Success." In *Prejudice, Politics, and the American Dilemma*, edited by Paul Sniderman, Philip Tetlock, and Edward Carmines. Palo Alto, Calif.: Stanford University Press.

McGuire, Gail M., and Barbara Reskin. 1993. "Authority Hierarchies at Work: The Impact of Race and Sex." *Gender & Society* 7(4): 487–506.

Morrison, Ann M., and Mary Ann Von Glinow. 1990. "Women and Minorities in Management." *American Psychologist* 45(2): 200–8.

Nelson, Jill. 1993. *Volunteer Slavery: My Authentic Negro Experience*. Chicago: Noble Press.

Nkomo, Stella M. 1988. "Race and Sex: The Forgotten Case of the Black Female Manager." In *Women's Career: Pathways and Pitfalls*, edited by Suzanne Rose and Laurie Larwood. New York: Praeger.

Northcraft, Gregory B., and Barbara Gutek. 1993. "Point-Counterpoint: Discrimination against Women in Management—Going, Going, Gone or Going but Never Gone?" In *Women in Management: Trends, Issues and Challenges in Managerial Diversity*, edited by Ellen Fagenson. Newbury Park, Calif.: Sage Publications.

Omi, Michael, and Howard Winant. 1994. *Racial Formation in the United States: From the 1960's to the 1990's*. New York: Routledge.

Phelan, Jo. 1994. "The Paradox of the Contented Female Worker: An Assessment of Alternative Explanations." *Social Psychology Quarterly* 57(2): 95–107.

Reskin, Barbara F., and Patricia A. Roos. 1990. *Job Queues, Gender Queues: Explaining Women's Inroads into Male Occupations*. Philadelphia: Temple University Press.

Sokoloff, Natalie. 1992. *Black Women and White Women in the Professions*. New York: Routledge.

Spelman, Elizabeth V. 1988. *Inessential Women: Problems of Exclusion in Feminist Thought*. Boston: Beacon Press.

Tickamyer, Ann, Susan Scollay, Janet Bokemeier, and Teresa Wood. 1989. "Administrators' Perceptions of Affirmative Action in Higher Education." In *Affirmative Action in Perspective*, edited by Fletcher Blanchard and Faye Crosby. New York: Springer-Verlag.

U.S. Department of Commerce. U.S. Bureau of the Census. 1983. "Detailed Population Characteristics: Tennessee." In *U.S. Census of Population, 1980*. Washington, D.C.: U.S. Government Printing Office.

Vanneman, Reeve, and Lynn Weber Cannon. 1987. *The American Perception of Class*. Philadelphia: Temple University Press.

Williams, Patricia. 1991. *The Alchemy of Race and Rights*. Cambridge, Mass.: Harvard University Press.

Woody, Bette. 1992. *Black Women in the Workplace: Impact of Structural Changes in the Economy*. New York: Greenwood Press.

Part III

NEW DIRECTIONS FOR SOCIAL THEORY AND POLICY

Chapter 11

Black Women and the New World Order: Toward a Fit in the Economic Marketplace

Delores P. Aldridge

African American women and men will face both challenges and opportunities at the dawn of the twenty-first century, which will be characterized by highly developed technology in the workplace. Many jobs traditionally held by women, particularly black and poor women, will be obsolete. And those women most in need will be the poorly educated without the skills necessary for a fit, or full engagement, within a highly technological world (Aldridge 1989, 1991, 1995).

Kweli (1983) observed that:

> The struggle for equity throughout the world is becoming increasingly technological in nature. No less than the survival, growth, and development of minority and poor communities, will depend on the successful engagement of this challenge. We must have equity if we are ever to master science and technology and control our destiny. (p. 8) Planning for the engagement of black people and, specifically, black women in the United States in response to this challenge is critical to making adjustments to what Toffler (1980) describes as the "Third Wave" of human development. Society has moved turbulently from agriculture (the first wave), to industry (the second wave), to the current wave of change or the new world order, which has brought with it dramatic transformations.

> A powerful tide is surging across much of the world today, creating a different, often bizarre environment in which to work, play, raise children or retire. . . . Old ways of thinking, old formulas, dogmas, and ideologies, no matter how useful in the past, no longer fit the facts. The world that is emerging from the clash of new values and technologies, new geopolitical relationships, new lifestyles and modes of communication, demands wholly new ideas, classifications, and concepts. (Toffler 1983a, 17)

As today's society considers the transformation of everyday life, historically oppressed people face even greater challenges.

The social and economic implications of the Information Age—the third wave—for the struggle of black Americans for survival, liberation, and development are ominous. Traditional strategies that served blacks well in the old industrial age will be more difficult to use effectively in a highly technological marketplace. Toffler (1983b, 18) argues that this new phase in the global marketplace must be characterized by efforts to ensure that a "technology" gap does not widen and consume the social and economic gains made thus far or threaten U.S. democracy by irrevocably dividing the nation into the technology rich and the technology poor. For blacks in America, claims of reverse discrimination and other retrenchment efforts are increasingly blurring the debate over equity. There is a real fear that, as these gains are being stripped away, a larger and more permanent black underclass is emerging. This new underclass is young and alienated, has no education or skills, and has few prospects for fulfilling the American dream. And many members are women serving as single parents (Wilson 1987).

Science and technology have been and continue to be potent components in the structure of inequality between women and men, between social classes, between regions, and between developed and developing nations. D'Ornofrio and Pfafflin (1982) contend that the poor have always been more than mere tools used functionally by their masters. Science and technology as a body of knowledge, a methodology, or a social activity can be viewed as a basis for power and control and as central to the dynamics of the global equity crisis. Thus an educational system designed to ensure and maintain the dominance of a privileged minority, that is, white males, conditions the transmission of scientific knowledge and the expertise derived from it. The historical pattern of race relations reveals efforts to stunt black intellectual growth and discourage the emergence of "scientific personalities" (Young 1974, 7). For example, because black youth were not perceived to possess strong abstract and cognitive reasoning abilities, curricula at schools in which they were a majority failed to have strong programs in the natural sciences and technology (Malcom et al. 1977).

Spight (1987, 8) provides insight into the challenge for black people:

It appears quite clear that neither the present welfare of blacks nor the long-term viability of blacks as a people (racial-cultural group) is presently on the agenda, public or hidden, of the power elite of the Western world. Moreover, there are no institutional forms or compelling legalisms that either have in the past, are now, will in the future provide such guarantees. Indeed, if the bilge from the mouths of the Shockleys, Jensens, Hernnsteins, et al., finds its logical expression in overt action, the very existence of black folks in the world-future is at stake. The danger of a new "scientific slavery" or systematic exclusion requires an appraisal and an action plan to ensure the engagement of black women and men within the new world order. How must the "mega-trends" be approached? How shall the future of black people be shaped and developed? These questions are critical for those interested in the role—if any—black women and black men will play in the scientific-technological twenty-first century.

Madhabuti (1978, 19) admonishes black people to consider basic survival issues as they evaluate their relationship to science and technology. He queries, "Where are our doctors, farmers, engineers, futurists, microbiologists? How many of our college graduates can build a house from the ground up, supply water to dry acreage, or pipe heat into a cold building?" Predicting the end of the Cold War, he insisted, "Our new danger will not necessarily come from the white Communist, Socialist, or Capitalist revolutionist, but from our inability to understand and function at a level comparable with life in the white scientific and technological world."

BLACK WOMEN'S ENGAGEMENT IN THE SCIENTIFIC-TECHNOLOGICAL REVOLUTION

Reflection on the current status of black women in America reveals that the issues and concerns confronting them confront all black people, both in the United States and globally, in their efforts to rise effectively to the challenge of science and technology. While the focus is upon the engagement of black women in America, their challenges must not be isolated from those of their men, families, and communities. Black women cannot afford to cower beneath the dinner table of society like ravenous dogs eager to feed upon whatever scraps that happen to fall their way. They must once and for all rise from the floor and take their place among those seated at the table. To understand that engagement, the questions to ask are: What kind of education do most black women have? What kinds of occupations do they hold? What is the relationship of their education and their occupations to the new world order, which is becoming increasingly dominated by a high-technology workplace?

BLACK WOMEN IN THE TWENTIETH-CENTURY ECONOMIC MARKETPLACE

The twentieth century has been characterized by many changes for women, not the least of which has been in the labor force. The three decades between 1960 and 1990, however, witnessed many major changes in the workplace and in the composition of the workforce. Perhaps the most pronounced change was the rapid increase in the labor force participation of white women. In 1960 fewer than a third of white women worked or sought work; by 1980 more than half participated in the labor force; and in 1990 an even greater number were participants. Thus, while overall employment grew by about 48 percent, or 32 million jobs, women's employment accounted for nearly 20 million of these new jobs. Most women moved into traditionally female jobs, such as clerical and service jobs, which suggests that many occupational barriers continued to exist. The increased rate of industrial production, particularly after World War II, created a greater demand for labor. Gross private domestic product increased at an annual average rate of 2.2 percent during 1955 to 1960 but stepped up to an annual average rate of 4.8 percent during 1960 to 1965. This increased productivity required more able-bodied men and women. And, of course, other changes in the social climate led to changes in the composition of the labor market.

The Civil Rights movement and legislation on fair employment practices of the 1960s significantly facilitated the entry into different categories of employment of all groups who previously had been blocked or limited in their involvement in the labor market. Clearly, African American women constituted one of these groups and, particularly if they were educated, accrued benefits from the efforts of the movement and from legislation.

Occupational Patterns

Education is one of the important variables often cited in explaining the labor market participation of various groups, as functioning in a variety of positions requires certain levels of education. The occupational patterns of black women have changed over the past three decades. The most dramatic and important movement has been away from agriculture. In 1910 over 85 percent of black women were employed as agricultural laborers or domestics, as contrasted with about 25 percent of white women (see table 11.1). By 1980, only 10 percent of black female workers were in farm employment, and virtually none were by 1990.

Between 1910 and 1940, black women made only slight occupational progress. Although the proportion employed as agricultural laborers declined by nearly three-fourths, apparently many black women moved into domestic service, as the proportion engaged in the latter increased more than 50 percent between 1910 and 1940. The move was but a horizontal one, for the two occupations were equally low in terms of remuneration. White women made significant gains during the same time span. The proportion of white women employed as clerical and sales personnel nearly doubled, reaching one-third of the white female labor force. In addition, the already small proportion engaged in domestics decreased nearly 40 percent, in contrast to the increase among African American women.

In terms of occupational gains, the 1940s were more favorable for black women than was the period from 1910 to 1940. The proportion of black women employed in clerical and sales positions quadrupled but still made up only one-twentieth of the total black female labor force. The proportion employed as semiskilled operatives in manufacturing rose two and one-

Table 11.1 / Occupational Status of Women Fourteen Years of Age and over, by Race, 1910 to 1990 (Percent)

Occupational Category	1910 Black	1910 White	1940 Black	1940 White	1950 Black	1950 White	1960 Black	1960 White	1970 Black	1970 White	1980 Black	1980 White	1990 Black	1990 White
Professional and technical	1.5	11.6	4.3	14.7	5.3	13.3	7.7	14.1	10.0	15.5	13.2	16.9	14.8	19.1
Managers, officials, and proprietors (except farm)	0.2	1.5	0.7	4.3	1.3	4.7	1.1	4.2	1.4	4.7	2.9	7.6	7.5	11.6
Clerical and sales	0.3	17.5	1.3	32.8	5.4	39.3	9.8	43.2	21.4	43.4	33.1	42.3	39.1	45.3
Craftsmen and foremen	2.0	8.2	0.2	1.1	0.7	1.7	0.7	1.4	0.8	1.1	1.2	1.8	2.3	2.1
Operatives	1.4	21.2	6.2	20.3	15.2	21.5	14.3	17.6	16.8	14.5	12.9	10.6	9.1	5.5
Nonfarm laborers	0.9	1.5	0.8	0.9	1.6	0.7	1.2	0.5	0.9	0.4	1.2	1.2	3.1	2.3
Private household workers	38.5	17.2	59.9	10.9	42.0	4.3	38.1	4.4	19.5	3.7	7.5	1.7	3.1	1.2
Service workers (except private household)	3.2	9.2	11.1	12.7	19.1	11.6	23.0	13.1	28.5	15.1	26.8	16.7	24.2	15.2
Farmers and farm managers	4.0	3.1	3.0	1.1	1.7	0.6	0.6	0.5	0.2	0.3	0.1	0.2	} 0.3	
Farm laborers and foremen	48.0	9.0	12.9	1.2	7.7	2.3	3.5	1.0	0.3	1.3	0.2	1.1		1.1

Sources: Data for 1910 are from U.S. Department of Commerce (1953, table 14); data for 1940 are from U.S. Department of Commerce (1953, table 52); data for 1950 are from U.S. Department of Commerce (1953, table 3); data for 1960 are from U.S. Department of Commerce (1963, table 3); data for 1970 are from U.S. Department of Commerce (1971, 1972); data for 1980 are from U.S. Bureau of Labor Statistics (1981); data for 1990 are from U.S. Department of Labor (1991, 184).

half times, while the percentage engaged in domestic work declined by 30 percent.

Most of the relative gain in the occupational status of African American women during the 1940s occurred during wartime, when severe labor shortages made it expedient for employers to reduce racial restrictions in hiring. The greatest gain in employment opportunities came in skilled and semiskilled manufacturing jobs, which few African American women had held prior to World War II. The largest increase was in the metals, chemicals, and rubber industries. Less than 3,000 African American women were employed in these industries in 1940, but less than five years later fifty times as many were employed (U.S. Department of Labor 1943, 18).

From 1950 to 1970, black women made appreciable gains in occupational distribution. Proportionately, by 1970 nearly four times as many black women were employed as clerical and sales workers as had been in 1950. The percentage of black professional women doubled, while the relative number of domestics declined by more than 50 percent. Nevertheless, the number of professional black women was still small compared with the number of white women and white men. Black women, unlike white women, were not primarily in white-collar occupations. Too many black women (19.5 percent) were still cleaning white women's houses. Much of whatever gains black women made could be attributed to the relatively high level of economic activity in the postwar period, to militant Civil Rights efforts, and to subsequent government legislation in the 1960s.

By 1980, nearly half of all black women who were employed worked in white-collar positions; approximately 15 percent held blue-collar jobs, and over one-third were still in service work, the majority in private households. But whereas in 1960 one in four black women workers was employed in a private household, in 1980 this was true for only about one in thirteen. More than a movement of a given set of women among occupations, this shift reflects a change in the composition of the labor force. As Aldridge (1989) explains, black women do not move up the occupational ladder at the same rate as their white counterparts do, and much of the "progress" over time in occupations reflects changes in labor force composition more than the advancement of the black women who remain in the labor force. Older women retired, and younger women entered the job market, filling clerical positions—jobs that relatively few older women held.

The Role of Education

Education plays a significant role in black women's employment, even though increased levels of education have not been accompanied by commensurate increases in the number of black women in top-level occupa-

Table 11.2 / Workers in Various Occupations, by Sex and Race or Ethnicity, 1993 (Percent)

Occupation	Whites		African American		Hispanic	
	Males	Females	Male	Females	Males	Females
Executive, administrative and managerial	17	14	8	10	7	8
Professional specialty	14	19	7	13	6	9
Technical, sales, and administrative support	20	42	18	36	15	38
Service	8	15	18	27	15	24
Precision production, craft, and repair	20	2	15	2	22	3
Operators, fabricators, and laborers	17	7	31	12	27	16
Farming, forestry, and fishing	4	1	3	0	8	2

Source: Kominski and Adams (1994, table 7).
Note: Data are for people aged twenty-five to sixty-four.

tions (see table 11.2). While the general measure of high school education is significant in relation to the workforce, there is little question that higher education is an important determinant of women's participation in more lucrative employment (Blitz 1974, 34; see table 11.3). Thus black women's educational gains in part account for their growing access to better positions in the labor market. Importantly, however, the majority of professional black women workers were employed as teachers and social service workers and not in communications or other highly technical fields.

Black Women and Technology

Black women's educational attainment, though steadily improving in terms of high school, college, and advanced degrees (see tables 11.4 and 11.5), has not resulted in significant numbers of women in the natural sciences, communications, communications technologies, computer science, engineering, or other technologies associated with the new world order and the fastest-growing occupations (see table 11.6).

The majority of black women have not worked in in high-technology fields. In the most prestigious occupational category (labeled "executive, administrative, and managerial" in table 11.2) are the people making deci-

Table 11.3 / Workers in Various Occupations Who Have College Degrees, by Sex, 1993 (Percent)

Occupation	College Degree	
	Males	Females
Executive, administrative, and managerial	55	39
Professional specialty	79	72
Technical, sales, and administrative support	33	16
Service	11	6
Precision production, craft and repair	6	9
Operators, fabricators, and laborers	4	4
Farming, forestry, and fishing	9	11

Source: Kominski and Adams (1994, table 7).
Note: Data are for people aged twenty-five to sixty-four.

sions in organizations—business executives and top-level bureaucrats. In the United States in 1993, 17 percent of white males fell into this category, followed by 14 percent of white females, 10 percent of African American females, 8 percent of African American males, 8 percent of Hispanic females, and 7 percent of Hispanic males. Just below that level are the "professional specialties," including physicians, nurses, lawyers, college professors and other teachers, engineers, and similar occupations. Once again, whites (both females and males) are more likely than blacks or Hispanics to be in these occupational categories. Furthermore, except for Hispanic females, black women are the least likely of all race-gender groups to work as engineers and college professors in the sciences.

Technical, sales, and administrative support occupations include an impressive number of black women. But the classic technician is a dental hygienist. The professions included in the sales part of this category are self-explanatory, and any consideration of administrative support occupations must recognize that mechanization and computerization have changed the nature of the long-used term "clerk." Secretaries, word processors, file clerks, bank tellers, and similar workers fall into this group. Women, especially black and Hispanic women, are far more likely than men are to be in these occupations and to work in the services category—waitresses and other food handlers, laundry workers, housekeepers, and so forth. These professions were among the fastest declining between 1984 and 1995, whereas the occupations that grew the fastest during that period employ relatively few women (table 11.6).

Thus the overwhelming majority of black women are not employed in high-technology fields. And, as Kweli (1983, 6) points out, computers and

Table 11.4 / Doctorates Conferred by Institutions of Higher Education, by Racial or Ethnic Group and Major Field, 1992 to 1993

Field	White	Black	Hispanic	Total
All	28,700	1,352	827	42,021
Agriculture and natural resources	564	13	20	1,173
Architecture and related programs	61	11	5	168
Area, ethnic, and cultural studies	114	11	5	178
Biological sciences/life sciences	2,810	63	84	4,435
Business management and administration services	815	29	10	1,346
Communications	196	21	8	293
Communications technologies	5	0	0	8
Computer and information sciences	383	6	7	805
Education	5,497	562	185	7,030
Engineering	2,210	42	51	5,823
Engineering-related technologies	9	1	1	20
English language & literature/letters	1,091	32	22	1,341
Foreign languages and literatures	468	8	65	830
Health professions & related sciences	1,205	66	26	1,767
Home & vocational home economics	255	16	6	345
Law and legal studies	11	1	0	86
Liberal arts and sciences, general studies and humanities	65	9	1	81
Library science	46	6	2	77
Mathematics	484	6	8	1,189
Multi/interdisciplinary studies	140	1	4	196
Parks, recreation, leisure & fitness studies	77	3	0	106
Philosophy and religion	340	17	5	448
Physical sciences & science technologies	2,405	37	68	4,393
Precision production trades	0	0	0	0
Protective services	22	2	0	32
Psychology	3,125	134	125	3,651
Public administration & services	318	47	9	459
R.O.T.C. and military technologies	0	0	0	0
Social sciences and history	2,201	91	85	3,460
Theological and material moving	1,065	102	12	1,417
Transportation and material moving	0	0	0	0
Visual and performing arts	695	23	16	882

Source: U.S. Department of Education, 1995.

Table 11.5 / Doctorates Conferred by Institutions of Higher Education, by Race or Ethnicity and Sex of Student, 1976 to 1977 Through 1992 to 1993, Various Years

Year and Sex	All Groups	Race or Ethnicity		
		White	Black	Hispanic
1976 to 1977				
Men and women	33,126	26,851	1,253	522
Percent	100	81.1	3.88	1.6
Women	8,090	6,819	487	139
Percent	24.4	25.4	38.9	26.6
1980 to 1981				
Men and women	32,839	25,908	1,265	456
Percent	100	78.9	3.8	1.5
Women	10,244	8,598	571	179
Percent	31.2	33.2	45.1	39.3
1986 to 1987				
Men and women	34,041	24,434	1,057	751
Percent	100	71.8	3.1	2.2
Women	11,980	9,522	572	310
Percent	35.2	39.0	54.1	41.3
1989 to 1990				
Men and women	38,113	25,880	1,153	788
Percent	100	67.9	3.0	2.1
Women	13,865	10,775	620	365
Percent	36.4	41.6	53.8	46.3
1991 to 1992				
Men and women	40,090	25,813	1,223	811
Percent	100	64.4	3.1	2.0
Women	14,922	11,139	647	353
Percent	37.2	43.2	52.9	43.5
1992 to 1993				
Men and women	42,021	26,700	1,352	827
Percent	100	63.5	3.2	2.0
Women	16,041	11,798	737	388
Percent	38.2	44.2	54.5	46.9

Source: U.S. Department of Education (1995).

Table 11.6 / Fastest-Declining and Fastest-Growing Occupations, 1984 to 1995

	Employment (Thousands)		
Occupation	1984	1995	Change (%)
Fastest-declining			
Stenographer	239	89	−63
Textile/sewing machine operator	955	607	−36
Farm worker	1079	797	−26
Private household worker	993	821	−17
Postal service clerk	317	301	−5
Fastest-growing			
Computer systems analyst	308	933	67
Correction officer and jailer	130	310	58
Medical assistant	128	206	38
Lawyer	490	894	45
Computer programmer	341	553	38
Registered nurse	1377	1977	30
Mechanical engineer	237	330	28
College and university faculty	731	823	11
Accountants and auditor	882	962	8
Computer operator, excluding peripheral	241	259	7

Sources: Data for 1984 are from U.S. Department of Commerce (1985); data for 1995 are from U.S. Department of Commerce (1996).

telecommunications are the key to these fields. He observes that telecommunications is the synthesizing technology for all of the information and transport technologies. Consequently, it represents a strategic industry for facilitating technological and social progress. Telecommunications will be the electronic highway over which the nation's new education, health care information, job-training, and financial management systems pass.

Freire (1983), in his revolutionary approach to "critical consciousness," finds that individuals can know (and subsequently do) to the extent that they problematize the natural, cultural, and historical reality in which they are immersed. He insists that "if men (women) are unable to perceive critically the themes of their times, and thus to intervene actively in reality, they are carried along in the wake of change. . . . They are submersed in that change and so cannot discern its dramatic significance" (Freire 1983, 7). For black women and men to intervene in the reality of the scientific-technological revolution, they will have to nurture this "critical consciousness" as well as actions or behaviors that will ensure their engagement in the new world order.

CURRENT THEORETICAL PERSPECTIVES

Three prevalent theoretical perspectives that are used to explain why more black people, particularly males, are not in upper-level jobs and educational programs that will be needed in the twenty-first century have centered around discrimination, lack of skills, lack of opportunities as a result of industrial restructuring, or disarticulation—a breakdown in the social processes or networks linking individuals to jobs and other mainstream institutions (Braddock and McPartland 1987; Bluestone, Stevenson, and Tilly 1992; Bound and Freeman 1992; Murray 1984; Peterson and Vroman 1992; Wilson 1987). These traditional labor market perspectives have been applied to the occupational participation of males and, therefore, they do not necessarily address the realities of the lives of black women because they look only at slices of black men's realities. Individuals, male or female, enter into areas of the job market that are receptive to them. Other theorists, such as Afrocentrics and feminists, have also sought to provide approaches to understanding phenomena relating to black life and women.

Afrocentrism

As a theoretical field, Afrocentrism, also known in some quarters as Africentrism, is not a new field, nor is it foreign to much of the significant work being done in the social sciences or cultural communications (Karenga 1988; Asante 1987). My own theoretical understanding of African-centered theory and its relationship to occupational participation and black women is made clear only in the context of the general field of Afrocentric theory. Leading proponents of Afrocentric intellectual ideas are Asante (1987, 1988) and Karenga (1980, 1988). Afrocentrism argues that the hegemonic Eurocentric epistemology, which sets the ideological foundation of U.S. society, needs to shift dramatically. However, Afrocentrists tend to reduce the issue of Eurocentric epistemological hegemony to one of racial biological determinism and ethnic bias, while ignoring economic and social structural analysis of the dynamics of domination.

African-centered research makes no grandiose claims of objectivity, though the African-centered researcher should maintain a critical stance and a commitment to accuracy. By consciously positioning or identifying themselves as such, African-centered researchers participate in the political and counter-hegemonic act of refusing to attempt to fit into the detached, empirically bound mode of the "traditional" (Eurocentric) researcher. African-centered research is not only research on or about black people, it is research for black people in the interest of black people's liberation.

In his theoretical perspective, Asante (1987) attempts to place the experiences and ideas of descendants of African peoples at the center of the discourse. Afrocentricity is a frame of reference wherein phenomena are viewed from the perspective of the African person.

A major weakness of Afrocentricity is that it limits its social critique to the role of white supremacist racism and to abstracting and dehistoricizing culture in its relationship to politics and power. Afrocentricity for the most part implicitly accepts the legitimacy of static, positivist epistemology. In its refusal to deepen the critique of existing capitalist social structure and capitalism's relationship to oppression and exploitation, Afrocentricity implicitly accepts the legitimacy of the politics of domination outside of the racial paradigm and fails to examine the relationship of other forms of oppression, such as sexism, heterosexism, and ecological destruction, to racism.

Feminism

Unlike Afrocentric theorists, feminist theorists have strongly contended that gender has held back women even though more attention is given to class and race. Feminism places women at the center of the discourse, attributing much of the inequity in the labor market to gender discrimination.

The agenda of feminism, a term conceptualized and adopted by white women initially, was designed to meet the needs and demands of white women and has their interests at the center. Feminism has become an established theoretical concept based on the notion that gender is primary in women's struggle in the patriarchal system. This prioritizing of female empowerment and gender issues may be justifiable for women who have not been plagued by powerlessness based on ethnic differences; however, that stance is questionable in the case of black women. The clear need for a distinct interpretation of the experiences of black women led Hudson-Weems to publish *Africana Womanism* (1993).[1]

In her article on feminism, Steady (1987, 3) contended that

> Various schools of thought, perspectives, and ideological proclivities have influenced the study of feminism. Few studies have dealt with the issue of racism, since the dominant voice of the feminist movement has been that of the white female. The issue of racism can become threatening, for it identifies white feminists as possible participants in the oppression of blacks.

At the heart of feminism is the battle of the white woman against her white male counterpart for subjugating her as his property. This struggle does not hold for black women, for black men have never had the same institutionalized power to oppress black women as white men have had to oppress white women (Ladner 1972).

Neither the Afrocentrists nor the feminists have adequately addressed the engagement of black women in the labor market. Each misses the essence of black women's struggle because it involves neither *simply* race nor *simply* gender but a combination of both, overlain and complicated by other "isms." Or, stated differently, black women are generally not at the center of studies focusing on blacks or on women but rather are viewed as a basis for comparison.

To understand and promote the engagement of black women in the labor market requires a rethinking of the traditional labor market paradigms, as well as those of the Afrocentrists and feminists. Hudson-Weems (1993), with her Africana Womanism, points in this direction as she centers women of African descent in their own experiences.

TOWARD A CRITICAL HEAL MODEL FOR BLACK WOMEN'S ENGAGEMENT IN THE LABOR MARKET

Any model that is designed to understand and promote the engagement of black women in the new world order must reflect the diversity of black women's historical-cultural experiences and provide an action plan. Such a model must (1) be centered in the historical-cultural experiences of black people yet meet the needs of the highly scientific and technological world of the twenty-first century; (2) focus on educational and employment equity issues at every level to maximize the potential of blacks in general— and black women specifically—in the scientific-technological professions by increasing their numbers in these areas; and (3) be action oriented so as to transform institutions and values both within and outside the black community that impede the promotion of science and technology with and for black people. In other words, a model should be African centered and have components that account for *h*istorical-cultural experiences, *e*quity, and *a*ction for the *l*abor market (HEAL).

Historical-Cultural Component

The introduction of Western science and technology dealt a serious blow to many of the traditional African economic and social institutions that provided prestige, support, and a livelihood for black women. These institutions, dismantled and destroyed through cultural imperialism, have not been replaced with sufficient outlets for providing equal access to the resources of scientific-technological development.

Steady (1981, 8–36), in her cross-cultural analysis of black women, highlights recurring or "unifying themes" that appear to be of critical importance in the lives of the majority of black women. All of these themes recognize that black women have gone into positions in the labor market that have been receptive to them. The themes are grounded in African heritage; economic exploitation and marginalization; negative imagery; a different perspective on male-female relationships; and self-reliance and the creation of survival imperatives. These themes are one link in the chain to under-standing black women's lives and their past, present, and future engage-ment in the workplace, particular societies, and the global context.

African Heritage, Economic Exploitation, and Marginalization Steady (1981) finds that these unifying themes have been interwoven throughout the historical-cultural experiences of black women internationally. For ex-ample, she observes that the development of Western civilizations has vic-timized black women in the diaspora through slavery; colonialism; new colonialism in Africa, the Caribbean, and South America; and the "internal colonialism" of the United States. The black woman from Africa became a key factor in the production of capital because of her capacity to produce slave labor:

> The manipulation of the fertility of black women is a good indicator of her exploitation. During slavery her fertility was highly valued. . . . Today the reverse is the case. Slave labor is no longer needed to produce wealth. . . . The fertility of the black woman, though still necessary to produce cheap labor, is increasingly viewed as unprofitable and from a racist point of view as threat-ening. (9)

Imagery and Black Women Exploitation and marginalization are intri-cately related to imagery—how women are perceived by others and how women perceive themselves. No single factor has any greater impact on the development of any group than the images that members hold of them-selves. Men and women respond not to a situation itself but to the "image situation": the situation as transformed by the images they carry in their minds. The image sees, the image feels, and the image acts, and for a situa-tion to change, the images men and women have of themselves must change (Bennett 1976).

If imagery is so powerful, then the engagement of black women in a new world order dominated by technology is tied to the image they have of themselves and their situation. How have black women both perceived themselves and been perceived within American society and globally? How have black women perceived the emergence of science and technol-ogy and their relationship to its dominance in the workplace? How have they been included or excluded from development processes, and what have been the consequences of the processes?

Within a given society, different perceptions and contradictory expecta-tions must be resolved. Women may have different perceptions of develop-ment than men in the same society do. Very little has been done to clarify the implications of these different perceptions. Conceivably, males and fe-males, having differing access to the new options, could give different meaning and value to them (Nelson 1981, 2).

These perceptions carry new meaning for the historical and cultural experiences of black women. Issues and concerns that are crucial to the analysis of women and development processes include dynamic factors, such as women's status and roles, their sexuality and fertility, historical rationalizations for women's status and inequality, the impact of political participation, sex-based stereotypes, and differences in educational opportunities (Tinker, Braasen, and Buvinio 1976, 224–44). Implicit in such an analysis is the need for an understanding of how social relations change and are changed by development processes.

Further, Steady (1981) explains how the projection of negative stereotypes through the literature, media, and societal practices has helped to limit women's choices throughout history. The most common stereotypes of black women are the "mammy," " the matriarch," the "tragic mulatto," and the "sensitive whore." These images, coupled with the severe lack of role models in scientific and technological professions, illustrate the historical potency of negative imagery in limiting the potential of black women in the United States and globally. The imagery is also very much a part of black women's relationships with males both in and outside their own racial group.

A Different Perspective on Male-Female Relationships Historical experiences and the role of imagery are critical to understanding the black female perspective on male-female relationships (Aldridge 1991). Clearly, images of real and idealized women abound, and male chauvinists come in all colors and societies. Thus within the context of most countries the choice and introduction of a technology aggravates the existing disparities between women and men. Changes in technology that accompany so-called modernization have for the most part led to a female concentration in domestic and service-related roles. Men seem universally to assume women's work when production changes from a subsistence to a production economy. Another universal trend appears to be that once a working operation becomes mechanized, it becomes a male domain. For women, this change results in a loss of control over the means of production and economic resources and reduces the women's ability to feed and care for their families (D'Ornofrio and Pfafflin 1982, 20). For black women, however, the issue of control over production is not the same as it is for white women, for it is not black men who control production in the United States.

Examining the historical inequities of the definition of women's work in the context of the continued survival of black families and communities shows that the antagonistic feminism of the women's movement is not realistic for black women. The struggles of black women cannot be isolated from the destinies of their families and communities. In the debate over women's rights, black women do not perceive their enemy to be the black man but rather the oppressive forces in the larger society that subjugate black women, men, and children (Ladner 1972, 49).

Self-Reliance and the Creation of Survival Imperatives   The politics of equity in the twenty-first century mandates increased political participation for black women if they are to survive and be fully engaged within a highly technological and scientific world. In 1985, the United Nations Decade for Women encouraged nations to distribute the benefits of scientific and technological development equitably to women and men. In doing so, it emphasized the importance of the contribution of women to the well-being and wealth of their families and societies. It advocated the participation of women in making decisions related to science and technology, including planning and setting priorities for research and development in the choice, acquisition, adaptation, innovation, and application of science and technology for development. And it also called for equal access for women and men to scientific and technological training and to the corresponding professional careers (U.N. Decade of Women 1985).

This overview of the historical-cultural experiences of black women, with emphasis on survival and development, serves as a point of departure for examining the facets of one component of the proposed model for promoting the engagement of black women in the new world order. This component seeks to demonstrate that the experiences, needs, the potentials, the survival skills and imperatives of black women require consideration.

Equity in Education and Employment

The equity component of the model is crucial because it is through educational and employment opportunities that people gain access to science and technology. Historically, improved education for black women has been linked to greater occupational access. Forces that led to the expansion or retrenchment of educational opportunity must figure into any analysis of black women in the labor market. In recent years within the United States, there has been a retrenchment of civil rights as a means for achieving equity. Progress has waned, and if efforts are not upgraded, equity will become even more elusive for black youth. McKenzie (1991) perceptively suggests strategies for transforming the nation's educational ills. If the nation is in crisis, what is the plight of black people in this scenario, and how do they respond more effectively to it? Spight (1987, 8) poses some serious questions about the relationship of blacks to the dynamics of science and technology :

1. To what extent do blacks currently possess scientific and technological expertise?

2. What current roles define their use of that expertise?

3. What alternative institutional forms exist in the black community for the expression of that expertise, and to what extent can and are they facilitating the mastery process?

4. What progressive new trends can be identified as being relevant to the development of institutional, scientific, and technological forums?

5. What aspects of Western science and technology militate its use in the struggle of blacks and thus require transcendence?

6. What would define this transcendent "Black Science" and its technological implications?

7. What is the current role and responsibility of black scientists and technologists?

These questions underscore the relevance of understanding the social and cultural dynamics necessary for nurture of "scientific personalities" among black youth. How do black scientists reach their goals? What motivates them? Which sociocultural dynamics of the black community are not conducive to the development of black scientists and technologists? The foregoing discourse suggests the need for action in order to enhance the potential of youth in the areas of science and technology.

Action Orientation

Malcom and colleagues (1977), McKenzie (1991) and Miller (1991) suggest ways to facilitate change in the pattern of representation of minorities in science and technology. Their focus is knowledge, resources, and mentors that motivate students and expose them to science and to high-technology opportunities, taking into consideration their experiences and the disparities in equity. But perhaps more important is for blacks and other minorities to take charge of their own destinies rather than wait to be empowered or engaged. Then they can keep their communities informed about scientific and technological issues that affect them, and decision makers will hear their voices and respond appropriately. With self-direction, blacks could devise strategies that incorporate particular sensitivity to black women at the center. Through these strategies, they would

Spread knowledge about different historical experiences, cultural values, and styles. This includes wide dissemination of information about the contributions of blacks to science and invention on college campuses and in the population as a whole. Minorities and whites (both women and men) need to hear the success stories of black women and men.

Tutor, counsel, and serve as role models for students throughout their educational careers from kindergarten through graduate school.

Identify the barriers to recruitment and retention of black women in science and technology and improve the counseling system to alert students of potential careers and capabilities and of job opportunities available in the sciences and high technology.

Give both female and male children positive exposure to quantitative careers at early ages and emphasize the development of good mathematical, reading, and communication skills early in their training.

Expand financial support for science research and training for students at both minority and majority institutions.

Encourage and expand special training programs for students who are interested in careers in science and technology,

Expand science-related, work-study, and undergraduate research experiences in the physical sciences and engineering.

Recruit more students for medical, graduate, and professional schools. Recruitment should pay adequate attention to assessing students' potential for graduate or professional school.

While crucial strategies for ensuring equity are grounded in historical-cultural experiences, the third component of the model—action orientation—completes it. As global changes continue, research should provide direction for action so as to ensure the social and economic well-being of black women and black people; recognize the growing interdependence of nations; and point the way toward strategies and programs that will insert black development interests and agendas into the national and international debate over U.S. reindustrialization, technological change, and development. Any action component of a model that is centered in the experiences of black women must also seek to educate black elected officials and other policy makers about policy choices that benefit and hinder them and their men, whose destinies are intertwined.

Finally, an action component must deal with values of black women and black people as well as those of white power brokers. Black reeducation and redevelopment are dependent upon new thoughts, values, and actions. The values must be livable, workable, and above all make sense while addressing the issues of the real world. The community must take hold of its individuals, giving them a sense of direction that ensures their progress and the respect of others.

SUMMARY

Many researchers of black women have successfully documented their status in the labor market, including their less-than-enviable relationship to white women. Many of the observations resulting from research over time lead one to believe that black women differ less from white women in their labor market participation and more in why and how they participate. Thus, to provide statistics that focus upon participation or lack of participation in the job market without also providing explanations of and action plans for altering inequity is of little value for ensuring black women's survival and full engagement in the labor market of the twenty-first century. Black women's historical-cultural imperatives have differed markedly from those of other groups, and any attempt to study black women must acknowledge these differences.

Understanding the historical-cultural experiences facilitates an examination of why black women have had difficulty achieving educational and occupational equity. The issue of equity in education and employment is an essential component of any model designed to ensure the engagement of black women and black people in the new world order. Education and employment are so interrelated that any model that does not consider the two will fail to capture vital components necessary for informing research and action for black women.

In sum, an African-centered (HEAL) model as presented here provides an alternative model for ensuring the engagement of black women in the new world order driven by science and technology. The livelihood and well-being of black women and their families and communities will to a great extent depend upon a model that shows an understanding of today's realities and thus is viable in the twenty-first century.

I thank Sharon Brown Bailey for her invaluable input in the development of an earlier draft of this work.

NOTE

1. According to Hudson-Weems (1993), Africana Womanism is neither an outgrowth of nor an addendum to mainstream feminism but rather a concept grounded in the culture and focused on the experiences, needs, and desires of Africana women. African womanists and feminists have separate agendas. Feminism is female centered; Africana Womanism is family centered. Feminism is concerned primarily with eliminating sexism from society; Africana Womanism is concerned with ridding society of racism first, then classism and sexism. Many feminists say their number-one enemy is the male; Africana womanists welcome and encourage male participation in their struggle. Feminism, Hudson-Weems says, is incompatible with Africana women, as it was designed to meet the needs of white women. In fact, the history of feminism reveals a blatant racism. For example, in reaction to the ratification of the Fifteenth Amendment to the Constitution in 1870, which granted Africana men voting rights, suffragist leader Carrie Chapman Catt asserted that middle-class white men recognize "the usefulness of woman suffrage as a counter-balance to the foreign vote, and as a means of legally preserving white supremacy in the South."

REFERENCES

Aldridge, Delores P. 1989. "Black Women in the Economic Marketplace: Continuing Struggle." *Journal of Black Studies* 20(2): 129–54.

———. 1991. *Focusing: Black Male-Female Relationships.* Chicago: Third World Press.

———. 1995. "Diversity in Higher Education and the Role of Historically Black Colleges and Universities." *Challenge* 6(2): 41–50.

Asante, Molefi K. 1987. *The Afrocentric Idea.* Philadelphia: Temple University Press.

———. 1988. *Afrocentricity.* Trenton, N.J.: Africa World Press.

Bennett, Lerone, Jr. 1976. *The Challenge of Blackness.* Chicago: Johnson.

Blitz, Rudolph C. 1974. "Women in the Professions, 1870–1970." *Monthly Labor Review* 97(5): 34–39.

Bluestone, Barry, Mary H. Stevenson, and Chris Tilly. 1992. "An Assessment of the Impact of 'Deindustrialization' and Spatial Mismatch on the Labor Market Outcomes of Young White, Black, and Latino Men and Women Who Have Limited Schooling." Working paper. Boston: University of Massachusetts, John W. McCormack Institute of Public Affairs.

Bound, John, and Richard Freeman. 1992. "What Went Wrong? The Erosion of Relative Earnings and Employment among Young Black Men in the 1980s." *Quarterly Journal of Economics* 107(1): 201–32.

Braddock, JoMills H., and James M. McPartland. 1987. "How Minorities Continue to Be Excluded from Equal Employment Opportunities: Research on Labor Market and Institutional Barriers." *Journal of Social Issues* 43(1): 5–39.

D'Ornofrio, Flores, and Sheila M. Pfafflin. 1982. *Scientific-Technological Change and the Role of Women in Development.* Boulder, Colo.: Westview Press.

Freire, Paolo. 1983. *Education for Critical Consciousness.* New York: Continuum Press.

Hudson-Weems, Clinora. 1993. *Africana Womanism: Reclaiming Ourselves.* Troy, Mich.: Bedford.

Karenga, Maulana. 1980. *Kawaida Theory: An Introductory Outline.* Inglewood, Calif.: Kawaida Publications.

———. 1988. "Black Studies and the Problematic of Paradigm: The Philosophical Dimension." *Journal of Black Studies* 18(4): 395–414.

Kominski, Robert, and Arthur Adams. 1994. "Educational Attainment in the United States: March 1993 and 1992." *Current Population Reports,* series P20, no. 476. Washington, D.C.: U.S. Government Printing Office for U.S. Bureau of the Census.

Kweli, Kujaatele. 1983. "The Information Age: Promise or Nightmare?" *Urban League Review* 1(1): 8.

Ladner, Joyce. 1972. *Tomorrows' Tomorrow: The Black Woman.* New York: Doubleday.

Madhabuti, Haki. 1978. *Enemies: Clash of the Races.* Chicago: Third World Press.

Malcom, Shirley M., Wayne Fortunato-Schwand, Franklin D. Hamilton, and Vijaya L. Melnick. 1977. "Science Education for Minorities: A Bibliography, Preliminary Report and Summary." In Vijaya L. Melnick and Franklin D. Hamilton, *Minorities in Science: The Challenge for Biomedicine.* New York: Plenum Press.

McKenzie, Floretta D. 1991. "Education Strategies for the '90s." In *The State of Black America 1991.* Washington, D.C.: National Urban League.

Miller, Warren F. 1991. "Developing Untapped Talent: A National Call for African American Technologists." In *The State of Black America 1991*. Washington, D.C.: National Urban League.

Murray, Charles. 1984. *Losing Ground: American Social Policy, 1950–1980*. New York: Basic Books.

Nelson, Nici, ed. 1981. *African Women and Development*. London: Frank Cass.

Peterson, George E., and Wayne Vroman. 1992. "Urban Labor Markets and Economic Opportunities." In *Urban Labor Markets and Job Opportunities*, edited by George E. Peterson and Wayne Vroman. Washington, D.C.: Urban Institute Press.

Spight, Carl. 1987. "Towards Black Science and Technology." *Black Books Bulletin* 5(3): 5–18.

Steady, Filomina Chioma. 1981. *The Black Woman Cross-Culturally*. Cambridge, Mass.: Schenkman Publishing.

———. 1987. "Africana Feminism: A Worldwide Perspective." In *Women in Africa and the African Diaspora*, edited by Rosalyn Terborg-Penn, Sharon Harley, and Andrea Benton Rushing. Washington, D.C.: Howard University Press.

Tinker, Irene, Michele Braasen, and Mayra Buvinio, eds. 1976. *Women and World Development*. New York: Praeger.

Toffler, Alvin. 1983. *The Third Wave*. New York: William Morrow.

———. 1983. "Civil Rights in the Third Wave." *Urban League Review* 8(1): 18.

United Nations Decade for Women. 1985. *Conference Proceedings: Women and Science and Technology*. New York: The United Nations.

U.S. Department of Commerce. U.S. Bureau of the Census.1953a. *1940 Census of Population*. Vol. 3, *The Labor Force*. Washington, D.C.: U.S. Government Printing Office.

———. 1953b. *1950 Census of Population: Occupational Characteristics*. Washington, D.C.: U.S. Government Printing Office.

———. 1963. *1960 Census of Population: Occupational Characteristics*. Washington, D.C.: U.S. Government Printing Office.

———. 1971. *Social and Economic Characteristics of the Population in Metropolitan and Nonmetropolitan Areas: 1970 and 1960 Current Population Reports*. Washington, D.C.: U.S. Government Printing Office.

———. 1972. "The Social and Economic Status of the Black Population in the United States: 1972." *Current Population Reports*, series P-23, no. 46. Washington, D.C.: U.S. Government Printing Office.

———. 1977. "Handbook of Statistics." *Current Population Reports*, series P-60, no. 132. Washington, D.C.: U.S. Government Printing Office.

———. 1985. *Monthly Labor Review*. Washington: U.S. Government Printing Office (November).

———. 1993. *1940 Census of Population: Comparative Occupation Statistics for the United States 1870–1940*. Washington: U.S. Government Printing Office.

———. 1996. *Statistical Abstract of the United States, 1996*. Washington: U.S. Government Printing Office.

U.S. Department of Education. National Center for Educational Statistics. 1995. *Integrated Postsecondary Education Data System Completion Survey*. Washington: U.S. Government Printing Office.

U.S. Department of Labor. U.S. Bureau of Labor Statistics. 1981. *Employment and Earnings*. Washington: U.S. Government Printing Office (January).

———. 1991. *Employment and Earnings.* Washington: U.S. Government Printing Office (January).

U.S. Department of Labor. U.S. Women's Bureau. 1943. *Handbook of Facts on Women Workers.* Washington: U.S. Government Printing Office.

Wilson, William Julius. 1987. *The Truly Disadvantaged: The Inner City, the Underclass, and Public Policy.* Chicago: University of Chicago Press.

Young, Herman. 1974. *Scientists in Black Perspective.* Louisville, Ky.: Lincoln Foundation.

Chapter 12

Now You See 'Em, Now You Don't: Race, Ethnicity, and Gender in Labor Market Research

Barbara F. Reskin and Camille Z. Charles

L abor market research has been one of the most fruitful approaches to understanding social inequality in contemporary American society. This is hardly surprising, given the fundamental role that labor market processes play in shaping social and economic inequality. Since paid employment is the primary way that most economic and many social resources are distributed to adults in the United States, access to paid employment influences a wide array of outcomes, including the acquisition of types of human capital distributed in the workplace, earnings, social status, and economic security for the postemployment years. Because they allocate workers to jobs, labor markets indirectly influence job conditions and various employment outcomes. In short, understanding labor markets is central to understanding social inequality.

Although researchers have established that workers' sex, race, and ethnicity affect virtually all their labor market outcomes, labor market research has not realized its potential to illuminate social and economic inequality because most research has not taken seriously the theoretical importance of sex, race, and ethnicity as interconnected aspects of the system of social stratification in the United States. This failure to appreciate why sex, race, and ethnicity affect labor market outcomes, we contend, has distorted social scientists' understanding of social stratification and limited their ability to propose policies to address labor market–mediated social inequality.

Two features of labor market research underlie its failure to appreciate the theoretical importance of these core ascriptive characteristics. The first is the balkanization of research on ascriptive bases of inequality. Research specialties on sex, race, and ethnic inequality in labor markets tend to involve different scholars, and the research literatures are almost totally independent. Publications focusing on one form of inequality rarely refer to the research literature on other forms. Some research on gender in labor markets, for example, treats workers as raceless by excluding race from explanatory models or focusing exclusively on whites.[1] Similarly, studies of race in labor markets often ignore gender by examining a single sex.[2] Although there are some signs of change, most scholars interested in one ascriptive characteristic disregard other ascriptive characteristics that affect the operation and outcomes of labor markets.

In reality, of course, the sex, race, and ethnicity that workers bring to labor markets simultaneously structure their labor market outcomes (Carlson 1992, 271). In the United States, it is inconceivable for an employer or supervisor to fail to notice whether a worker is female or male; white, African American, or Asian. Ignoring these statuses in models of labor market outcomes is likely to distort the results. A constellation of sex, race, and sometimes ethnic status affects whether one belongs to the group that controls the operation of labor markets and where one falls in the labor queue. Treating sex, race, and ethnicity as if their effects were independent ignores the collective role these attributes play in labor market outcomes.

Second, research that disregards the configuration of workers' ascriptive characteristics tends to be based on incomplete theoretical models and precludes observing the joint effects of certain variables. Such omissions—whether at the theoretical or the analytic level—represent specification errors. Notwithstanding the highly sophisticated statistical analyses that are common in labor market research (Sorensen 1996, 1334), misspecified models can produce biased estimates of the relationships under examination.

Ignoring the various ways that sex, race, and ethnicity affect labor market outcomes can lead to problems in several circumstances:

1. when researchers exclude significant segments of the labor force, thereby limiting the generalizability of the studies' results,

2. when researchers omit race from regression analysis if race is correlated with other independent variables,

3. when the analytic model assumes that the causal processes for nonwhite and nonmale groups are identical to those for white men,

4. when the analysis omits measures of factors that affect workers' labor market outcomes and are correlated with race or sex, and

5. when researchers treat variables whose values are influenced by social institutions that are inextricably linked to the labor market as if they were causally independent of the labor market (in statistical terms, as if they were exogenous rather than endogenous).[3]

By identifying problems in the ways that quantitative researchers study labor markets, we hope to encourage scholars to build models that more fully capture the effects of sex-based, racial, and ethnic diversity in labor markets. After discussing the problems in labor market research, we consider ways to improve labor market research, including developing data sets that represent the diversity of the labor force, supplementing analyses of standard quantitative data sets with qualitative data, and grounding research in cultural and historical contexts.

ERRORS IN LABOR MARKET RESEARCH

The previous generation of researchers often omitted race- or sex-defined groups from studies of labor market outcomes, sometimes without justification (for example, Blau and Duncan 1967). Over the past quarter century, the compositions of research populations have come closer to that of the labor force. Although studies based on a single sex or race are no longer common, contemporary labor market research remains unsystematic in its treatment of sex, race, and ethnicity. We base this claim on our review of seventy-three articles that appeared between 1993 and 1996 in high-quality, peer-reviewed journals that report sociological research on labor markets (see the reference section on recently published research at the end of this chapter). Because our objective was to get a sense of the field, we did not attempt an exhaustive review of all published labor market research.[4] Nonetheless, we believe that the articles we reviewed constitute a substantial proportion of sociology articles on U.S. labor markets that analyzed individual-level data and in which sex, race, and ethnicity are all theoretically relevant. We surveyed most 1993 to 1996 issues of the *American Sociological Review*, the *American Journal of Sociology*, *Demography*, *Research in Social Stratification and Mobility*, *Social Forces*, and *Work and Occupations*, as well as other recent articles on labor markets that were in the senior author's reprint file.[5] Although we do not claim that these articles are a representative sample, there is no reason to believe they substantially misrepresent contemporary sociological labor market research.

Excluding Sex or Race Groups from the Data

As researchers have long recognized, a study's conclusions can be generalized only to the population from which the research sample is drawn. The proportionally larger the excluded groups and the more they differ from the group under study, the more a study's external validity is compromised.

How often do contemporary researchers exclude from the data races or sexes whose labor market experiences may differ fundamentally from those of the research subjects? Of the seventy-three quantitative studies of labor market processes we examined, 34 percent excluded men, women, nonwhites, or whites from the database (see the top row and the left-hand column of table 12.1). Of these studies, four were limited to a single sex

Table 12.1 / The Treatment of Sex and Race in Labor Market Studies, 1993 to 1996 (n = 73)

Race as a Variable	Sex as a Variable					
	Data Included for Only One Sex	Data Included for Sex, But Sex Not in Model	Sex Included as Additive Term	Slopes Allowed to Differ by Sex	Total	Percentage of Total
Data included for only one race	4	—	—	3	7	9.6
Data racially diverse but race not in model	—	—	—	9	9	12.3
Race included as an additive term	5	—	4	16	25	34.3
Slopes allowed to differ by race	13	1	1	17	32	43.8
Total	22	1	5	45	73	100.0
Percent of total	30.1	1.4	6.8	61.6	99.9[a]	

[a]Percentages do not add to 100 because of rounding.

and a single race (two studied white men, and two studied white women); fifteen studied just men, and seven studied only women; three investigated the effect of sex among whites but not among people of color; and eighteen examined the effect of race among members of just one sex (thirteen focused on men, five studied women; data not shown tabularly).

Of course, researchers sacrifice no generalizability if their interest extends only to the group they are studying. Sometimes researchers' objectives are sufficiently narrow that external validity is not a problem. But studies that seek to explicate basic labor market processes will misinform to the extent that they exclude groups among whom these processes operate differently than they operate among the groups that are studied. A full understanding of ascription in labor markets, for example, depends on studying samples that represent the U.S. labor force. Duncan, Featherman, and Duncan (1972, 15) omitted women from their study of the effects of socioeconomic background on occupational achievement because they expected that different variables might be relevant for women or that the same variables might have different effects for the sexes. Although subsequent research proved they were right, the decision of many early status-attainment researchers to exclude women yielded an image of the labor market that was far more meritocratic—at least in the processes that allocated workers to occupations—than was the case. In view of the pervasive sex-based inequality in the labor market, studying men—especially white men—exaggerates the extent to which labor market processes are meritocratic. In addition, researchers' understanding of race-based ascription derives largely from research on men. With the recognition that patterns of racial inequality differ by sex (see, for example, chapter 1) comes the need to reexamine the knowledge of racial inequality in labor markets.

The increasing heterogeneity of the U.S. labor force has correspondingly limited the generalizability of findings based on sexually and racially homogeneous research samples. When Duncan and his collaborators omitted women from their influential status-attainment studies, they excluded about 35 percent of the labor force. Although contemporary researchers are less likely to exclude women (just over one-fifth of those we reviewed did so), limiting their subjects to men restricts the generalizability of findings to just over half of the labor force. Nonwhites' and non-Anglos' shares of the labor force have also grown substantially over the last twenty years. In 1970, omitting nonwhites from labor market research excluded 13 percent of the labor force; in 1990, restricting samples to whites excluded 18 percent of the labor force (calculated from U.S. Department of Commerce 1973, 1992).

In sum, excluding substantial segments of the labor force reduces the generalizability of a study's conclusions. One-third of the labor market studies from the 1990s that we surveyed excluded important segments of the labor force.

Misspecifying Causal Processes

The validity of research results based on regression analysis depends on properly specified models. Properly specified models include relevant variables, omit irrelevant variables, and specify the correct functional form of independent variables' effects on the dependent variable. In misspecified models, the error term is correlated with the independent variables, producing biased estimates of the latter's effects (Hanushek and Jackson 1977, 101). Four types of specification errors are common in research on the operation of labor markets: (1) the omission of a variable denoting race; (2) the omission of a race-sex interaction to allow the effect of race to differ for men and women; (3) the failure to allow race and sex to affect the coefficients for other explanatory variables; and (4) the omission of other explanatory variables that are related to race or sex and that affect people's labor market outcomes. Because such specification errors produce biased estimates of the parameters in the model, they call a study's results into doubt.

Omitting Race   By including variables for sex and race in their analyses, researchers model a process in which employers give members of different races or sexes different amounts of a dependent variable (such as earnings), net of other factors that determine its allocation. These additive models allow different race or sex groups to have an across-the-board advantage or disadvantage with respect to the dependent variable. Researchers often treat significant additive effects of sex or race, net of other variables, as signaling discrimination in which employers base rewards on group membership.[6] Studies that omit relevant variables are subject to omitted-variable bias, a type of specification error. Two types of omitted variables are of concern here: variables that indicate racial group membership and relevant variables that are correlated with race or sex. Omitting relevant variables that are correlated with independent variables in the model yields biased estimates of the effects of the correlated independent variables (Kennedy 1985).[7]

From a theoretical standpoint, omitting a variable to denote race assumes that the labor market is race neutral and that employers are indifferent to workers' race. Thus it does not allow for the possibility that employers practice conventional or statistical discrimination.[8] In view of substantial evidence that contemporary U.S. labor markets are not race neutral, omitting race is rarely justified on theoretical grounds (Holzer 1996; Fix and Struyk 1993; Wilson 1996; Reskin 1998). Whenever employers give members of different races or sexes different "amounts" of the dependent variable, net of factors that are thought to legitimately affect one's amount of the dependent variable, analyses need to allow for this possibility by including race in the model.[9] This "additive" model allows for the possibility that one or more groups enjoy across-the-board advantages with respect to the dependent variable.[10] Omitting race precludes assessing the assumption that sex-based differences have different causes than racial differences do. For instance, the overrepresentation of female law professors in teaching family law has been attributed to differences in men's and women's teaching interests. However, research that looked at how teaching specialties varied by both sex and race revealed that minority men and women were also significantly more likely than white men to teach family law, net of other factors (Merritt and Reskin 1997). The overrepresentation of women as well as minority men in family law, a low-status subject, suggests that power and status rather than gender-based preferences dictated teaching assignments. This finding has implications for the broader debate on the causes of occupational segregation.

Of the sixty-six quantitative studies of labor market processes that were based on racially diverse samples, nine did not include a variable for race (see table 12.1). (We located just one study that included both sexes in the data but that all but ignored sex in the analysis.) Most of those that included a variable for race used a single dichotomy (black-nonblack or white-nonwhite); almost none included a set of dummy variables to distinguish among nonwhites.[11] All of the nine studies in our review that omitted race included standard human capital variables, which are all correlated with race. The omission of race from one-eighth of the studies in which the sample was racially diverse means that a nontrivial number of studies were at risk of specification error that rendered the estimated parameters for the human capital variables and other variables inaccurate and called into question their conclusions.

Omitting Race-Sex Interactions   Of the thirty-eight studies that included variables for both race and sex, only seventeen allowed race and sex to interact, despite theoretical reason to believe that minority women might be particularly disadvantaged or white men uniquely privileged in labor markets (for example, Almquist 1975; Jones 1986). If race and sex interact, excluding an interaction term from the model yields inaccurate estimates of the effects of sex and race. For example, according to a model that did not allow race and sex interactions in predicting the prestige of the schools where law faculty members worked, minorities began teaching at significantly more prestigious schools than whites, although sex was unrelated to the prestige of the first law school job. Adding a sex-race interaction revealed that both minority men and white women had an initial prestige advantage over white men and minority women (Merritt and Reskin 1997).

Misspecifying the Effects of Race or Sex   Although sex- or race-based ascription may occur because labor market actors favor one or another sex or race in the total amount of awards, most ascription probably occurs when members of different sex or race groups receive different rates of return for their values on independent variables. To model the possibility that employers reward members of different sex or race groups differently for the same independent variables, researchers must allow their slopes to vary for different races and sexes. They do this either by including sex and race interaction terms for variables whose effects may differ or by estimating separate equations for each sex and race group and then testing whether the coefficients for independent variables differ significantly across the groups. Studies that do not allow causal parameters to differ for different race and sex groups may misrepresent the way that sex or race affects workers' outcomes and may be subject to model specification error resulting in biased estimates of coefficients (Hanushek and Jackson 1977, 101).

There are both theoretical and empirical reasons to question whether discrimination operates exclusively or even primarily by giving some groups an across-the-board advantage or disadvantage (that is, through an additive effect of sex or race). To operationalize the legal definition of discrimination—unequal treatment of similarly situated persons—one must compare whether the characteristics that are supposed to yield an outcome do so at the same rate for members of different groups.[12] Considerable empirical evidence demonstrates the existence of race and sex interactions in the predictors of some labor market outcomes. The effects of experience and organizational location on earnings, for example, are often stronger for white males than for other race-ethnicity-sex groups (Montgomery and Wascher 1987; Beck and Colclough 1988; Cotton 1988; Jaynes and Williams 1989; Hirsch and Schumacher 1992; Tomaskovic-Devey 1993; Beggs 1995; Averett and Hotchkiss 1996). In addition, white men receive more authority for their qualifications than do white women and people of color. If white women, black women, and black men received the same authority payoffs to education and experience that white men garnered, these groups' authority gaps with white men would narrow by 60 to 90 percent (McGuire and Reskin 1993).

In sum, labor markets may fail to be sex and race neutral in two ways. First, one group can enjoy an advantage, net of all of the factors that affect the outcome of interest. Allowing for this type of nonneutrality requires a model in which sex and race and their interaction have across-the-board effects. However, treating the additive effects of sex and race (or a sex and race interaction) as indicating discrimination without testing for sex and race interactions can mask the ways that sex- and race-based ascription actually occurs in labor markets. Labor markets probably confer unequal payoffs for credentials or location for black and white women and men. To model this possibility, analyses must allow the slopes of independent variables to differ for the sexes and races included in the sample, unless they are known not to differ. Failing to allow the slopes to differ constrains the independent variables to operate identically for all race and sex groups. If they do not, the coefficients for the independent variables will represent averages of their varying effects for different races and sexes, and the coefficients for the additive terms for sex and race are likely to misstate the extent to which employers directly reward or punish workers based on their sex or race.[13] Until researchers establish that independent variables do not affect different groups differently, models of labor market processes should allow their slopes to vary. Although including sex and race interactions complicates the task of the data analyst, omitting them can obscure the ways that race and sex shape the operation of labor markets.

Omitting Theoretically Relevant Independent Variables that Are Correlated with Sex or Race   Because few studies assign equal theoretical weight to race and sex, few include both the variables that typically appear in analyses of sex differences and those that appear in analyses of racial differences. As a result, models of the operation of labor markets often omit variables that affect workers' outcomes and are correlated with included variables. This omission usually happens when researchers are interested primarily in explaining a sex or a race difference but not in explaining both. In this situation, researchers usually omit variables that lack theoretical centrality for explaining sex differences despite those variables' theoretical importance for explaining racial differences—or vice versa. Commonly omitted variables include those thought to affect the outcomes of women (for example, family status) or of people of color (precise measures of skill) but not of white men.

Omitting variables is problematic for three reasons. First, if the omitted variables are correlated with variables in the analysis, the latter will "explain" variation in the outcome of interest that is actually due to the omitted variable. Second, the omission of theoretically important variables can distort the understanding of the processes that generate the outcomes under study, an important problem for studies that aim to understand the determinants of labor market outcomes. Third, as noted, omitting relevant variables that are correlated with independent variables in the model yields biased estimates of the effects of the correlated independent variables.

An instance of this omission is the way many researchers treat family status in labor market research. Most researchers assume that sex differences in domestic and family roles contribute to sex differences in labor market outcomes (such as labor force attachment, hours worked, promotions, and earnings, among others). Many assume that women's commitments to their families reduce their attachment to the labor force.[14] As a result, studies of sex differences in labor market outcomes routinely include measures of family status. However, studies that are restricted to men, studies that include sex only as a control variable, and studies that include both sexes but focus on race often exclude family status from the model, despite the fact that family status affects the labor market outcomes of both sexes, regardless of color (Blau and Duncan 1967; O'Neill and Polachek 1993; Hsueh and Tienda 1995; Carr 1996).

Just as researchers interested in men or in racial differences often assume that family status is irrelevant for explaining differences in employment outcomes, researchers interested in sex differences tend to ignore skill, apart from education and experience, although they routinely invoke measures of skill to explain the employment and earnings gap between whites and people of color (for example, Farkas and Vicknair 1996; Moss and Tilly 1996). If explaining racial disparities in employment outcomes requires operationalizing skill more fully than simply years of education or experience, then why not measure skill with equal care in all studies of labor market outcomes? If employers are choosing among workers based on their English fluency, why not include English fluency in all analyses? If African American men's lack of "soft skills" really explains some employers' aversion to them (Moss and Tilly 1996) and soft skills aren't simply a proxy for being black, then researchers interested in sex-based differences in employment or even in white men's occupational outcomes should take into account measures of soft skills.

In sum, researchers' failure to recognize the importance of race and sex subjects research on labor markets to statistical and theoretical errors that undermine its value by yielding biased results, masking the extent of race- and sex-based ascription and leading to incorrect policy implications.

Treating Endogenous Variables as Exogenous

The logic underlying much research on race and sex differences in labor market outcomes is to determine how much of a difference in an outcome can be explained by differences in human capital, other personal attributes, and other controls and how much persists net of these variables. This analytic strategy tends to construe the portion of the disadvantaged labor market positions of women and people of color that can be statistically explained by group differences in education, skills, experience, English language fluency, nativity, parental education, place of residence, and the like as being caused by the differences between groups on these variables. In other words, this strategy treats measures of human capital and, more recently, social capital as exogenous variables.[15]

The variables enumerated in the previous paragraph can statistically account for a substantial portion of race and sex differences in labor market outcomes. African Americans, Mexican Americans, and Puerto Ricans average fewer years of education than whites (Bean and Tienda 1987; Jaynes and Williams 1989; O'Hare 1992; see chapter 3) and tend to score lower than whites on the measures of cognitive skill in some standard data sets. Women of all races, Latinos, and African American men average less employment experience than white men do. Thus education, cognitive skill,

/ **389**

and experience help statistically to explain group differences in labor force participation, unemployment, earnings, promotions, and the like.

We argue, however, for treating these indicators of human and social capital as a result of as well as a cause of racial and gender inequality. These differences result from a variety of stratification processes, including the different circumstances surrounding the arrival and incorporation of groups into the United States; their families' economic, social, and physical locations; social barriers to their full participation in society; and dominant groups' stake in maintaining the status quo. These factors are inextricably linked to the roles that race and sex have played and continue to play as fundamental organizing principles in American society (Blauner 1972; Lieberson 1980; Reskin 1988; Steinberg 1989; Hacker 1992; Massey and Denton 1993).

Stepping back in the causal chain allows a large portion of the racial differences in education and experience to be explained by African Americans' and Hispanics' different histories in the United States and in their concentration in families with low income and little wealth and in neighborhoods with poor schools, limited job opportunities, and high unemployment. All of these circumstances reduce the acquisition of the kinds of social capital that enhance individuals' chances of securing a good job (Wilson 1987, 1996; Bean and Tienda 1987; Jaynes and Williams 1989; Oliver and Shapiro 1989; Fernandez Kelly 1995).

European immigrants came to the United States voluntarily and, despite initial hardship and exclusion, were encouraged to rapidly assimilate into American society (Gordon 1964; Lieberson 1980; Steinberg 1989). In contrast, African Americans, Latinos and Latinas, and Asian immigrants have faced and continue to encounter substantial barriers to assimilating into and full participation in mainstream American society relative to *all* white ethnic groups (Gordon 1964; Blauner 1972; Barrera 1979; Lieberson 1980; Steinberg 1989; Glenn 1991; Amott and Matthaei 1991).[16] In ignoring the social and historical contexts from which the disadvantages of people of color originate, the standard human-capital approach implicitly suggests that racial disparities in labor market outcomes would disappear "if they'd just get more . . . education/experience/skills . . ." or "if they'd just expand their social networks . . ." or "if they'd just move to the suburbs . . . ."

At present, people of color get lower returns to their education than whites (Montgomery and Wascher 1987; Beck and Colclough 1988; Cotton 1988; Jaynes and Williams 1989; Orfield 1992; Tomaskovic-Devey 1993), in part because the former are disproportionately educated in urban public schools, many of which suffer from low teacher-student ratios, outdated textbooks, antiquated equipment, disciplinary problems, overworked and underpaid faculty and staff, and few extracurricular activities (Entwisle, Alexander, and Olsen 1994; King 1987; Roscigno 1995; Wise and Gendler

1989; Sutton 1991; Fernandez Kelly 1995). These conditions ensure that the high school diplomas that many African American and Latinos and Latinas take into the job market are worth less than those from primarily white suburban schools (Kirschenman and Neckerman 1991; Kozol 1991). Indeed, a ghetto education teaches young people to be appropriately skeptical about the payoffs to public education (Fernandez Kelly 1995, 231). Although education does enhance the labor market outcomes of some people of color, for persons in hyperghettos more years of the same sort of education are unlikely to improve the kinds of labor market outcomes researchers study.

Similar problems exist in terms of the effectiveness of social networks for obtaining better jobs, at least for racially segregated young people. Researchers have repeatedly established that employers rely on social networks to recruit workers and that social networks affect the kinds of jobs workers get (Granovetter 1974; Marsden 1994; Miller and Rosenbaum 1997). However, hiring by means of informal networks is also known to disadvantage women and people of color because workers' informal ties tend to be segregated by race and sex (Brass 1985; Campbell and Rosenfeld 1985; Braddock and McPartland 1987; Ibarra 1992; Bell and Nkomo 1994, 40; Browne and Hewitt 1995). For social networks to be useful, they must be diversified so that individuals can take advantage of weak ties with persons connected to the labor market. Residents of hyperghettos lack these ties, however, largely because of the factors that have relegated them to ghettos (Kasinitz and Rosenberg 1996, 189, 192; Fernandez Kelly 1995, 242; Wilson 1996).

Treating education, experience, and other credentials as exogenous ignores the fact that people of color and women are denied access to these credentials (including entry-level jobs) because of their race and sex (Cose 1993; Feagin and Sikes 1994; Bell and Nkomo 1994). Using these credentials to explain labor market outcomes without taking into account groups' historical and social contexts yields erroneous conclusions regarding the factors that contribute to groups' disadvantage and hence to ineffective policy interventions. And simply mentioning past and current discrimination does not justify the misspecification of models.

Ignoring the advantages that white men accrue from racial and gender stratification seriously limits the value of much research on labor markets. Researchers need to consider the possibility that the real exogenous variables are not race and sex differences in credentials but race- and sex-differentiated labor market *outcomes*. Middle- and upper-class white men created and maintain the labor market structures that reward education. Thus, while education and job experience are associated with positive labor market outcomes for those at the top of the social and economic hierarchy, there is no reason to expect more education and experience to benefit blacks and Hispanics and white women. As Lieberson (1985, 185–87) argued, although "superficial causes" may seem to affect a dependent variable, changing a superficial cause will not lead the dependent variable to change, no matter how strong their association. Consider racial differences in education, for example. If educational differences between the races are a "basic cause" of the racial earnings gap, then blacks' converging education with whites should narrow the earnings gap. But if educational differences are a superficial cause, narrowing the educational gap will not reduce the earnings gap at the rate that the regression coefficient for education implies. As Lieberson (1985, 189) observed, the United States' formal commitment to an achievement ideology means that the superficial cause of an earnings gap between more and less powerful groups—in other words, the mechanism through which the earnings gap is generated at any time—will probably involve some form of achievement (for example, education, experience, skills, continuity of labor force participation, hours worked per week, and the like). To the extent that the propensity of members of advantaged groups to safeguard their advantages is a *basic* cause of the earnings gap, large numbers of blacks or Hispanics will not be able to catch up with whites' earnings by matching whites' educational attainments.[17] Thus, as more minorities complete high school, the quality of their education has deteriorated, employers insist on skills not taught in ghetto schools, jobs that require only a high school degree have moved away from the ghettos, and urban employers use recruitment methods that exclude people of color (Wilson 1987, 1996; Kasarda 1989; Johnson and Oliver 1991; Delpit 1995; Holzer 1996). In fact, according to a recent study, Chicago employers reported they disregard high school records and recommendations in deciding whom to hire (Miller and Rosenbaum 1997).

In sum, in treating human and social capital as exogenous, labor market research ignores the systematic differences in the access of other race and sex groups to the positions or credentials that affect white men's labor market outcomes. Implicitly, these studies assume that African Americans and Latinos and Latinas can work their way up the socioeconomic ladder the same way that European immigrants did a century ago (Glazer and Moynihan 1970; Lieberson 1980; Steinberg 1989). Ignoring minorities' and women's unequal access to the opportunities to acquire human capital disregards both America's history of systematically excluding African Americans and Hispanics from institutional mainstreams and the exclusionary barriers that continue to exist in labor markets. At best, this disregard produces only narrow bits of knowledge; at worst, it yields erroneous theoretical and policy conclusions. Race and sex differences in labor market inputs and outcomes exist within a context in which white men both benefit from race, sex, and ethnic inequality in the labor market and control the mechanisms through which people obtain these inputs and outcomes. In ignoring the incentive powerful groups have to maintain inequality, researchers fail to realize their potential to illuminate the operation of labor markets.

INCORPORATING RACE, SEX, AND ETHNICITY IN LABOR MARKET RESEARCH

In this final section, we discuss ways that researchers can incorporate race, sex, and ethnicity into research on labor markets, thereby advancing the understanding of the ways that labor markets operate. We stress the need to create more inclusive data sets, to place the results of quantitative research in context and to combine quantitative and qualitative research.

Creating More Comprehensive Data

The limitations of widely available data sets constrain researchers' ability to take into account race, ethnicity, and gender.[18] The decennial census asks women but not men how many children they have ever had. The General Social Survey, on which some labor market studies draw (for example, Kalleberg and Reskin 1995; Rowe and Snizek 1995; Logan 1996), has too few respondents to permit analysts to go beyond black and white.[19] Reports published by the U.S. Census Bureau usually provide tabulations on labor market outcomes by sex or race or Hispanic ethnicity but seldom tabulate data by both sex and race or ethnicity (for example, U.S. Department of Commerce 1996, tables 615, 617, 618, 623). None of these limitations in publicly funded data will change until researchers demand more ethnic detail, and researchers are unlikely to demand more detail until they take seriously the idea that sex, race, and ethnicity jointly shape workers' labor market outcomes.

Supplementing Quantitative Analysis with Qualitative Analysis

Researchers can circumvent some of the limitations in data sets by supplementing quantitative analysis with qualitative analysis. Dual labor market theory originated in a set of qualitative impressions of local labor markets in Boston, Chicago, Detroit, and Harlem in studies conducted by institutional economists concerned with the high levels of poverty and underemployment of African American men who lived in urban ghettos. Their qualitative observations revealed that the attributes that economists and sociologists view as indicators of productivity or human capital had little effect on urban blacks' labor market outcomes. They concluded that the range of African American men's qualifications was broader than the range of jobs available to them, which were almost invariably menial, isolated jobs that neither required nor rewarded skill or experience (Gordon 1972, 44–45).[20] By turning to qualitative research to understand quantitative findings that were anomalous within the framework developed to explain the labor market outcomes of white men, these institutional economists discovered that labor markets are segmented, an important theoretical advance in the conceptualization and understanding of labor markets.

Labor market researchers should follow the example of the institutional economists by using qualitative research to examine both the supply and the demand sides of the labor market. In the past decade, researchers have demonstrated how much research that includes both quantitative and qualitative components can reveal about labor market discrimination. Several ambitious studies of employers' hiring practices have illuminated how and why employers discriminate against people of color (Kirschenman and Neckerman 1991; Waldinger and Bailey 1991; Holzer 1996; Kasinitz and Rosenberg 1996; Wilson 1996; Miller and Rosenbaum 1997; Moss and Tilly 1996; see chapter 9). These studies have demonstrated, for example, that urban employers imposed more rigorous requirements on new hires than suburban employers did, thus holding urban—largely minority—youth to higher standards (Holzer 1996); that employers often passed over African American women and men who lived nearby in favor of blacks who lived farther away, in part because the former lacked social ties with current workers and in part because employers viewed them as more problematic employees (Kasinitz and Rosenberg 1996); that Detroit employers admitting moving to the suburbs to escape black workers (Turner 1996); and that employers' sex-based stereotypes of blacks shaped their hiring practices (see chapter 9).

Qualitative studies on the supply side also reveal the conditions under which labor markets are and are not race and sex neutral, and the ways that they deviate from neutrality. For example, interviews with people of color and white women and men show the importance of perceptions of opportunity for labor market–related behavior. In one such study, Fernandez Kelly (1995) showed that the decisions by African American teenage girls to have babies were the only rational path to adult status, since employment was not a viable option. Another example of what qualitative research that focuses on workers can show is the finding in chapter 10 that 15 percent of the African American women and 11 percent of the white women in a sample of professionals aspired to self-employment in order to avoid negative workplace experiences (see also Cose 1993; Feagin and Sikes 1994). This qualitative research makes sense of what strictly quantitative research would show only as sex and race differences in job attachment. Finally, in chapter 8 Kathryn Edin and Kathleen Mullan Harris use qualitative data to supplement their quantitative analysis, showing that African American women had a harder time staying off welfare than white women did even though the former were more likely than white women to remain continuously employed. The qualitative data explain this difference: African American women's more limited access to nonwage income made it harder for them to support their families on the poverty-level wages many single mothers earn.

Placing Labor Market Research in Social, Cultural, and Historical Contexts

Research on labor markets would benefit from greater attention to the social, cultural, and historical contexts in which labor markets operate. Such grounding is available in ethnographies, autobiographies, and commentary by people from diverse racial, ethnic, and sex groups. "No standpoint is neutral because no individual or group exists unembedded in the world" (Collins 1990, 33). Just as the life experiences of white men affect their assumptions about how labor markets operate, so too do the experiences of white women, men of color, and women of color. Although one need not be a person of color, a white woman, or a white man to understand the experiences of members of those groups, members of each group are likely to have valuable insights into the opportunities open to them and the barriers they encounter and into how they view and are viewed by labor market actors from other groups (Collins 1990; DuBois 1990).[21] Drawing on a variety of sources that puts labor markets into the cultural and social milieu in which they operate will enhance the understanding of fundamental labor market processes.

CONCLUSIONS

In the late 1970s, Feldberg and Glenn (1979, 524) wrote that "while issues of work are framed as universal ones, the actual study of work has proceeded along sex-differentiated lines." They characterized studies framed as universal as employing "job models" and those concerned with sex differences as employing "gender models." Our review of research published in the 1990s indicates that research can still be classified as focusing on jobs (or labor markets) or gender. Researchers almost invariably consider workers' family status when their object is to explain sex differences in labor market outcomes and ignore it when their focus is exclusively on men or on race differences in labor market outcomes. Moreover, research that includes women is likely to be about gender whereas some studies of jobs or labor markets continue to exclude women. Indeed, of the contemporary quantitative sociological studies on labor markets that we surveyed, almost one-third excluded one sex from the analysis by focusing on just one sex (men over women by more than two to one).

In the early 1980s, the book *All the Women Are White, All the Blacks Are Men, But Some of Us Are Brave* (Hull, Scott, and Smith 1982) pointed out the invisibility of women of color in scholarship as well as in American life. Of contemporary quantitative sociological studies on labor markets, only one-fifth allowed the experiences of women of color to differ from those of white women or men of color. Although labor market researchers no longer study exclusively white women, research on people of color is substantially more likely to be on men than on women, and although we located studies focused solely on white men, white women, and minority men, we found none that was concerned exclusively with women of color. The social marginality of women of color almost certainly contributes to their invisibility in research on labor markets.

We argue that the value of research that ignores race, ethnicity, and gender and the way they interact is limited because it lacks external validity, is subject to specification error, and fails to observe the links between labor markets and racial and sex stratification. We do not believe that nothing can be learned from careful studies that focus on subpopulations, if such subpopulations are the appropriate group in which to observe the processes of interest and researchers attend to the limitations associated with studying subsets from a diverse labor force.[22] But such studies cannot illuminate why and how labor markets work or their role in perpetuating and reducing inequality among the diverse groups composing the labor force. Framing research designs that look like the United States is no simple matter. However, in a specialty area that has drawn some of the most methodologically creative and statistically proficient sociologists, what is stopping researchers is not the problem of developing research designs or analyzing data but the failure to demand more from their own research and that of others. Only by placing research questions in cultural and historical contexts, allowing the labor market processes of interest to differ for different groups, and drawing on both quantitative and qualitative research designs, can research fulfill its promise of promoting theoretical understanding and effective public policy.

We are especially grateful to Irene Browne, Paula England, Lowell Hargens, Jerry Jacobs, Irene Padavic, and an anonymous reviewer for their comments on this chapter and to Vincent Roscigno for directing us to research on racial inequality in education. We are grateful to Debra McBrier and Naomi Cassirer for research assistance, to Julie Kmec for library assistance, and to Dolores McGee for clerical and editorial assistance. Of course, we bear responsibility for any flaws in our argument or other errors.

NOTES

1. More than one-fifth of the studies reviewed below did not include race as a variable; 5.5 percent were limited to whites.

2. Of the thirty-two studies that focused on race differences, fourteen were limited to one sex.

3. Exogenous variables are variables whose causes are treated as external to an analysis; endogenous variables are treated as dependent variables within an analysis.

4. Although we focus on sociology, we suspect that our argument generally applies to labor market research published in nonsociology journals.

5. We omitted a few issues that were not available.

6. This inference can be unwarranted. Depending on the model's specification, an effect of sex or race may mean that employers treat one group more or less favorably than others. However, the size of the effect of group membership is a function of the other variables in the equation. For example, if one is interested in sex differences in managers' earnings, including a dummy variable for managerial level would explain that part of the sex difference in pay that resulted from male managers' concentration in higher-level posts than female managers. However, if an undergraduate degree in accounting affects managers' earnings and is correlated with sex, excluding whether sample members had an accounting degree would overestimate the effect of sex.

7. This biases upward the estimator of the variance-covariance matrix for the regression coefficients, thereby producing inaccurate estimates of the effects of the variables (Kennedy 1985, 69).

8. Statistical discrimination occurs when employers treat characteristics that they associate with a group as if they apply to all members of the group. Unlike conventional discrimination, in which employers allegedly pay costs in order to indulge their biases, statistical discrimination originates in employers' desire to avoid the costs of obtaining information about specific individuals. When the employer's beliefs about a group's characteristics are wrong (what England 1992 termed "error discrimination"), the resulting discrimination is closer to conventional discrimination than statistical discrimination.

9. In economic terms, this unearned positive effect is a "rent."

10. This may occur because members of some race-sex groups receive rewards without the qualifications or performance required of others.

11. Studies that include race typically dichotomize it as black-nonblack, white-nonwhite, or black-white. Only nine of the seventy-three studies included Hispanic as a variable, and only two of these took into account ethnic diversity among Hispanics. Asians and American Indians are the least visible groups in recent quantitative labor market research (for exceptions, see Tang 1993; Portes and Zhou 1996; Reskin and Cassirer 1996), and only two studies examined ethnic diversity among Asian workers (Portes and Zhou 1996; Reskin and Cassirer 1996).

12. Although the definition of discrimination as unequal treatment implies a single employer, observing different slopes in data for workers with different employers can help to identify the channels through which groups receive different returns to the same credentials or organizational characteristics.

Even though the slopes for two or more groups may differ, if they intersect within the range of values for the independent variable of interest, then—assuming they are positive and linear—members of the group with the steeper slope whose values on the independent variable are below the point of intersection will experience discrimination by virtue of group membership relative to members of the group with the flatter slope whose values on the independent variable are below the point of intersection on the dependent variable. (The logic in this scenario resembles that in an explanation for occupational sex segregation that was current in the 1980s: that women, assuming only short-run labor force participation, opted for occupations, such as nursing, that yielded a steep return to their human capital, while men, assuming long-term labor force participation, chose occupations that offered lower initial returns on earnings but higher long-run returns; Polachek 1976.) Thus, before concluding that a lower slope signals discrimination, analysts must assess whether the point where the slopes intersect falls within either group's range on the independent variable.

13. If the direction of a variable's effect differs for different groups (for example, the effect of number of children on women's and men's labor force participation), its average effect will be weaker than its effect for either group.

14. However, as chapters 6 and 8 show, the opposite is true for women whose partner or family members make it possible for them to participate in the labor force.

15. See note 3.

16. See also Cose (1993) and Feagin and Sikes (1994) for difficulties surrounding the incorporation of middle class African Americans; see Massey and Mullan (1984), Massey and Denton (1985), and Yinger (1995) for examples specific to residential segregation and spatial assimilation.

17. This assumes no change in whites' perception that the disparity is in their best interest. Change has occurred when powerful whites perceive real costs associated with denying economic opportunities to people of color, as happened in the aftermath of the urban riots in the late 1960s.

18. Of course, data limitations sometimes result from forms of race- and ethnicity-based exclusion that limit the number of members of ethnic and racial groups in some populations. The substantial underrepresentation of groups is itself an important finding that deserves attention in research reports.

19. The principal investigators of the General Social Survey have proposed a survey that will oversample Hispanics, but at this writing funding was not available.

20. Although the theory of segmented labor markets recognized that labor markets were racialized, its inattention to gender and to sex-race interactions reduced its utility.

21. Persons from subordinate groups may have an advantage in this respect because they must understand dominant groups to function in an environment that the latter control, whereas members of dominant groups can thrive without any special insight into subordinate groups.

22. The problem of external validity is similar to that of well-designed experimental research in social psychology, which elucidates behavior among white, middle-class college undergraduates but may not hold for other groups. Experimentalists have the excuse of limited research populations.

REFERENCES

Almquist, Elizabeth. 1975. "Untangling the Effects of Race and Sex: The Disadvantaged Status of Black Women." *Social Science Quarterly* 56(1): 129–42.

Amott, Teresa L., and Julie A. Matthaei. 1991. *Race, Gender, and Work*. Boston: South End Press.

Averett, Susan L., and Julie L. Hotchkiss. 1996. "Discrimination in the Payment of Full-Time Wage Premiums." *Industrial and Labor Relations Review* 49(2): 287–301.

Barrera, Mario. 1979. *Race and Class in the Southwest: A Theory of Racial Inequality*. South Bend, Ind.: Notre Dame Press.

Bean, Frank D., and Marta Tienda. 1987. *The Hispanic Population of the United States*. New York: Russell Sage Foundation.

Beck, E. M., and Glenna Colclough. 1988. "Schooling and Capitalism: The Effect of Urban Economic Structure on the Value of Education." In *Industries, Firms, and Jobs: Economic and Sociological Approaches*, edited by George Farkas and Paula England. New York: Plenum.

Beggs, John J. 1995. "The Institutional Environment: Implications for Race and Gender Inequality in the U.S. Labor Market." *American Sociological Review* 60(4): 612–34.

Bell, Ella, and Stella M. Nkomo. 1994. *Barriers to Work Place Advancement Experiences by African Americans*. Momograph prepared for the Glass Ceiling Commission, U.S. Department of Labor.

Blau, Peter M., and Otis Dudley Duncan. 1967. *The American Occupational Structure*. New York: John Wiley and Sons.

Blauner, Robert. 1972. *Racial Oppression in America*. New York: Harper and Row.

Braddock, Jomills Henry II, and James M. McPartland. 1987. "How Minorities Continue to Be Excluded from Equal Employment Opportunities: Research on Labor Market and Institutional Barriers." *Journal of Social Issues* 43(1): 5–39.

Brass, Daniel J. 1985. "Men's and Women's Networks: A Study of Interaction Patterns and Influence in Organizations." *Academy of Management Journal* 28(June): 327–99.

Browne, Irene, and Cynthia Hewitt. 1995. "Networks, Discrimination or Location? Explaining Job Segregation among African Americans." Paper presented to the Russell Sage Conference on the Multi-City Survey of Urban Equality. New York (February 1996): 1.

Campbell, Karen E., and Rachel A. Rosenfeld. 1985. "Job Search and Job Mobility: Sex and Race Differences." *Research in the Sociology of Work* 3: 147–74.

Carlson, Susan M. 1992. "Trends in Race/Sex Occupational Inequality: Conceptual and Measurement Issues." *Social Problems* 39(3): 268–90.

Carr, Deborah. 1996. "Two Paths to Self Employment?" *Work and Occupations* 23(1): 26–53.

Collins, Patricia Hill. 1990. *Black Feminist Thought: Knowledge, Consciousness, and the Politics of Empowerment*. Boston: Unwin Hyman.

Cose, Ellis. 1993. *The Rage of a Privileged Class: Why Are Middle Class Blacks So Angry? Why Should America Care?* New York: HarperCollins.

Cotton, Jeremiah. 1988. "Discrimination and Favoritism in the U.S. Labor Market: The Cost to a Wage Earner of Being Female and Black and the Benefit of Being Male and White." *American Journal of Economics and Sociology* 47(1): 15–27.

Delpit, Lisa. 1995. *Other People's Children.* New York: New Press.

Du Bois, W. E. B. [1903] 1990. *The Souls of Black Folk.* New York: Vintage Books.

Duncan, Otis Dudley, David L. Featherman, and Beverly Duncan. 1972. *The American Occupational Structure.* New York: Seminar Press.

England, Paula. 1992. *Comparable Worth: Theories and Evidence.* New York: Aldine de Gruyter.

Entwisle, Doris R., Karl L. Alexander, and Linda S. Olsen. 1994. "The Gender Gap in Math: Its Possible Origin in Neighborhood Effects." *American Sociological Review* 59(6): 822–38.

Farkas, George, and Keven Vicknair. 1996. "Appropriate Tests of Racial Wage Discrimination Require Controls for Cognitive Skill." *American Sociological Review* 61(4): 557–60.

Feagin, Joe R., and Melvin P. Sikes. 1994. *Living with Racism: The Black Middle Class Experience.* Boston: Beacon Press.

Feldberg, Rosyln L., and Evelyn Nakano Glenn. 1979. "Male and Female: Job versus Gender Models in the Sociology of Work." *Social Problems* 26(5): 524–38.

Fernandez Kelly, M. Patricia. 1995. "Social and Cultural Capital in the Urban Ghetto: Implications for the Economic Sociology of Immigration." In *The Economic Sociology of Immigration,* edited by Alejandro Portes. New York: Russell Sage Foundation.

Fix, Michael, and Raymond J. Struyk, eds. 1993. *Clear and Convincing Evidence: Measurement of Discrimination in America.* Washington, D.C.: Urban Institute Press.

Glazer, Nathan, and Daniel P. Moynihan. 1970. *Beyond the Melting Pot: The Negroes, Puerto Ricans, Jews, Italians, and Irish of New York City.* Cambridge, Mass.: MIT Press.

Glenn, Evelyn Nakano. 1991. "Cleaning Up/Kept Down: A Historical Perspective on Racial Inequality in 'Women's Work.'" *Stanford Law Review* 43(July): 1333–56.

Gordon, David M. 1972. *Theories of Poverty and Unemployment.* Lexington, Mass.: Lexington Books.

Gordon, Milton. 1964. *Assimilation in American Life.* New York: Oxford University Press.

Granovetter, Mark. 1974. *Getting a Job: A Study of Contacts and Careers.* Cambridge, Mass.: Harvard University Press.

Hacker, Andrew. 1992. *Two Nations: Black and White, Separate, Hostile, Unequal.* New York: Charles Scribner's Sons.

Hanushek, Eric A., and John E. Jackson. 1977. *Statistical Methods for Social Scientists.* San Diego: Academic Press.

Hirsch, Barry T., and Edward J. Schumacher. 1992. "Labor Earnings, Discrimination, and the Racial Composition of Jobs." *Journal of Human Resources* 27(4): 602–28.

Holzer, Harry J. 1996. *What Employers Want: Job Prospects for Less-Educated Workers.* New York: Russell Sage Foundation.

Hsueh, Sheri, and Marta Tienda. 1995. "Earnings Consequences of Employment Instability among Minority Men." *Research in Social Stratification and Mobility* 14: 39–70.

Hull, Gloria, Patricia Bell Scott, and Barbara Smith. 1982. *All the Women Are White, All the Blacks Are Men, But Some of Us Are Brave.* Old Westbury, N.Y.: Feminist Press.

Ibarra, Herminia. 1992. "Homophily and Differential Returns: Sex Differences in Network Structure and Access in an Advertising Firm." *Administrative Science Quarterly* 37(3): 363–99.

King, Mary C. 1992. "Occupational Segregation by Race and Sex, 1940–88." *Monthly Labor Review* 115(4): 30–37.

Jaynes, Gerald David, and Robin M. Williams, Jr. 1989. *A Common Destiny: Blacks in American Society.* Washington, D.C.: National Academy Press.

Johnson, James H., Jr., and Melvin L. Oliver. 1991. "Economic Restructuring and Black Male Joblessness in U.S. Metropolitan Areas." *Urban Geography* 12(6): 542–62.

Jones, Edward. 1986. "Black Managers: The Dream Deferred." *Harvard Business Review* 64(May–June): 84–93.

Kalleberg, Arne L., and Barbara F. Reskin. 1995. "Gender Differences in Promotion in the United States and Norway." *Research in Social Stratification and Mobility* 14: 237–64.

Kasarda, John D. 1989. "Urban Industrial Transitions and the Underclass." *Annals of the American Academy of Political and Social Science* 501(1): 26–42.

Kasinitz, Philip S., and Jan Rosenberg. 1996. "Missing the Connection: Social Isolation and Employment on the Brooklyn Waterfront." *Social Problems* 43(2): 180–96.

Kennedy, Peter. 1985. *A Guide to Econometrics* (2d ed.). Cambridge: MIT Press.

King, R. A. 1987. "Rethinking Equality in Computer Access and Use." *Educational Technology* 27(4): 12–18.

Kirschenman, Joleen, and Kathryn M. Neckerman. 1991. " 'We'd Love to Hire Them But . . . ' The Meaning of Race for Employers." In *The Urban Underclass,* edited by Christopher Jencks and Paul Peterson. Washington, D.C.: Brookings Institution.

Kozol, Jonathan. 1991. *Savage Inequalities: Children in America's Schools.* New York: Crown.

Lieberson, Stanley. 1980. *A Piece of the Pie: Blacks and White Immigrants since 1880.* Berkeley: University of California Press.

———. 1985. *Making It Count.* Berkeley: University of California Press.

Logan, John Allen. 1996. "Opportunity and Choice in Socially Structured Labor Markets." *American Journal of Sociology* 102(1): 114–60.

Marsden, Peter V. 1994. "The Hiring Process: Recruitment Methods." *American Behavioral Scientist* 7(7): 979–91.

Massey, Douglas S., and Nancy A. Denton. 1985. "Spatial Assimilation as a Socioeconomic Outcome." *American Sociological Review* 50(1): 94–105.

———. 1993. *American Apartheid.* Cambridge, Mass.: Harvard University Press.

Massey, Douglas S., and Brendan P. Mullan. 1984. "Processes of Hispanic and Black Spatial Assimilation." *American Journal of Sociology* 89(4): 836–73.

McGuire, Gail M., and Barbara F. Reskin. 1993. "Authority Hierarchies at Work: The Impacts of Race and Sex." *Gender and Society* 7(4): 487–506.

Merritt, Deborah J., and Barbara F. Reskin. 1997. "Sex, Race, and Credentials: The Truth about Affirmative Action in Law School Hiring." *Columbia University Law Review* 97(2): 199–311.

Miller, Shazia Rafiullah, and James E. Rosenbaum. 1997. "Hiring in a Hobbesian World." *Work and Occupations* 24(4): 498–523.

Montgomery, Edward, and William Wascher. 1987. "Race and Gender Wage Inequality in Services and Manufacturing." *Industrial Relations* 26(3): 284–90.

Moss, Philip, and Chris Tilly. 1996. "'Soft' Skills and Race." *Work and Occupations* 23(3): 252–76.

O'Hare, William P. 1992. "America's Minorities—The Demographics of Diversity." *Population Bulletin* 47(4): PS2–46.

O'Neill, June, and Solomon Polachek. 1993. "Why the Gender Gap in Wages Narrowed in the 1980s." *Journal of Labor Economics* 11(1): 205–28.

Oliver, Melvin L., and Thomas M. Shapiro. 1989. "Race and Wealth." *Review of Black Political Economy* (Spring): 1–25.

Orfield, Daniel. 1992. "Urban Schooling and the Perpetuation of Job Inequality in Metropolitan Chicago." In *Urban Labor Markets and Job Opportunities*, edited by George Peterson and Wayne Vroman. Washington, D.C.: Urban Institute Press.

Polachek, Solomon. 1976. "Occupational Segregation: An Alternative Hypothesis." *Journal of Contemporary Business* (Winter): 1–12.

Portes, Alejandro, and Min Zhou. 1996. "Self-Employment and Earnings of Immigrants." *American Sociological Review* 61(2): 219–30.

Reskin, Barbara F. 1988. "Bringing the Men Back In: Sex Differentiation and the Devaluation of Women's Work." *Gender and Society* 2(1): 58–81.

———. 1998. *The Realities of Affirmative Action*. Washington, D.C.: American Sociological Association.

Reskin, Barbara F., and Naomi Cassirer. 1996. "Occupational Segregation by Gender, Race, and Ethnicity." *Sociological Focus* 29(3): 231–43.

Roscigno, Vincent J. 1995. "The Social Embeddedness of Racial Educational Inequality: The Black-White Gap and the Impact of Racial and Local Political-Economic Contexts." *Research in Social Stratification and Mobility* 14: 137–68.

Sorensen, Aage. 1996. "The Structural Basis of Social Inequality." *American Journal of Sociology* 101(5): 1333–65.

Steinberg, Stephen. 1989. *The Ethnic Myth: Race, Ethnicity and Class in America*. Boston: Beacon Press.

Sutton, R. 1991. "Equity and Computers in the Schools: A Decade of Research." *Review of Educational Research* 61(4): 475–503.

Tang, Joyce. 1993. "Whites, Blacks and Asians in Science and Engineering: A Reconsideration of Their Economic Prospects." *Research in Social Stratification and Mobility* 12: 249–94.

Tomaskovic-Devey, Donald. 1993. *Gender and Racial Inequality at Work: The Sources and Consequences of Job Segregation*. Ithaca, N.Y.: ILR Press.

Turner, Susan. 1996. "Barriers to a Better Break: Wages, Race, and Space in Metropolitan Detroit." Paper presented to the Russell Sage Conference on the Multi-City Survey of Urban Inequality. New York (January 1996).

U.S. Department of Commerce. U.S. Bureau of the Census. 1973. "United States Summary. Subject Reports. Occupational U.S. Summary." In *1970 Census of Population*, vol. 1. Washington, D.C.: U.S. Government Printing Office.

———. 1992. *1990 Census of Population and Housing: Public Use Microdata Sample*. Washington, D.C.: U.S. Government Printing Office.

———. 1996. *Statistical Abstract of the United States 1996*. Washington, D.C.: U.S. Government Printing Office.

Waldinger, Roger, and Thomas Bailey. 1991. "The Continuing Significance of Race: Racial Conflict and Racial Discrimination in Construction." *Politics and Society* 19(3): 291–323.

Wilson, William Julius. 1987. *The Truly Disadvantaged: The Inner City, the Underclass, and Public Policy.* Chicago: University of Chicago Press.

———. 1996. *When Work Disappears: The World of the New Urban Poor.* New York: Alfred A. Knopf.

Wise, Arthur E., and Tamar Gendler. 1989. "Rich Schools, Poor Schools: The Persistence of Unequal Education." *Education Digest* 55(4): 3–8.

Yinger, John. 1995. *Closed Doors, Opportunities Lost: The Continuing Cost of Housing Segregation.* New York: Russell Sage Foundation.

RECENTLY PUBLISHED RESEARCH ON RACE AND SEX INEQUALITY

Adler, Marina A. 1993. "Gender Differences in Job Autonomy: The Consequences of Occupational Segregation and Authority Position." *Sociological Quarterly* 34(3): 449–65.

Andersen, Deborah, and David Shapiro. 1996. "Racial Differences in Access to High-Paying Jobs and the Wage Gap between Black and White Women." *Industrial and Labor Relations Review* 49(2): 273–86.

Anderson, Cynthia, and Donald Tomaskovic-Devey. 1995. "Patriarchal Pressures: An Exploration of Organizational Processes that Exacerbate and Erode Gender Earnings Inequality." *Work and Occupations* 22(3): 328–56.

Ascheffenburg, Karen. 1995. "Rethinking Images of the Mobility Regime: Making a Case for Women's Mobility." *Research in Social Stratification and Mobility* 14: 201–35.

Averett, Susan L., and Julie L. Hotchkiss. 1996. "Discrimination in the Payment of Full-Time Wage Premiums." *Industrial and Labor Relations Review* 49(2): 287–301.

Baldi, Stephane, and Debra Branch McBrier. 1997. "Do the Determinants of Promotion Differ for Blacks and Whites? Evidence from the U.S. Labor Market." *Work and Occupation* 24(4): 478–97.

Beggs, John J. 1995. "The Institutional Environment: Implications for Race and Gender Inequality in the U.S. Labor Market." *American Sociological Review* 60(4): 612–33.

Bernhardt, Annette, Martina Morris, and Mark S. Handcock. 1995. "Women's Gains or Men's Losses? A Closer Look at the Shrinking Gender Gap in Earnings." *American Journal of Sociology* 101(2): 302–28.

Browne, Irene. 1997. "Explaining the Black-White Gap in Labor Force Participation among Women Heading Households." *American Sociological Review* 62(2): 236–52.

Burr, Jeffrey A., Michael P. Massagli, Jan E. Mutchler, and Amy M. Pienta. 1996. "Labor Force Transitions among Older African American and White Men." *Social Forces* 74(3): 963–82.

Cancio, A. Silvia, T. David Edwards, and David J. Maume. 1996. "Reconsidering the Declining Significance of Race: Racial Differences in Early Career Wages." *American Sociological Review* 61(4): 541–56.

Carlson, Susan M. 1992. "Trends in Race/Sex Occupational Inequality: Conceptual and Measurement Issues." *Social Problems* 39(August): 268–90.

Carr, Deborah. 1996. "Two Paths to Self Employment?" *Work and Occupations* 23(1): 26–53.

Cassirer, Naomi. 1996. "Race Composition and Earnings: Effects by Race, Region, and Gender." *Social Science Research* 25(4): 375–99.

Cohn, Samuel, and Mark Fossett. 1995. "Why Racial Employment Inequality Is Greater in Northern Labor Markets: Regional Differences in White-Black Employment Differentials." *Social Forces* 74(2): 511–42.

D'Amico, Ronald, and Nan L. Maxwell. 1995. "The Continuing Significance of Race in Minority Male Joblessness." *Social Forces* 73(3): 969–91.

DiPrete, Thomas A., and Margaret L. Krecker. 1991. "Occupational Linkages and Job Mobility within and across Organizations." *Research in Social Stratification and Mobility* 10: 91–132.

DiPrete, Thomas A., and Patricia A. McManus. 1993. "Tenure, Mobility, and Incumbency: Comparing Observed Patterns of Earnings with Predictions from an Elaborated Theory of Occupational and Firm Labor Markets." *Research in Social Stratification and Mobility* 12: 45–82.

———. 1996. "Institutions, Technical Change, and Diverging Life Chances: Earnings Mobility in the United States and Germany." *American Journal of Sociology* 102(1): 34–79.

Duncan, Greg J., Johanne Boisjoly, and Timothy Sneeding. 1996. "Economic Mobility of Young Workers in the 1970s and 1980s." *Demography* 33(4): 497–510.

Eliason, Scott. 1995. "An Extension of the Sorensen-Kalleberg Theory of the Labor Market Matching and Attainment Processes." *American Sociological Review* 60(2): 247–71.

England, Paula, Melissa S. Herbert, Barbara S. Kilbourne, Lori L. Reid, and Laurie M. Megdal. 1994. "The Gendered Valuation of Occupations and Skills: Earnings in 1980 Census Occupations." *Social Forces* 73(September): 65–100.

England, Paula, Lori L. Reid, and Barbara Stanek Kilbourne. 1996. "The Effect of Sex Composition on the Starting Wages in an Organization: Findings from the NLSY." *Demography* 33(4): 511–22.

Farkas, George, and Kevin Vicknair. 1996. "Appropriate Tests of Racial Wage Discrimination Require Controls for Cognitive Skill." *American Sociological Review* 61(4): 557–60.

Felmlee, Dianne. 1995. "Causes and Consequences of Women's Employment Discontinuity, 1967–1973." *Work and Occupations* 22(2): 167–87.

Figart, Deborah, and June Lapidus. 1996. "The Impact of Comparable Worth on Earnings Inequality." *Work and Occupations* 23(3): 297–318.

Firebaugh, Glenn, and Brian Harley. 1995. "Trends in Job Satisfaction in the United States by Race, Gender, and Type of Occupation." *Research in the Sociology of Work* 5: 87–104.

Gill, Andrew. 1989. "The Role of Discrimination in Determining Occupational Structure." *Industrial and Labor Relations Review* 42(4): 610–23.

Gyimah-Brempong, Kwabena, and Rudy Fichtenbaum. 1993. "Black-White Wage Differential: The Relative Importance of Human Capital and Labor Market Structure." *Review of Black Political Economy* 21(4): 19–52.

Hachen, David. 1993. "Intergenerational Mobility Regimes in the United States and

Canada: A Comparative Analysis." *Research in Social Stratification and Mobility* 14: 3–44.

Henretta, John C., and Jyunkee Lee. 1996. "Cohort Differences in Men's Late Life Labor Force Participation." *Work and Occupations* 23(2): 214–35.

Hersch, Joni. 1991. "Male-Female Differences in Hourly Wages: The Role of Human Capital, Working Conditions, and Housework." *Industrial and Labor Relations Review* 44(4): 746–59.

Hirsch, Barry T., and Edward J. Schumacher. 1992. "Labor Earnings, Discrimination, and the Racial Composition of Jobs." *Journal of Human Resources* 27(4): 602–28.

Hsueh, Sheri and Marta Tienda. 1995. "Earnings Consequences of Employment Instability among Minority Men." Research in Social Stratification and Mobility 14: 39–70.

Jacobs, Jerry A. 1992. "Women's Entry into Management: Trends in Earnings, Authority, Values, and Attitudes among Salaried Managers." *Administrative Science Quarterly* 37(2): 282–301.

Jacobs, Jerry A., Marie Lukens, and Michael Useem. 1996. "Organizational, Job, and Individual Determinants of Workplace Training: Evidence from the National Organizations Survey." *Social Science Quarterly* 77(1): 159–76.

Jacobsen, Joyce P. 1994. "Trends in Work Force Sex Segregation, 1960–1990." *Social Science Quarterly* 75(1): 204–21.

Kalleberg, Arne L., and Barbara F. Reskin. 1995. "Gender Differences in Promotion in the United States and Norway." *Research in Social Stratification and Mobility* 14: 237–64.

Kalleberg, Arne L., and Mark van Buren. 1996. "Is Bigger Better?" *American Sociological Review* 61(1): 47–66.

Kilbourne, Barbara, Paula England, and Kurt Beron. 1994. "Effects of Individual, Occupational, and Industrial Characteristics on Earnings: Intersections of Race and Gender." *Social Forces* 72(4): 1149–76.

Kilbourne, Barbara Stanek, Paula England, George Farkas, Kurt Beron, and Dorothea Weir. 1994. "Returns to Skill, Compensating Differentials, and Gender Bias: Effects of Occupational Characteristics on the Wages of White Men and Women." *American Journal of Sociology* 100(3): 689–719.

Kreft, Ita G., and Jan de Leeuw. 1994. "The Gender Gap in Earnings: A Two-Way Nested Multiple Regression Analysis with Random Effects." *Sociological Methods and Research* 22(3): 319–41.

Leicht, Kevin T., and Norma Shepelak. 1994. "Organizational Justice and Satisfaction with Economic Rewards." *Research in Social Stratification and Mobility* 13: 175–202.

Lichter, Daniel T., and David J. Landry. 1991. "Labor Force Transitions and Underemployment: The Stratification of Male and Female Workers." *Research in Social Stratification and Mobility* 10: 63–90.

Logan, John Allen. 1996. "Opportunity and Choice in Socially Structured Labor Markets." *American Journal of Sociology* 102(1): 114–60.

Lorence, Jon, and Joel Nelson. 1993. "Industrial Restructuring and Metropolitan Earnings Inequality: 1970–1988." *Research in Social Stratification and Mobility* 12: 145–84.

Marsden, Peter V., Arne L. Kalleberg, and Cynthia R. Cook. 1993. "Gender Differences in Organizational Commitment: Influences of Work Positions and Family Roles." *Sociology of Work and Occupations* 20(3): 368–90.

McGuire, Gail M., and Barbara F. Reskin. 1993. "Authority Hierarchies at Work: The Impacts of Race and Sex." *Gender and Society* 7(4): 487–506.

O'Neill, June, and Solomon Polachek. 1993. "Why the Gender Gap in Wages Narrowed in the 1980s." *Journal of Labor Economics* 11(1): 205–28.

Oppenheimer, Valerie K., and Matthijs Kalmijn. 1995. "Life-Cycle Jobs." *Research in Social Stratification and Mobility* 14: 1–38.

Petersen, Trond, and Laurie A. Morgan. 1995. "Separate and Unequal: Occupation-Establishment Sex Segregation and the Gender Wage Gap." *American Journal of Sociology* 101(2): 329–65.

Phelan, Jo, Evelyn J. Bromet, Joseph E. Schwartz, Mary Amanda Dew, and E. Carroll Curtis. 1993. "The Work Environment of Male and Female Professionals: Objective and Subjective Characteristics." *Work and Occupations* 20(1): 68–89.

Portes, Alejandro, and Min Zhou. 1996. "Self-Employment and Earnings of Immigrants." *American Sociological Review* 61(2): 219–30.

Presser, Harriet. 1995. "Job, Family, and Gender: Determinants of Nonstandard Work Schedules among Employed Americans in 1991." *Demography* 32(4): 577–98.

Presser, Harriet B., and Elizabeth Bamberger. 1993. "American Women Who Work at Home for Pay: Distinctions and Determinants." *Social Science Quarterly* 74(December): 815–37.

Presser, Harriet B., and Joan M. Hermsen. 1996. "Gender Differences in the Determinants of Work-Related Overnight Travel among Employed Americans." *Work and Occupations* 23(1): 87–115.

Reskin, Barbara F., and Naomi R. Cassirer. 1996. "Occupational Segregation by Gender, Race, and Ethnicity." *Sociological Focus* 29(3): 231–44.

Reskin, Barbara F., and Catherine E. Ross. 1992. "Jobs, Authority, and Earnings among Managers: The Continuing Significance of Sex." *Work and Occupations* 19(4): 342–65.

Rosenfeld, Rachel A., and Kenneth I. Spenner. 1992. "Occupational Sex Segregation and Women's Early Career Job Shifts." Work and Occupations 19(4): 424–49.

Rowe, Reba, and William E. Snizek. 1995. "Gender Differences in Work Values." *Work and Occupations* 22(2): 215–29.

Sakamoto, Arthur, and Meichu D. Chen. 1991. "Sample Selection and the Dual Labor Market." *Research in Social Stratification and Mobility* 10: 171–98.

Shenhav, Yehouda. 1992. "Entrance of Blacks and Women into Managerial Positions in Scientific and Engineering Occupations: A Longitudinal Analysis." *Academy of Management Journal* 35(4): 889–901.

Spilerman, Seymour, and Harris Shrank. 1991. "Responses to the Intrusions of Family Responsibilities in the Workplace." *Research in Social Stratification and Mobility* 10: 27–62.

Tang, Joyce. 1993. "Whites, Blacks and Asians in Science and Engineering: A Reconsideration of Their Economic Prospects." *Research in Social Stratification and Mobility* 12: 249–94.

Thomas, Melvin E. 1993. "Race, Class, and Personal Income: An Empirical Test of the Declining Significance of Race Thesis, 1968–88." *Social Problems* 40(3): 328–42.

Thomas, Melvin E., Cedric Herring, and H. D. Horton. 1993. "Discrimination over the Life Course: A Synthetic Cohort Analysis of Earnings Differences between Black and White Males." *Social Problems* 41(4): 608–28.

Tomaskovic-Devey, Donald. 1993a. "The Gender and Race Composition of Jobs and the Male/Female, White/Black Pay Gaps." *Social Forces* 72(1): 45–76.

———. 1993b. "Labor-Process Inequality and the Gender and Race Composition of Jobs." *Research in Social Stratification and Mobility* 12: 215–47.

Waldfogel, Jane. 1997. "The Effect of Children on Women's Wages." *American Sociological Review* 62(2): 209–17.

Wellington, Allison J. 1994. "The Male/Female Wage Gap among Whites: 1976 and 1985." *American Sociological Review* 59(6): 839–48.

Wenk, DeeAnn, and Rachel A. Rosenfeld. 1992. "Women's Employment Exit and Re-entry: Job-Leaving Reasons and Their Consequences." *Research in Social Stratification and Mobility* 11: 127–50.

Wilson, Franklin, Marta Tienda, and Larry Wu. 1995. "Race and Unemployment: Labor Market Experiences of Black and White Men, 1968–1988." *Work and Occupations* 22(3): 245–70.

Witkowski, Kristine M., and Kevin T. Leicht. 1995. "The Effects of Gender Segregation, Labor Force Participation, and Family Roles on the Earnings of Young Adult Workers." *Work and Occupations* 22(1): 48–72.

Chapter 13

Latinas and African American Women in the Labor Market: Implications for Policy

Joya Misra

Almost 30 percent of all African Americans and Latinos and Latinas live in poverty, whereas only 10 percent of whites do. This number includes almost half of all African American children and more than one-third of Latino and Latina children. The poverty rates calculated for children living in households headed by women are even more dramatic. Two-thirds of African American and Latino and Latina children in families headed by single mothers live in poverty (compared with 20 percent of white children in such families) (Danziger and Weinberg 1994, 35, 37).

To make sense of these disturbing figures, scholars have explored variations in the labor market, as it is a key mechanism for the distribution of resources. The studies consistently show a wage disadvantage for African American women and Latinas. For example, the findings in chapter 4 show that employed Latinas and African American women earn 73 percent and 67 percent, respectively, of employed white men's earnings. Yet most labor market analyses that address race have focused on the problem of minority men's joblessness and falling wages and address minority women only as unmarried mothers (Wilson 1987; Mincy 1994). For example, Mincy (1994, 139) argues that "race conscious policies . . . must . . . help low-skilled black workers to compete against low-skilled women and immigrants," without acknowledging that these women workers may also be African American.

Gender, race, and ethnicity and their intersections affect all labor market outcomes. Yet few studies, even among those published in the mid-1990s in top sociology journals, utilize gender and race analytically to understand these labor market outcomes. As the survey described in chapter 12 shows, research that fails to recognize the theoretical centrality of race, ethnicity, and gender to labor market processes and outcomes evidence four significant problems: the studies (1) often omit important variables (such as family status); (2) assume equivalent effects across racial and gender groups when they do not exist, leading to the misspecification of causal processes;

(3) suffer from sample selection bias when some groups are left out of analyses based on attributes that correlate with the dependent variable; and (4) treat as exogenous, or independent from factors in the model, factors that are actually endogenous, or caused by independent factors in the model. As stated in chapter 1,

> Simply borrowing from models originally developed for African American men or white women will not be enough. The experiences of African American women in the labor market are very different from those of African American men or white women. African American women need and deserve their own models.

This volume offers an in-depth analysis of African American women's and Latinas' participation in the labor market, employment opportunities, and economic prospects. By analyzing in detail the Latinas and African American women who make up 8 percent of the U.S. labor force (see chapter 12), the contributors to this volume help answer the troubling question of why these women and their children are so likely to live in poverty. In this chapter, I first summarize the key insights provided by these authors and then draw out the policy implications of these insights.

SUMMARY OF LABOR MARKET OUTCOMES AND PROCESSES

As Irene Browne suggests in the introduction, "Economic hardship among Latinas and African American women is often framed as a welfare issue or a problem of the lack of a male wage earner rather than a question of female labor market dynamics." Such scholarship has often assumed that because the wage gap between minority and white women narrowed during the 1970s, minority women have attained parity with white women (chapter 1). Therefore, other problems, such as low marriage rates, have been blamed for minority women's poverty. Yet in the 1980s wage differentials actually increased more for African American and Mexican-origin women than for white women (see the introduction). Using data from the 1990s, the contributors to this volume highlight the importance of understanding minority women's position in the labor market. Some of the critical issues that African American women and Latinas face are described below.

Labor Force Participation

Over the 1980s and 1990s white women's labor force participation has expanded rapidly. In contrast, African American women and Latinas' participation rates have remained steady or increased less rapidly, leading to larger employment gaps between these groups and white women. While the work commitment of young African American women has shown no signs of decline, labor force participation stagnated through the 1970s and 1980s (chapter 1). Labor force participation rates for young Mexican-origin women have similarly held steady, though they have expanded in some regions (chapter 4; chapter 7). Young Puerto Rican women have increased their labor force participation, although they still lag considerably behind young white women (chapter 3; chapter 6).

Wages

The hourly wages of young African American women were relatively stable during the 1970s. However, throughout the 1980s, young African American women's wages decreased while young white women's wages increased.[1] This difference led to a widening wage gap between these groups (chapter 1, figure 1.1; chapter 2, figures 2.1 and 2.2). For young Mexican-origin women, wages were low and declining. Although young Mexican-origin women with less than a high school education attained wage parity with white women, those with higher levels of education earned considerably less than white women did. In addition, Mexican-born women, recent immigrants, and nonproficient English speakers were at a wage disadvantage. Wages have been more equitable for young Puerto Rican women compared with white women of the same educational levels.

Unemployment

Unemployment rates for African American, Mexican-origin, and Puerto Rican women are twice the rates for white women (introduction, table I.3). In addition, the gaps in the unemployment rates have grown over time, widening in particular during recessions, indicating that African American and Latina women are more vulnerable to economic shifts (chapter 1; chapter 3). At every educational level, African American and Latina women have higher unemployment rates than white women. For example, even minority women who are college graduates face higher levels of unemployment: in 1990, 3.5 percent of young college-educated African American women were unemployed, and 4.5 percent and 4.3 percent of young, college-educated Puerto Rican and Mexican-origin women, respectively, are unemployed, compared with 1.7 percent of young white women (chapter 1, table 1.2; chapter 3, tables 3.5, 3.8). Among less educated minority women, Puerto Rican and African American women face much higher levels of unemployment than white women, although Mexican-origin women are closer to parity with white women at *lower* educational levels (chapter 1, table 1.2; chapter 3, tables 3.5, 3.8).

Increased Competition with White Women

The rapid influx of young white women into the labor market has increased the level of job competition faced by African American women and

Latinas. During the 1980s, for the first time in the twentieth century, young white women's labor force participation rates exceeded those for young minority women (introduction; chapter 1; chapter 2). The increase of white women workers has expanded the employment gap between white and minority women (chapter 1; chapter 3).

Increased Competition with Immigrants

Immigrant workers may compete with Latinas and African American women for jobs. For example, in 1980 wages in areas with a high concentration of Mexican-born women were lower for Mexican immigrant and Mexican American women than in other areas. However, white women's wages were not affected, while African American women's wages were higher in these areas. In 1990, areas with a high concentration of Mexican-born women showed lower wages for Mexican-origin women, no effect for Mexican-American women, and higher wages for African American and white women. This pattern may be due to the fact that Mexican-origin women are employed in domestic positions, which allow African American and white women to spend more time working outside of the home. These findings suggest that competition with immigrants actually only affects members of the immigrating group (chapter 7, tables 7.5, 7.6).

Education and Skills

Differences in educational attainment and the increasing returns to education explain some of the employment and wage differences for young Latinas and African American and white women (chapter 2, table 2.2; chapter 11). Although educational attainment rose for young African American, Latina, and white women during the 1980s, it expanded more rapidly for white women. African American women and Latinas are also less likely to receive training in the science and technology necessary for employment in the most expansive and well-paying sectors of the economy (chapter 11). Among Latinas, Puerto Rican women have attained the highest levels of educational attainment, followed by Mexican American women and Mexican immigrant women (chapter 2, table 2.1; chapter 3, table 3.1; chapter 7, table 7.1). However, the educational gap between white women and Latinas remains sizable.

Of all women, education has the greatest payoffs for whites. Among high school graduates and women with some college, young white women are more likely to be employed than are young African American women or Latinas. Even among college graduates, white women have a slight employment edge (chapter 1, tables 1.1, 1.2; chapter 3, tables 3.4, 3.7). In addition, the wage gap between African American and white women has widened in recent years. For example, African American *college-educated* women have faced the greatest decline in relative wages (chapter 1, figures 1.2, 1.3; chapter 2, figure 2.3). The wage gap has also widened between Mexican-origin women and white women at every educational level, although it has narrowed between Puerto Rican and white women (chapter 3, tables 3.4, 3.7).

The work experience of white women has also increased vis-à-vis African American women and Latinas (chapter 1, figure 1.4). African American women once had much higher levels of work experience, since they were less likely to leave the labor market for extended periods. Yet white women have increased their commitment to remaining in the labor market in recent years. Mexican-origin women have also increased their work experience but have on average significantly less experience than both African American and white women do (chapter 7, table 7.1). Full-time experience and seniority at a firm significantly raise the wages of young African American women and Latinas (chapter 4, table 4.2). However, experience and seniority do not explain wage differences between African American women or Latinas and white women (chapter 4, table 4.7).

Another key factor in employment outcomes may be the development of cognitive skills through work experience and education (chapter 4, tables 4.3, 4.4). Yet skills and educational attainment explain differences between whites and African American women or Latinas better than they explain differences between men and women within the same ethnic category (chapter 4, table 4.7). For example, young African American women and Latinas show higher levels of educational attainment relative to African American men and Latinos but earn only 90 percent and 82 percent, respectively, of those men's wages (chapter 4, table 4.1).

Restructuring of the Economy

With deindustrialization has come a reduction in the number of low-skill manufacturing jobs. Traditionally, these jobs paid better than clerical and service sector jobs did. Latinas and African American women were more concentrated in blue-collar jobs than white women were, so deindustrialization has affected these groups more severely (chapter 2, table 2.2; chapter 6; chapter 11).[2] As jobs in blue-collar manufacturing have decreased, jobs in information services, administration, and professional sectors have grown. Since white women have traditionally been more likely to be employed in these now-growing areas, African American women and Latinas face stiff competition for these jobs (introduction; chapter 2). Women may be more able to compete for these positions if they have social support in the form of a family member's income, so that when restructuring hits, they are able to search for a good job (chapter 6). Weaker unions may also play a role in the worsening position of minority women (chapter 2). The declining real value of the minimum wage has additionally worsened the position of African American women and Latinas (chapter 2, table 2.2).

Industry

In terms of occupations, white women are most strongly represented in clerical and professional-technical positions; African American and Mexican American women, in clerical and service positions; and Mexican-born women, in service and operative positions (chapter 7; chapter 11, table 11.1). In the Southwest, Mexican-born women continue to work primarily in manufacturing, even though it is a declining sector. When they leave this sector, they usually enter domestic service. African American women, however, have been leaving domestic service, while white women have made clear advances in professional and managerial fields (chapter 7, table 7.3; chapter 10).

Because African American women and Latinas are less likely to be employed in industries with high demands for cognitive skills, their wages are lower than white women's wages. However, this difference in industry does not explain the wage gap between African American men and women or between Latinos and Latinas, since women work in industries with higher demands for cognitive skills (chapter 4, tables 4.1, 4.2, 4.7).

Gender Segregation of Jobs

Gender segregation, or the employment of women in jobs and occupations that primarily employ other women, has been one of the key factors in women's lower wages (chapter 5). Gender segregation is associated with lower wages, because jobs seen as women's or seen as requiring nurturant skills are often devalued.

Women earn less in jobs dominated by women, regardless of the education and skills necessary for the position (chapter 4). The level of gender segregation in both jobs and occupations has remained steady and quite high since 1980. In 1988, almost two-thirds of men would have had to change occupation to eliminate gender-based occupational segregation (chapter 1; King 1992). However, these figures do not explain differences between white women and African American women or Latinas (chapter 4, tables 4.6, 4.7). Both Latinas and African American women pay greater penalties for working in gender-segregated or nurturant jobs than white women (chapter 4, tables 4.6, 4.7).

Segregation of Jobs by Race or Ethnicity

Just as analyses of gender segregation illustrate the ways that women have often been concentrated in low-paying occupations, analyses of racial or ethnic segregation have shown that minority women are often concentrated in certain low-paying occupations and jobs (introduction; chapter 5). In 1988, almost one-third of white women would have needed to change their occupations to eliminate occupational segregation by race (chapter 1; King 1992). Using a detailed analysis that includes twenty-six different ethnic groups, Reskin (chapter 5) shows that certain groups of women (Southeast Asian, Central American) are found in most racially segregated jobs, while other groups of women are found in moderately segregated jobs (African American, Mexican-origin, Puerto Rican) or less segregated jobs (British, German). Workers in the most racially segregated jobs suffer clear wage disadvantages and may be more vulnerable during economic recessions (chapter 5).

Geographic Differences

Employment and wages vary significantly between regions. The racial gap in wages is lower in the Northeast and higher in the South than in other regions. In the Midwest, African American women have seen their wages decline the most, in part because of deindustrialization. As a result, the racial wage gap has widened significantly, although it has not surpassed the southern wage gap (introduction; chapter 1, figure 1.3; chapter 2, figure 2.4, table 2.2). Despite these regional differences, region does not serve as a strong predictor of racial differences in wages (chapter 4, tables 4.2, 4.3, 4.4). Latinas also have better employment outcomes when they are more geographically dispersed. For example, Puerto Rican women concentrated in New York and New Jersey and Mexican-origin women concentrated in California and Texas have lower earnings relative to white women than Latinas living elsewhere do (chapter 3). Similarly, Mexican-born women pay wage penalties when they live in areas with a high concentration of Mexican immigrants (chapter 7).

Spatial Mismatch and Residential Segregation

The availability of low-skilled jobs has declined in urban centers (introduction; chapter 2, table 2.2; chapter 6). Yet this decline has hurt African American women and Latinas more than it has hurt white women. Employment rates for African American women in suburban areas have increased, while they have declined radically for those in center cities. For white women, employment opportunities have been expanding in both center cities and suburban areas (chapter 1, figure 1.7). In addition, the industries that are expanding are more likely to locate in suburban areas rather than center cities (chapter 2). Because many African American women and Latinas reside outside suburban areas, they are at a disadvantage for getting these jobs (chapter 6). The location of subsidized housing in center-city areas and other forms of residential segregation contribute to Latinas' and African American women's declining job opportunities (chapter 2).

Family Responsibilities

Since 1980, labor force participation has grown rapidly among all married women. Among young white, Mexican-origin, and Puerto Rican women, single women without children have the highest rates of labor force participation. However, for young African American women, participation rates are higher for *married* women than single women without children. Marriage has a dampening effect on labor force participation for every group except African American women (chapter 1, figure 1.5; chapter 3, tables 3.4, 3.7). Single motherhood has been increasing among every group. African American women have the highest levels of single motherhood, followed by white, Mexican American, and Mexican-born women. Yet the employment of single mothers also *decreased* since the mid-1970s for every group except Puerto Rican women (chapter 1, figures 1.6a, 1.6b; chapter 3, tables 3.4, 3.7).

Family structure may play a key role in determining how economic restructuring affects wages. For example, married Puerto Rican women who are laid off are more likely to find another well-paying job than single women, who often must take the first job they find (chapter 6). When women search for new jobs, the economic resources provided by their husbands actually allow married women to earn higher wages (introduction). The positive effect of marriage on young African American women's labor force participation suggests a similar effect for African Americans. This finding indicates one of the ways in which minority women's labor market experiences may differ from white women's experiences.

Job-Search Networks

Both residential segregation and family structure affect connections to the informal networks that are critical for finding jobs, particularly well-paying jobs. In neighborhoods with greater unemployment, women are less likely to know other workers who can provide an entrée to new jobs. Husbands and other adult family members also provide these connections but are similarly limited by residential segregation (chapter 2; chapter 11). Successful integration into the U.S. labor market requires the support of a network of family or neighbors who can lead workers to jobs (chapter 6).

Welfare

Social support networks and family are also key to determining who is able to exit welfare successfully. Structural factors such as residential context, unemployment rates, and differences in recipients' education and skills are often emphasized, but these factors do not explain why African American women are more likely to return to welfare than whites are. One key to this puzzle is that, although African American women are more likely to work continuously and receive wages similar to those of white women, both groups generally find jobs that pay wages lower than necessary for survival. When in need, African American women draw upon their social networks, but the members of these networks are less likely to have extra resources. White women face many of the same financial crises but are more likely to cohabit or marry after leaving welfare and have other sources of social capital to draw upon (introduction, chapter 8). These findings suggest the importance of wealth discrepancies between groups, and these effect exiting welfare.

Discrimination

Because the labor force participation of white women has increased, employers have found it easier to engage in statistical discrimination in recent years. Statistical discrimination refers to employers' choosing workers by substituting characteristics they associate with groups for information about individuals. In addition, with an increased supply of women workers, employers have found it easier to engage in pure discrimination (introduction, chapter 1).

Among women in professional, managerial, and administrative positions, a majority of both African American and white women agreed that sexism occurs in the workplace, although African American women were more likely to agree (chapter 10). Among these same women, more than two-thirds of the African Americans also perceived racism, while less than a third of white women did so. Perceptions of gender and racial discrimination differed for white and African American women. For example, while one-quarter of white women argued that they themselves had been treated unfairly because of their gender, more than 40 percent of African American women believed they had been (chapter 10).

In terms of entry-level workers, many employers clearly engage in statistical discrimination. African American women are characterized as primarily "single mothers," even though the majority (80 percent) are not (chapter 9, table 9.1). In addition, employers believe that African American women are more likely to have child-care problems, even though white and African American women report similar rates and white and African American men also report notable problems arising from child-care concerns (chapter 9, table 9.3).

Variations Among Ethnic Groups

Although many studies treat Latinas as one group, the contributors to this volume point out the wide divergence among Latinas based on differences in country of origin, immigration status, geographical location, English proficiency, and marital status. For example, Cuban women find jobs with wages very similar to those of whites, Puerto Rican and Mexican American women do somewhat worse, and Mexican-born women are in the lowest-paying jobs (introduction; chapter 7). Puerto Rican women fare very poorly economically compared with other Latinas, even though they have the added bonus of U.S. citizenship and higher educational levels (chapter 3). Analyses of twenty-six different ethnic groups show that significant differences in women's educational attainment, occupation, immigration rate, and fluency clearly affect earnings (chapter 5).

Summary

The chapters in this volume analyze in detail the labor market opportunities and outcomes of Mexican-origin, Puerto Rican, and African American women. Studies have noted the widening gaps between the labor force participation and wages of white women, Latinas, and African American women.

The greater returns that white women receive for education and their increasing levels of educational attainment have limited the positive impact of increases in educational attainment for African American women and Latinas. Deindustrialization has also contributed to the relative decline of Latinas and African American women in the labor market, since they are more likely to be employed in the weakening sectors of the economy. White women have been better represented in the expanding sectors, such as professional and technical services, while African American women and Latinas have been represented more heavily in service and operative positions. Gender segregation and racial segregation also affect the types of jobs that Latinas and African American women take, with more highly segregated jobs paying lower wages. Wages differ by geographic region, and racial wage gaps are larger in the South and increasing in the Midwest. Latinas receive higher wages if they live outside highly concentrated Latino and Latina areas.

Declining job opportunities in urban areas and residential segregation also have led to worsening labor market outcomes for African American women and Latinas. Family structure has led to some surprising effects: married women particularly have expanded their labor force participation and seem to garner rewards relative to single women. Single mothers in all groups face declining job opportunities. Residential segregation and family structure also affect connections to job search networks that join workers with jobs. Both statistical and pure gender and racial discrimination continue to strongly affect labor market outcomes, although white and African American women have somewhat different perceptions of discrimination. Finally, different groups of Latinas evidence very different labor market opportunities and outcomes.

IMPLICATIONS FOR POLICY

Policy makers can take a number of critical lessons from the analyses in this volume. Most important is that *Latinas' and African American women's labor market opportunities and outcomes cannot be assumed to reflect white women's, Latinos', and African American men's opportunities and outcomes.* Even among Latinas, significant differences between groups require exploration. As Mary Corcoran, Colleen M. Heflin, and Belinda Reyes remark in chapter 3, "Public policies must be formulated to address the relative labor market disadvantage Latinas [and African American women] face." The most well-intentioned policies will suffer from inefficiency if incomplete models are used to design them. In drawing a more detailed picture of the Latinas and African American women in the U.S. labor market, this volume contributes to a more in-depth understanding of labor market models.

Several suggestions clearly arise from the evidence presented here. As Blank (1994, 188) has cogently noted,

> Given that social and economic changes are continuing to move more women in the labor market, policy efforts designed to supplement and support that trend may be more successful than efforts expended on men, whose labor force participation has steadily fallen.

Certainly men's and women's lives are interconnected, and policy making should reflect that interrelationship. However, focusing policy on raising men's incomes will not necessarily increase women's economic well-being, particularly in light of the increase in the number of families headed by single mothers. In addition, as a result of gender segregation, most men and women do not compete for the same positions. Therefore, I focus my attention on the policies that might best help African American women and Latinas achieve greater success in the labor market, with the understanding that these policies will for the most part also support the economic chances of African American men and Latinos.

Improve Educational Attainment and Job Training

Improving the educational attainment and skills of Latinas and African American women is a critical prerequisite to enhancing their labor market opportunities. While white women receive greater returns from their education, Latinas and African American women do clearly benefit from greater educational attainment. In particular, both groups need access to college education. In addition, job-training programs need to be expanded and funded both to help young women make the transition from schools to jobs and to upgrade workers' skills so that they can find jobs in the skill-intensive, expanding sectors of the economy (chapter 8; Blank 1994; Garfinkel and McLanahan 1994; Murnane 1994; Tobin 1994).

Since the 1960s, the government has developed and funded programs directed at educational opportunities, job counseling, and training. These programs were expanded until the 1980s, when funding for education and training programs was drastically reduced. Outlays on federally targeted job-training programs dropped from $9.6 billion in 1980 to only $3.5 billion in 1992 (Burtless 1994, 57). Most evidence suggests that these programs have made good progress in combating poverty and encouraging employment. The effects of educational programs can be difficult to assess, since benefits accrue long after outlays have been made. However, educational attainment has risen among targeted populations, and educational programs have been shown to increase college attendance and to decrease dropout rates, special education needs, teen pregnancies, unemployment, and crime (Murnane 1994). These programs need to be expanded, improved, and more generously funded.

Summer programs and other targeted programs should have the explicit goal of reducing ethnicity-related gaps in cognitive skills (chapter 4).[3] Educational enrichment programs need to encourage and support efforts to increase academic achievement and attainment (Mincy 1994). For example, while college entrance rates are relatively similar for white and African American women, degree attainment rates are not. Programs should focus on addressing this problem. To encourage competencies in science and technology, notes Delores Aldridge (chapter 11), important steps are to develop curriculums that reflect the contributions of minority members, make tutors and counseling available for all students, improve the recruitment of minority students, expose students to lab-based science curricula and science and math careers, and expand special training programs for careers in science and research experience for undergraduates. Educational reforms should also ensure that every student, regardless of class background, receives a high-quality education (Blank 1994; chapter 4; chapter 7).

Training programs have also shown direct positive effects, particularly for women (Bassi and Ashenfelter 1986; Blank 1994; Burtless 1994). Programs that prepare high school students for work, joint high school–community college vocational programs, school-to-work programs, and youth apprenticeship programs all play important roles in stimulating employment and increasing wages (Blank 1994). In addition, language training classes for immigrants can greatly improve their wages (chapter 3; chapter 7). Burtless (1994, 74) argues that "one dollar spent on training ultimately raises the incomes of participating adults by more than one dollar. Effective training thus not only redistributes slices of the economic pie from the nonpoor to the poor, but increases the size of the pie."

Desegregate Occupations, Institute
Comparable Worth Policies

One of the clearest contributors to African American women's and Latinas' lower wages is their segregation in jobs and industries that are heavily populated by white and minority women. One method of desegregating industries and jobs should be to develop educational curricula that encourage girls to enter traditionally male-dominated occupations and encourage African American girls and young Latinas to enter occupations traditionally dominated by white women (chapter 4). In addition, boys should be encouraged to enter fields traditionally dominated by women. Job-training programs should also be carefully developed and evaluated to ensure tracking into nontraditional but well-paying and expanding industries.

A more immediate approach to this problem is through comparable worth policies. Occupations held by women now often require high levels of cognitive skills, but wages do not reflect these higher skill levels. Comparable worth policies mandate setting occupational pay levels in accordance with the comparable worth of an occupation, ensuring that wages are pegged to the skills required (chapter 4; England 1992; England et al. 1994). One recent study shows that implementing comparable worth would decrease overall earnings inequality, earnings inequality between men and women, and earnings inequality between groups of women (Figart and Lapidus 1996). While comparable worth policies do not desegregate occupations, instituting comparable worth would contribute to placing a greater value on and more fairly rewarding the work that African American and Latina women do.

Lessen Residential Segregation

Residential segregation also plays a key role in limiting African American women's and Latinas' occupations. In the 1990s, jobs became more rare in city centers but proliferated in the suburbs. However, Latinas and African American women are more likely to live in center-city areas, which also is where most low-income or subsidized housing is located. Therefore, poverty is reinforced, as residential segregation helps maintain the relative lack of labor market opportunities (chapter 4; Massey and Denton 1993; Massey and Eggers 1990). In addition, residential segregation often results in neighborhoods with fewer middle- or working-class families and fewer infrastructural resources. Such segregation has numerous ill effects. Wilson (1987, 57) recounts one effect:

> Thus, in a neighborhood with a paucity of regularly employed families and with the overwhelming majority of families having spells of long-term job-

lessness, people experience a social isolation that excludes them from the job network system that permeates other neighborhoods and that is so important in learning about or being recommended for jobs that become available in various parts of the city.

One solution to residential segregation is to develop low-income housing in areas outside city centers. Latinas and African American women who settle in suburban areas will have increased labor market opportunities. Another possibility is housing vouchers that allow poor women to choose the area that they live in while still receiving housing subsidies (Blank 1994). Expanding public transportation may also be an important solution to this problem. For Latinas and African American women living in center-city areas, affordable, quick, and available transportation to suburban areas can make an enormous difference in work opportunities. Because cars are beyond the budgets of many poor families, public transportation is not a simple convenience but a crucial part of getting and maintaining jobs (Blank 1994; Lehman 1994).

Another solution to residential segregation is to develop new industries within city centers and to develop integrated communities that include both middle-class and working-class workers (Lehman 1994; Wilson 1987). If African American women and Latinas live in neighborhoods that are entirely poor, they have fewer resources available to serve as job search networks. Enterprise zones are one approach to redeveloping city centers through spatial targeting. For example, businesses may receive tax incentives for conducting business in a zone and employing workers from that zone. While businesses in such zones have been criticized for not truly expanding employment opportunities, even limited expansion holds some possibility of lifting neighborhoods out of despair (Lehman 1994).

Improve Wages and Tax Policy

Another difficulty faced by African American women and Latinas is that their wages are frequently too low to support themselves and their families. At a very basic level, wages for all workers must be improved (chapter 8; Blank 1994). Real wages have declined since the mid-1970s, making survival more and more difficult for poor women (Blank 1994; Garfinkel and McLanahan 1994). Although the minimum wage increase in 1996 provided some relief, raising the minimum wage to levels that allow survival is critical. In addition, wage policy should seek to create a more egalitarian wage distribution (chapter 4; Burtless 1994). Comparable worth policy may also reduce wage gaps.

Another support for wages may be through the Earned Income Tax Credit (EITC), which structures the tax system to reward work effort (Blank 1994; Tobin 1994; Garfinkel and McLanahan 1994). First designed in the mid-1970s, the EITC provides work incentives for low-wage workers in the form of a refundable tax credit for families with children, so that families who do not owe taxes can receive tax refunds. Yet this program helps families with incomes between $8,000 and $20,000 a year but has little or no benefit for families who earn less than this amount. Potential recipients apply for the EITC on their federal income tax forms, and if they owe less than the credit, they receive the difference in cash. Between 10 percent and 20 percent of those eligible do not receive the benefit (Bergmann 1996, 101, 102). Although the expansion of the EITC in 1986 and 1993 benefited low-wage workers, the program needs to be publicized more widely and expanded, particularly to poor families who earn so little that they do not file taxes and who are not currently covered by the program. Along with a higher minimum wage, the EITC could move poor families closer to the poverty line (Blank 1994).

Improve Access to Health Care

Health care is one of the most pressing needs of Latinas and African American women (chapter 7; Bergmann 1996; Blank 1994; Burtless 1994; Garfinkel and McLanahan 1994; Tobin 1994; Wolfe 1994). Because they are more likely to live in poverty, these women are less likely to have any sort of medical insurance or receive regular medical care. As a result, and as a result of poor nutrition and living conditions, they face more serious health problems than white women do (Wolfe 1994). Poor health puts additional limits on the earnings of the poor.

In 1989, less than 5 percent of individuals living in poverty had access to private insurance (Wolfe 1994, 254–55). Even those who are eligible for Medicaid by virtue of disability or status as a welfare recipient often have difficulty finding health care because services are not readily available in their neighborhoods (Wolfe 1994). For women trying to leave welfare, health care is often the key stumbling block. Since many recipients lose the right to receive Medicaid soon after leaving welfare, and since most low-paying jobs do not include health insurance benefits, one illness can be catastrophic (chapter 8).

One plan is to provide universal health care for all citizens (chapter 4). However with the defeat of President Clinton's health care plan in 1994, universal health insurance has seemed out of reach. More limited plans may meet with greater success (Starr 1986; Wolfe 1994). For example, Wolfe (1994) suggests developing a "healthy kid" program that would cover all children under the age of nineteen for a specific set of services and would be administered through community care centers. Basic care would be free, and additional care or care for adults would require an income-conditioned copayment. This plan would most likely be relatively cheap and would increase immunization rates, family planning, and prenatal care (Bergmann

1996). Another plan is to allow women and their families to remain on Medicaid for a full year after leaving welfare (Garfinkel and McLanahan 1994). Clearly, Latinas and African American women would be best served by a more comprehensive solution, but these limited plans would most likely give many women a chance to keep themselves and their families healthy and economically stronger.

Provide Subsidized Day-care

Even middle-class women in the United States worry about the availability and cost of child care. Poor Latinas and African American women face even greater difficulties obtaining day-care. Single motherhood increases the need for child care, and women's lower level of earnings decreases the resources available to pay it. Day-care costs can quite easily consume much of a woman's wages, making labor force participation less feasible. In addition, even women who can afford some child care may have difficulty finding high-quality care. Decreasing expenses for and ensuring the availability of child care is also a critical factor in women's leaving welfare successfully (chapter 8; Burtless 1994).

One solution would be the provision of public child care, analogous to the provision of public education in the United States (chapter 4; Kamerman and Kahn 1991). Currently, child care is in very short supply, but the existence of publicly funded child-care centers could ensure that high-quality care is available (Kamerman and Kahn 1991). Another solution would be to subsidize high-quality child care provided by large centers, employers, or family child-care centers that would charge fees on a sliding scale (Garfinkel and McLanahan 1994; Blank 1994; Kahn and Kamerman 1987; Kamerman and Kahn 1991; Bergmann 1996). Middle-class families already benefit from child-care subsidies in the form of income tax deductions. Poor families, however, do not earn enough for these deductions to matter. Child-care providers, who earn very low wages and rarely receive health benefits, might also receive subsidies (Blank 1994).

Ensure a Safety Net

Because Latinas and African American women have fewer opportunities and earn lower wages in the labor market, they need a safety net to rely upon when they cannot find work, cannot find day-care for their children, or face health problems. From 1935 to 1996, that safety net was Aid to Families with Dependent Children (AFDC), a means-tested welfare program for families with children.

Even before AFDC was terminated and replaced with the more limited Temporary Aid to Needy Families (TANF) program, welfare benefits were so low that they did not serve as a true safety net for poor families (Blank

1994). Benefits usually kept families well below the poverty threshold (41 percent of the threshold with AFDC and 72 percent of the threshold with AFDC and food stamps; Danziger and Weinberg 1994, 39). In addition, rates of participation in AFDC were low: in 1989, the ratio of children who received AFDC to all poor children was only 59 percent (compared with 80 percent in 1973; Danziger and Weinberg 1994, 39). However, means-tested programs like AFDC are among the most efficient poverty-reducing programs. Burtless (1994, 63) remarks, "These transfers are the nation's least costly mechanism for reducing the gap between market-provided incomes and the resources required for a standard of living above the poverty level."

In 1992, AFDC cost $22.9 billion, compared with $238 billion spent on Social Security's Old Age Insurance program. These figures, along with the fact that AFDC was not indexed to the cost of living, partly explain why the poverty rate for the elderly has drastically declined since the 1960s (from 35.2 percent in 1960 to 12.2 percent in 1990) while increasing for children since the 1970s (from 14.9 percent in 1970 to 19.9 percent in 1990) (Danziger and Weinberg 1994, 37). One reason that Social Security has expanded while AFDC has been eliminated is the means-tested nature of AFDC benefits. Social Security, a universal program, benefits all workers, but AFDC benefited only the poorest and had less public support.

One way to ensure a safety net for poor families would be to institute a universal children's allowance (Bergmann 1996; Garfinkel and McLanahan 1994). These allowances, in line with policies in European welfare states and provided in every industrialized country except the United States, partly subsidize the costs of raising children and represent an investment in the future workers of the country by ensuring that they receive adequate nutrition and care (chapter 4). Allowances serve as a significant source of income for the average family with children but constitute an even more important part of the income of poor families and families headed by single mothers (Kamerman and Kahn 1983). Along similar lines, Garfinkel and McLanahan (1994) suggest a refundable tax credit that would subsidize child-rearing costs. As an extension of the EITC, such a credit would be easily administered and would greatly help poor families.

Another way to provide a safety net would be to restructure the welfare system so that it rewards work more than the current system does and to combine job training, job placement, child care, transportation to jobs, and health care into a comprehensive program for women (Ellwood and Summers 1986; Blank 1994). AFDC was inherently flawed in that it did not reward work; most women receiving AFDC were not able to earn more than the program paid even when working because of AFDC's low levels of earnings disregard ($30 per month) and because of child-care costs (Blank 1994). However, the time limits placed on receiving TANF will not help women solve the difficulties that keep them from finding and keeping jobs (Blank 1994). Poor Latinas and African American women need a comprehensive safety net that addresses their multiple dilemmas: low wages, inadequate day care and health care, and inadequate job training, among others (Blank 1994).

Address the Family Support Gap

Family structure is a key issue for policy makers, particular in terms of poor African American women and Latinas. Rates of single motherhood have been rising among all groups of women, and single motherhood contributes to higher poverty rates and difficulty finding and keeping well-paying jobs. Even for women without children, marriage benefits employment chances. For example, African American married women are more likely to be employed than single women without children are; if laid off, Puerto Rican married women are more likely to find good jobs than single women are (chapter 1; chapter 6). Some scholars have focused on increasing employment opportunities for African American men and Latinos, with the assumption that income-producing men would lead to higher marriage rates (Wilson 1987; Mincy 1994; Wilson and Neckerman 1986). Yet families headed by single mothers are poor also because women receive lower wages. Since the labor force participation rate among men has been shrinking, a more direct approach is to address women's wage rates (Blank 1994). Simply put, women should be able to earn enough to support their families.

Other family support programs include child support assurance that would guarantee the payment of child support by noncustodial parents. In 1990, only half of all mothers awarded child support by the courts actually collected it all. One-quarter received no support at all (Kamerman and Kahn 1995, 52). A federal child support assurance plan would require parents to share in the costs of maintaining their children, paying the higher of either a minimum benefit or a percentage of their gross income (Garfinkel and McLanahan 1994; Kamerman and Kahn 1995; Bergmann 1996). If a nonresident parent did not pay ordered or agreed-on child support, the government would pay that sum and could then recover it through the garnishment of wages, liens, or seizures (Garfinkel 1992). Federal law already allows the government to withhold the award automatically from an absent and delinquent spouse, but the law is not enforced systematically.

Another approach is the development and expansion of community-defined and -administered, broad-brush family support services directed at educating parents about children's health, child development, the prevention of child abuse, and other child-rearing issues (Kamerman and Kahn 1995). Evidence shows that social support networks are critical in women's finding employment and becoming self-sufficient (chapter 8; Wilson, Ellwood, and Brooks-Gunn 1995). Family support services can simulate more informal networks and provide another safety net for Latina and African American mothers.

Expand Antidiscrimination Policies

Despite common convictions that racial discrimination no longer hampers the work opportunities of African American women and Latinas, evidence continues to show that discrimination affects both their labor market opportunities and their outcomes (Cancio, Evans, and Maume 1996). For example, Duncan (1996) found that women with similar skills, experience, and seniority continue to receive lower earnings than men.

Affirmative action for many years served as a way of countering this discrimination by promoting equal opportunity and recruiting talented minority candidates. However, recent attacks on affirmative action have resulted in the dismantling of many programs, despite the fact that affirmative action is a critical means of recruiting promising Latinas and African American women into schools and businesses (chapter 4; chapter 9; chapter 11; Duncan 1996; Stein 1995). Yet affirmative action, while necessary, is not enough. Affirmative action programs do not always reach the lowest-paid and most marginal workers who face discrimination. Antidiscrimination legislation must also be expanded and vigilantly implemented (chapter 4).

Some scholars have suggested that race-neutral policies not specifically targeted at minorities are more effective than antidiscrimination laws. Wilson (1987) has focused on universal policies that are more likely to garner support from a majority of the population. For example, if employers utilize more formal methods of hiring workers, such as skills tests, African American women and Latinas may actually benefit (Holzer 1987; Neckerman and Kirschenman 1991). Neckerman and Kirschenman (1991) found that employers who used skills tests were more likely to hire African Americans, in part because their other methods for hiring were based on subjective criteria, such as employee referrals or interview skills.

Other theorists have insisted upon at least some race-conscious policies (Darity and Myers 1983). For example, since most employers rely on subjective criteria for hiring, affirmative action policies can help level the playing field for quality minority applicants. In summarizing Darity and Myers' (1983) research, Mincy (1994, 116) argues, "Policies that ignore the legacy of racism in this country have no hopes of ameliorating the (black) underclass." Identifying and demolishing both pure and statistical discrimination requires race-conscious programs (Mincy 1994).

Restructure Work

Family responsibilities create difficulties for all workers in the U.S. labor market. The model for work assumes a breadwinning husband and a homemaker wife, who cares for the children and home. Yet, as the studies in this volume show, that model no longer exists for any group. Restructuring work to allow more flexibility and enabling parents to balance their family and work responsibilities more successfully would benefit all workers (Smith 1997). As Irene Browne and Ivy Kennelly show in chapter 9 (table 9.3), both men and women report that family issues affect their ability to work. Other studies suggest that all workers have been stretched to their limits in trying to balance work and home responsibilities (Schor 1991; Hochschild 1997).

The restructuring of work could take many forms. Some workplaces already allow greater flexibility in the hours that people work and have developed meaningful part-time positions (Smith 1997; Moen and Firebaugh 1994). Relative to U.S. workers, employees in many European countries work fewer hours per week, receive more vacation time each year, and have greater access to paid sick leave. In addition, workers who take either paid or unpaid sick leave benefit from job and seniority guarantees. The provision of family leave so that workers can care for newborn babies or sick children and other family members is also critical (Bookman 1991; Bravo 1991; Hantrais and Letablier 1996; Kamerman and Kahn 1991). The Swedish system has found ways to reward men who take parental leave. As a result, women who take parental leave are not as disadvantaged in the labor market, and both men and women feel responsible for caring for their children (Sundström 1991; Trzcinski 1994).

Flexible work may improve options for all U.S. workers, but it has little chance of significantly improving the lives of poor Latinas and African American women without many of the other changes discussed in this chapter (McLaughlin, Millar, and Cooke 1989). Improving wages, raising the level of educational attainment and skills, addressing occupational and residential segregation, providing child and health care, ensuring a safety net and family support for poor women, and enforcing antidiscrimination legislation are also critical steps in bringing about equality in the labor market.

IS THIS VISION POSSIBLE?

Although the programs outlined above would require time and resources, their benefits would be well worth their costs. Creating a more equitable society through the mechanism of the labor force is in line with the goals of many legislators, scholars, and activists. Two key pieces of evidence support adopting or expanding the programs discussed in the preceding sections. One is simply that the benefits of these programs, if executed effectively, will almost certainly outweigh their costs. Another is that many of these programs have worked in the European context without sacrificing economic growth (Blank 1994).

Macroeconomically, there is no reason to limit spending on these programs. The radical growth of the budget deficit during the 1980s was due primarily to increased spending on defense and biomedical research, the savings and loan bailout, and the expansion of Social Security insurance without a tax increase (Burtless 1994). Implementing the programs discussed here would require raising taxes—but not enough to impair work incentives or economic growth. In addition, these programs will certainly lead to increased earnings, higher tax revenues, and even greater economic health while yielding important returns in poverty and crime reduction (Blank 1994; Mincy 1994; Burtless 1994). As Blank (1994, 203) notes, "Evidence already exists that [these programs] can produce benefits that can outweigh their costs if they are effectively implemented."

One way to judge the impact of increasing spending on social programs is to examine Western European "welfare states," which all spend a higher proportion of gross domestic product on social programs. As studies have consistently shown, higher outlays do not seem to stifle economic growth. Many European nations were hit by the same economic recession that the United States faced during the 1980s, but this recession was not due to social spending. In fact, the economic growth rates of European nations have been similar to and at times higher than that of the United States. This is not to suggest that such spending carries no economic penalty, but that spending does not hamper long-term growth (Burtless 1994).

Even though African American women and Latinas face many obstacles in the labor market, they have increased their labor market participation rates, educational attainment, and skills since the 1970s. Because of the rapid expansion of white women's education and employment, the gains of African American women and Latinas in these areas have not always received the attention they deserve. It is time for policy makers to recognize the impressive progress of African American women and Latinas and create new and better programs directed at encouraging even greater successes for these women in the labor market.

I appreciate the very detailed and thoughtful comments of Irene Browne, Cynthia Hewitt, Marina Karides, Ivy Kennelly, and Stephanie Moller.

NOTES

1. Many of the analyses reported in this volume compared groups of young women, with a potential for less than ten years of experience. An analysis of the employment and wages of young African American women and Latinas women better reflects the changing economic conditions than one that includes such information for older cohorts of women.

2. However, Waldinger (1996) suggests that African American women were traditionally not as heavily represented in manufacturing jobs.

3. As Dahrendorf (1959) and Kohn (1980) argue, these skills are often acquired through experience on the job, rather than formal training. Gaps in cognitive skills may then be an outcome rather than a cause of lower levels of labor market participation.

REFERENCES

Bassi, Laurie J., and Orley Ashenfelter. 1986. "The Effect of Direct Job Creation and Training Programs on Low-Skilled Workers." In *Fighting Poverty: What Works and What Doesn't*, edited by Sheldon H. Danziger and Daniel H. Weinberg. Cambridge, Mass.: Harvard University Press.

Bergmann, Barbara R. 1996. *Saving Our Children from Poverty: What the United States Can Learn From France*. New York: Russell Sage Foundation.

Blank, Rebecca M. 1994. "The Employment Strategy: Public Policies to Increase Work and Earnings." In *Confronting Poverty: Prescriptions for Change*, edited by Sheldon H. Danziger, Gary Sandefur, and Daniel H. Weinberg. New York: Russell Sage Foundation.

Bookman, Ann. 1991. "Parenting without Poverty: The Case for Funded Parental Leave." In *Parental Leave and Child Care: Setting a Research and Policy Agenda*, edited by Janet Shibley Hyde and Marilyn J. Essex. Philadelphia: Temple University Press.

Bravo, Ellen. 1991. "Family Leave: The Need for a New Minimum Standard." In *Parental Leave and Child Care: Setting a Research and Policy Agenda*, edited by Janet Shibley Hyde and Marilyn J. Essex. Philadelphia: Temple University Press.

Burtless, Gary. 1994. "Public Spending on the Poor: Historical Trends and Economic Limits." In *Confronting Poverty: Prescriptions for Change*, edited by Sheldon H. Danziger, Gary Sandefur, and Daniel H. Weinberg. New York: Russell Sage Foundation.

Cancio, A. Silvia, T. David Evans, and David J. Maume, Jr. 1996. "Reconsidering the Declining Significance of Race: Racial Differences in Early Career Wages." *American Sociological Review*. 61(4): 541–56.

Dahrendorf, Ralf. 1959. *Class and Class Conflict in Industrial Society*. Stanford: Stanford University Press.

Danziger, Sheldon H., and Daniel H. Weinberg. 1994. "The Historical Record: Trends in Income, Inequality, and Poverty." In *Confronting Poverty: Prescriptions for Change*, edited by Sheldon H. Danziger, Gary Sandefur, and Daniel H. Weinberg. New York: Russell Sage Foundation.

Darity, William A., and Samuel L. Myers. 1983. "Changes in Black Family Structure: Implications for Welfare Dependency." *American Economic Review* 73(May): 59–64.

Duncan, Kevin C. 1996. "Gender Differences in the Effect of Education on the Slope of Experience/Earnings Profiles: National Longitudinal Survey of Youth, 1979–1988." *American Journal of Economics and Sociology* 55(October): 457–71.

Ellwood, David T., and Lawrence H. Summers. 1986. "Poverty in America: Is Welfare the Answer or the Problem?" In *Fighting Poverty: What Works and What Doesn't*, edited by Sheldon H. Danziger and Daniel H. Weinberg. Cambridge, Mass.: Harvard University Press.

England, Paula. 1992. *Comparable Worth: Theories and Evidence.* New York: Aldine de Gruyter.

England, Paula, Melissa S. Herbert, Barbara Stanek Kilbourne, Lori L. Reid, and Lori McCreary Megdal. 1994. "The Gendered Value of Occupations and Skills: Earnings in 1980 Census Occupations." *Social Forces* 73(September): 65–99.

Figart, Deborah M., and June Lapidus. 1996. "The Impact of Comparable Worth on Earnings Inequality." *Work and Occupations* 23(3, August): 297–318.

Garfinkel, Irwin. 1992. *Assuring Child Support.* New York: Russell Sage Foundation.

Garfinkel, Irwin, and Sara McLanahan. 1994. "Single Mother Families, Economic Insecurity, and Government Policy." In *Confronting Poverty: Prescriptions for Change,* edited by Sheldon H. Danziger, Gary Sandefur, and Daniel H. Weinberg. New York: Russell Sage Foundation.

Hantrais, Linda, and Marie-Thérèse Letablier. 1996. *Families and Family Policy in Europe.* New York: Longman.

Hochschild, Arlie Russell. 1997. *The Time Bind: When Work Becomes Home and Home Becomes Work.* New York: Metropolitan Books.

Holzer, Harry. 1987. "Informal Job Search and Black Youth Unemployment." *American Economic Review* 77(June): 446–52.

Kahn, Alfred J., and Sheila B. Kamerman. 1987. *Child Care: Facing the Hard Choices.* Dover, Mass.: Auburn House.

Kamerman, Sheila B., and Alfred J. Kahn. 1983. *Income Transfers for Families with Children: An Eight Country Study.* Philadelphia: Temple University Press.

———. 1991. "A U.S. Policy Challenge." In *Child Care, Parental Leave, and the Under 3s: Policy Innovation in Europe,* edited by Sheila B. Kamerman and Alfred J. Kahn. New York: Auburn House.

———. 1995. *Starting Right: How America Neglects Its Youngest Children and What We Can Do About It.* New York: Oxford University Press.

King, Mary. 1992. "The Evolution of Occupational Segregation by Race and Gender, 1940–1988." *Monthly Labor Review* 115(April): 30–37.

Kohn, Melvin. 1980. "Job Complexity and Adult Personality." In *Themes of Work and Love in Adulthood,* edited by Neil J. Smelser and Erik H. Erikson. Cambridge, Mass.: Harvard University Press.

Lehman, Jeffrey S. 1994. "Updating Urban Policy." In *Confronting Poverty: Prescriptions for Change,* edited by Sheldon H. Danziger, Gary Sandefur, and Daniel H. Weinberg. New York: Russell Sage Foundation.

Massey, Douglas S., and Nancy A. Denton. 1993. *American Apartheid: Segregation and the Making of the Underclass.* Cambridge, Mass.: Harvard University Press.

Massey, Douglas S., and Mitchell L. Eggers. 1990. "The Ecology of Inequality: Minorities and the Concentration of Poverty." *American Journal of Sociology* 95 (March): 1153–88.

McLaughlin, Eithne, Jane Millar, and Kenneth Cooke. 1989. *Work and Welfare Benefits.* Aldershot, England: Avebury.

Mincy, Ronald B. 1994. "The Underclass: Concept, Controversy, and Evidence." In *Confronting Poverty: Prescriptions for Change,* edited by Sheldon H. Danziger, Gary Sandefur, and Daniel H. Weinberg. New York: Russell Sage Foundation.

Moen, Phyllis, and Francille M. Firebaugh. 1994. "Family Policies and Effective Policies: A Life Course Perspective." *International Journal of Sociology and Social Policy* 14(1–2): 29–52.

Murnane, Richard J. 1994. "Education and the Well-Being of the Next Generation." In *Confronting Poverty: Prescriptions for Change*, edited by Sheldon H. Danziger, Gary Sandefur, and Daniel H. Weinberg. New York: Russell Sage Foundation.

Neckerman, Kathryn M., and Joleen Kirschenman. 1991. "Hiring Strategies, Racial Bias, and Inner-City Workers." *Social Problems* 38(4): 433–47.

Schor, Juliet. 1991. *The Overworked American: The Unexpected Decline of Leisure*. New York: Basic Books.

Smith, Vicki. 1997. "New Forms of Work Organization." *Annual Review of Sociology* 23: 315–39.

Starr, Paul. 1986. "Health Care for the Poor: The Past Twenty Years." In *Fighting Poverty: What Works and What Doesn't*, edited by Sheldon H. Danziger and Daniel H. Weinberg. Cambridge, Mass.: Harvard University Press.

Stein, Nancy. 1995. "Questions and Answers about Affirmative Action." *Social Justice* 22, 3(61, Fall): 45–52.

Sundström, Marianne. 1991. "Sweden: Supporting Work, Family, and Gender Equality." In *Child Care, Parental Leave, and the Under 3s: Policy Innovation in Europe*, edited by Sheila B. Kamerman and Alfred J. Kahn. New York: Auburn House.

Trzcinski, Eileen. 1994. "Family and Medical Leave, Contingent Employment, and Flexibility: A Feminist Critique of the U.S. Approach to Women and Family Policy." *Journal of Applied Social Science* 18(1): 71–87.

Tobin, James. 1994. "Poverty in Relation to Macroeconomic Trends, Cycles, and Policies." In *Confronting Poverty: Prescriptions for Change*, edited by Sheldon H. Danziger, Gary Sandefur, and Daniel H. Weinberg. New York: Russell Sage Foundation.

Waldinger, Roger. 1996. *Still the Promised City? African-Americans and New Immigrants in Postindustrial New York*. Cambridge, Mass.: Harvard University Press.

Wilson, Julie Boatright, David T. Ellwood, and Jeanne Brooks-Gunn. 1995. "Welfare-to-Work through the Eyes of Children." In *Escape from Poverty: What Makes a Difference for Children?* edited by P. Lindsay Chase-Lansdale and Jeanne Brooks-Gunn. New York: Cambridge University Press.

Wilson, William Julius. 1987. *The Truly Disadvantaged*. Chicago: University of Chicago Press.

Wilson, William Julius, and Kathryn M. Neckerman. 1986. "Poverty and Family Structure: the Widening Gap between Evidence and Public Policy Issues." In *Fighting Poverty: What Works and What Doesn't*, edited by Sheldon H. Danziger and Daniel H. Weinberg. Cambridge, Mass.: Harvard University Press.

Wolfe, Barbara L. 1994. "Reform of Health Care for the Nonelderly Poor." In *Confronting Poverty: Prescriptions for Change*, edited by Sheldon H. Danziger, Gary Sandefur, and Daniel H. Weinberg. New York: Russell Sage Foundation.

Index

Numbers in **boldface** refer to tables or figures.